Interact with your textbook

* each book in the _DIRECTIONS_ series offers free teaching and learning solutions online

www.oxfordtextbooks.co.uk/orc/directions/

 online resource centre

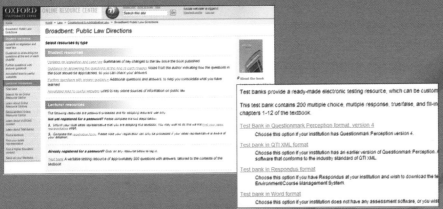

www.oxfordtextbooks.co.uk/orc/broadbent_directions/

Visit the website for access to additional resources.

For Lecturers

* A test bank of approximately 200 questions with answers

For Students

* Updates on legislation and case law

* Guidance on answering the questions at the end of each chapter

* Further questions with answer guidance

* Annotated links to useful websites

See the **Guide to the Online Resource Centre** on p. xxvi for full details.

public law

DIRECTIONS

GRAEME BROADBENT

OXFORD
UNIVERSITY PRESS

OXFORD
UNIVERSITY PRESS

Great Clarendon Street, Oxford OX2 6DP

Oxford University Press is a department of the University of Oxford.
It furthers the University's objective of excellence in research, scholarship,
and education by publishing worldwide in

Oxford New York

Auckland Cape Town Dar es Salaam Hong Kong Karachi
Kuala Lumpur Madrid Melbourne Mexico City Nairobi
New Delhi Shanghai Taipei Toronto

With offices in

Argentina Austria Brazil Chile Czech Republic France Greece
Guatemala Hungary Italy Japan Poland Portugal Singapore
South Korea Switzerland Thailand Turkey Ukraine Vietnam

Oxford is a registered trade mark of Oxford University Press
in the UK and in certain other countries

Published in the United States
by Oxford University Press Inc., New York

© Graeme Broadbent 2009

British Library Cataloguing in Publication Data

Data available

Library of Congress Cataloging in Publication Data

Data available

Typeset by Newgen Imaging Systems (P) Ltd., Chennai, India
Printed in Great Britain
on acid-free paper by
Ashford Colour Press Ltd, Gosport, Hampshire

ISBN 978–0–19–928972–1

10 9 8 7 6 5 4 3 2 1

Outline contents

v

Detailed contents

Chapter 3 Parliamentary sovereignty

Chapter 4 Parliament

Table of cases

Table of statutes

Table of European materials

Guide to the book

Public law Directions is enriched with a range of features designed to support and reinforce your learning. This guided tour shows you how to fully utilize your textbook and get the most out of your study.

Learning objectives

> ## Learning Objectives
>
> While reading this chapter, you should aim to understand:
>
> - who the members of the government (the executive) are and what they do;
> - the relationship between the Prime Minister and other members of the government;
> - the relationship between Ministers and their departments;

Each chapter begins with list of learning objectives. These serve as a helpful signpost to what you can expect to learn by reading the chapter.

Thinking points

thinking point
Do you think that the merit of flexibility outweighs the value of having a statement of fundamental principles?

One consequence of this is that, in countries with a written c⃰ arguments about matters central to the major functions of the ⃰ the Prime Minister or the monarch, are legal arguments because⃰ pretation of the legal rules contained in the constitution, and, ⃰ the courts. The position is different in Britain, for, while such ma⃰ of legal argument before the courts, they are also matters of pol⃰ the rules, whether legal or otherwise, are capable of being chan⃰ and political processes.

Thinking points allow you to pause and reflect on what you have been reading. They give you the opportunity to form your own views on the issues discussed in the book, and provide valuable practice in critical thinking.

Definition boxes

The functions exercised by local authorities are largely executi⃰ tive, though, given the amount of direction from central gover⃰ described as administrative. Local authorities also have limited leg⃰ can make delegated legislation where Parliament delegates a spe⃰ eral legislation. They also have the power to make a specific form ⃰ known as **bylaws**.

bylaws
laws that relate to the local authority area only

The thinking behind both of these is that local authorities are bes⃰ legislation is appropriate to their location and circumstances.

Key terms are highlighted in colour when they first appear and are clearly, concisely explained in definition boxes. These terms are collected in a glossary which can be found at the end of the book.

Case close-ups

> **case close-up**
>
> **R v Gloucestershire County Council ex p Barry [1997] AC 584**
>
> Mr. Barry had been assessed by the council as needing community care serv
> were provided for him. The council then became concerned about its finan
> decided that it could not longer afford to provide services for Mr. Barry. It th
> that it was withdrawing the services, citing its lack of resources as the reaso
> lenged this decision on two grounds. One was that the council was not er
> resources into account when assessing need. On this point, Mr. Barry lost, th
> rowest of margins. The House of Lords held, by 3: 2, that a council could tak
> resources when assessing need, even though the statute was silent on this po
> first instance, Mr. Barry won on his other point, which was that, once he had

Summaries of cases are boxed throughout so you can easily pick out the significant facts and details.

Statute boxes

> **statute**
>
> **Public Order Act 1986, s.12**
>
> (1) If the senior police officer, having regard to the time or place a
>   circumstances in which any public procession is being held or is
>   held and to its route or proposed route, reasonably believes that-
>
>   (a) it may result in serious public disorder, serious damage to pro
>   disruption to the life of the community, or
>
>   (b) the purpose of the persons organising it is the intimidation
>   view to compelling them not to do an act they have a right to
>   act they have the right not to do,

Boxed extracts from legislation are provided throughout for ease of reference.

Cross-references

> **cross reference**
> *See Chapter 4 for delegated legislation.*
>
> Under the Government of Wales Act 1998, the powers of the N
> Wales were limited to those powers formerly exercised by the S
> Wales, and as such were effectively limited to the making of regu
> egated legislation. As this was the case, there was no need for pro
> those in Scotland outlining legislative competence, because the sco
> the National Assembly for Wales was seeking to exercise was mor
>
> Provision was made for the appointment of a First Secretary, elec
> who was then able to appoint other members known as Assembl
> on specific areas with in the Assembly's jurisdiction. The lack of le

Connections between topics are cross-referenced so you can see how they interlink. Links are highlighted to aid quick and accurate navigation through the book.

End-of-chapter questions

> **Questions**
>
> If you answer the following questions, you will have appreciated the main
> in this chapter. Check your answers against the notes provided at the back o
>
> **1** Who are the members of the executive?
>
> **2** What mechanisms exist to prevent abuses of power by the executive?
>
> **3** What is the nature of the relationship between Ministers and their civil

Questions at the end of each chapter allow you to check that you have understood the material covered and provide a useful summary of what you have learned. You will find guidance on answering these questions at the back of the book and on the online resource centre, so you can check your answers.

Further reading

> **Further reading**
>
> To further your understanding of the topics covered in this chapter, have a look at
> reading materials mentioned below. Useful web links are also provided on the On
> Resource Centre.
>
> Rodney Brazier, *Constitutional Reform* (Oxford University Press, 3rd ed., 2008) ch.4
> This provides you with a critical review of the current and possible future voting sy
>
> Jeffrey Jowell and Dawn Oliver (eds), *The Changing Constitution* (Oxford University P
> 6th ed., 2007) ch.7

Selected further reading is included at the end of each chapter to provide a springboard to further study.

Guide to the Online Resource Centre

The Online Resource Centre that accompanies this book provides students and lecturers with ready-to-use teaching and learning resources. They are free of charge and are designed to maximize the learning experience.

www.oxfordtextbooks.co.uk/orc/broadbent_directions/

For Students

Accessible to all, with no registration or password required, these resources enable you to get the most from your textbook.

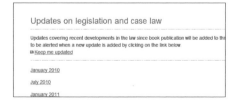

Updates to the law

An indispensible resource allowing you to access changes and developments in the law that have occurred since publication of the book. These are linked to the book by page number, so you can easily identify which material has been supplemented or superseded.

> 1. What mechanisms exist to prevent abuses of power by the executive?
>
> Think about ways of challenging the government both through the courts as well as in Parliame courts there are the processes of judicial review relating to the exercise of statutory powers, or damages where the executive commits, for example, a breach of contract or a tort. Parliament of mechanisms designed to subject the executive to scrutiny, including questions, committees, debates etc.

Guidance on answering the end of chapter questions

All the questions that appear at the end of each chapter are supplemented with notes from the author indicating how they should be approached, so you can check your answers. Where relevant, the author points out the difficulties and controversies you will need to be aware of when tackling questions on this topic. This guidance is provided both as text and in downloadable podcast format.

> 4. How have the EU and the Human Rights Act impacted on parliamentary sovere
>
> You should note that their impact has been different. Joining the European Community (as it entailed subscribing to the idea of Community sovereignty. This means that European legislat over any inconsistent law of a member state and is a necessary principle in order to promote application of European law across all member states. This has been achieved legally by virt European Communities Act 1972 and as such it can be argued that parliament has approved limitation on its sovereignty. The position is very different with regard to the Human Rights Ac specifically incorporated the European Convention on Human Rights within the framework of sovereignty, in particular by not giving the courts the power to overturn inconsistent legislatio refer it back to Parliament by means of a declaration of incompatibility. The power balance be government, Parliament and the courts is clearly affected by these changes and you might thi

Further questions with answer guidance

These extra questions allow you to consolidate what you have learned and stretch yourself that little bit further. Answer guidance is provided so you can check you are on the right lines.

> Annotated links to useful websites
>
> Parliament
> www.parliament.uk
>
> Government
> www.direct.gov.uk
>
> Prime Minister
> www.number10.gov.uk
>
> The Monarchy

Web links

A selection of annotated web links chosen by the author allows you to research easily those topics that are of particular interest to you. These links are checked regularly to ensure they remain up-to-date.

For Lecturers

Password-protected to ensure only lecturers can access this resource; each registration is personally checked to ensure the security of the site. Registering is easy: click on 'lecturer resources' on the Online Resource Centre and complete a simple registration form which allows you to choose your own username and password. Once you are registered, you can download this resource to your university's Virtual Learning Environment.

> Test banks provide a ready-made electronic testing resource, which can be customized to me
>
> This test bank contains 200 multiple choice, multiple response, true/false, and fill-in-the-blank chapters 1-12 of the textbook.
>
> Test Bank in Questionmark Perception format, version 4
> Choose this option if your institution has Questionmark Perception version 4.
>
> Test bank in QTI XML format
> Choose this option if your institution has an earlier version of Questionmark Perception. Also choose software that conforms to the industry standard of QTI XML.
>
> Test bank in Respondus format

Test bank

A fully customizable resource containing ready-made assessments that you can use to test your students. This resource offers versatile testing tailored to the contents of the textbook, with questions in several different formats.

The British constitution

Learning Objectives

While reading the chapter, you should aim to understand:

- the nature and characteristics of the British constitution;
- how the British constitution differs from constitutions of other countries;
- the structure of British government, both national and local; and
- the impact of British membership of the European Union.

Introduction

Any organization needs to have rules as to how it is to be run. What those rules are, who draws them up, how they can be changed and what form they take are, amongst others, matters that need to be determined at the outset. It is no different when that organization is a state. A state, whether large or small, needs to have some fundamental organizing principles in order that it might run effectively. Those principles will reflect the nature of the state and those values that it regards as fundamental. How they are expressed—whether as laws or simply as understandings as to how things should be done—will be significant in determining the character of the state. Whilst each state will have its own set of fundamental principles, however expressed, certain common characteristics may be identified in the ways in which states generally, or at least particular types of states, are organized. The first sections thus identify ways of describing the characteristics of how states are organized and then apply those terms to the situation in Britain. Before embarking on this, it is perhaps helpful to indicate at the outset the nature of constitutional arrangements in Britain.

(1.1) The governance of Britain

Britain, unlike most other countries in the world, does not have a formal document setting out the arrangements by which it is to be governed, nor does it have a set of core values by which the state is to be run. Instead, the central focus of the British system of governance is Parliament. Parliament comprises the House of Commons and the House of Lords. The House of Commons, as the democratically elected House, is the more powerful and important of the two. Parliament not only passes laws but also acts as a focus for debate and discussion of matters of national importance. Members of both Houses generally belong to one of the leading political parties—the Labour, Conservative and Liberal Democrat parties—though some belong to smaller parties whilst others sit as independent members with no party affiliation. After the last general election in 2005, the composition of the House of Commons was as follows:

thinking point
Should the government be located in Parliament?

General Election 2005

	Seats	% of vote
Labour	355	35.2
Conservative	198	32.4
Liberal Democrat	62	22.0
Other	31	10.4
Total	646	100

Source: House of Commons Research Paper 05/33 (2005)

cross reference
See further
Chapter 4.

It can be seen that the Labour Party had a working majority in the House of Commons. They thus formed the government, which is also located in Parliament. The members of the government have a dual role as Ministers and as Members of Parliament. Parliament thus has as another of its functions the task of holding the government to account.

It may seem odd to begin by talking about Parliament and the government rather than about the Queen. Although the Queen is the head of state, her functions are largely ceremonial, although to an outsider, she may appear to be the most important person in the country. In practice, however, power is largely exercised by the government, with the Prime Minister at its head. A key characteristic of the British constitution is that the appearance and reality are often different.

thinking point
If the Queen is not the most powerful person in the country, who is?

An important part of the government of a state is that law is used as an instrument to regulate relationships within the state and also to prevent abuses of power by the state. The courts have a key role to play in adjudicating on disputes whether between citizen and citizen or between citizens and the state. Disputes between individuals are governed by private law, typically involving aspects of the law of contract, tort or family law. Disputes involving the state are matters of public law, which includes the criminal law. The aspects of public law with which this book is concerned are those commonly labelled constitutional and administrative law. Constitutional law is concerned with the structures which create and allocate powers to the government, in its broadest sense, of the state. Administrative law is concerned with the way in which powers are exercised by government at all levels.

3

cross reference
Parliamentary supremacy is discussed in Chapter 3.

The courts in Britain do not enjoy as much power as their counterparts elsewhere. The principle of parliamentary supremacy means that Parliament is the supreme law making body in the United Kingdom, and its laws cannot be held to be invalid by the courts. This is in contrast to many other countries in the world where the highest courts have the power to declare legislation that conflicts with the constitution to be invalid. The absence of such a power for the courts in Britain is in part because of the absence of a formal constitution but largely because of the principle of parliamentary supremacy, which, as we shall see, is at the heart of British constitutional arrangements.

1.2 The nature of constitutions

1.2.1 What is a constitution?

In almost all countries in the world there has been some event that has caused that country to make a fresh start, for example:

- attaining independence, as has been the case, for example, with the former British colonies such as many Caribbean and African states;

- following a revolution, which historically brought about the constitutions of the United States of America and the former Union of Soviet Socialist Republics;

- recovery from warfare (internal or external) as happened in many countries such as Germany, Japan and other states following World War II;

- reconstruction as a new state as has occurred in many of the states of eastern Europe following the collapse of the USSR, and the reconstruction of former independent states such as Russia, Ukraine, Estonia and Georgia;

- internal reorganization such as has occurred in South Africa or Zimbabwe.

Following such events, the opportunity has been taken to make a statement of the fundamental principles by which the government of the state is to be organized and of the values that the state regards as important to its identity. The constitution is the vehicle through which this occurs, and it is thus a fundamental political statement proclaiming the nature of the state as a dictatorship, democracy, or whatever else it might be. The nature of the state will be reflected in its organisation, and so constitutional provisions will typically relate to the head of state, the executive government, law making, the judicial system and individual rights for its citizens. How these are constituted will depend on the nature of the state. For example, those who are to be active in the government of the state—such as the head of state, members of the government (the executive), of the law making body (the legislature) or the courts—may be elected or appointed depending on the nature of the state. Whether elections are held at all; and where they are, who can be elected and who can vote are all likely to form part of the constitution. The rights guaranteed to citizens by the constitution are an important indicator of the nature of the state.

These fundamental political principles tend to be expressed in a legal document which is the constitution and which forms the basis of how the state operates. The word 'constitution' does not, however, have a single meaning. In the present context, Sir Kenneth Wheare (*Modern Constitutions* (Oxford University Press, 2nd ed., 1966) p.1) offers a helpful explanation:

> The word 'constitution' is commonly used in at least two senses in any ordinary discussion of political affairs. First of all it is used to describe the whole system of government of a country, the collection of rules which establish and regulate or govern the government... In almost every country in the world except Britain however, the word 'constitution' is used... to describe not the whole collection of rules, legal and non-legal, but rather a selection of them which has usually been embodied in one document or in a few closely related documents.

Much depends, then, on the sense in which the word is used. It is by using the word in the second, narrower, sense described by Wheare that has led some commentators to deny that Britain has a constitution, and, by implication, any constitutional law. A constitution in this second sense is often called a written constitution. In that Britain does not have a single document or collection of documents that contain 'the constitution', this is correct. However, as Wheare explains, if we adopt a broader view, and use the term in the first sense he identifies, then it becomes much easier to accept the view that Britain has a constitution. As we shall see, however, it does not follow necessarily from this that we can readily identify a body of law as 'constitutional'.

1.2.2 The British constitutional model

One of the reasons that Britain has not adopted a written constitution is that there has never been an event in British history that has led to a new beginning: the last time that happened was in 1066, when the adoption of constitutions was not part of the political discourse. The nearest Britain came to such an event after that was in the civil war in the mid 17th century. A document, called the Instrument of Government, was drawn up in 1653 (see J.P. Kenyon *The Stuart Constitution* (Cambridge University Press, 1966) p.342), and would have provided the basis for the future government of the country without a monarchy but with matters firmly under the control of Parliament. However, this was abandoned following the restoration of the monarchy in 1660.

Since then, there have been piecemeal changes to aspects of the way in which the country is run and the values that underpin it, but there has never been a comprehensive attempt to do so. The British constitution has simply developed in accordance with the needs as they are perceived at the time. This may be seen as both a strength and a weakness. It is a strength in that it enables the British constitution to evolve to meet changing circumstances: it does not have to retain aspects of the constitution that may have been appropriate to the period in which it was drawn up but which have become inappropriate in the light of changing values and experience. It may be seen as a weakness in that the British constitution has no clear statement of the fundamental principles on which it is based and lacks the stability of other constitutions.

thinking point
Do you think
that the merit of
flexibility outweighs
the value of having
a statement of
fundamental
principles?

One consequence of this is that, in countries with a written constitution, many of the arguments about matters central to the major functions of the state, such as the role of the Prime Minister or the monarch, are legal arguments because they relate to the interpretation of the legal rules contained in the constitution, and, as such, are decided by the courts. The position is different in Britain, for, while such matters may be the subject of legal argument before the courts, they are also matters of political argument because the rules, whether legal or otherwise, are capable of being changed by the normal legal and political processes.

1.2.3 The nature of constitutional laws

Simply taking a more all embracing view of a constitution still leaves a number of matters to be considered, and these are discussed below.

What are constitutional laws?

There is a question as to what amounts to constitutional law. Where a country has a written constitution this is a relatively simple matter, as the constitutional laws are the laws contained in the constitution as interpreted by the courts. There is a finite body of material to which the description 'constitutional' can be applied. The problem with the British constitution is defining which laws are constitutional and which are not when this distinction is not formally recognized in English law. It is thus open to commentators such as Professor Griffith ('The Political Constitution' (1979) 42 MLR 1) to argue that, as all laws in some way alter the balance of power in Britain, and as constitutions exist to regulate power relationships within the state, then it follows that all laws can properly be described as constitutional. This is one solution. Equally, it might be argued that as no laws are capable of being identified as constitutional on the basis that they differ in some significant respect from other laws, and that as all laws are capable of being changed in the same way, Britain therefore has no laws properly called constitutional. One solution to this is to adopt a pragmatic approach and identify those laws that might otherwise appear in a written constitution as the proper subject matter of constitutional law. This is the approach adopted by most textbook writers and will be adopted here. We will thus examine the laws that govern the operation of the institutions of British government.

The legal sources of the British constitution

It follows from this that, in the absence of a formal constitution, the legal sources of the British constitution are the same as the sources of law generally:

- European Union law
  The law of the European Union is incorporated into English law by virtue of the European Communities Act 1972, which came into force on 1 January 1973. In order to enable European Union law to apply uniformly across the Union, it prevails over the law of individual member states.
- Acts of Parliament
  For matters not affected by the European Union, Acts of Parliament have the highest status in the United Kingdom.
- Equity
  The principles of equity were originally designed to correct deficiencies in the common law, and developed into a system of its own.
- Common law
  This is the law developed by the judges in cases coming before the courts.

The status of laws

In countries with a written constitution the constitutional laws enjoy a higher status than other laws. Ordinary laws are often required to comply with the constitutional laws and in the event of a conflict between a constitutional law and an ordinary law the constitutional law will prevail. In Britain, all laws generally enjoy the same status: laws dealing with litter are Acts of Parliament with no greater status than Acts regulating the succession to the throne, as they can all be created and changed in the same way. This is a further reason why it is difficult to identify laws that can be described as constitutional and why different rules have had to be adopted as to how to resolve conflicts between Acts of Parliament.

cross reference
See Chapter 3.

There are exceptions to this idea that all laws enjoy equal status. Under s.2(4) European Communities Act 1972, Acts of Parliament, whether passed before or

cross reference
This is also discussed further in Chapter 3.

after 1973 (the date the European Communities Act 1972 came into force) must be given effect subject to the requirement of European law, which includes the principle that the laws of the European Union must take precedence over the domestic laws of member states. This applies both to Parliament which must not pass laws that conflict with European union requirements, and the courts, who, when faced with a conflict between an Act of Parliament and a rule of European union law must give effect to the European rule and if necessary suspend the operation of the relevant Act of Parliament.

cross reference
See further Chapters 3 and 7.

A further partial exception occurs under the Human Rights Act 1998. All new law must comply with the rights protected by virtue of the 1998 Act, and the Minister introducing new law into Parliament must make a statement to this effect (see s.19 Human Rights Act 1998). The courts must try to interpret legislation so as to comply with the rights guaranteed by virtue of the 1998 Act.

In enacting these two pieces of legislation, it may be that the United Kingdom is moving toward identifying particular laws as having a special status such as that enjoyed by constitutional laws in countries governed by a written constitution, but this process is not formalized so as to create clear dividing lines between different types of law in terms of their status.

Changing the law

In countries with a written constitution the laws contained in the constitution are usually more difficult to change than other laws. This is because the constitution contains the fundamental principles by which the state is to be governed and these would not be embedded into the fabric of the state if they could be altered too easily. In order to enshrine these fundamental principles they are protected against change. In Britain, all laws may be changed in the same way, so that the most fundamental aspects of the government of Britain can be changed in just the same way and just as readily as the most minor.

The power of the courts

The absence of a written constitution changes the balance of power within the state, especially as far as the courts are concerned. In countries with a written constitution the courts usually have a power to strike down legislation that is contrary to the constitution. This thus limits the powers of the legislature. The courts in Britain, however, do not have power to strike down laws made by Parliament.

Legal and non-legal rules

There is a significant difference between Britain and countries with a written constitution in that Britain has both legal and non-legal rules as part of its constitution. In countries with a written constitution, constitutional rules are necessarily legal as they form part of the legal document that is the constitution. In Britain, however, non-legal rules form a significant part of the constitution and play a significant role in the way in which it operates. It is surprising that major parts of the British constitution are not governed by law but depend instead on a series of non-legal rules or practices, which are generally called '**conventions**'. There is, for example, no statutory provision for virtually the whole of cabinet government.

. . . .

conventions

non-legal rules which are followed as a matter of political practice

. . . .

1.2.4 **Conventions**

The inclusion of non-legal rules, or conventions, as part of the constitution has a number of implications.

First, these conventions are capable of being changed very easily. They are simply practices that have been followed, with no particular mechanisms for changing them or creating new ones. As such they enable the British constitution to change to meet changing conditions and needs. This is usually not possible under a written constitution as the constitution is generally protected against change and usually requires elaborate procedures to effect any alterations.

Secondly, under a written constitution a person acts unconstitutionally when acting contrary to the constitution. Where this occurs the person also acts illegally because breaching the constitution necessarily involves breaking the law. In Britain, however, the two are not inextricably bound together. A person can act unconstitutionally but not illegally by failing to follow an accepted convention. Such action would be unconstitutional in that the person would not have acted in ways required by the constitution but not illegal because the unconstitutional behaviour did not involve a breach of the law.

cross reference
See further Chapter 5.

thinking point
Should all constitutional principles be enacted as legal rules or are more informal rules beneficial?

Thirdly, the presence of conventions affects the role of the courts. In a country with a written constitution, all matters relating to the constitution are matters of law and therefore capable of being determined by the courts. It is immediately apparent that the courts in such countries have a great influence on how the state runs and is governed. In Britain, however, the presence of conventions means that there are areas relating to the government of the state in which the courts play no part, as they can only adjudicate on matters of law. The impact of conventions is confined to the political sphere, and arguments relating to them have to be resolved through political processes. For example, an allegation that a Minister has acted incompetently, and thus in breach of the individual responsibility that he owes to Parliament, could lead to questions being asked in the House of Commons or to a motion calling for his resignation.

1.2.5 **Sources of the British constitution**

We can now identify the sources of the British constitution, both legal and non-legal, as follows:

- European Union law
- Acts of Parliament
- Equity
- Common law
- Conventions

1.2.6 **Classifying constitutions**

Although each constitution is unique to the state to which it relates, it is possible to identify certain characteristics that particular types of constitution have.

Written and unwritten

We have seen that they may be described as written where they are set out in a document or series of documents. The constitutions of almost every country in the world fit this description. Constitutions which are not expressed in a document or set of documents, such as the British constitution, are described as unwritten. This description must not be taken too literally and is not, as a description, very helpful. Parts of what may be identified as the British constitution are, of course, written down. The terms written and unwritten really refer to the form the constitution takes and the essence of the distinction is whether the constitution is set out in a single document or set of documents or is merely assembled from a variety of disparate sources.

Rigid and flexible

An allied aspect of constitutional form is the ease with which the constitution can be changed. In this regard, constitutions may be described as rigid if they are subject to some special process before they can be altered, which is usually more restrictive than the way in which other law can be changed. As we have seen, this is quite common, as the constitution contains the fundamental principles and values on which the state is based and making those aspects difficult to change is an important aspect of their special status.

By contrast, the absence of a written constitution in Britain leads us to ask how it might be changed. Two features may be mentioned. First, all laws may be changed in the same way under the British constitution: there is no special procedure for changing particular laws. Any bill passed by Parliament and receiving the royal assert is effective, subject to certain limitations, to change the law. If Parliament tried to make it more difficult to change a particular law, this restriction would be ineffective because no higher body

cross reference
See further
Chapter 4 on the law
making powers of
Parliament.

thinking point
Is the ability to
change law easily
necessarily a good
thing?

than Parliament is recognized as having the power to make law. Secondly, the British constitution includes non-legal rules, which can be changed without any formal procedures being followed. The ability to change the constitution without any form of special procedure leads to the constitution being described as flexible.

The terms 'rigid' and 'flexible' must not be taken too literally. They simply refer to the nature of the process for changing the constitution. In general terms it follows that a rigid constitution will normally be more difficult to change than a flexible one. But this need not necessarily be so. If there is sufficient political will in favour of the change, an apparently rigid constitution can be changed quite quickly. Conversely, the absence of such will can make an apparently flexible constitution difficult to change.

Presidential and premiership

Constitutions may also be classified according to the nature of the head of state. In countries where the head of state is also the head of government, the constitution is said to be presidential. This does not tell us how a person becomes head of state, only what functions that person performs. There may be certain advantages attached to this type of arrangement in that the head of state exercises real power and is not simply a figurehead: there is one voice speaking on behalf of the country and doing so with clear authority. There is often the added advantage (as some would see it) that there is usually a limit to the time that a person can hold presidential office and thus the country does not have the same leader indefinitely. However, where this is not the case, the state has a person in office for a long time exercising power, which the experience of history has shown is not always a desirable state of affairs, whatever the gains in terms of stability.

Where the functions of head of state and head of government are performed by different people the constitution is said to be a premiership. Again, this description merely describes the functions and does not indicate how the head of state and head of government come to hold those posts. Nor does it give any indication of whether the head of state is a monarch or is some other type of individual. The advantages of this arrangement include the ability of the head of state and the head of government to concentrate on their own particular functions, without having one person trying to do both, which may not be efficient. Also, this arrangement combines stability and continuity with flexibility in that it is unlikely that both postholders will change at the same time.

Britain's constitutional monarchy

The British constitution is characterised by having the monarch as head of state. Succession to the monarchy occurs, other than in the most exceptional cases, where the monarch dies and this provides continuity as the normal life expectancy ensures that a monarch is likely to occupy that position for a number of years. The present Queen, for example, has been on the throne for more than 50 years and has provided the British constitution with continuity and stability over a long period of time. Prime Ministers occupy their posts for a much shorter time period, typically five years. The present Queen has thus seen a large number of Prime Ministers come and go.

The nature of the monarchy differs across the world. In Britain there is said to be a constitutional monarchy. What this means is that the Queen exists within a legal framework that defines her powers and role, together with a number of conventions as to how she is expected to act in particular situations. As we shall see, a description of the powers apparently enjoyed by the Queen as part of the royal prerogative (the common law powers enjoyed by the Crown) makes it look as though the monarch has considerable power within the British constitution. However, this is tempered by conventions as to how these legal powers are to be exercised. For example, the Queen, as a matter of law, has to give the royal assent to bills that have been passed by Parliament before they can become law. Taken on its own this would imply that the Queen has a choice as to whether to give her assent or to refuse to do so. The convention is, however, that she will always give her assent, and despite arguments from time to time as to whether it would be appropriate for her to refuse to assent to particular types of legislation, the monarch has always done so in modern times.

cross reference
See Chapter 5.

Similarly, the Queen has the power in law to appoint the Prime Minister and other Ministers. Again, conventions dictate that she exercises these powers in particular ways. So, by convention, she appoints the leader of the party with a majority of seats in the House of Commons as Prime Minister. Other ministerial appointments are made in accordance with the wishes of the Prime Minister. There may, perhaps, be more scope for intervention by the monarch in the appointment of the Prime Minister if it happened that no single party had a majority of seats in the House of Commons. This situation has not yet arisen, as general elections tend to produce a clear result (which is said to be one of the strengths of the electoral system) but could happen if the balance of support between the parties were to alter radically or if the electoral system were to change. In such a situation, the existing convention could not apply, and the question would be how the matter might proceed, something about which we can only speculate at this juncture.

thinking point
If the monarchy does not have any real power, then what is the purpose of it?

11

Bi-cameral and unicameral

A further way in which constitutions may be classified is according to the structure of the legislature. Where the legislature is divided into two bodies, it is said to be bi-cameral. This is the most common form, with nearly all countries adopting it as the preferred model. As most countries have adopted this form of legislature, there are evidently advantages to this structure. The division into two chambers fulfils a number of functions. First, it allows for an internal balance which is designed to prevent an excessive concentration of power over something as important as the law making function. Secondly, it allows for a different perspective to be taken by each chamber. There would be no point in having each chamber being composed in the same way, and the practice is that there are differences in the composition of each chamber. How that composition differs varies from country to country, with different forms of election or appointment commonly used to signify the differences. Thus, in Britain, the House of Commons contains elected Members of Parliament, whilst the House of Lords comprises individuals whose membership depends on a combination of direct appointment, membership by

cross reference
On membership of Parliament see Chapter 4.

virtue of holding a particular post, or by birth (though now supplemented by election). These differences mean that some members are subject to political pressures by virtue of having to win a seat in a popular election whilst others are in a more secure position as they are members for life. Thirdly, and very practically, this arrangement allows for a division of labour between the two chambers.

Legislatures that do not have this division and only have one chamber are said to be unicameral. This type of legislature might be appropriate in small states where government is necessarily on a small scale, and is, for example, seen in the devolved bodies in Scotland and Wales as well as in small island states across the world, but is hardly found at all in larger developed states. It may be more efficient to have only one chamber in a legislature, but it is generally regarded as more democratic and more effective to have two.

thinking point

Might it be more efficient to have only one chamber in the legislature as it concentrates discussion in one place instead of dissipating it into two?

Unitary and federal

A further way in which constitutions may be regarded relates to the way in which power is divided internally within the state. In all states, power is exercised at a number of levels—central, regional, local etc. The question is how that power is divided. In a unitary state, only the central government has primary law making powers. Any lower tiers of government only exercise delegated powers—that is powers given to them rather than powers that are theirs by right. The position is different in a federal state, where both the central government and the individual territories comprising the federation have primary powers, the exact configuration of which varies from state to state. It is usual for certain powers relating to what are essentially national interests to be reserved for the central government whilst the regional governments will have autonomy over matters that reflect regional differences.

1.3 The structure of the United Kingdom and devolution

At this point it would be appropriate to examine the structure of the United Kingdom. The term 'United Kingdom' refers to Great Britain and Northern Ireland, which form an entity for international as well as internal purposes. Great Britain comprises England, Scotland and Wales, though the term is often used when referring to the United Kingdom. The arrangements for government of the constituent parts of the United Kingdom have been subject to quite dramatic change in recent years. Historically, power gradually became centred on the Parliament at Westminster, which retains the ability to legislate for the whole of the United Kingdom. Recently, however, there has been a devolution of power, in varying degrees to the other constituent countries of the United Kingdom. As the history of Northern Ireland is so complex as to require disproportionately lengthy discussion, the focus will be on Scotland and Wales.

1.3.1 **Scotland**

Whilst the accession of James I, already James VI of Scotland, to the throne of England marked a personal union of the monarchy of the two countries, it was not until the Act of Union with Scotland Act 1707 that the union of the two countries was completed and the combined nation Great Britain created with the Westminster Parliament as its law making body. Notwithstanding this union, Scotland, under the terms of the Treaty of Union, retained some of its own distinctive features, including its legal and judicial system. Despite intermittent separatist tendencies, the union remained in place into the 20th century. Reassertions of nationalism led to the passing of the Scotland Act 1978, which paved the way for devolution of power to Scotland in the event of a referendum producing the requisite majority in favour of such a move. In the event, the referendum did not result in a sufficient majority to bring the legislation into force and the matter receded into the background without ever disappearing completely from the political agenda. The incoming Labour government of 1997 was committed to devolution and introduced the bill that became the Scotland Act 1998.

The Scottish Parliament

The Act (in s.1) creates the Scottish Parliament, which is, unlike the Westminster Parliament composed of a single chamber. The 129 Members (Members of the Scottish Parliament, or MSPs) are elected by a mixture of first past the post (or simple majority—the person who gains the most votes in the constituency is elected) and proportional representation under an additional member system, with voters having two votes each: one is cast for the individuals who are elected by simple majority in the 73 constituencies; the second is cast for a party and contributes toward the election of members in the 56 regional seats contained in 8 regions, each returning 7 MSPs. These are worked out using a complex formula that allocates regional seats on the basis of constituencies won in that region. Once the number of regional seats to be allocated to each party has been calculated, the individual members are allocated to those seats on the basis of a party list. This is a list drawn up by each party of its members, in the order of the party's preference, who then fill up the number of seats allocated to that party. The 129 members thus comprise a mixture of those representing constituencies and those representing regions, unlike the Westminster Parliament which only contains constituency Members of Parliament (MPs) elected by a simple majority in each constituency. The result has been that the Scottish Parliament has not mirrored the Westminster Parliament in having one party with a substantial majority able to use its power to dominate the legislature. The 2007 election produced the following results:

Party	Seats
Scottish National Party	47
Scottish Labour	46
Scottish Conservative	16
Scottish Liberal Democrat	16
Scottish Green Party	2
Other	2
Total	**129**

(Source: The Scottish Parliament <http://www.scottish.parliament.uk/apps2/msp/msphome/default.aspx#top>)

cross reference

See further Chapter 4 on electoral systems.

This has implications for the way in which government in Scotland is run, as each of the two major parties is dependent on support either from each other or from one or more of the smaller parties.

thinking point

Is this state of affairs better than the situation in the Westminster Parliament where the government can use its voting strength to ensure that it achieves the results it wants?

Unlike local government in England and the National Assembly for Wales, the Scottish Parliament has primary legislative powers and, subject to limitations imposed by the 1998 Act, has wide powers to legislate for the people of Scotland (s.28) in ways that have led to significant differences between England and Scotland in areas such as education and law and order. However, whilst the Westminster Parliament has no limits on its ability to pass laws (subject to the requirements of European Union Law and the Human Rights Act 1998) the Scottish Parliament has explicit limits placed on it in this respect. By virtue of s.29, an Act of the Scottish Parliament cannot be treated as law if it is outside the legislative competence of the Scottish Parliament. The term 'legislative competence' is used to express the idea that the Scottish Parliament has limits on its ability to make laws. This means that Acts passed by the Scottish Parliament can be subjected to scrutiny by the courts against the terms of the 1998 Act to ensure that the Scottish Parliament is not going beyond the powers it has been given. The 1998 Act does not contain a statement explaining which matters the Scottish Parliament can make laws about, but rather provides a list of matters on which the Scottish Parliament cannot make laws. Matters falling outside the legislative competence of the Scottish Parliament include, for example, matters relating to:

- the relationship between England and Scotland;
- the Crown;

- defence; and

- foreign affairs.

Such reservations are understandable, as these are matters having an impact outside Scotland and are appropriately dealt with by the Westminster Parliament acting on behalf of the country as a whole. The Scottish Parliament may also not legislate in ways that are incompatible with the European Convention on Human Rights or with European Union law. The courts have jurisdiction to hear issues such as these with a final appeal to the **Judicial Committee of the Privy Council**. The Act also (in s.28) leaves untouched the power of the Westminster Parliament to make laws for Scotland.

· ·

Judicial Committee of the Privy Council

this was originally created as a committee of the Privy Council to hear appeals from overseas countries with a connection with the United Kingdom, latterly as members of the Commonwealth. It is now the final court of appeal in matters relating to devolution issues. The judges sitting in it are usually the judges of the House of Lords. See further Chapter 6

· ·

In addition to its legislative functions, the Scottish Parliament contains members of the Executive, headed by the First Minister, who is appointed by the Queen but is put forward by the Scottish Parliament itself. Following the 2007 election the First Minister is a member of the Scottish National Party, which has already led to renewed interest in the relationship between Scotland and the rest of Great Britain. As with the government at Westminster, the First Minister nominates other Ministers and together they comprise the executive. Their functions broadly parallel those of the government at Westminster in that they formulate policy and oversee its implementation whether by securing the passing of legislation through the Scottish Parliament or by carrying out executive acts, which include exercising powers under the royal prerogative where it is appropriate to do so. The sources of executive power are the same as for the government at Westminster, namely statute and the common law powers enjoyed under the royal prerogative. There are also powers under the Act allowing for powers to be transferred to Scottish Ministers.

cross reference
See Chapter 5.

The question of whether a legislative or executive activity is within the competence of the Scottish Parliament or the Executive is known as a 'devolution issue' by virtue of the provisions in Schedule 6 of the 1998 Act. Depending on when it arises, the issue may be referred directly to the Judicial Committee of the Privy Council for its determination in respect of a potential problem, or brought before the courts for determination by them, with a final appeal to the Judicial Committee of the Privy Council.

It seems clear, now that the Scottish National Party is prominent in the Scottish Parliament, that the question of further devolution of power, and possible outright separation will be on the political agenda for the foreseeable future, which clearly has implications for the continuation of the United Kingdom.

1.3.2 Wales

After the various military campaigns in Wales in the Middle Ages the position of Wales remained subject to a variety of forms of governance until an Act of 1536 formally joined Wales to England. Unlike Scotland, which was to retain much of its distinctive administrative and legal structure, the systems applying in England were largely applied to Wales, and England and Wales became a unit for purposes of legal jurisdiction. Later, the distinctiveness of certain aspects of Welsh life and culture was recognized and legislation peculiar to Wales passed, with the post of Secretary of State for Wales being created in 1964. Nationalist tendencies revived in the 20th century, and, as with Scotland, the government paved the way for devolution to a Welsh governing body by passing the Wales Act 1978 in similar terms to that for Scotland in requiring support in a referendum before it could come into effect. As with Scotland, insufficient support was forthcoming and devolved government did not come into effect. The Labour Party, sympathetic to the claims of Wales, also included a manifesto commitment to devolved government, and when elected in 1997 subsequently introduced the bill that became the Government of Wales Act 1998. This has latterly been amended in significant ways by the Government of Wales Act 2006.

The devolution of government to Wales differs significantly from that devolved to Scotland and the Scottish Parliament, in that much less power has been passed to the National Assembly for Wales and its members, though this may change if the trend indicated in the Government of Wales Act 2006 is continued. The Government of Wales Act 1998 provided for the creation of the National Assembly for Wales, but this body, unlike its Scottish counterpart was essentially an executive and administrative body. The legislative powers delegated to it were secondary rather than primary, though the Government of Wales Act 2006 has now paved the way for the National Assembly for Wales to make laws in their own right in the future.

The National Assembly for Wales

The National Assembly for Wales is, like the Scottish Parliament, composed of a single chamber whose members are elected by a combination of first past the post and proportional representation again in the form of the additional member system. The 60 members of the National Assembly for Wales, called Assembly Members (AMs) are elected on the basis of voters casting two votes, one for a candidate in a constituency and the other for a party. AMs are elected on the basis of a simple majority in 40 constituencies, whilst the party votes are subject to a complex calculation which results in the election of 4 members for each of 5 regions, allocated by a list drawn up by the party and filled according to the proportion of votes received. Whilst this system produced a finely balanced result in the 2007 election in Scotland, the result in Wales, whilst not producing an overall majority for any one party, did produce a more decisive result.

thinking point

Is there any justification for treating Wales in a different way to Scotland?

Party	Seats
Labour	26
Plaid Cymru	15
Welsh Conservatives	12
Welsh Liberal Democrats	6
Independent	1
Total	60

(Source: National Assembly for Wales: <http://www.assemblywales.org/memhome/mem-party-group-seating/mem-party-groups.htm>)

cross reference
See Chapter 4 for delegated legislation.

Under the Government of Wales Act 1998, the powers of the National Assembly for Wales were limited to those powers formerly exercised by the Secretary of State for Wales, and as such were effectively limited to the making of regulations by way of delegated legislation. As this was the case, there was no need for provisions comparable to those in Scotland outlining legislative competence, because the scope of any powers that the National Assembly for Wales was seeking to exercise was more clearly identified.

Provision was made for the appointment of a First Secretary, elected by the Assembly, who was then able to appoint other members known as Assembly Secretaries to work on specific areas within the Assembly's jurisdiction. The lack of legislative competence, however, meant that the National Assembly for Wales was performing only executive functions, and so there was no real separation between the executive and the rest of the Assembly, the executive simply constituting a committee of the National Assembly. The Government of Wales Act 2006 makes significant changes to these arrangements. It establishes a Welsh Assembly Government, a title that had been used informally by Assembly Secretaries, who had also used the term 'Ministers' to style themselves, and makes it a separate entity from the National Assembly for Wales whilst still remaining located within the National Assembly. This changes the relationship between the Executive and ordinary members of the National Assembly, with the ordinary members now exercising functions analogous to those exercised elsewhere of holding the government to account. The head of the executive is now the First Minister and appoints other members of the executive, now known as Welsh Ministers. Functions previously transferred to the National Assembly and exercised by the executive as a committee within that body are now transferred to the Welsh Assembly government directly.

The National Assembly for Wales also now has, by virtue of the Government of Wales Act 2006, primary legislative powers. The National Assembly is now able to make laws, which will be known as Assembly Measures. This will, however, only operate on the basis of agreement with the Westminster Parliament, whose power to legislate for Wales remains unaffected by the changes in the 2006 Act. This means that the issue of legislative competence which affects the Scottish Parliament will not arise as the National Assembly will only be allowed to legislate on particular and specific matters, though this might change as the powers under the 2006 Act extend greater legislative competence to the National Assembly. Also, as with the Scottish Parliament, the 2006 Act seeks to identify the legislative competence of the National Assembly of Wales by the concept of a 'devolution issue'. A devolution issue is identified as a question of competence in executive and legislative activities. Devolution issues relating to the National Assembly of Wales may be considered by the courts, and ultimately by the new Supreme Court in London which will become operational in 2009.

1.3.3 **Local government**

There has always been a system of local government, though its nature and functions have changed over the years. The modern system of local government was created by statute and, as a result, Parliament has, from time to time, changed the structure, powers and duties of local authorities but the basis of the current position remains the Local Government Act 1972, though this has been significantly amended. The system of local government is not uniform across the country, with Scotland, for example, having its own distinctive system. Even within England, different types of local government exist. In some parts of the country local government is divided between county councils and district councils, whilst elsewhere the functions of both of these bodies are exercised by larger bodies called unitary authorities. In some areas, smaller and more localized parish councils exist to deal with purely parochial matters.

The functions exercised by local authorities are largely explicable on historical grounds: there is no inherent reason why the matters dealt with by local authorities should be dealt with by them. A range of functions are the responsibility of local authorities, including housing, social care, public health, highways, public transport, planning, and refuse collection and disposal. Some authorities have additional functions under local legislation such as licensing markets or levying tolls on tunnels or bridges. There has, over the years, been a change in the role of local authorities in respect of service provision, with local authorities moving form the position of being providers of services to being bodies that enable services to be provided by, for example, private enterprises.

Local authority revenue has always been a contentious issue. Central government has readily used its power to put forward legislation designed to reduce spending by local authorities. The income of local authorities is divided unevenly between money raised directly by the local authority and central government. The former is currently in the form of the council tax, which contains components relating to individuals and to property. The latter is in the form of money allocated by central government, which forms the bulk of local authority income. As a result, central government has considerable influence over the finances of local government.

There has generally between a tension between local government and central government especially when the party in power nationally differs from the majority party at local level. This may be seen in a number of the cases discussed in Chapter 12. The balance between the two has changed over the years with the general tendency for local government to become increasingly required to act under the direction of central government, so that even where a matter is the responsibility of local government it has to be undertaken in accordance with the policies of central government. So, for example, education in schools has to be in accordance with the requirements of the national curriculum laid down by the Department for Children, Families and Schools.

thinking point

Given the control exercised by central government over local government, is there any point in having a separate institution of local government?

The functions exercised by local authorities are largely executive rather than legislative, though, given the amount of direction from central government, they might be described as administrative. Local authorities also have limited legislative functions. They can make delegated legislation where Parliament delegates a specific power under general legislation. They also have the power to make a specific form of delegated legislation known as **bylaws**.

bylaws
laws that relate to the local authority area only

The thinking behind both of these is that local authorities are best placed to know what legislation is appropriate to their location and circumstances.

 1.4 # The European Union

Government in Britain is not just concerned with internal organization. It also has an international dimension, most significantly arising from its membership of the European Union, which may now be considered.

As Europe had been so torn apart during World War II, it was not surprising that, after the end of the war, enormous efforts were made to try to prevent any recurrence. One aspect of this was in the form of a series of treaties relating to coal and steel (1951), atomic power (1957) and the establishment of an economic community (1957). As the war receded in time, the focus of European cooperation became more focused on economic activity and a move toward greater integration in matters associated with this. The United Kingdom was a late entrant into this endeavour, with membership of what was then the Common Market only becoming effective on 1 January 1973. This was the date when the European Communities Act 1972 came into force. The Act was necessary because when the United Kingdom signs a treaty with another country or countries, this only binds the United Kingdom as an entity in international law. It has no effect on English law unless and until it is incorporated into English law by means of an Act of Parliament.

Membership of what is now the European Union has a significant impact on those areas of law which European Union law affects. As an organization focusing on economic activity, its core activities have been those things most closely associated with this, such as trade and employment. Thus its effect on English law, while significant in those areas it affected, was not felt across many areas of English law which thus remained untouched by membership of the European Union. More recently however, the European Union has developed an interest in areas allied to economic activity, and its emerging social agenda may yet spread its influence into areas of law hitherto unaffected. A further influence has come from the growth of the European Union, as the addition of new members necessarily affects the way in which the Union operates, with implications for both new and existing members.

In terms of its structure, the European Union has four main institutions:

The Council of the Union

The Council of the Union is a key body in the structure of the Union. It is composed of Ministers from each of the member states and, as such, is the forum where national interests are most keenly debated. It has the power to enact legislation, though in some areas it must act in cooperation with the European Parliament.

The European Commission

The interests of the Union are most apparent in the workings of the European Commission, which consists of commissioners nominated by the member states who work across the range of European Union activities. Its role is traditionally expressed in its description as the guardian of the treaties, signifying that its role is primarily supranational rather than national. As part of its function, it ensures that member states comply with European Union law, if necessary bringing a state before the European Court of Justice where it believes that state is not complying with its obligations under European Union law. It can initiate legislation which may then be enacted by the Council or can legislate on matters which the council has delegated to it.

The European Parliament

As the European Union and its predecessors have developed, the European Parliament has come to play a more prominent role, and can no longer be dismissed as a mere 'talking shop'. It is now an important component in the internal balance that is said to characterize the workings of the European Union, especially with regard to legislation in a range of powers requiring it to be consulted, to be involved in the decision making process, or to be a part of the process in deciding whether legislation should be passed.

The European Parliament comprises representatives from the member states who are elected directly by voters in constituencies in rather the same way that national elections are conducted. Members of the European Parliament (MEPs) sit in their political groupings rather than in national groups.

The European Court of Justice

As the European Union involves not just political cooperation but also legal relationships, it needs a court to adjudicate over disputes as to the application of that law. It does this in two broad ways. One is by hearing cases brought directly to it, where, for example, it is alleged that a member state has failed to comply with European Union law. Another is to hear cases referred to it by national courts under Article 234 of the Treaty. This occurs where a national court is unsure of the interpretation of European Union law and seeks a ruling on this by the European Court of Justice. As such rulings are binding on member states, the process helps to provide coherence within the European Union by providing uniform interpretation of European Union law across all member states.

cross reference
This is discussed
further in Chapter 3.

1.4.1 **European Union law**

European Union law comprises a number of different types of measure. Of primary significance are the various treaties, especially the European Economic Community Treaty 1957 (the Treaty of Rome), the Treaty of European Union 1992 and the Amsterdam Treaty 1997, each of which has developed the process of integration which has always been an objective of the enterprise.

Secondary legislation of the European Union comes in a variety of forms, the main forms of which are regulations and directives. Regulations are said to be of general application and directly applicable. They are described as generally applicable because they apply as law in all member states and as directly applicable because they automatically become law in all member states without the member state having to do anything in order to implement them. In English law, s.2(1) European Communities Act 1972 provides for this. In English law, it would not be possible for a law made outside the United Kingdom to be effective in English domestic law without an Act of Parliament making provision for this. Directives recognise the diversity of legal systems across the member states. They generally provide for a result to be achieved and a date by which that result is to be achieved, both of which are binding on member states, but it is left to the member state to decide how to achieve that result.

A further source of European Union law comes in the form of case law of the European Court of Justice. As well as providing rulings on the interpretation of matters of European Union law and thus ensuring that its application is uniform across all the member states of the European Union, the European Court of Justice also enables the law, and especially that contained in the treaties, to develop in line with current needs and thinking, thus preventing it from becoming outdated.

(1.5) **Inward and outward looking**

As we have seen, in terms of its government, the United Kingdom is both inward and outward looking. It has assumed obligations relating to its membership of a number of international organisations, with the European Union having a significant legal impact domestically due to both its legal and political dimensions. Internally, the division of government into various tiers has changed the legal relationship between the various bodies that have governmental functions. The constitutional history of the United Kingdom has been one of constant change, and so these relationships are not static but rather evolve.

This state of constant evolution is perhaps the most defining characteristic of all those attributed to the British constitution.

Questions

If you answer the following questions, you will have appreciated the main issues raised in this chapter. Check your answers against the notes provided at the back of the book.

1 What are the main characteristics of the British constitution?

2 How does the British constitution differ from constitutions of other countries?

3 Describe the structure of British government, both national and local.

4 What is the impact of British membership of the European Union?

Further reading

To further your understanding of the topics covered in this chapter, have a look at the reading materials mentioned below. Useful web links are also provided on the Online Resource Centre.

A.W. Bradley and K.D. Ewing, *Constitutional and Administrative Law* (Pearson Longman, 14th ed., 2007) chs.1 and 3
These chapters will give you a detailed account of the nature of constitutions and of government in the United Kingdom and the devolution of power within it.

Michael Allen and Brian Thompson, *Cases and Materials on Constitutional and Administrative Law* (Oxford University Press, 9th ed., 2008) ch. 3
This provides you with extracts from primary sources relating to the European Union together with commentary.

Features of the constitution

Learning Objectives

While reading this chapter, you should aim to understand:

- the theory of the separation of powers;
- how the separation of powers applies (or does not apply) to the British constitution;
- the meanings of the rule of law;
- the nature of constitutional conventions; and
- the part played by conventions in the British constitution.

Introduction

In this chapter we examine two ideas that are said to provide theoretical underpinnings of the British constitution, namely the separation of powers and the rule of law, and also constitutional conventions, which occupy an unusual position in the British constitution.

 2.1 # The separation of powers

One of the most fundamental questions for any state is how power is to be exercised and by whom. It has been recognized since as far back as ancient Greece that it is undesirable to have all the power of the state concentrated in one person or body as this carries with it the potential for abuse. Writers from Aristotle onwards have sought to analyse state power in terms of a number of different functions and have argued that in order to prevent undue concentration of power, these various functions should be distributed amongst a number of persons or bodies thus creating a balance of power in the state. In other words, there should be a separation of the various powers of the state among a number of persons or institutions. This is a question of identifying ways in which power might be exercised within a state and by whom.

Montesquieu

....

Charles-Louis de Secondat, later Baron de Montesquieu, was born in 1689 into a wealthy and noble family. He studied law and engaged in the activities of government typical of members of the nobility, but his interest in political organization culminated in *The Spirit of the Laws* (*L'Esprit des Lois*) of 1748, the work for which he is best known, in which he viewed the British constitution in a favourable light as a model for preventing the state from exercising excessive power. He died in 1755.

With regard to the British constitution this idea is linked with the French writer Montesquieu, though he has no monopoly of thought on the subject nor was he the first to have considered it. In his work, translated as *The Spirit of the Laws* (1748), he considered the British constitution and made a number of observations regarding its nature and operation. He identified three functions of the state: the executive, the legislative and the judicial. As a broad generalization, these functions may be identified as follows:

- the executive function involves the formulation and execution of policy;
- the legislative function is concerned with the making of laws; and
- the judicial function relates to adjudication over disputes.

We will return to these functions in more detail later. Montesquieu argued that to concentrate more than one of these functions in any individual or body posed a threat to individual liberty. He argued instead that these functions should be kept separate to prevent excessive concentration of power. He further argued that the way to prevent abuses of power was to have a system of checks and balances whereby each of the bodies exercising one of these functions would be subject to the influence of the bodies exercising the other two functions. Thus, the executive would be kept in check by the legislature and the judiciary; the legislature by the executive and the judiciary; and the judiciary by the executive and the legislature. In diagrammatic terms, it might look like this:

Figure 2.1

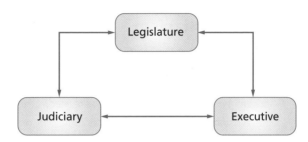

The idea of the separation of powers is thus essentially prescriptive: it is concerned with what ought to happen rather than being descriptive of what actually happens in any given state. The theory is easy to state in general terms and as such is perhaps unexceptional as a political ideal. However, difficulties arise when trying to translate these notions into practice. First, the functions of the state do not translate neatly into the categories identified by Montesquieu. Secondly, there are really three issues to be considered:

• whether the functions should be kept separate;

• whether the institutions exercising those functions should be kept separate; and

• whether the personnel in those institutions should be kept separate.

Thirdly, the theory tells us nothing about the way in which this system of checks and balances might operate. How much power should each exercise? How far should each be subject to the others? Fourthly, it does not tell us how this matter is to be decided. Whilst under a written constitution the functions and powers may be set out in the constitution itself, that cannot be the case in the unwritten British constitution which Montesquieu was supposedly describing. Here, the matter is regulated by a mixture of law and convention. Further, under a written constitution these matters are fixed by the constitution itself and are maintained because the constitution is generally protected against change. Under the British constitution, by contrast, the relationship between the legislature, executive and judiciary are not fixed and are subject to change. Even in those states with a written constitution, the formal allocation of functions and powers is only a skeleton and does not tell us how the system works in practice.

thinking point

Does the idea of the separation of powers seem a desirable principle for states to follow? Is it compatible with the efficient running of the state?

These points may be illustrated by examining the extent to which the separation of powers exists in the British constitution, focusing initially on the institutions of Parliament, the government and the courts, which represent the legislature, executive and judiciary respectively. The British constitution has, as we have seen, evolved in an unplanned way and continues to evolve. Thus the manifestation of the separation of powers owes more to political and legal developments than to any blueprint.

2.1.1 **Parliament**

The legislative role in Britain is largely taken by Parliament, which comprises the House of Commons, containing elected Members of Parliament, and the House of Lords, comprising a mixture of appointed and hereditary peers. Whilst its primary function may be the passing of legislation, it has other functions, notably, in the present context, holding the government to account. It also controls national finance and is a forum for debate and the redress of grievances. In terms of its personnel, many of its members sit in more than one capacity. It is a convention that Ministers must be members of one or other of the Houses of Parliament, and so all the political members of the government are also MPs or peers. The archbishops and certain bishops of the Church of England sit in the House of Lords by reason of the post they hold.

cross reference
Parliament is discussed more fully in Chapter 4.

Also, for the time being, Parliament houses the highest court in the land in the House of Lords with the result that its judges are also members of the House of Lords. As full members of the House of Lords they could theoretically take part in its legislative activities. However, by convention, they refrain from involvement in politically controversial matters as this might compromise their judicial neutrality. This may, however, be a difficult distinction to sustain, as hardly anything is immune from political controversy of some kind. The convention does seek to emphasize the importance attached to the separation of powers, recognising the potential conflict between the two roles of judging and legislating.

thinking point
Is there a conflict between judging and legislating?

One of the changes that have occurred under the Labour government from 1997 onwards has been to make aspects of the separation of powers a matter of legal structure rather than convention. This has, in this context, been achieved by the creation of a Supreme Court separate from Parliament, which then removes the need for the highest court to be part of Parliament and judges to be members of the House of Lords. There is thus a clear concentration on the judicial function in the new Supreme Court.

One of the notable features of the British constitution is the requirement that members of the government are also Members of Parliament. Were it only the case that members of the government were also members of the legislature, the objection to this dual role might be reduced. The problem, however, is that under the British system of government, the party with the majority of seats in the House of Commons also forms the government. This means that, not only is there an overlap between members of the government and Parliament, but also that the government dominates Parliament to the extent that it can ensure that its legislative proposals become law. Given the importance of the principle of **parliamentary sovereignty**, or supremacy, in the British constitution, this has significant implications to which we will return later.

. . . .

parliamentary sovereignty

the principle of parliamentary sovereignty, or supremacy, is that Parliament is the law making body with the highest authority in the UK and can make laws subject to no prior restraints; and that the courts cannot overturn laws made by Parliament: see further Chapter 3

. . . .

2.1.2 **The executive**

The executive in Britain is constituted in part by the government, that is, those members of the majority party in Parliament who hold some form of ministerial office and are concerned in policy formulation and overseeing its execution. Members of the government, as we have seen, also have to be members of one or other of the Houses of Parliament. The executive also comprises those parts of the state machinery that are concerned with carrying out government policy such as the civil service, the army and the police. In contrast to the political members of the executive, those involved in the administration of law and executive policy are barred from membership of the House of Commons under s.1 House of Commons Disqualification Act 1975. In addition to these functions members of the executive carry out legislative functions by making **delegated legislation**.

. . . .

delegated legislation

an Act of Parliament may contain powers enabling an individual, usually the Secretary of State or a named organization such as a local authority, to make law. This is called delegated legislation because Parliament has delegated the law making power to the person or body. Delegated legislation takes many forms, including Statutory Instruments and bylaws

. . . .

It has been a feature of legislative activity that increasingly, in the interests of efficiency, Parliament has delegated to Ministers or local authorities the power to make law. Essentially Parliament lays down a framework which is then fleshed out by regulations and other forms of delegated legislation, which provide a more detailed form of law. Thus, the power to make law is, in principle, governed by Parliament which can set limits on the power to make delegated legislation by the terms it uses when passing the Act which confers the power to make it.

Ministers also exercise functions that could be classified as judicial in deciding on disputes over matters such as planning, tax or immigration. Whilst all of these are subject to an appeal to the courts, the initial decision rests with someone whose primary function is executive. Again, there have been moves to try to separate out this function by creating a legal framework more appropriate to such disputes. Until recently, tribunals came under the relevant government department. However, in line with the requirement in Article 6 of the European Convention on Human Rights, that adjudication must be by an

cross reference
See further Chapters 5 and 10.

cross reference
See further Chapters 5 and 10.

independent and impartial tribunal, under the Tribunals, Courts and Enforcement Act 2007 the tribunal service is now constituted as a body wholly separate from the relevant government department.

2.1.3 **The judiciary**

The function of the judges and the courts in which they sit is to resolve disputes and, in the process of doing so, rule on the interpretation of the law. At one level this appears self contained. However, whilst the courts may not seem to be involved in legislative activities, the line between interpretation and development of the law and law making is one which is difficult to draw in practice. The theory is that judges do not make law but simply declare what the law is. Lord Reid exploded this particular idea in a lecture in 1972 ('The Judge as Law Maker' (1972) 12 JSPTL 22) where he argued that the courts clearly were involved in law making: developing the common law or interpreting an Act of Parliament were clearly creative activities which took the judges beyond the realms of merely declaring what the law is. The real question, therefore, is how much creativity should the judges properly exercise. Much of the answer to this lies in how far the judges are prepared to exercise self restraint and to recognize their constitutional position *vis-à-vis* the executive and the legislature. This is discussed further below.

cross reference
See Chapter 6.

thinking point
Would it be possible to devise a system where legislative, executive and judicial functions were totally separate?

It is, so far, apparent that the institutions identified above are not confined to one area of operation only. Parliament does more than simply legislate; the government does more than simply formulate and administer policy; the courts do not simply adjudicate. The compartments are not watertight. It may be questioned whether they ever can be. Can a clear line, for example, be drawn between the functions of legislating and of scrutinizing the executive in Parliament as presently constituted? Perhaps some overlap of functions and personnel is necessary to achieve workability: each of these institutions working in isolation may not function as effectively. The matter may be further explored by looking at the relationships each institution has with the other two.

2.2 Relationships between the organs of government

2.2.1 **Parliament and the government**

One of Parliament's key roles is to call the government to account. It does so in a variety of different ways. It is an integral part of the legislative process, in that every stage through which a **bill** passes has to conclude with a vote which must be favourable in order for the bill to proceed further.

. . . .

a bill

a bill is the form in which an instrument which ultimately becomes an Act of Parliament starts while it is
under discussion in Parliament

. . . .

The very process of consideration of a bill, whether in the House or in a committee,
involves questioning the desirability of the government's proposals and deciding whether
to support them or not. There are other mechanisms whereby the activities of the executive can be subject to scrutiny, however. The most visible, from the public perspective, is
Question Time in which the Prime Minister and other Ministers are required to answer
questions in the House of Commons. This activity is largely about the political relationship between the parties with the government trying to defend its policies in the face
of questions, which are often hostile, from members of opposing parties and questions,
which are often friendly, from their own back bench members. More searching, though
not as visible, are written questions, the answers to which may provide more information than an oral answer might provide. This is often because they are seeking more
detailed information, thus requiring a longer time to compile. A written reply may well
also require longer than the time available to reply orally to a question. Further, the information may not be readily digestible as part of an oral answer.

The ultimate accountability in Parliament comes in the form of a vote of no confidence
in the government, which will normally be initiated by the opposition. Such a vote is
rare and even more rarely successful, as a government can usually survive on the basis
of the support it enjoys from its own party members. The last time a government lost a
vote of no confidence was in 1979: the Labour government was then forced to resign
and call a general election. For the same reason calls for Ministers to resign can usually
be resisted. Less dramatic forms of accountability occur through the operation of parliamentary committees and their reports which can provide critical analysis of the policies
and practices of government.

cross reference
See Chapter 4.

However, as the government comprises the party with the largest number of seats in the
House of Commons, it can ensure that its measures will, unless there is a serious back
bench revolt, pass into law as it can muster enough votes to secure its passage. Thus,
whilst, in theory, one of Parliament's functions is to act as a check on the executive, in
practice, the executive in its turn acts as a check on Parliament, for it can prevent the
passing into law of anything of which it disapproves.

thinking point
*If the government
has a majority in
Parliament, can
it be truly said to
be accountable to
Parliament?*

2.2.2 **Parliament and the courts**

The relationship between the courts and Parliament is conditioned by a number of factors, of which two are particularly notable. First, Article 9 of the Bill of Rights 1689
provides (in modern spelling) 'that the freedom of speech and debates or proceedings
in Parliament ought not to be impeached or questioned in any court or place outside
Parliament'. This, on its face, inhibits the courts from any inquiry as to the way in which

Parliament conducts itself and hence limits the courts' ability to scrutinize its operations. This becomes particularly significant when coupled with the second key factor which is the idea of parliamentary sovereignty. In the absence of a written constitution, parliamentary sovereignty is fundamental to the operation of the British constitution. It is a legal idea which means that the validity of legislation passed by Parliament cannot be challenged in the courts. This only works if the courts accept the limitation on their powers. The evidence is that on the whole the courts recognize the respective position of themselves and Parliament in constitutional arrangements and respect the boundaries between them. This is partly in recognition of the separation of powers and may be illustrated with reference to some decisions of the House of Lords.

In *Pickin v British Railways Board* [1974] AC 765, it was held that once a document had been identified as an Act of Parliament the courts could not go behind it to examine the way in which it had been passed to see if, as the plaintiff asserted, there had been a procedural irregularity. This approach was recently followed in *(R)Jackson v Attorney General* [2006] 1 AC 262, where again the courts maintained that the validity of an Act of Parliament could not be challenged. This principle has been qualified with regard to statutes in conflict with European Union law. Here, the courts have held that such legislative provisions must be set aside in order to comply with the obligation of the UK resulting from EU membership. Thus, in *Factortame v Secretary of State for Transport* [1990] 2 AC 85; [1991] 1 AC 603, the House of Lords set aside provisions in the Merchant Shipping Act 1988 which were in conflict with European Community law. At one level, this gives the courts greater power to check the activities of the legislature by having the capacity to set aside conflicting laws. However, this is carried out under parliamentary authority, as s.2(4) of the European Communities Act 1972 requires that Acts of Parliament are to be given effect subject to European law, including the principle of European sovereignty.

This may be contrasted with the position under the Human Rights Act 1998 where the courts are not able to set aside legislation which is incompatible with the European Convention on Human Rights. They are required, by s.3, as far as possible to interpret legislation so as to be compatible with the convention rights. If this is not possible, then, under s.4, they have the power to issue a declaration of incompatibility. The effect of this is, however, simply to indicate that, in the view of the court, there is an incompatibility between the Act and the convention rights. The Act remains in force untouched, unless and until Parliament changes it.

The courts have considerable latitude as to the meaning of Acts of Parliament under the guise of interpretation. Although they cannot rewrite the legislation, they can, by the approach they take to the interpretation of the words used, significantly influence the scope of a piece of legislation. An extreme example is provided by the decision of the House of Lords in *Anisminic v Foreign Compensation Commission* [1969] 2 AC 147. Here, the Foreign Compensation Act 1950 provided that the decisions of the Foreign Compensation Commission were final and were not to be questioned in any court whatsoever. The House of Lords held, however, that this exclusion of the courts could only

cross reference
See further Chapter 3.

cross reference
See Chapter 7.

thinking point
Should the courts have the power to overrule legislation?

thinking point

Does the decision in Anisminic v Foreign Compensation Commission constitute an abuse of power by the courts?

thinking point

Does the passing of the War Damage Act 1965 constitute an abuse of power by Parliament?

apply to a correct determination by the Commission, and not to one that was incorrect as Parliament could not have meant to deny a remedy through the courts to someone in respect of whom an incorrect decision had been reached.

Parliament does, however, have the final word, for it can alter by legislation decisions of the courts that are not felt to be satisfactory. Thus, for example, in *Burmah Oil Co v Lord Advocate* [1965] AC 75, the House of Lords decided that damage caused in wartime by British troops, acting under the royal prerogative, destroying oil installations to prevent them falling into enemy hands was an activity in respect of which compensation was payable. The government introduced, and Parliament passed, the War Damage Act 1965 which reversed this decision, and did so retrospectively: not only was compensation not payable in respect of such damage, it had never been payable.

2.2.3 **The executive and the courts**

As with their relationship with Parliament, the courts have, to some extent, been self determining in their approach to their relations with the government with regard to checks on the exercise of executive power. The legislative prohibition on questioning the activities of Parliament does not have a counterpart with regard to the government. Major obstacles, such as the ability to review powers exercised under the royal prerogative or the immunity of the Crown in litigation, have been gradually dismantled so as to allow the courts to rule on the lawfulness of government action across almost the full range of its activities. The Crown Proceedings Act 1947 removed many of the obstacles to Crown liability in contract and tort, whilst the decision of the House of Lords in *Council of Civil Service Unions v Minister for the Civil Service* [1985] AC 374 paved the way for the courts to review the way in which powers under the royal prerogative are exercised, though subject to the significant limitation that the subject matter has to be something on which the courts can meaningfully adjudicate: the previous prohibition on questioning matters relating to national security or foreign affairs for example remain. These are not matters on which a court could sensibly pronounce as they involve sensitive policy considerations.

thinking point

Should there be any limitations on matters over which the court can adjudicate? Should a court, for example, be able to declare whether a declaration of war was lawful?

Subject to this and similar areas of sensitive subject matter, the courts are able to review the ways in which the executive acts. They are thus able to act as a check on executive action, though the extent to which they do so in practice varies. The judges may take a wide or narrow view of the legislation they are considering. Depending on what standpoint they adopt with regard to interpretation of the particular piece of legislation, they can intervene to declare executive action to be unlawful or can decline to do so.

Relationships between the organs of government

31

Whilst the role of the courts is to decide whether the executive has acted lawfully or not, the courts inevitably become enmeshed in questions that have a political undercurrent. The line between law and politics is difficult to draw: some would argue that there is no line between them and that there is a political dimension to all legal decisions, at least with regard to those involving the state. A few examples serve to illustrate the point.

case close-up

Bromley London Borough Council v Greater London Council [1983] 1 AC 768

The Labour group on the GLC had fought an election manifesto including a pledge that, if elected, they would reduce fares on London Transport by 25%. Once elected, they implemented this pledge. Bromley LBC challenged the legality of the rate precept that had been levied and argued that the GLC was in breach of its statutory duty to provide efficient and economic transport for London. The House of Lords held that the GLC had failed to give sufficient weight to the requirement to run the transport system economically. They could not lawfully devise policies that would lead to the system making a loss and thus need to be financed by higher rate precepts. They had also failed to give sufficient weight to the fact that the money they were spending was public money deriving from ratepayers across London. Further, they had given too much weight to the manifesto commitment and to the requirement to run services efficiently. Reducing the fares in this way was thus unlawful.

thinking point

Do you think it is significant that the ruling group on the GLC was the Labour Party and on Bromley LBC it was the Conservative Party?

case close-up

Secretary of State for Education v Tameside MBC [1977] AC 1014

This case concerned what was essentially a dispute between central and local government. Under s.68 Education Act 1944, the Secretary of State was empowered to give such directions to a local education authority 'as appear to him to be expedient' provided he was satisfied that the authority 'have acted or are proposing to act unreasonably'. The council had put forward a scheme for the implementation of comprehensive schools within its area. This had been approved by the Secretary of State. Following an election, however, the ruling group on the council changed, and the newly constituted council proposed to abandon the comprehensive scheme, retain grammar schools and operate a selective regime. The Secretary of State gave directions under s.68 requiring the council to implement the previously approved comprehensive scheme. The House of Lords held that the directions were unlawful. The local authority had a scheme which was capable of implementation. It could not, therefore, be said that they were acting unreasonably, and therefore the Secretary of State had no basis for issuing directions.

thinking point
In both the GLC and the Tameside cases, were the views of the voters relevant?

case close-up

Congreve v Home Secretary [1976] QB 629

The issue here was whether the Home Secretary had acted lawfully in demanding an additional payment from television licence holders who had renewed their licences early to avoid a price increase previously announced. Under the Wireless Telegraphy Act 1949, a television licence may be issued subject to such terms as the Minister may think fit and may be revoked on giving written notice to the holder. The Minister had announced an increase in licence fees. Mr. Congreve, and a number of like-minded people, had bought new television licences before their existing ones expired in order to avoid the increased fee which would be payable if they waited for their licences to reach the expiry date. The Home Office wrote to these people stating that they could not renew their licences early and demanding the difference between the fee they had paid and the increased fee. It was held that the Home Office was acting unlawfully. The object of the licensing scheme was to regulate broadcasting and not to make money. The licence holders were acting lawfully as there was nothing in law to stop them acting as they had.

These examples serve to illustrate that the courts have a pivotal role in determining whether the executive is acting lawfully or not in exercising its powers. However, the executive can attempt to restrict the amount of scope the courts have to declare executive action to be unlawful by inserting provisions into legislation restricting the ability of the courts to intervene and then using their majority to ensure that it passes through Parliament. The attempt to use the Foreign Compensation Act 1950, in *Anisminic* (above), to exclude the jurisdiction of the courts is just one example.

2.2.4 Conclusion: the separation of powers

It will have become apparent from the discussion above that there is a degree of uncertainty in the exact nature of the relationship between the institutions of the legislature, executive and judiciary and their respective functions. This is almost inevitable given the unwritten nature of the British constitution. It means, however, that the exact scope of the separation of powers under the British constitution is hard to determine and inevitably, in the circumstances, opinions differ as to this.

The judges have been very positive in their assertions that the constitution is based on a separation of powers. In *Duport Steels Ltd v Sirs* [1980] 1 WLR 142 at 157, for example, Lord Diplock said: '...it cannot be too strongly emphasised that the British constitution, though largely unwritten, is firmly based upon the separation of powers'. However, this may in part be due to the perspective of the judges, who may be expected to see the separation of powers with a particular emphasis on the independence of the judiciary, which is a feature of the British constitutional arrangements and, as we have seen in Chapter 1, has been strengthened by the changes brought about by the Constitutional Reform Act 2005. At the other extreme, the complete overlap between the political wing of the executive and the legislature would provide evidence that the separation of powers is not a feature of the British constitution. Perhaps the true position is most accurately expressed by Sir David Williams, who has written that the doctrine is 'at best selective in application' ('Bias, the Judges and the Separation of Powers' [2000] PL 45 at 47).

2.3 The rule of law

The rule of law is a slippery concept. No doubt those using the term know what they mean by it, but the difficulty lies in the fact that usages differ. There is a confident statement in s.1 Constitutional Reform Act 2005:

statute

> **Constitutional Reform Act 2005, s.1**
>
> This Act does not adversely affect—
>
> (a) the existing constitutional principle of the rule of law, or
> (b) the Lord Chancellor's existing constitutional role in relation to that principle.

This is asserted as if the phrase 'the rule of law' had a fixed and commonly understood meaning. As the following discussion will illustrate, this is far from being the case. Unravelling the meaning of the term is not easy as there is a tendency, in many discussions of the rule of law, to be prescriptive rather than descriptive. In this section, a number of possible meanings of the term will be explored, each of which commands a certain degree of support.

2.3.1 Order v Anarchy

At its most basic, the concept can be taken to express a preference for society functioning within a framework of law in order to prevent anarchy. In *Heaton's Transport v Transport and General Workers' Union* [1973] AC 15 at 23, Sir John Donaldson said:

> . . . Without the rule of law and courts to enforce it, each one of us would be free to push and bully our fellow citizens and (which may be thought more important) our fellow citizens would be free to push and bully us. In a free for all none of us could hope to be the winner. The justification for the law, the courts and the rule of law is that they protect us from unfair and oppressive actions by others; but if we are to have that protection we must ourselves accept that the law applies to us too, and limits our freedom.

thinking point

Is Sir John Donaldson correct? Why do you think some areas of human interaction are regulated by law whilst others are not?

2.3.2 **Everyone subject to law**

> ### Dicey
> ....
> Albert Venn Dicey was born in 1835 and embarked on practice as a barrister but later returned to Oxford, where he had been a student, to pursue an academic career, becoming Vinerian Professor of English Law in 1882. His inaugural lecture *Can English Law be Taught in the Universities?* (1883) (to which the answer was that it could) was followed by other publications, including his work *Conflict of Laws* (first published in 1896 and now published as *Dicey, Morris and Collins on the Conflict of Laws*) and his Harvard lectures of 1898, later published as *Lectures on the Relation Between Law and Public Opinion in England During the Nineteenth Century* (1905). His major work on the constitution is his *Introduction to the Study of the Law of the Constitution* (first published in 1885).

As Sir John Donaldson indicates, however, there is a related dimension to this idea: where a society is to be governed by law, as opposed to any other forces, this will necessarily involve the notion that everyone agrees to be subject to that law. Dicey (*Introduction to the Study of the Law of the Constitution* (Macmillan, 10th ed., 1959) p.193) expressed this idea thus:

> No man is above the law . . . every man is subject to the ordinary law of the realm and amenable to the jurisdiction of ordinary tribunals.

It may seem self evident that in a system governed by law, all should be subject to the law. However, this is not always borne out in practice. At common law, the Crown was exempt from much of the law, so that it could not be sued in contract or tort. This immunity was largely reduced by the Crown Proceedings Act 1947, which removed most of these immunities. The Crown remains exempt from the operation of Acts of Parliament unless the Act is stated to apply to it, or it applies by necessary implication. Some immunities from the operation of the law are conferred by statute: diplomatic immunity is an obvious example.

It could be argued that immunities conferred by statute are not strictly examples of individuals being above the law because it is the law itself which has determined that they enjoy this immunity. However, conferring immunity goes against the spirit of the rule of law if not its letter. Some immunities seem to flout the principle quite openly. In *R v Secretary of State for Home Affairs ex p O'Brien* [1923] 2 KB 361, the Home Secretary had ordered the deportation of a number of Irish nationals on the ground that they were undesirable. The Court of Appeal held that the Home Secretary had misinterpreted his powers. His action was unlawful as he had no power to order deportation on this ground. He should have been subjected to penalties as a result, but the government secured the passage of an Act of indemnity, the Restoration of Order in Ireland (Indemnity) Act 1923, to prevent him becoming subject to any penalty.

thinking point

Is passing an indemnity Act contrary to the spirit of the rule of law?

2.3.3 **Equality before the law**

Dicey writes of the importance not only of no one being above the law but of all being equal before the law (*Introduction to the Study of the Law of the Constitution* (Macmillan, 10th ed., 1959)). This is very different to saying that individuals should be equal within the law. This is clearly impossible, as one of the roles of the law is not only to mediate power relationships to prevent anarchy, as Donaldson J explains in the passage quoted earlier, but also to confer power on those who need it. Consequently different individuals have different powers. So, for example, government, whether central or local, police officers and other officials have greater powers than individual citizens in order to carry out their functions effectively.

2.3.4 **Adjudication in the ordinary courts**

In the last part of the statement quoted above, Dicey was contrasting the position in Britain with that in France and other continental countries which have special courts and tribunals to deal with constitutional matters. He is expressing a preference for the British model as he suggests that the specialist continental tribunals may favour the government against the citizen whereas the ordinary courts in Britain are, he believes, neutral as between the parties. Similarly, his reference to the ordinary law is indicative of his scepticism about the ability of a written constitution to offer protection to individuals, preferring instead the system based on parliamentary sovereignty which, he suggests, means that the rights of individuals can be better protected by legislation which addressed individual issues rather than the more generalized pronouncements in written constitutions.

2.3.5 **Government according to law**

Dicey's faith in the ability of a parliamentary democracy to deliver greater protection than a written constitution also leads him to put forward the idea that government should be conducted according to law. Professor Graham Zellick has written (*The Guardian* 15 February 1988) that '[t]here is no more important principle in British constitutional law than the doctrine of legality under which the government in all its guises must conform scrupulously to the letter of the law'.

thinking point
Following this decision, how would you have responded if you had been Home Secretary?

The courts have subscribed to the principle in requiring the government to justify any action it takes by reference to the law authorizing the action. The principle was upheld in a series of cases in the 17th and 18th centuries which provided the foundations of the modern law.

Entick v Carrington (1765) 19 St Tr.1030

· ·

Government officials entered the home of the plaintiff in order to search for seditious and other materials. When sued in trespass, they relied on a warrant issued by the Home Secretary and also a claim that their actions were justified on the ground of state interest. These arguments were rejected. The Home Secretary had no power to issue a warrant couched, as here, in general terms. Further, the law did not recognize state interests as a justification for entry to premises and conducting a search of them. In a celebrated passage, Lord Camden CJ said:

> By the laws of England, every invasion of private property . . . is a trespass. No man can set his foot upon my ground without my licence, but he is liable to an action, though the damage be nothing . . . If he admits the fact, he is bound to shew by way of justification that some positive law has empowered or excused him. The justification is submitted to the judges, who are to look into the books; and see if such a justification can be maintained by the text of the statute law or by the principles of common law. If no such excuse can be found or produced, the silence of the books is an authority against the defendant and the plaintiff must have judgment.

(This passage only appears in the State Trials version of the report from which an extract appears in Michael Allen and Brian Thompson *Cases and Materials on Constitutional and Administrative Law* (Oxford University Press, 9th ed., 2008) ch.4 at p.158.)

thinking point
As the council had given more than 24 hours' notice, does this decision seem reasonable?

The courts have often, though not universally, taken a strict approach to the interpretation of powers given to the state, especially where they involve depriving individuals of their liberty or entering premises. In *Stroud v Bradbury* [1952] 2 All ER 76, for example, the Public Health Act 1936 allowed council officials to enter premises on giving 24 hours' notice. They sought to enter a week later. It was held that they were acting unlawfully. The notice had expired due to the delay in executing it.

Most people would subscribe to the idea of government according to law, but like the notion of the rule of law itself it is not easy to apply. The law is often ambiguous and open to competing interpretations.

Further, as the government has a majority in the House of Commons, and more often than not a working majority, the government is able to secure the passage through Parliament of legislation in the form it wants that legislation to be: the government essentially creates the rules by which it is governed.

2.3.6 **Discretion: arbitrary authority?**

A particular feature of modern legislation, to which Dicey would take exception, is that it gives government or other state officials the choice (discretion) to decide how to act in particular circumstances: for example, to grant planning permission or not to do so; to arrest or not to arrest. Dicey (*Introduction to the Study of the Law of the Constitution* (Macmillan, 10th ed., 1959) p.188) contrasted government according to the rule of law with government by arbitrary or discretionary authority. It must be remembered that at the time Dicey was writing government was on a much smaller scale than today. The considerable expansion in the scale of government that has occurred in the last 50 years has brought with it a corresponding expansion in the law. Governments, if they are to act in conformity with the law in order to uphold the rule of law, need to be given powers to carry out their functions, especially if those functions impact on the ordinary citizen. Indeed, under the European Convention on Human Rights, which, it will be recalled, is part of English law by virtue of the Human Rights Act 1998, any limitations on the Convention rights have to be effected by law.

Central government has some powers deriving from the common law, which were formerly exercised by the monarch as part of the royal prerogative. The courts have, however, set strict limits on the availability and exercise of those powers, with the result that the vast majority of governmental powers are created by statute. The same is true, for example, of the police, who, whilst enjoying some powers by virtue of the common law, are again mainly dependent on statutory powers in order to carry out their functions. Local government was created by statute and is entirely dependent on statutory authority to enable it to function.

thinking point
Can modern government operate solely on the basis of fixed rules?

Two models for legal regulation

Legal regulation follows two broad models, though in practice, as will be seen throughout this book, legislation often has characteristics of both. In the first, everything is regulated by detailed rules which leave little scope for the exercise of individual judgement on the part of those administering them. This is advantageous in that it promotes certainty and consistency, with no individual idiosyncrasies taken into account and it operates mechanistically, eliminating any personal bias on the part of the person administering it. The major disadvantage of this model is that it is very generalized and cannot be tailored to individual circumstances. In the second model, the rules are much more loosely drafted leaving scope to those administering the law to consider individual circumstances and mould the law to address them. The existence of discretion is said to be the great strength of this type of legislation, but is also its weakness in that it leaves scope for individual views to affect the way in which powers are used. There are examples of both types of regulation in English law, but it is clear that Dicey preferred the first type. In this, he was dealing with a situation radically different from today where the variety of activities undertaken by government necessitates the exercise of discretion. Discretion was not completely absent in Dicey's time either: decisions to detain aliens or exercise powers of arrest have always been subject to the exercise of discretion.

2.3.7 The problem of retrospective laws

Leaving scope for discretion does, however, mean that the exact parameters of the law are uncertain. This causes problems with regard to one of the other principles denoted by the idea of the rule of law. It is that a person should not be subject to any sanction unless he has broken the law (see Dicey, *Introduction to the Study of the Law of the*

Constitution (Macmillan, 10th ed., 1959) p.188), and that, in order for this principle to operate, the law must exist prior to the alleged breach. This has a particular application in the criminal law and it is no surprise that it finds expression in Article 7 of the European Convention on Human Rights:

> No one shall be held guilty of any criminal offence on account of any act or omission which did not constitute a criminal offence under national or international law at the time when it was committed. Nor shall a heavier penalty be imposed than the one that was applicable at the time the criminal offence was committed.

It is self evidently unjust to punish someone for something that was lawful at the time it was done. This may, however, be contentious. In *Shaw v DPP* [1962] AC 220, the defendant had published the *Ladies' Directory*, a publication listing prostitutes and the services they provided. He was charged with conspiracy to corrupt public morals, an offence which, it was argued, was unknown in English law. That its existence was by no means certain is demonstrated by the fact that the House of Lords held by a majority of 4:1, with a powerful dissent from Lord Reid, that the offence existed and that consequently Mr. Shaw could be convicted of it.

The idea of law informing and attempting to modify behaviour is also relevant here in that the state must make known the conduct it is seeking to prohibit. This is something of a fiction, for no one can know every law that prohibits certain forms of conduct, but nevertheless it is influential on the ability of the state to impose sanctions.

Whilst it might be especially important, in view of the consequences, to prohibit retrospective criminal legislation, the principle has considerable force in the civil law also, where, again, retrospective legislation is frowned upon. The notion that legal change should be prospective rather than retrospective is regarded as an important principle.

It is this thinking that explains the criticism surrounding *Burmah Oil v Lord Advocate* [1965] AC 75, discussed earlier, and its aftermath. The issue, it will be recalled, was whether compensation was payable under the royal prerogative in respect of property requisitioned and destroyed during wartime. The government had taken over oil installations during World War II which had then been destroyed to prevent them falling into the hands of the enemy. The government claimed that as this was damage caused in the conduct of war, compensation was not payable. The House of Lords held that there was a distinction between different types of damage caused in wartime. Whilst compensation might be payable in respect of damage caused in battle, this was damage caused to prevent the installations falling into the hands of the enemy and there was no rule recognized as part of the prerogative that provided that such damage could be caused without compensation being payable. The government however subsequently introduced a bill into Parliament which became the War Damage Act 1965 and provided that compensation was not payable where damage had been caused in the conduct of war. Strikingly, the Act was given retrospective effect: not only was compensation not payable for such acts in the future but it was not payable for such acts in the past. Whilst this might have been strictly within the rule of law in that the law was used to make this

thinking point
Does this violate the spirit of the rule of law?

change and was formally correct, it went against the spirit of the rule of law in that the law had been effectively manipulated to achieve the result the government wanted.

2.3.8 **The content of laws**

So far, the discussion has concentrated on the rule of law as simply requiring formal compliance: so long as the law is used to regulate behaviour and everyone is subject to it then the requirements of the rule of law are satisfied. However, some writers have argued that formal compliance is only part of what the rule of law means. Rousseau, for example, argued that rules should only make laws that are morally reasonable and socially acceptable. Once we move to consideration of the content of rules then the scope for debate widens instantly. Who is to judge whether rules are morally reasonable? In a democracy, that role is undertaken by the legislature whose members are elected to make decisions about the laws by which the country will be governed and are accountable to the electorate for their actions in doing so. Matters become more difficult in a dictatorship or totalitarian regime, where the democratic mandate is not present.

thinking point
Who, ultimately, should decide these matters?

2.3.9 **Obedience to the law**

A related issue here is whether it is ever acceptable to break the law. Civil disobedience has long been a course of action taken by those opposed to particular laws, whether in the form of the mass trespass in the 1930s on private land around Kinder Scout in the Peak District or the refusal to pay the poll tax (as the community charge was more popularly known) in the 1980s and early 1990s. Where ideas of the rule of law are confined to purely formal matters, it becomes easier to argue that the law should be obeyed by everyone because it is the law. It is in this sense that politicians often invoke the rule of law. Where the content of the law is seen as part of the rule of law, then it becomes easier to justify disobedience to repugnant laws.

2.3.10 **Access to justice**

cross reference
See Chapter 12.

An important feature of the rule of law, alluded to earlier, is that there should be access to the means of resolving legal disputes. Although most disputes are settled without recourse to the courts, the rule of law might be said to require that the courts are accessible to all. This has long been a contentious issue, with the financial barriers to using the courts prominent in debates in this area. Restrictions on the availability of financial assistance are cited as denying citizens the benefits of adjudication they should enjoy under a system based on the rule of law. Further, the rule of law is said to require that the courts hear cases fairly: that there is a fair hearing before an unbiased judge. These are the minimum requirements of the rules of natural justice which are discussed later.

2.3.11 Conclusion: rule of law

The rule of law is thus a concept capable of having a variety of meanings. To say what it does mean is more difficult than to suggest what it should mean. A particularly helpful contribution to the debate is provided by Joseph Raz ('The Rule of Law and its Virtue' (1977) 93 LQR 195). He argues that the rule of law *should* have a number of characteristics: his account is prescriptive rather than descriptive. In his view, laws should be prospective and not retrospective; clear; stable—that is not change too frequently; laws should be made by processes that are open and clear; courts should be accessible; court proceedings should be open and fair with legal disputes determined by independent and impartial judges. It will be seen that he places emphasis on openness, clarity and fairness in law making and adjudication. However, as Raz would concede, these aspirations are not always easy to realize in practice and it is the detail of the idea of the rule of law that is so difficult to pin down. Most would agree that adherence to the rule of law is a good idea in general terms but would disagree as to what it means in detail.

thinking point

If it is so difficult to provide a clear and universally accepted definition of the phrase 'the rule of law', does it fulfil any useful purpose in constitutional theory?

 2.4

Conventions

The term 'convention' is used in two distinct senses in constitutional discussion which need to be clearly differentiated. On the one hand, it is the term used to describe an international treaty, such as the European Convention on Human Rights. The second is the term to describe certain non-legal practices that are part of the British constitution and are in consequence often described as constitutional conventions. It is this second type of convention that is considered here.

2.4.1 Nature of conventions

Dicey described constitutional conventions as '... habits or practices which regulate the conduct of members of the sovereign power'. (*Introduction to the Study of the Law of the Constitution* (Macmillan, 10th ed., 1959) p.24). More recently, Professor Hood Phillips (*Constitutional and Administrative Law* (Sweet & Maxwell, 8th ed., (2001) p.2) says that constitutional conventions are 'rules of political practice which are regarded as binding by those to whom they apply but which are not laws as they are not enforced by the courts or by the Houses of Parliament'. These non-legal rules or practices form a distinctive feature of the British constitution. For example, almost the whole of cabinet government—the existence, appointment and resignation of the Prime Minister, the size and membership of the cabinet, the responsibility of Ministers, etc.—is based on convention rather than law. Other examples of conventions include those relating to the monarch, especially those that determine how she should act in particular situations. For example, the convention that she should give the royal assent to legislation; that she should appoint the leader of the party with the majority of seats in the House of Commons as Prime Minister; that she should grant a dissolution of Parliament when the Prime Minister requests it; that she should appoint and dismiss Ministers in accordance with the wishes of the Prime Minister. Conventions attach to other key figures in British constitutional practice: for example, the law lords refrain from participating in any activity that could be construed as political; the Speaker of the House of Commons maintains a stance of strict impartiality.

cross reference
See further
Chapter 4.

42

thinking point
Which is preferable: stability or flexibility in constitutional arrangements?

Under a written constitution, only those things forming part of the constitution can be described as constitutional. Such things are necessarily legal rules given that the constitution is a legal document. They are also fixed rules because the constitution will usually contain provisions designed to prevent it being easily changed. The effect of such provisions is to make the constitution not only difficult to change but also ensuring that any changes will be infrequent, giving it a currency and stability appropriate to something which lies at the foundation of the state. The British constitution is not subject to such constraints and can embrace both legal and non-legal elements. As a result it enjoys both flexibility and the capacity to adapt to changing circumstances. Constitutional conventions contribute to providing this flexibility as they govern the way in which individuals are required to act in particular situations. As with other aspects of the operation of the British constitution, individuals, on the whole, act in ways expected of them. It is for this reason that many of the rules remain as conventions rather than rules of law.

It is possible to identify legal rules as such because they can only come from particular sources: those sources and what comes out of them are capable of being clearly identified. They can only be changed in particular ways and have mechanisms for enforcement and adjudication available. Conventions share none of these features and are consequently more difficult to pin down whilst offering greater flexibility than legal rules. Each of these issues may be considered in turn.

2.4.2 **Establishing and changing conventions**

The first issue to consider is how conventions are established. Unlike a law which is promulgated fully formed, conventions tend to emerge over a period of time. Dicey's description of them as habits or practices is helpful in understanding this point. What turns something that has happened once into a convention is not only repetition, but as Professor Hood Phillips indicates, the idea that the practice should be followed. This suggests that a measure of acceptance of the practice amongst those affected is necessary.

As long as those concerned carry on doing the same things in the same ways, and that this is accepted as correct by all those affected, then it becomes possible to say that a convention has been established. Analysis of what the practice is may reveal the contents of the convention, which are obviously necessary in order to both identify and practise it. Difficulties arise, however, when someone deviates from what has happened previously. There is a problem of interpretation necessarily involved, with two possibilities. First, the different practice is in fact a step toward the establishment of a new convention; or, secondly, that it is a deviation from the previous convention which will be re-established as it formerly was in the future. As with the establishment of a convention the true situation will only emerge over time as practices are followed or not followed.

In any event the precise content of a convention may be difficult to pin down. Changes may be subtle rather than dramatic, affecting the details but not the overall parameters of the convention. Again, it will only be over time that such issues may be resolved. However, it is this flexibility and ability to adapt to changing circumstances that forms one of the most positive features of conventions and gives them an advantage over legal rules. Legal rules have to adopt a particular formula of words which remains until it is changed. Any change has to come about by some formal means such as the passing of an amending piece of legislation. Conventions are not susceptible to this formal process and can alter subtly as time goes on.

thinking point
Is vagueness an acceptable price to pay for flexibility?

Conventions come to an end when they cease to be followed over a period of time. Or there may be a deliberate change, perhaps involving the convention being translated into law. A dramatic example occurred in 1909–1911 (the events are explained in detail in Elizabeth Wicks *The Evolution of a Constitution* (Hart Publishing, 2006) ch.5). The House of Lords refused to pass the Finance Bill containing the measures proposed in the budget presented by the government and passed by the House of Commons. The convention was that the House of Lords should pass measures that had been approved by the House of Commons on matters of government policy. The government threatened that they would create sufficient peers to ensure the passage of the Bill if the Lords did not give way, which they eventually did. Using the same threat, the government then secured the passage of the Parliament Act 1911 which provides for bills to become law in certain circumstances, notwithstanding that they have not been passed by the House of Lords. This is now a legal rule, though a convention still exists (the Salisbury agreement) that the House of Lords should not obstruct a measure forming part of the government's manifesto commitments when it has been passed by the House of Commons.

The situation described above arose because of the failure of the House of Lords to follow a convention. The consequence was both political and legal in that instance. Ordinarily, however, the consequence will only be political. The convention of ministerial responsibility provides an example. If a Minister has failed to follow collective responsibility when required to do so or has acted in a way that casts doubt on his fitness to hold ministerial office or his department has made an error for which the Minister can be held responsible, he might be expected to resign. That this is not universally the case is illustrated in Chapter 5 where this issue is discussed further.

thinking point
Would converting all conventions into legal rules be an improvement on the present situation

2.4.3 **Conventions and the law**

Enforcement of conventions exists through the political process as the courts have no power to enforce something that does not involve the breach of a legal rule. They cannot adjudicate on whether a convention has been breached. This does not mean, however, that the courts completely disregard conventions as there might be purposes for which they are relevant to a legal dispute. The court may need to consider conventions when resolving a legal dispute in order to understand properly the legal question or to put it into a context. The availability of a political solution may lead the courts to a particular conclusion. In *Liversidge v Anderson* [1942] AC 206, for example, the fact that a Minister was accountable to Parliament provided some justification for the conclusion of the majority in the House of Lords that the words 'if the Minister has reasonable grounds for believing a person to be of hostile origins or associations' meant that as long as the Minister was satisfied that he had reasonable grounds to detain someone he was acting lawfully rather than requiring him to have objectively reasonable grounds for a decision to detain that person (see Viscount Maugham at p.222 and Lord Wright at p.270).

thinking point

Should the possibility of a political solution be a reason for refusing a remedy in law?

The desirability of upholding a convention may lend support to an argument that a particular legal position should be adopted.

> ## case close-up
>
> ### *AG v Jonathan Cape* [1976] QB 752
>
> This case concerned the publication of the diaries of Richard Crossman, a former Cabinet Minister. He had kept a diary during his time as a Minister in the Labour government of 1964–70 which revealed, among much else, the contents of cabinet discussions. These are supposed to be secret and part of the justification for this is to support the convention of collective responsibility, which requires that Ministers support government policy as formulated by the cabinet. The convention, it was argued, depends on the deliberations of cabinet being kept secret as otherwise this might inhibit discussion if members of the cabinet knew that their true views were likely to be revealed publicly, and also that the credibility of a convention that requires that all minsters agree to the policy decided by cabinet would be damaged. On this ground, amongst others, the Attorney General sought to prevent publication of the diaries.
>
> The Court of Appeal held, however, that the argument against publication based on the convention of collective responsibility could not be sustained. The evidence was that the convention was not universally followed, and, therefore, much of the force of the Attorney General's argument was lost on this point. If the convention was not universally followed then it could not support an argument that damage would be done to the convention, as it was already being breached in other circumstances. The court ultimately decided that the diaries could be published, as there was no overwhelming argument for continuing confidentiality and the time between the events recorded in the diaries and the date of publication was sufficient that no harm would result from publication.

> ***thinking point***
>
> *If it cannot be shown that a convention is universally followed, can it be said that the convention exists in any meaningful sense?*

In any argument about the possible effect of a convention on a legal rule, the legal rule will prevail as that is the court's primary focus. Thus, for example, in *Madzimbamuto v Lardner-Burke* [1969] 1 AC 645 the Privy Council was asked to rule on the validity of an Act passed in breach of a convention. The convention was that Parliament would not pass an Act relating to a colony without its consent. Parliament passed an Act affecting Southern Rhodesia (as it then was) without first obtaining its consent, which was hardly surprising given that this was during the period when Southern Rhodesia had made a unilateral declaration of independence from the UK. The Privy Council held that the Act was valid notwithstanding the alleged breach of convention, as that was not a ground on which it could be invalidated. Arguments based on convention can only, at best, have a supporting role in deciding a legal point.

There is a relationship between some conventions and particular laws, however, in that the convention explains how the law should work. Sir Ivor Jennings (*Law and the Constitution* (Hodder & Stoughton, 5th ed., 1959) pp.81–2) makes the point with colourful imagery: 'The short explanation of the constitutional conventions is that they provide the flesh which clothes the dry bones of the law; they make the legal constitution work; they keep it in touch with the growth of ideas.' This relationship is clearly seen with regard to conventions affecting the monarch. For example,

- the power to give the royal assent to legislation is a matter of the royal prerogative, and it is therefore possible in law that the Queen might refuse to assent to a particular bill notwithstanding that it has passed through both Houses of Parliament. However, there is an extremely strong convention that she will always assent to legislation: the last time a monarch refused to do so was in 1714, so it is almost unthinkable that the Queen would refuse her assent. Indeed so certain is this convention that there is legislative provision for assent to be signified on her behalf;

- the power to appoint a Prime Minister is also part of the royal prerogative, but there is a convention that the Queen will always appoint as Prime Minister the leader of the party with the majority of seats in the House of Commons;

- Ministers are technically appointed and dismissed by the Queen acting under the royal prerogative. By convention she accedes to the wishes of the Prime Minister in this matter; and

- the power to dissolve Parliament, which results in a general election, is also a matter of the royal prerogative, but there is a convention that the Queen will always dissolve parliament when requested to do so by the Prime Minister.

cross reference

An interesting question of what would happen if an election produced a result in which there was not a party with a majority is discussed in Chapter 4.

thinking point

These are important parts of the constitution; should they be legal rules or are there advantages in their status as conventions?

2.4.4 **Unconstitutional behaviour**

Under a written constitution, a person acting unconstitutionally also acts illegally, because the only way of acting unconstitutionally is to violate the constitution which is a legal document. The two therefore go hand in hand. As the British constitution embraces both legal and non-legal sources it is possible for a person to act unconstitutionally but not illegally. This is because acting contrary to a convention does not involve acting unlawfully.

2.4.5 **Conventions or legal rules?**

Two matters may be considered in conclusion. First, there is the question whether conventions should be replaced by legal rules; and secondly, if they are not to be replaced by legal rules, should they be codified?

As to the first of these, converting conventions into legal rules would have the advantages of certainty—it would be possible to ascertain whether a rule existed and what its precise contents were. It would also be possible to know whether it had been changed, when it had been changed and what its new contents were or even whether it had been abolished. Drawbacks would include the loss of flexibility—a precise formula of words would have to be adopted and a new formula of words devised when there was any change; any changes would have to be made using a formal process; changes would be staged rather than subtle. Laws also do not disappear when they have outlived their usefulness, whereas conventions have this capacity. Laws also need some form of impetus to be changed. The example of legislation shows that Parliament cannot be relied on to change things unless there is some political or other imperative. Conventions by contrast may be changed merely by changing practice without the need for any formal process.

A major change would be the involvement of the courts and the prevalence of legal, as opposed to political, considerations attaching to determination of matters relating to any particular convention, including interpretation of what the convention (now converted into law) involved. It is doubtful, in any case, whether some conventions would be capable of translation into law in their present form. Whilst it is almost impossible to imagine the Queen refusing to appoint as Prime Minister the leader of the party with a majority of seats in the House of Commons and appointing someone else instead, it is even more difficult to conceive of the courts exercising jurisdiction over such a matter. It is, like aspects of the royal prerogative, not subject matter that is appropriate for determination by a court. To make the issue one which a court would be capable of trying, a new set of rules would have to be devised to avoid the spectre of leaving the possibility of a challenge in the courts to a decision of the Queen.

However, the opportunity could be taken to provide for matters such as the appointment of the Prime Minister, perhaps removing the matter from the Queen altogether, which, in many other countries is part of the legal framework of the constitution. It could provide

thinking point

a good opportunity to bring aspects of the constitution into the modern age rather than preserving historical legacies of a previous age.

Similar arguments apply to the idea of codifying conventions. To be effective, such an exercise would again necessarily involve reducing conventions to particular forms of words and would need to have clear mechanisms for recording any changes; again the subtlety possible under the present arrangements would be lost in this process. Issues relating to application and enforcement of conventions would however remain in the political sphere, which would retain greater flexibility than is possible through the courts.

Conventions essentially work under the present arrangements because those to whom they apply feel obliged to observe them not only for reasons of constitutional propriety but also because in most cases it is in the person's interests to act in this way. The example of the House of Lords in the 1909 budget crisis, discussed earlier, is exceptional, but also shows that the result of not following a convention may be more drastic and result in a diminished constitutional standing subsequently. However, there may be better ways of doing things in the modern era.

thinking point

If the present system works well in practice, why change it?

? Questions

If you answer the following questions, you will have appreciated the main issues raised in this chapter. Check your answers against the notes provided at the back of the book.

1 Explain the theory of the separation of powers.

2 To what extent does the separation of powers apply to the British constitution?

3 What does the phrase the rule of law mean?

4 What are the characteristics of constitutional conventions?

5 What part do conventions play in the British constitution?

Further reading

To further your understanding of the topics covered in this chapter, have a look at the reading materials mentioned below. Useful web links are also provided on the Online Resource Centre.

A.W. Bradley and K.D. Ewing, *Constitutional and Administrative Law* (Pearson Longman, 14th ed., 2007) chs.5 & 6
These chapters consider the separation of powers and the rule of law in detail.

Joseph Jaconelli, 'Do Constitutional Conventions Bind?' [2005] CLJ 149
This provides an in depth analysis of the role played by conventions in the constitution and in particular addresses the question of their binding force.

Michael Allen and Brian Thompson, *Cases and Materials on Constitutional and Administrative Law* (Oxford University Press, 9th ed., 2008) chs.4 & 5
This provides you with a selection of primary source material together with commentary.

Chapter 2 Features of the constitution

Parliamentary sovereignty

Introduction

As we have seen, most countries have a written constitution which is at the centre of that country's constitutional arrangements and which is the basis of all consideration of constitutional matters. Britain does not have a written constitution, but must have something that is at the heart of its constitutional arrangements. This role is taken by the doctrine of parliamentary sovereignty, or supremacy, as it is sometimes termed. Some commentators (e.g. A. Bradley and K. Ewing, *Constitutional and Administrative Law* (Pearson Longman, 14th ed., 2007) ch.4 generally, but particularly at pp.54–5; M. Allen and B. Thompson, *Cases and Materials on Constitutional and Administrative Law* (Oxford University Press, 9th ed., 2008) ch.2 generally, but especially at p.41) prefer the term supremacy, not least because it does not become enmeshed in discussions about national sovereignty. However, many judges and commentators use the term sovereignty in this context, and this is the term used here for the avoidance of confusion, though its limited meaning in this particular context should be borne in mind.

Sovereignty, in this sense and context, is conceived very much in legal terms. Under its classical formulation, the theory is that Parliament has the right to legislate on any matter it chooses and is subject to no legal limitations on its ability to do so. This extreme form of the doctrine is no longer tenable as, over the years, limitations on parliamentary sovereignty have been recognized. In common with other changes to British constitutional arrangements, this has been a gradual process. As Lord Hope says (*R(Jackson) v Attorney General* [2006] 1 AC 262 at 303): 'Step by step, gradually but surely, the English principle of the absolute legislative sovereignty of Parliament which Dicey derived from Coke and Blackstone is being qualified.' This chapter explores the concept of parliamentary sovereignty and those changes to which Lord Hope alludes.

> Parliamentary sovereignty is the principle in law that Parliament can legislate on any subject matter without any prior legal limitations and that an Act of Parliament cannot be declared to be invalid by the courts. However, this principle is, as this chapter illustrates, qualified by modern developments and continues to be qualified by the courts.

3.1 Parliamentary sovereignty: the traditional view

The traditional statement is provided by Dicey who explained the concept as follows (*Introduction to the Study of the Law of the Constitution* (Macmillan, 10th ed., 1959 pp.39–40)):

> The principle of parliamentary sovereignty means neither more nor less than this, namely that Parliament thus defined has, under the English constitution, the right to make or unmake any

law whatever, and further, that no person or body is recognised by the law of England as having a right to override or set aside the legislation of Parliament.

Under the constitutional arrangements in most countries, the legislature is limited in what it can do by the terms of the constitution. This is not, as the above quotation from Dicey indicates, the position under the British constitutional arrangements. Parliament is, in law, unencumbered by pre-existing constitutional limitations. However, Dicey goes on (*ibid.*) to identify one limitation to which Parliament is subject: it cannot legislate to bind itself for the future. This idea contains an important feature of parliamentary sovereignty, namely that Parliament is only sovereign at any given moment. A later Parliament can undo anything or everything its predecessors have done. This only works, however, where Parliament does this by means of an Act of Parliament, which, as will be seen, is also generally immune from legal challenge through the courts. This is not the case with regard to, say, delegated legislation or resolutions of either House which have neither the same effect nor carry the same immunity.

thinking point
Does this make the British constitution unstable? Does it matter?

3.1.1 **Express and implied repeal**

Thus, Parliament can pass an Act to repeal either the whole or part of a previous Act. The easiest way for Parliament to signal its intentions here is to repeal the earlier Act in an express way, by including a provision stating that the relevant previous legislation is repealed in whole or in part, specifying the part in the latter case. This puts the matter beyond doubt. Unfortunately, Parliament does not always follow this course. Sometimes it will simply pass legislation that conflicts with previous legislation. The courts will assume that Parliament did not intend to repeal previous legislation in the absence of an express provision to this effect, and will ordinarily attempt to interpret both pieces of legislation so that they are compatible. If, however, this is not possible and the two pieces of legislation are in irreconcilable conflict, then the principle is that the later legislation prevails, as it is the latest expression of the will of Parliament. The earlier legislation is repealed by the later, even though this is not expressly stated in the later Act. This is the principle of implied repeal: the later Act impliedly repeals the inconsistent parts of the earlier Act.

These points may be illustrated by two cases from the 1930s.

case close-up

Vauxhall Estates Ltd v Liverpool Corporation **[1932] 1 KB 733**

The Acquisition of Land (Assessment of Compensation) Act 1919 provided for a scheme of compensation for compulsory purchase. It further provided that anything inconsistent with this scheme was of no effect. The Housing Act 1925 created a different scheme for compensating those whose property had been subject to compulsory purchase. It did so without expressly repealing the 1919 Act. A dispute arose as to the proper basis for assessing compensation for compulsory purchase. Two particular issues arose. One was whether the provision in the 1919 Act to the effect that Parliament could not enact a scheme inconsistent with that provided in the 1919 Act was effective to override the 1925 scheme. The second was whether, by enacting the

Housing Act 1925, Parliament had effectively repealed inconsistent provisions in the 1919 Act notwithstanding the absence of an express provision to this effect.

The King's Bench Division held that, insofar as the terms of the 1925 Act were inconsistent with those of the 1919 Act, they prevailed and the inconsistent terms on the 1919 Act were impliedly repealed. Avory J said (at p.743):

> ...we are asked to say that by a provision of this Act of 1919 the hands of Parliament were tied in such a way that it could not by any subsequent Act enact anything which was inconsistent with the provisions of the Act of1919. It must be admitted that such a suggestion as that is inconsistent with the principle of the constitution of this country. Speaking for myself, I should certainly hold, until the contrary were decided, that no Act of Parliament can effectively provide that no future Act shall interfere with its provisions.

Thus, if there is any inconsistency, the later Act will impliedly repeal the earlier to the extent of the inconsistency.

This was confirmed soon after in *Ellen Street Estates Ltd v Minister of Health* [1934] 1 KB 590.

case close-up

***Ellen Street Estates Ltd v Minister of Health* [1934] 1 KB 590**

This concerned the conflict between the same 1919 and 1925 Acts that had been the subject matter of the *Vauxhall Estates* case. A further factor was that a subsequent Act, the Housing Act 1930, said that compensation for compulsory purchase should be in accordance with the 1919 Act. The Court of Appeal held that compensation should be calculated in accordance with the scheme under the 1925 Act, which had impliedly repealed the 1919 Act, as had been decided in *Vauxhall Estates*. The reference in the 1930 Act to the scheme in the 1919 Act was a reference to something that had ceased to exist, as it had been repealed by the 1925 Act. There was thus no 1919 scheme and that part of the 1930 Act was meaningless. The only scheme left in existence by this series of Acts was thus the 1925 scheme and it was this that should be followed.

thinking point

Are the courts correct to recognize implied repeal or should they only recognize repeal of earlier legislation where Parliament has expressly provided for this?

3.1.2 Practical limitations

Although in theory, subject to the limitation that it may not bind future Parliaments, Parliament can legislate as it wishes, including repealing, expressly or impliedly, any earlier legislation, the matter is not as clear cut as might at first appear from Dicey's statement. Firstly, he is referring to the absence of legal limitations on the legislative power of Parliament. There are clearly practical limitations on Parliament's ability to legislate. As the business of Parliament is controlled by the government, which almost always enjoys a working majority in the House of Commons, the political priorities of the government will predominate at the expense of the political priorities of other parties and individuals. The result of this is that the government's legislative programme, which gives effect to its policies, will be largely implemented. It is worth remembering that it is Parliament that passes primary legislation, though much of this legislation will be initiated by the government and the government will ensure that its measures pass successfully through Parliament.

Secondly, the government's scope to promote legislation will also, in practice, be limited by forces such as economic reality and international obligations. The influence of public opinion varies: governments have to propose legislation, and Parliament has to pass it, to do things that are unpopular but necessary, such as raising taxation or imposing limits on individual freedom in order to secure wider benefits such as social welfare or environmental protection. Laws also need to be capable of enforcement in order to prevent bringing the law, and with it Parliament, into disrepute. Whilst, in theory, Parliament could pass an Act to recolonise America or laws that criminalise thought, these are things it would never do.

3.1.3 Legal limitations

Even turning to legal limitations, the position is not as clear as Dicey suggests and has certainly become less so in the years since he wrote. We can consider this in relation to another matter relevant to the issue, namely the role of the courts. As the earlier examples of *Vauxhall Estates* and *Ellen Street Estates* illustrate, where Parliament fails to signal its intentions clearly by repealing earlier legislation expressly, it falls to the courts to determine whether it has done so impliedly. The position is complicated further where, as in those examples, the relevant legislation suggests that its terms are to be binding as to the future. The matter is resolved, ultimately, as a matter of statutory interpretation in the courts.

3.1.4 Challenging the validity of an Act of Parliament

The most fundamental question the courts have to answer is whether the validity of an Act of Parliament can successfully be challenged. Dicey asserts that it cannot. His view has received a measure of support from the courts at the highest level.

case close-up

***British Railways Board v Pickin* [1974] AC 765**

This case concerned a private Act of Parliament promoted by British Railways Board, the British Railways Act 1968, which deprived Mr. Pickin of some land. He argued that the Act was invalid as, he alleged, British Railways Board had misled Parliament in certain respects and, therefore, the provisions depriving him of the land were invalid. The House of Lords held that his claim must fail. The courts had no power to declare an Act of Parliament to be invalid. Three lines of reasoning supported the decision of the House of Lords. First, there was an important constitutional issue relating to the respective functions of the courts and Parliament. The courts exist to interpret and apply the law made by Parliament and not to question its validity. As Lord Reid pointed out (at p.788), it was important for the avoidance of conflict between them that both the courts and Parliament recognized their respective functions and the limits of their activity. The underlying theory that he is recognizing here is that of the separation of powers.

A second line of argument supporting the decision concerned the integrity of parliamentary procedure. It was for Parliament to determine what its procedures were and whether they had been followed or not, and not for the courts to interfere in this. The exclusive right to determine its own proceedings was one of the privileges of Parliament. This is reflected in Art.9 of the Bill of Rights 1688, which provides 'that freedom of speech and debates or proceedings in Parliament ought not to be impeached or questioned in any court or place out of Parliament'. It followed from these first two lines of reasoning that any allegation of impropriety in parliamentary proceedings should be pursued through Parliament and political channels rather than through the courts (see Lord Simon of Glaisdale at pp.798–9). The third important determination by the House of Lords in this case is that, for the purpose of a challenge to validity, there is no difference between a private Act of Parliament and a public Act. The sole issue is whether the instrument in question is an Act of Parliament. If it is then the courts cannot, insofar as it concerns solely domestic matters, challenge its validity. If it is not, as we shall see, then they may inquire further.

thinking point

If the House of Lords had decided that the Act in question was open to challenge on grounds of procedural irregularities, how might that have affected relations between Parliament and the courts?

Pickin involved a challenge based on an allegation of a procedural flaw in the way in which the Act was passed by Parliament. The House of Lords was not concerned with the substance of the British Railways Act, although underlying the challenge was dissatisfaction with the contents of the legislation. There had been suggestions in some early cases that Acts might be challenged on the basis that their content was immoral or unethical. Lord Reid ([1974] AC at 782) made it clear that the courts would not entertain a challenge to the validity of an Act of Parliament based on the contents of that legislation:

> In earlier times many learned lawyers seem to have believed that an Act of Parliament could be disregarded in so far as it was contrary to the law of God or the law of nature or natural justice, but since the supremacy of Parliament was finally demonstrated by the Revolution of 1688 any such idea has become obsolete.

thinking point

How do the courts know an instrument is an Act of Parliament?

The outcome of *Pickin* is thus essentially a formal rule. As long as an instrument is an Act of Parliament the courts will not question its validity, whatever the basis of the challenge. *Pickin* was, however, a decision of its time and was limited in its application even at the time it was decided, and subsequent cases have sought to test the application of the decision in differing contexts.

The application of *Pickin*

Instruments that are not Acts of Parliament

Despite the extensive discussion of the issues in the speeches in the House of Lords, *Pickin* still leaves scope for the courts to determine issues not squarely raised by that case. First, the decision in *Pickin* relates only to Acts of Parliament, whether public or private, and holds that the courts cannot question their validity. In order to bring that principle into play the instrument in question must be an Act of Parliament. The courts, therefore, have to make this preliminary determination as a precondition to applying *Pickin*. Once the court has determined that the instrument in question is an Act of Parliament, then the court is bound to give effect to it. Megarry VC explains the point succinctly:

> ... the duty of the court is to obey and apply every Act of Parliament and ... the court cannot hold any such Act to be ultra vires. Of course there may be questions about what the act means, and of course there is power to hold statutory instruments and other subordinate legislation ultra vires. But once an instrument is recognised as being an Act of Parliament, no English court can refuse to obey it or question its validity. (*Manuel v Attorney General* [1983] Ch 77 at 86)

cross reference
See further
Chapter 5.

Thus, anything short of an Act of Parliament is not within *Pickin*. So the principle in that case does not apply, for example, to a resolution of either House, constitutional conventions, delegated legislation, the royal prerogative, or treaties. Where the matter in question is something other than an Act of Parliament, the courts can either question its validity (for example, where it is a piece of delegated legislation or part of the royal prerogative) or simply refuse to give effect to it (for example where it is a resolution, convention or treaty). Some examples serve to illustrate the point. In *Commissioners of Customs and Excise v Cure & Deeley Ltd* [1962] 1 QB 340, regulations (a form of delegated legislation) had the effect, as Sachs J saw it, of excluding the court from deciding disputes between the commissioners and the taxpayer and indeed substituting the commissioners for the court as the body to determine such matters. This was something that went beyond the general power given under the Finance (No. 2) Act 1940 to make regulations to enable the commissioners to do their job and the regulations were therefore ultra vires.

---

thinking point

Given that so much law is now in the form of delegated legislation and therefore open to challenge, does the decision in Pickin *have less of an impact than it might at first appear?*

Also, as we have seen, in *Burmah Oil v Lord Advocate* [1965] AC 65, the House of Lords held that the prerogative of destruction of property in wartime without payment of compensation did not extend to the destruction of oil installations owned by Burmah Oil where this was done to prevent them falling into the hands of the enemy.

In *Stockdale v Hansard* (1840) 9 Ad & E 1; 112 ER 1112, a resolution of the House of Commons could not be used to defend an action for libel, while in *Bowles v Bank of England* [1913] 1 Ch 57 a resolution of a committee of the House of Commons could not authorize the Crown to levy income tax. As we have seen, in *Attorney General v Jonathan Cape* [1976] QB 752, the Court of Appeal refused to recognize the convention of collective ministerial responsibility as a ground for prohibiting the publication of the diaries of Richard Crossman, the former Cabinet Minister. In *R v Home Secretary ex p Brind* [1991] 1 AC 696, the House of Lords reiterated the general principle that the courts could not give effect to the provisions of a treaty unless and until it was brought into English law by means of an Act of Parliament. So in that case they were unable, when determining the legality of a ban on broadcasts involving terrorists, to consider the European Convention on Human Rights because, at that time, it had not been incorporated into English law.

Interpretation of Acts of Parliament

Secondly, as Megarry VC indicates, in the passage from *Manuel* quoted above, the courts still retain the power to interpret statutes. This is a power with limits, however, for the courts may not rewrite the statute in question: they can only interpret the words that are there. However, this limitation should not perhaps be as great as might at first appear, for the way in which the courts interpret a particular provision can affect its scope, in some cases quite dramatically. The interpretation of statutes may be said to leave the courts with considerable power, if not to rewrite what Parliament has passed, to determine its effect. This is especially true in relation to their enhanced duty under s.3 Human Rights Act 1998 to interpret legislation as far as it is possible to do so as to be compatible with the Convention rights.

cross reference
*See further
Chapter 7.*

Limitation to domestic law

Thirdly, *Pickin* is concerned with a matter of domestic law, and indeed a matter concerning one individual and one organization. It did not deal with a law aiming to lay down fundamental rights, especially one seeking to determine a particular situation in the future. For example, s.4 of the Statute of Westminster provides that the United Kingdom cannot legislate for a Dominion unless the Act in question states that the Dominion has requested and consented to it. The issue arises whether a court can question the validity of a statute allegedly made in violation of this provision. This was one of the issues in *Manuel v Attorney General* [1983] Ch 77.

case close-up

Manuel v Attorney General [1983] Ch 77

A group of Canadian Indians sought to challenge the validity of the Canada Act 1982, an Act passed by the United Kingdom Parliament, on the basis that the requirements of the Statute of Westminster had not been complied with. They also argued that the United Kingdom Parliament had no power to amend the Canadian constitution so as to prejudice the Indians without their consent as required by a number of treaty obligations incorporated into a series of 19th century statutes.

At first instance, Megarry VC held, on the authority of *Pickin*, that an English court could not question the validity of an Act, duly passed in proper form by the United Kingdom Parliament. His decision was upheld by the Court of Appeal, who said (at pp.99ff) that, even if the Statute of Westminster had not been complied with (something of which they found no evidence), no cause of action was disclosed, as this would mean challenging the validity of an Act of Parliament and *Pickin* precluded this. The case thus amounts to a restatement of the traditional view of the English courts toward an Act of Parliament.

The courts in *Manuel* were only concerned with statutes passed by the British Parliament, although the Act in question, the Statute of Westminster, was of a more fundamental nature than that under consideration in *Pickin*. The outcome in *Manuel* thus strengthened the views expressed in *Pickin* because the Court of Appeal was dealing with a public Act of constitutional significance rather than a private Act of limited application and could, perhaps, have sought to distinguish between different types of Act. However, as we have seen, the House of Lords in *Pickin* had apparently closed off that possibility by ruling that there was no difference in this context between a public Act and a private Act.

The additional significance of an Act concerned with major constitutional matters did not affect the outcome as far as the judges, both at first instance and in the Court of Appeal in *Manuel* were concerned. In *Thoburn v Sunderland City Council* [2003] QB 151, Laws LJ seemingly sought to revive this distinction, but, as discussed below, this was in the context of the application of EC law, and is, outside that context, a difficult distinction to sustain given the absence of a written constitution and a differentiation between constitutional and other laws. If there was a problem relating to the passing of the Act, then that was a matter for Parliament and not for the English courts. As long as the Act had been passed by the Queen in Parliament, the courts could not question its validity. The Court of Appeal did, however, recognize that if there was an irregularity disclosed on the Canadian side, this might give rise to an action in the Canadian courts.

thinking point

Do you think the possibility of a remedy in Canada is a satisfactory outcome for the applicants who were complaining about a British statute?

However, whilst reinforcing *Pickin*, Megarry VC (in *Manuel* at p.86) confined his remarks to Acts of Parliament passed by both the House of Commons and the House of Lords and relating to non-EC matters. He specifically exempted from his remarks about the inviolability of Acts of Parliament legislation passed under the terms of the Parliament Acts and any legislation connected with the European Communities Act 1972. The Court of Appeal considered and rejected an argument that Parliament had, under the Statute of Westminster and similar legislation, given up its sovereignty in whole or in part. The Court of Appeal did not have to decide this point as it decided that the Indians had not shown any failure to comply with the requirements of the Statute of Westminster. However, the Court of Appeal expressed the view (at p.109) that such an argument would fail, even if there was evidence of non-compliance with the terms of the Statute of Westminster, because of the decision of the House of Lords in *Pickin* which recognized that matters of procedure were for Parliament and that, subject to the limitations identified by Megarry VC, an Act duly passed by Parliament was immune from challenge in the courts.

cross reference
See Chapter 4 for general discussion of the Parliament Acts.

3.1.5 **The Parliament Acts**

The position of legislation passed under the terms of the Parliament Acts and of legislation concerned with EC matters has subsequently come squarely before the courts. As to the first of these, the validity of legislation passed under the terms of the Parliament Acts was considered by a bench of nine judges in the House of Lords in *(R)Jackson v Attorney General* [2006] 1 AC 262. The issue here was whether the Hunting Act 2004, which had been passed under the terms of the Parliament Acts, was a valid Act of Parliament.

The main argument in the House of Lords turned on the interpretation of the Parliament Act 1911 and whether it could be used to amend its own terms. If it could, then the Parliament Act 1949 was valid and consequently the Hunting Act 2004, which was passed under the terms of the Parliament Act 1911 as amended by the Parliament Act 1949, was also valid. If, on the other hand, the Parliament Act 1949 was invalid then the Hunting Act 2004 was also invalid. The key provision was s.2 of the Parliament Act 1911, which allowed any public bill, except a money bill or a bill to extend the life of Parliament, to be passed using the general procedure under the 1911 Act notwithstanding that the bill had not been passed by the House of Lords. The House of Lords in *Jackson* held that there was no limitation on the type of bill that could be passed under the Parliament Act procedure other than those stated in s.2 (which were not relevant to the issue before the House of Lords) and therefore the use of the Parliament Act 1911 to pass the Parliament Act 1949 was a legitimate exercise of power. The fact that Parliament, in s.2, specifically excluded money bills and bills to extend to the life of Parliament from the general scheme of the Parliament Act 1911 suggested that everything else might be included. Subsequent use of the Parliament Act 1911 to pass, for example, the Government of Ireland Act 1914 and the Welsh Church Act 1914 fortified this view as both measures effected significant constitutional change. Thus, the Parliament Act 1949 was valid and the Hunting Act 2004 was valid also.

The effect of all of this appears to be that if an Act of Parliament dealing with purely domestic matters is valid on its face then the courts cannot challenge its validity, and that this remains true whether the Act was passed in the normal way by the House of Commons and House of Lords before receiving the royal assent, or whether it has been passed in accordance with the terms of the Parliament Acts. If there is an allegation of a procedural defect within Parliament, then the remedy lies in Parliament and not through the courts.

thinking point

If Parliament can legitimately reduce the requirements for the purposes of enacting legislation, as it has done in the Parliament Acts, can it increase them, by, for example, requiring a referendum or specific majority vote?

3.1.6 Parliamentary sovereignty and European law

cross reference
See further Chapter 1.

If, however, the Act of Parliament is concerned with matters affected by the European Union then the situation is rather different. British membership of the European Economic Communities, as it then was, was given legal effect by the European Communities Act 1972. The measures in s.2 provide for EC law to have effect as part of English law either directly by virtue of s.2(1) or, for those parts of EC law that are not of direct effect, for their implementation under the terms of s.2(2). This is reinforced by s.3, which provides, in effect, that where a domestic court is considering a matter on which EC law impacts, then it must determine the effect of the Treaties or EC law 'in accordance with the principles laid down by and any relevant decision of the European Court'. The combined effect of this is to bring into English law not only those parts of EC law created in the form of legal instruments but also decisions of the European Court of Justice (ECJ). This includes decisions of the European Court of Justice establishing the principle of the sovereignty of the EC. Thus, in *Costa v ENEL* [1964] ECR 585, the ECJ held that, in the event of a conflict between EC law and the domestic law of a member state, EC law prevails. This is not a surprising conclusion. In order for the EC to operate effectively there must be uniform application of EC law across all the member states. If this were not the case, then there would be chaos as each member state would be able to pick and choose which laws to abide by.

Impact in English law

However, this clearly impacts on traditional notions of parliamentary sovereignty as laid down by Dicey and the courts in cases such as *Pickin*, *Vauxhall Estates* and *Ellen Street Estates*. Once the UK became a member of the EC, a situation would inevitably arise whereby there would be a clash between parliamentary sovereignty and EC sovereignty. The key provision in this context is s.2(4). This contains the following: 'any enactment passed or to be passed . . . shall be construed and have effect to the foregoing provisions of this section . . .' In other words, all Acts of the UK Parliament, whether past, present or future, should be given effect subject to EC law. In an ideal world, Parliament would have gone through every Act of Parliament that had been passed prior to 1 January 1973, the date on which the European Communities Act 1972 came into force, and amended it accordingly. Clearly, this was not possible given the volume of existing legislation at that date, and so s.2(4) provides a mechanism for achieving the incorporation of EC sovereignty. Thus, any pre-1973 legislation that is in conflict with EC law is affected by s.2(4) on the normal principles of implied repeal as explained in *Vauxhall Street Estates* and *Ellen Street Estates* and takes effect subject to prevailing EC law.

The real problem comes with post-1972 Acts of Parliament. Under the normal principles of implied repeal, as recognized in *Vauxhall Estates* and *Ellen Street Estates*, a later Act of Parliament that is in conflict with an earlier Act takes precedence: Parliament cannot bind itself as to its future action, as those cases illustrate. On this basis, we would expect post-1972 Acts that are in conflict with EC law to prevail because EC law is part of English law by virtue of the European Communities Act 1972 and could thus be modified by later legislation to the extent of any conflict because s.2(4) could not be binding as to the future. However, this approach would itself conflict with the principles of EC sovereignty, which would demand that s.2(4) is protected against implied repeal, thus forming an exception to the position established in *Vauxhall Estates* and *Ellen Street Estates*. How have the courts resolved this dilemma?

Resolving conflicts

The issue only becomes critical where there is conflict between EC law and English law. A first issue for the courts is, therefore, whether there is in fact a conflict or whether the relevant pieces of legislation can be interpreted in such a way as to be in harmony. The courts do not go out of their way looking for conflict, but equally there is a question as to how far the courts ought to try to achieve an interpretation of English law that is compatible with the relevant EC law. The courts cannot rewrite the words of the Act of Parliament, and may only work within the words Parliament has used. Within those parameters, however, there is a degree of latitude, as words may have a range of meanings. Unlike the Human Rights Act, Parliament gave no guidance to the judges as to how they should approach the task of interpretation of the European Communities Act 1972. Under s.3 of the Human Rights Act 'so far as it is possible to do so, primary legislation and subordinate legislation must be read and given effect in a way which is compatible with the Convention rights'. There is no comparable provision in the European Communities Act 1972. The use of the words 'so far as it is possible to do so' in s.3 of the Human Rights Act 1998 encourages the judges to go further than was previously the norm in terms of how much latitude they have in the interpretation of words, and certainly further than was the norm in 1972. Judges have, of course, always been entitled to choose between meanings where a word has more than simply its primary meaning, but were not expected to strain the construction of a term. So the question of how far the judges could go in seeking to arrive at an interpretation that made English law and EC law compatible was an open question.

cross reference
See further
Chapter 7.

In *Garland v British Rail Engineering Ltd* [1983] 2 AC 751, Lord Diplock said (at p.771) that the courts should be prepared to read the statute in question in such a way as to achieve consistency with a treaty obligation or other rule of EC law, as long as the words were reasonably capable of bearing the meaning necessary to achieve this. Taking this approach, the House of Lords held that the Sex Discrimination Act 1975 was to be construed, if it was reasonably capable of bearing such meaning, so as to be consistent with the UK's obligations under what was then Article 119 of the Treaty of Rome (now Article 141). Some inconclusive case law followed in which courts argued as to whether different approaches should be taken depending on whether the particular rule of EC law in question was or was not directly effective.

thinking point

Is it better to produce a strained interpretation of legislation in order to achieve consistency with EC law than simply to concede that the legislation is incompatible and give effect to EC law?

The *Factortame* litigation

A significant development on this and other issues took place in the litigation around the Merchant Shipping Act 1988. This had been passed in response to the fixing of quotas for national fishing fleets as part of the EC common fisheries policy. The Act provided for limits on the size of the British fishing fleet and enabled the Secretary of State to make regulations providing for the registration of British fishing vessels. He produced regulations which specified that only those ships whose owners were British either by citizenship or domicile could be registered. This had the effect of excluding a number of boats formerly registered as British but owned by Spanish nationals. In *Factortame v Secretary of State for Transport* [1990] 2 AC 85; [1991] 1 AC 605, it was alleged that the Merchant Shipping Act and regulations made under it were invalid as they were contrary to EC law. The Secretary of State contended that this was not so and that the Act and regulations were compatible.

The Divisional Court made a reference under what was then Article 177 of the Treaty of Rome (now Article 234) and made an order suspending the operation of the offending parts of the 1988 Act pending a ruling from the European Court of Justice. The House of Lords held, however, that the courts had no power to make an order suspending the operation of a statute pending a reference to the European Court of Justice, as to allow this would mean that if the applicants' claim ultimately failed the court would in effect have been granting them rights contrary to the wishes of Parliament. The courts would thus be undermining parliamentary sovereignty. Their caution is understandable as, both legally and politically, it appears desirable for the European Court of Justice to rule on this matter rather than the House of Lords reach a conclusion which may be out of step with legal regimes elsewhere in Europe.

However, the House of Lords referred to the European Court of Justice the question whether a court was able to, or even was obliged to, provide interim relief pending rulings of the European Court of Justice on the substantive issues involved. The European Court of Justice held that laws should be suspended pending a ruling, as long as there was a prima facie case, in that the point that had been referred to the ECJ was at least arguable, and that there was a degree of urgency involved. Both these criteria were satisfied here. The point put forward by the fishermen was arguable and as their livelihood was affected, and possibly irreparably if the UK view were to prevail, the requirement of urgency was satisfied also. The European Court of Justice decided in favour of the Spanish fishermen on the substantive issue and required the UK to disapply the offending parts of the Merchant Shipping Act 1988 and regulations made under it. Regulations were subsequently made to give effect to the ruling of the European Court of Justice.

The effect of the extensive litigation in this matter is twofold. First, it established, in a case directly concerned with the relationship between English and EC law, that the principle of the primacy of EC legal sovereignty prevailed over parliamentary sovereignty in the event of a conflict between the two regimes. This, in turn, means that s.2(4) European Communities Act 1972 is protected against implied repeal and forms an exception to the principles laid down in *Vauxhall Estates* and *Ellen Street Estates*. Secondly, it established principles whereby statutes could be suspended pending a ruling from the European Court of Justice and disapplied if found to be in conflict with provisions of EC law. It does not, however, give the English courts the right to strike down or invalidate Acts of Parliament that are found to be in conflict with EC law: all the courts can do is to recognize the incompatibility and give effect to EC law in preference to the domestic legislation.

Subsequent developments

In the light of the series of rulings coming out of the *Factortame* litigation, the English courts were able to develop the law without necessarily having to refer the matter to the European Court of Justice, and have done so in subsequent cases. In *R v Secretary of State for Employment ex p Equal Opportunities Commission* [1995] 1 AC 1, for example, the Commission challenged the validity of provisions in the Employment Protection (Consolidation) Act 1978 on the ground that they discriminated against women and thus infringed Article 119 of the Treaty of Rome (now Article 141) and associated Directives. This was because the thresholds for payments for unfair dismissal and redundancy were based on hours worked with a minimum threshold of eight hours, which meant that part-time workers were less likely to qualify for such payments. As significantly more women worked part-time, the provisions were likely to impact more on them than on men. The House of Lords agreed that the provisions were incompatible with both Article 119 and the associated Directives and made declarations to that effect.

thinking point

Is the effect of the Factortame *litigation to give more power to the English courts and alter the balance between the courts and Parliament?*

An important subsequent discussion of the doctrine of implied repeal in the context of EC law is found in *Thoburn v Sunderland City Council* [2003] QB 151.

---

case close-up

Thoburn v Sunderland City Council [2003] QB 151

In a series of cases heard together, the issue common to them all was whether it was lawful to sell loose foodstuff by reference to imperial measures of pounds and ounces as the primary indicator of weight. The Weights and Measures Act 1985 permitted sale by reference to imperial measures. However, regulations made by virtue of ss.2(2) and 2(4) of the European Communities Act 1972 and made subsequently to the 1985 Act required that produce should be sold by reference to metric units of weight, although imperial measures could be used as a supplementary indication of weight. The question, therefore, was whether the Regulations were effective to modify the 1985 Act. Although the Regulations were made after 1985, they were made under the authority of a statute which was passed prior to 1985 (i.e., the European Communities Act 1972). The issue was therefore whether the 1985 Act had impliedly repealed the 1972 Act insofar as the 1972 Act permitted the making of regulations contrary to the provisions of the 1985 Act.

The Divisional Court held that the Weights and Measures Act 1985 did not impliedly repeal the European Communities Act 1972. The ordinary rules of implied repeal did not apply to the European Communities Act 1972, which was not affected by subsequent legislation in the absence of some express provision. The Divisional Court widened the discussion and regarded this principle as deriving from the view that the 1972 Act was a constitutional statute to which the doctrine of implied repeal, as laid down in *Vauxhall Estates* and *Ellen Street Estates*, did not apply. Giving the leading judgment, with which Crane J agreed, Laws LJ stated (at p.189) the relationship between Community law and domestic English law as a series of propositions:

(1) All the specific rights and obligations which EU law creates are by the 1972 Act incorporated into our domestic law and rank supreme: that is, anything in our substantive law inconsistent with any of these rights and obligations is abrogated or must be modified to avoid the inconsistency. This is true even where the inconsistent municipal provision is contained in primary legislation. (2) The 1972 Act is a constitutional statute: that is, it cannot be impliedly repealed. (3) The truth of (2) is derived, not from EU law, but purely from the law of England: the common law recognises a category of constitutional statutes. (4) The fundamental basis of the United Kingdom's relationship with the EU rests with the domestic, not the European, legal powers.

thinking point

Should the exception to the principle of implied repeal be confined to EC law or should more exceptions be created in the way suggested by Laws LJ?

Is the 1972 Act protected against express repeal?

It is clear from a series of cases that the provisions of the European Communities Act 1972, and especially s.2(4), are protected from implied repeal. However, there is a more fundamental question as to whether Parliament could pass an Act which expressly sought to override EC law. The question would be whether the courts should give effect to parliamentary sovereignty or EU sovereignty. The situation has never arisen, for it would represent a fundamental repudiation of the UK's membership of the EU, with unimaginable political repercussions. Such views as have been expressed by judges would suggest that, in this instance, the courts would be bound to give effect to parliamentary sovereignty. In *Macarthys Ltd v Smith* [1979] ICR 785, Lord Denning said (at p.789):

If the time should come when our Parliament deliberately passes an Act—with the intention of repudiating the Treaty or any provision of it—or intentionally of acting inconsistently with it—and say so in express terms—then I should have thought it would be the duty of our courts to follow the statute of our Parliament.

However, as Lord Denning goes on to indicate, the judges would be slow to accept that this was Parliament's intention as this would amount to a repudiation of the UK's membership of the EU. In *Garland v British Rail Engineering Ltd*, Lord Diplock indicated that the wording that Parliament would have to use to express such an intention would have to be 'clear'. This may require Parliament to refer, in an explicit way, to a wish to override EU law in particular respects. As this has never happened, the point is inevitably speculative, but it is an important indicator of the ultimate power of Parliament and the courts' recognition of this.

'Constitutional statutes'

cross reference
See Chapter 1.

cross reference
See further
Chapter 7.

The reference to constitutional statutes by Laws LJ in *Thoburn* is problematic in that, as we have seen, English law does not formally divide laws into constitutional laws and other laws in the way that countries with a written constitution are able to. Consequently, it becomes possible to argue, on the one hand, that all laws are constitutional in the sense that they affect and reconfigure the power relationships within the state. On the other hand, others deny that, in the absence of a formal constitution, there is such a thing as constitutional law in Britain. A middle position is occupied by those who would, pragmatically, draw the line by considering laws analogous to those that would ordinarily appear in a written constitution as constitutional, and this may be what Laws LJ has in mind. This is an issue that will need to be worked out in subsequent case law, but one statute that would self-evidently be regarded as constitutional is the Human Rights Act 1998. The object of this Act, was to bring the provisions of the European Convention on Human Rights into English domestic law. The question of how this was done has implications for parliamentary sovereignty.

thinking point
Is it possible to identify constitutional statutes in a country with an unwritten constitution?

3.1.7 **Parliamentary sovereignty and the Human Rights Act**

The Human Rights Act 1998 creates a framework for the incorporation of provisions of the European Convention on Human Rights (which are called 'the Convention rights' in the Act: see s.1(1)) which is designed to preserve parliamentary sovereignty. In countries with a written constitution, the courts have the power to strike down legislation which is contrary to the constitution, which includes, of course, those parts of the constitution that establish individual rights. This power is notably absent from the Human Rights Act 1998. Where legislation is in conflict with the Convention rights, s.4 allows the higher courts to make a declaration of incompatibility. It is not mandatory for them to do so. Section 4 provides that a court 'may' make such a declaration if it is satisfied that the provision in question is incompatible with the convention rights. Such a declaration is subject to limitations in that, by virtue of s.4(6) the legislation in question remains in force and its validity is unaffected by the declaration; further, the declaration is not binding on the parties in the proceedings in which it is made. It is really a case of the court giving notice to Parliament that it believes that there is an incompatibility between the legislation in question and the Convention rights. It then falls to Parliament, if it agrees with the assessment of the court that there is indeed an incompatibility, to decide what to do to remove the incompatibility.

thinking point
Should the courts have been given a power under the Human Rights Act to strike down incompatible legislation?

Should a court decide to make a declaration of incompatibility, the effect is that it is then for Parliament to decide whether to amend the legislation in question and, if so, how to do this. Parliament may pass an amending Act to rectify the defect. However, there is a 'fast track' procedure under s.10 whereby an amendment can be effected by means of delegated legislation, which essentially leaves the matter under the control of the government, subject to parliamentary intervention. The Act also makes provision to address the matter of compatibility for the future by providing, in s.19, that the Minister in charge of a bill that has been introduced into either house of Parliament must make a statement prior to the second reading of the bill to the effect that the provisions of the bill are compatible with the Convention rights, or, in a highly unlikely alternative, that although he is unable to make a statement of compatibility the government nevertheless wishes to proceed with the bill. This statement, in whatever form, cannot be binding on the courts, which are entitled to exercise their own independent judgment on this issue.

thinking point

Would it be more satisfactory to give the courts the power to strike down legislation in order to speed up the process of dealing with incompatible legislation, especially from the point of view of the public authorities who are required to continue to administer legislation that has been found to be incompatible?

As far as the courts are concerned, the power to make a declaration of incompatibility in s.4 needs to be read alongside the powers given to the courts and the duties imposed on them by ss.2 and 3. Under s.3(1), primary and secondary legislation must be read and given effect in a way which is compatible with the Convention rights. In doing so, the courts are required, under s.2, to take into account, amongst other things, decisions of the European Court of Human Rights. Putting ss.2, 3 and 4 together produces the duty on the courts to try as far as possible to read domestic legislation so that it complies with the Convention rights, taking into account decisions of the European Court of Human Rights, but that if they are unable to do so, then they may make a declaration of incompatibility.

cross reference

The relationship between ss.2, 3 and 4 is explored further in Chapter 7.

There is plenty of scope for the courts to exercise their discretion in how they approach these tasks. Whilst s.3 is strongly worded in requiring courts to seek to make domestic legislation compatible, there are limits. The courts may not rewrite the statute: their task is interpretation not redrafting. The more arguable issue is what the limits of interpretation are, and drawing the line between interpretation and rewriting. Also, whilst s.2 requires them to take account of decisions of the European Court of Human Rights, they are not bound by those decisions. It is thus open to the courts to develop a line of interpretation that is appropriate to Britain and in some instances to reject the approach taken by the European Court of Human Rights to a particular issue. As we have seen, the courts also have the discretion as to whether to issue a declaration of incompatibility where, despite following s.3, they are unable to reach an interpretation that produces compatibility.

Thus, whilst the drafting of the Human Rights Act appears to preserve the sovereignty of Parliament by giving itself the exclusive right to amend legislation, it has also handed to the courts a new power that could be used creatively to enable the courts, always bearing in mind the often stated duty to recognize the proper functions of the courts and Parliament, to take an active role in determining the effect of legislation. It has also given the government the power, by virtue of s.10, to amend primary legislation by means of secondary legislation.

3.1.8 **Parliamentary sovereignty in transition?**

More generally, the concept of parliamentary sovereignty retains a degree of fluidity in terms of both its principle and application. As the quotation from Lord Hope at the beginning of this chapter recognizes, the absolute principle of parliamentary sovereignty as propounded by Dicey and others has been reduced over the years, if it was ever true at all, and will continue to be limited further, particularly if the statement of Laws LJ in *Thoburn* is developed further. The European Communities Act 1972 and the Human Rights Act 1998 are, on any definition, constitutional statutes, which Laws LJ would hold, are protected against implied repeal though perhaps not against express repeal. The as yet unanswered question if the courts are to proceed down this path is: which statutes may be described as constitutional? This may not be the only relevant issue here, for the constitutional changes that may be pursued by the present government may further redefine the relationship between the courts and Parliament.

? Questions

If you answer the following questions, you will have appreciated the main issues raised in this chapter. Check your answers against the notes provided at the back of the book.

1 What is the principle of parliamentary sovereignty?

2 Why is this principle so important in the British constitution?

3 What is the significance of the difference between Acts of Parliament and other forms of law?

4 How have the EU and the Human Rights Act impacted on parliamentary sovereignty?

Further reading

To further your understanding of the topics covered in this chapter, have a look at the reading materials mentioned below. Useful web links are also provided on the Online Resource Centre.

A.W. Bradley and K.D. Ewing, *Constitutional and Administrative Law* (Pearson Longman, 14th ed., 2007) ch.4
This provides you with a detailed discussion of the issues raised here.

Jeffrey Jowell, 'Parliamentary Sovereignty under the New Constitutional Hypothesis' [2006] PL 562
This article provides you with an examination of the changing nature of parliamentary sovereignty with particular reference to the *Jackson* case.

Michael Allen and Brian Thompson, *Cases and Materials on Constitutional and Administrative Law* (Oxford University Press, 9th ed., 2008) ch.2
This provides you with a selection of primary source material together with commentary.

Parliament

Introduction

This chapter and the two that follow, on the legislature and judiciary, consider the three branches of government of the state. This chapter examines Parliament: what it does, how people become Members of it and what they contribute to its overall functioning when they get there. Parliament consists of two houses, the House of Commons and the House of Lords. Members of the House of Commons are elected and represent a particular town, city or location. Members of the House of Lords become members by appointment or, in some cases, by birth. A Member of the House of Commons is called a Member of Parliament, usually abbreviated to MP. There are currently 646 MPs, though the number changes from time to time for reasons explained below. Members of the House of Lords have a variety of titles depending on the nature of their membership. A brief summary of the functions of each house will provide an initial idea of matters that will be explored further. The Select Committee on Procedure in 1977 (*First Report of the Select Committee on Procedure 1977–78* HC 588) identified the following functions of the House of Commons:

- Legislation (both primary and secondary)
- Scrutiny of the executive
- Control of finance
- Redress of grievances

The White Paper on the House of Lords in 1968 (*House of Lords Reform* Cmnd. 3799) identified the following functions:

- Supreme Court of Appeal
- Forum for debates on matters of public interest
- Revise public bills passed by the House of Commons
- Initiate less controversial public bills and Private Members' Bills
- Consider subordinate legislation
- Scrutinize the activities of the executive
- Consider private legislation

Not surprisingly, the two lists largely coincide, though do hint at some significant differences. The membership and functions of each house will be considered in turn.

4.1 The House of Commons: the electoral system and electoral reform

Taking the House of Commons first, we can consider the way a person becomes a Member of Parliament (MP), which also requires us to look, in a critical way, at the electoral system.

4.1.1 The electoral system

The system for electing Members of Parliament is basically quite simple. The country is divided into a number of areas, called constituencies, each of which returns one Member of Parliament. Each elector casts one vote, the votes are counted and the candidate with the most votes is elected to serve as Member of Parliament for that constituency. Because of this, the system is often referred to as 'first past the post'. We can now examine the elements of the system in more detail before attempting an evaluation of it.

> The United Kingdom is divided into areas called constituencies (or seats), each of which returns one Member of Parliament (MP). An MP is elected by electors casting one vote only for their preferred candidate. The candidate with the most votes is elected.
>
> The system also leads to the election of a government. This will be the party with the most seats in the House of Commons. Its leader will become Prime Minister.

The right to vote

This might be seen as one of the fundamental features of a democracy and something we would expect to find embedded in the constitution. As we have seen, the lack of a formal constitution makes the UK unusual in having no guaranteed rights that are protected against change. Thus, the history of the development of the electoral system was characterized by a gradual move to a generally universal right to vote (though, as we shall see, even now the right to vote is not completely unqualified, with certain individuals disqualified), and the system, whilst remaining basically intact, has been subject to a number of amendments over the years.

The basic requirements to vote in parliamentary elections are contained in the Representation of the People Act 1983 (as amended). The basic requirements are that the voter must be:

- over the age of 18 at the date of the poll;
- a British subject; and
- resident in and appear on the register of electors for the constituency.

This last category is a requirement: it is an offence not to register. These minimal positive qualifications are qualified by a number of categories of person disqualified from voting, which includes:

- aliens (non-UK subjects);
- peers (other than Irish peers and hereditary peers no longer sitting in the House of Lords);
- those in prison following conviction of a criminal offence; and
- those convicted of corrupt or illegal electoral practices (ss.1, 3–7).

thinking point
Why should anyone be disqualified from voting?

These are not without controversy: the European Court of Human Rights has recently ruled that disqualifying all those in prison from voting is excessive and as such a breach of the right to free elections under Article 3 of Protocol 1 of the European Convention on Human Rights (*Hirst v UK* [2006] 42 EHRR 41). The European Court emphasized the importance of the right to vote as a basic right in a democracy.

The elector may exercise the right to vote in one of three ways. The elector may turn up at the polling station and cast a vote in person; or apply for a postal vote, or enable a proxy to cast a vote for him (s.19 as amended). At present voting is not compulsory. This has meant that the number of votes cast has varied considerably in elections, with, on the whole, general elections seeing a better turnout than local or European elections. The turnout is also not uniform across the country. There are thus issues, to which we will return, about the representativeness of governments and questions of how to encourage greater participation in elections.

thinking point

Would compulsory voting make people take a greater interest in how the country is governed? Or are there better ways of encouraging participation in elections?

Candidates

Turning from the elector to look at the candidates, we again find surprisingly few positive requirements. Those that do exist derive from both common law and statute but membership is subject to the overriding right of the House of Commons to determine its own membership.

Formally, candidates must be over 21 and British citizens. They must not, for example, be Members of the House of Lords or hold one of the offices described in the House of Commons (Disqualification) Act 1975, which covers a range of public appointments such as membership of the judiciary or members of public services such as the civil service, the police or the armed forces. Those who are bankrupt, suffering from mental illness or convicted of treason or convicted of corrupt or illegal electoral practices are also excluded. In practice, however, the main positive requirement for being elected is to be nominated by one of the leading political parties. The process of nomination is entirely within the competence of the party itself, being subject to the party's own rules. Thus, in effect, the party can determine who is elected as in many cases it is the party's nomination rather than any intrinsic merits of the candidate that secures election.

Ultimately, however, it is one of the privileges of the House of Commons to control its own membership. This includes not only the power to determine who can be admitted to membership of the House, it also includes the power to expel or suspend those it feels are unfit to serve as Members.

Constituencies

The constituency is the focus of the series of individual elections that take place across the country. The fixing of boundaries for constituencies is the task of the Boundaries Committee, an independent part of the Electoral Commission. It exercises its functions in accordance with the principles laid down in the Parliamentary Constituencies Act 1986 (as amended) and the Political Parties, Elections and Referendums Act 2000. Under this legislation it is required to keep the boundaries under review and recommend change where appropriate. This is a necessary power to enable changes to be made where, for example, there are significant changes in the population of a particular area, as well as, in the longer term, to reflect more gradual population growth and change.

We might expect that, if each constituency is returning one Member in the interests of equality, each constituency should be made up of approximately the same number of voters on its electoral roll. This is the essential working principle for the Boundary Committee, but it is allowed to depart from the principle of numerical equality on the basis of one or more subsidiary guidelines. There are first of all numbers of seats allocated to the constituent parts of the United Kingdom. Thus, England has to have 529 seats, Scotland 59 seats, Wales 40 seats and Northern Ireland 18 seats. This distribution reflects geography as well as constituency size, as both Wales and Scotland have a number of seats covering large areas which are not densely populated. Further, the committee is to observe local government boundaries, and respect any natural boundaries such as rivers or artificial boundaries such as housing estates. In order to keep the size of constituencies manageable for the elected Member and his constituents, sparsely populated areas may contain fewer electors than more densely populated areas. Thus, rural constituencies might be smaller than urban and areas such as the Scottish islands will have smaller numbers.

Within these guidelines the Boundaries Committee has a wide discretion when drawing up boundaries. One factor it cannot take into account is the political impact of its decisions, which forms no part of its discretion. This is not surprising, given the nature of its functions. This was illustrated in *R v Boundaries Commission ex p Foot*. [1983] QB 600.

R v Boundaries Commission ex p Foot [1983] QB 600

. . . .

Prior to the general election of 1983, there had been an extensive set of changes made to the boundaries. Mr. Foot, as leader of the Labour Party, argued that the effect of these changes would be to lead to the loss of a number of seats for Labour. He argued that the Boundaries Commission (as it then was) had failed to take into account the political impact of its proposals. The Court of Appeal held, however, that the Boundaries Commission, in order to exercise its function properly, had to have a wide discretion and in order to preserve its political neutrality could not take into account the political impact of its decisions. Mr. Foot not only lost the case but also, as he predicted, the general election.

The conduct of elections

Once the election is announced, Parliament is dissolved and the process of nomination of candidates begins. A candidate must submit a properly completed nomination paper supported by ten electors in the constituency, together with a deposit of £500. This may seem anti-democratic, and was originally introduced to deter frivolous candidates. Today, with most candidates enjoying party support, it is not so much of an issue. The host of 'fringe' candidates who stand in elections might suggest that the sum is not prohibitively high. In any event, the deposit is returned as long as the candidate gets more than 1/20 of the total votes cast in that constituency.

Under s.22 Political Parties, Elections and Referendums Act 2000, provision is made whereby political parties may be registered as such. This carries with it advantages including the right to describe candidates as belonging to that party, and to party election broadcasts during an election and also accounts for the small number of independent candidates in any election.

There are limits on the amounts of money candidates are allowed to spend on their campaign. The limits change from time to time, and depend on factors such as the size and nature of the constituency. Any expenditure has to be authorized by the candidate or the candidate's agent, and a return of expenditure has to be made once the election is concluded. It is always difficult to distinguish between the campaign being run by individual candidates and the party campaign at national level. The law recognizes this (s.76 Representation of the People Act 1983 and Part V Political Parties Elections and Referendums Act 2000) and caps both individual and party expenditure in order to limit the impact of financial advantage between the parties. There is inevitably a degree of artificiality in this as some smaller parties may struggle even within the limits to match the larger parties.

Parties are also entitled to an election broadcast, though this does not entitle them to put across their views in any way they wish.

R(Prolife Alliance) v BBC [2004] 1 AC 185

The claimants were a party opposed to, amongst other things, abortion and euthanasia. They fielded sufficient candidates in Wales to secure a party election broadcast there. The tape submitted for the broadcast contained material which the BBC felt would be offensive to viewers, and rejected it on the grounds that it would amount to a breach of their duty not to broadcast material which offends against good taste or decency. The Prolife Alliance sought judicial review of this decision which they argued was an impediment to freedom of speech in the political arena and also a breach of their rights under Article 10 of the European Convention on Human Rights. The case thus represented a clash of values between free political speech on the one hand and the duty of the media not to broadcast offensive material. Put another way, was political speech above the ordinary law in terms of the protection afforded to it? The House of Lords held that the same criteria should apply to all broadcast material and that the decision of the BBC to refuse to broadcast this particular material was not unlawful. This was legitimately within the discretion of the BBC exercising their judgement within the legal framework. Further, Article 10 did not provide a right to a broadcast of this nature.

thinking point
Should parties be prevented from putting across their views in any way they wish?

These rules are all designed to provide, as far as possible, that parties and their candidates have an equal opportunity to present themselves and their views to the electorate both at constituency and national level. The system is, however, seemingly weighted in favour of the larger and more established parties who have a longstanding national profile and are always going to field large numbers of candidates. The current legal framework also ignores the influence of the media in the election campaign. The media is required to be impartial in its reporting of the election campaign, but in terms of newsworthiness, the major national parties are likely to receive the most extensive coverage. The requirement of impartiality probably has the greatest impact at constituency level where the media must be careful when discussing particular candidates to ensure that they are not favouring that candidate, or selection of candidates, as against the other standing in that constituency. In practice, the media is aware of its obligations, but this ignores its more general influence on electors and this almost inevitably favours the larger parties.

Voting

Voting in person

The right to vote has traditionally been exercised in person by means of a secret ballot, which Article 3 of Protocol 1 of the European Convention on Human Rights recognizes as a hallmark of a democratic society. This means that the way people vote remains confidential to them, unless they choose to disclose this information. The system remains relatively secure where this is the case, as the ballot paper is handed to the individual who remains in reasonably close proximity to the election officials while completing it. The risk of interference with the casting of the vote is limited. The main problem associated with voting in person is the possibility of someone impersonating the elector, but recorded instances of this have been few and far between: this is not to say, however, that it does not occur. The fact that the actual voting process takes place in a controlled environment limits the possibilities for fraud. There is, of course, the possibility that the delivery of polling cards could be abused, so that cards do not reach the voter to whom they belong but end up in other hands.

Other methods of voting

Once the system moves away from voting in person to voting by proxy or by postal ballot, it inevitably becomes less secure as it becomes possible for third parties to interfere not only in the delivery of electoral communications but also in the completion of official documents. For many good reasons, the system of postal voting has been extended in recent years. Prior to 2001, it was only available to persons who could show they had good reason for not voting in person. The Representation of the People Act 2000 and associated regulations changed this to a system of postal votes being available on demand. Making voting easier may be thought to encourage more voters to vote, thus increasing the democratic nature of the process. It also enables the less mobile members of society, such as older people or the disabled, to participate in the electoral process.

The potential problems associated with this development were illustrated by events in the local elections in parts of Birmingham in 2004, which resulted in a case before the election court (*In the matter of a Local Government Election for the Bordesley Green Ward of the Birmingham City Council held on 10th June 2004* (Election court: Commissioner Mawrey QC; unreported). In two wards of the city, there were allegations of fraud involving misuse of the postal voting system. Two examples of such frauds were by intercepting ballot packages that were sent to those who had applied for a postal vote and then, in some cases completing and returning them. The system was insecure as there were insufficient checks to ensure that the ballot paper had been completed by the person to whom it had been addressed. A second tactic involved intercepting completed ballot papers and checking them to ensure that the person had voted for the correct party, and destroying those that had not. There are various ways of carrying out these practices, from the removal of packages from mailboxes where they have been left protruding to collusion with postal workers to offers to help individuals complete their ballot papers.

Undue influence and fraud

This last shades into the possibility of undue influence, which is an offence under s.115 of the Representation of the People Act 1983, whereby members of a household may be influenced by other family members or members of a wider community to vote in particular ways. This tendency is increased, it was suggested in the Birmingham case, where families are large and/or contain voters who do not have a good command of English. The issue becomes critical where, as in the Birmingham wards, the result of the election is likely to be close. In the Birmingham case, Mr. Commissioner Mawrey, sitting in the election court, endorsed the comment that the system invited fraud. As a result of this case and of examples of alleged abuse elsewhere the government instigated a series of reports and measures in an attempt to limit fraud by tightening up the administration of the present system and reforming the law to make the system more secure in future. The Electoral Administration Act 2006 attempts to address the deficiencies of the present system, not least by trying to ensure that there are more elaborate systems in place to verify the identity of those both applying for and exercising postal votes. One of the ways that the authorities were alerted to the possibility of fraud was instances of voters turning up to vote and finding that they were listed as having exercised a postal vote which they had never received.

thinking point

Is there any way of making it easier for people to vote without compromising the security of the electoral system?

Membership of the House of Commons

Once the votes have been counted, the person with the most votes is declared to be the Member of Parliament for that constituency. However, membership of the House of Commons is, in the last resort, a matter for the House of Commons itself. One of the privileges of Parliament, as we shall see, is the ability to determine its own membership. This includes the power to determine whether individuals are legally disqualified from sitting as Members. In practice, however, the House accepts rulings of the election court on such matters.

Two examples may serve to illustrate the powers of the House of Commons in this regard.

case close-up

Re Parliamentary Election for Bristol South East **[1964] 2 QB 257**

Mr. Anthony Wedgwood Benn was elected as MP for the constituency. He then inherited his father's peerage, becoming Viscount Stansgate. As he was now a member of the House of Lords, he could not sit in the House of Commons, and a by-election was called. Mr. Benn did not wish to take up his seat in the House of Lords, preferring to sit in the House of Commons as an elected Member of Parliament. He therefore stood as a candidate in the by-election and was duly re-elected. One of the losing candidates challenged the result of the election arguing that Mr. Benn could not be returned as an MP because of his membership of the House of Lords, notwithstanding Mr. Benn's wish not to take up his seat in the Lords. The election court held that even though Mr. Benn did not wish to sit in the House of Lords, his inheritance of a peerage meant that he was ineligible for membership of the House of Commons and declared the by election result to be void, a decision supported by the House of Commons. It was not until the passing of the Peerage Act 1963, which Mr. Benn was instrumental in sponsoring, that a peer became able to disclaim his peerage thereby making him eligible for membership of the House of Commons. Mr. Benn duly disclaimed the Stansgate peerage and was later re-elected as a member of the House of Commons.

The second example is a decision of the House of Commons Committee of Privileges which, even though it is quite old, provides a useful illustration of the House exercising its power of determining its membership. Mr. Allighan was a member of the House of Commons. He alleged that Members of Parliament had been leaking information to the press because they had been bribed or were drunk, or both. On investigation, the only members guilty of this were Mr. Allighan himself and another MP, Mr. Walkden. They were both expelled from the House as being unfit to serve as Members of Parliament (HC 138 (1947)).

4.1.2 **Electoral reform**

The system as described above has been in operation for the best part of a century. The last major reforms were effected in the early 20th century to achieve a universal right to vote, though questions about whether the system should be reformed have never been far away. Supporters of the present system, however, point to what they regard as its merits. Four particular factors may be noted.

Virtues of the current system

The virtues may be summarized as:

- Simplicity
- Speed
- Produces definite result
- Strong link between MP and constituency

First, the system is simple. Voters cast their votes by marking one cross on the ballot paper. Votes are added up with no complicated calculations to be performed, and the Member is the person with the most votes. There are no real difficulties either for the voter or the election officials in understanding and operating the system. A second virtue, following from this is that it produces a swift result both in individual constituencies and nationally. This means that the identity of the government is known by the day after the election, thus eliminating the possibility of uncertainty. Thirdly, the system tends, because of the concentrations in voting discussed below, to produce a definite result, with one party acquiring a clear majority. Thus, a strong government is produced which, by means of its majority in the House of Commons, is able to carry through its policies into law. Fourthly, by having only one representative for each constituency, a strong link and identity are forged between the Member and the constituency. Members of Parliament in particular argue the merits of this last factor.

Deficiencies of the current system

The deficiencies of the present system may be summarized as:

- Not truly representative
- Government does not need to enjoy majority support from popular vote
- Wasted votes
- Lack of voter choice

One peculiarity of the system is the extent to which a proportion of the seats are 'safe seats'. By this is meant that they will, in the ordinary course of things, return a Member from one particular party, it being unlikely that a person from any other party would be returned for that constituency. The reason for this is the way in which support for the main political parties is concentrated in particular clusters; a crude division (modified as the century progressed and the Liberal Democrats became a growing presence in elections) was that significant support for Labour was concentrated in major towns and cities, especially those of an industrial nature located in the north, whereas support for the Conservatives tended to be concentrated in rural areas and towns within such areas, and also suburbs, especially, in both cases, in the south of the country, particularly in the affluent counties surrounding London. So, for example, an inner city constituency in the industrial north might be expected to return a Labour Member, whilst a constituency in an affluent part of Surrey might return a Conservative Member.

In such circumstances, critics have argued that the system is not truly representative. The votes cast are not reflected in the result nationally, as a government can be elected notwithstanding that it does not have a majority of the vote nationally. One reason for this is the electoral geography, as illustrated in the previous paragraph. A further reason is the fact that an individual only needs one more vote than the nearest rival in order to be elected. So it is possible that, say, 20,000 voters supported a candidate who lost the election to another candidate who polled 20,001. This also illustrates a further criticism of the present system, which is that the 20,000 who voted for the second placed candidate, together with those who voted for lower placed candidates, will not be represented by a candidate of their political persuasion. Nor will their votes have counted towards the election of a successful candidate. To this extent their votes are said to be wasted. This can have the effect of dissuading them from voting, thus reducing the turnout at an election and, in democratic terms, reducing participation in the electoral process. Further, the fact that the major parties, for obvious reasons, only field one candidate per constituency means that voters who might incline to a different wing of the party have no real choice of candidate. In effect, given that the candidates most likely to be elected are those from the leading parties, the choice is effectively made by the party itself rather than the voters. Thus in the 'safe' seats, the party to all intents and purposes, determines who will be elected. Yet, argue critics, there are no real controls over the way in which the party chooses its candidates other than those imposed by the party itself.

thinking point

Do you think the virtues of the present system are outweighed by its deficiencies?

Proposals for reform

It is one thing to criticize the present system, but wholly another to find an alternative that would command widespread support, not least because of different views as to the values that should predominate in any system of voting. There is also the matter of whether there is any impetus for reform at national level: the present system works satisfactorily in its own terms and there is no guarantee that any alternative would be any better in terms of representation and government.

One solution which is seen as addressing these and other perceived problems with the present system is to adopt some form of proportional representation. This is an umbrella term for a number of electoral systems which have as their basic objective securing a correlation between the votes cast and the seats obtained by the parties. This, it is argued, the present system fails to achieve because of the concentration of support for the major parties, or, in the case of the Liberal Democrats, because its support is spread across the country in ways that do not allow it to make an impact in those parts of the country where there is solid support for the Labour and Conservative parties.

The adoption of a system of proportional representation would radically alter the British electoral system. It would require larger constituencies as one of the objects is to ensure that representation by a Member for a party of an elector's choice would not be confined to those who voted for the candidate securing the most votes, but would be spread amongst those who voted for candidates securing significant numbers of votes. Candidates on the fringes of the political spectrum would still, as now, be unlikely to secure representation.

Single Transferable Vote

One example of a system of proportional representation is the Single Transferable Vote. This works by having multi-Member constituencies. Voters cast their votes for a number of candidates in order of preference. A candidate reaching the quota—the number of votes where, mathematically, she must be elected—is elected and the excess votes are redistributed to the second preferences of the voters who voted for the now elected candidate. In this way, the system seeks to address the 'wasted votes' syndrome. The process continues until all the seats are filled. One advantage for the voter is that it allows for the expression of preferences within and across parties as the voter is presented with a range of candidates. However, this additional complexity could lead to an increase in **spoiled ballot papers** to a higher degree than happens under the present system. Also, the result is not deliverable as quickly as the current system, but proponents argue that this is a small price to pay for a greater degree of representation.

spoiled ballot papers
ballot papers which are incorrectly completed

The system also tends to level out party support so that no one party is likely to hold an absolute majority. This is a significant problem with proportional representation for many critics as they argue that the system tends to produce governments that do not have a majority to govern effectively. However, proponents argue that the system produces consensus, which it is said, more truly represents the feeling of the electorate, by requiring parties to take into account the views of others. They also argue that the 'strong government' argument is overplayed, since the present system tends to produce large swings as one party is replaced by another, which means that whilst a government might be strong whilst it is in office the system is in the long term unstable. Thus, it is argued, STV produces greater long term stability and protects the electorate against government by extremists.

For some, a fundamental objection to proportional representation is that it breaks the link between the MP representing a manageably sized constituency. This, it is said, enables the MP to identify with those residing in it, and the electors have an individual representative with whom they can identify. Given that MPs would be representing a much larger area, the whole process would become much more anonymous. Proponents argue that at least electors would have a greater chance of being represented by someone of their own political persuasion.

Party List

A second example is the Party List system. Here, voters simply cast a vote for the party they wish to see in government and the Members are drawn from a list for each party. The seats are filled and allocated to the constituencies. This system has the advantage of simplicity, in that, as with the present system, voters are simply asked to cast one vote rather than the multiple choices that STV ballot papers would present. Also, electors are voting for a party rather than for individuals, which makes the process more impersonal. The link between the individual and the constituency is again broken or at least weakened. However, as the party retains, to a degree, control of which of its candidates is elected, the possibility of an upset whereby a leading figure within the party fails to be elected, is considerably reduced. This is one of the quirks of the present system and, some might argue, provides a degree of spice, on election night. A party with a realistic chance of being in a position to govern would have planned ahead and would not want its plans disrupted by a freak election result. The results are deliverable more swiftly under a party list system than under STV, which might be felt to be advantageous. However, as with STV, the system is more likely to produce a situation where no one party has an overall majority and thus is unable to govern without the cooperation of other parties.

Hybrid systems

A further possibility is to combine one or more systems. Thus for example, a certain proportion of seats could be filled by 'first past the post' with the remainder topped up by a party list. Any permutation of systems could be used. In the end, as the above examples illustrate, much depends on what are felt to be the key qualities the system needs to have. Those who regard representativeness as the main requirement will favour systems of proportional representation that deliver that. Those who feel that a system that secures for a party election to government with a working majority and which promotes a strong personal link between a Member of Parliament and the constituency will tend to favour the present system notwithstanding its inability to produce a strong correlation between votes cast and seats won. Those who would like some balance in the objectives of the system might favour a combined or hybrid system.

Other aspects of electoral reform

Recently, the focus of electoral reform has switched to reforming the operation of the system. Voting is not compulsory, and, as a result, not every elector chooses to exercise the right to vote. This, in turn, means that Members of Parliament, and consequently the government, are only elected by a proportion of the total electorate. In the 2005 general election, for example, there was nationally a 61% turnout, though this was unevenly spread across the country. The Labour government was elected to office by 35% of the electorate who actually voted. This gives rise to arguments about how far their views had been endorsed by the population as a whole and thus how far they had a mandate to carry through their policies. However, as the number of seats gained is not dependent on the number of voters actually casting their votes, Labour gained 356 seats in that election, putting it in a position where it had an overall majority of seats ahead of the Conservatives party who secured 32% of the vote—only 3% below Labour—and 192 seats, and the Liberal Democrats who secured 22% of the vote and 62 seats. In each case the disparity between the percentage of the votes and the percentage of the seats is due to the way in which voting strength is concentrated in different parts of the country.

General Election 2005

	Seats	percentage of vote
Labour	355	35.2
Conservative	198	32.4
Liberal Democrat	62	22.0
Other	31	10.4
Total	646	100

Source: House of Commons Research Paper 05/33 (2005)

On this basis it could be argued that making voting compulsory would at least mean that Members of Parliament, and thus the government, were elected by the electorate as a whole rather than a fraction of it. This would in turn enhance the credibility of the claims of government to have a mandate to implement its policies. Alternative strategies for improving the turnout include making it easier to vote. As discussed above, making postal votes more widely available has been tried, with mixed success. The figures quoted in the *Bordesley* case show that once postal voting on demand was introduced, the number of postal votes increased dramatically, from 7,000 in 2001 to just over 20,000 in 2002 with a further rise to just over 28,000 in 2003. There was a further dramatic increase to around 70,000 in 2004. It was this startling rise that contributed to a feeling that fraudulent activity was occurring. Nevertheless, these figures, even allowing for possible fraud, from one ward in a major city suggest that voting by post rather than in person at the polling station may be a popular option which would have the effect, if these sorts or figures were replicated nationally, of increasing significantly the percentage of the electorate voting in a parliamentary election. The major drawback is to prevent the various types of fraud revealed by the investigations in that case. Unless this can be secured, then there are serious questions raised about the integrity of the system which would be damaging to the electoral system.

The more radical proposals for reform such as the introduction of proportional representation have as part of their appeal the notion that they would promote increased participation in elections because voters would feel they had a greater say in the outcome. This is especially true of systems such as STV which allow for a greater degree of voter choice and hence influence on the outcome.

thinking point
What reforms of the electoral system would you advocate? Why?

The options for electoral reform basically involve making alterations to the present system without altering its underlying framework, or embarking on a more radical reform of the system and putting something entirely new in its place. There have, over the years, been a number of reports, both official and unofficial. The Labour and Conservative Parties appear to wish to continue with the 'first past the post' system and try to make it operate more effectively. As things stand at present, it would only be if the Liberal Democrats were to form a government, something the current system makes unlikely, that any major reform of the electoral system would become part of government policy.

4.2 The House of Commons: organization and functions

Once Members of Parliament arrive at Westminster and take up their seats, what do they do? There are currently 646 Members of Parliament in the House of Commons. Some Members of Parliament will have a dual role as both constituency MPs and holders of some government office as Ministers. The House of Commons Disqualification Act 1975 (s.2) limits the number of Ministers who can sit in the House of Commons to 95. The effect of this is that some Ministers will be Members of the House of Lords. The Speaker presides over the House as an independent Member whose role is to ensure the proper conduct of the business of the House. The Leader of the House, who is a member of the government, organizes the business of the House on a weekly basis. Organization within the House depends very much on party organization. Each party has officials called whips whose functions are essentially concerned with party discipline, ensuring, for example, that Members will be in the House for important votes.

4.2.1 Duration

The House sits for a maximum of five years, which, by convention, is divided into annual sessions. The combined effect of the Septennial Act 1715 and the Parliament Act 1911 is that the House is automatically dissolved after this time. In practice, Parliaments do not always run for the full five years, as a general election is often called before this automatic termination occurs. The Prime Minister will ask the monarch for Parliament to be dissolved, and by convention, the monarch will concur. A general election will be held either where the life of Parliament ends automatically or there is a dissolution of Parliament.

thinking point

Should the government be able to decide when to hold an election or should the dates for elections be fixed?

4.2.2 **Functions**

The main functions of the House relate to:

- Legislation
- Scrutiny of the executive
- Control of finance
- Redress of grievances

There is a considerable overlap in these functions, but each may be examined in turn.

Legislation

An Act of Parliament begins as a bill. Bills are classified in a number of ways. They may be classified by type into, principally, public bills and private bills. Public bills are those of general application. Private bills are more limited in their application; they may, for example, apply to a particular location or even to particular individuals. The classification is important, not least because bills follow a different procedure according to their type. This section focuses on public bills.

Alternatively, bills may be classified according to the way in which they are introduced. Here the principal division is between government bills and Private Members' Bills. Most bills are introduced into Parliament by the government and will implement their major policies. However, individual Members of Parliament may introduce bills on matters that are important to them. Parliamentary procedure is organized so that individuals have an opportunity to present bills, but as the business of the House is organized by the government, who also have the party whips under their control, the chances of a Private Member's Bill becoming law are slim unless it receives government backing.

Private Members' Bills

Nonetheless, individual Members may present a bill by a number of means. There is a ballot for Private Members' Bills, with time allocated for their presentation, and a Member coming high in the ballot has the certainty of being able to introduce a bill. Such Members are understandably very popular with pressure groups who will seek to lobby those coming high in the ballot to try to persuade them to introduce a bill in their area of interest. Alternatively, individual Members can seek to introduce a bill under the 10 minute rule, whereby individual Members have ten minutes to present a bill, after which a vote is taken as to whether the bill should be allowed to proceed. Very few bills get beyond being introduced by this method.

Legislative procedure for public bills

Once a bill has been introduced, it goes through a series of stages before finally emerging, as an Act of Parliament. Briefly, the procedure generally followed for public bills is that the bill is introduced and given a first reading in the House of Commons. This is largely a formality. The bill is then sent for printing and a date fixed for its second reading. The second reading is a debate on the general principles of the bill, following which there is a vote as to whether the bill should proceed. Many bills fall at this stage and proceed no further. A bill that has had a successful second reading is then sent to a standing committee for detailed scrutiny. The composition of the committee reflects membership of the whole House, so the government always has a majority. The committee goes through the bill clause by clause, making detailed amendments, including the addition of new material and deletion of existing material. Following the committee stage, as it is called, the bill returns to the full House. The bill as amended is reported back to the House—hence the name 'report stage' for this part of the process—and is given a third reading. If the bill is successful at this stage it then goes to the House of Lords for their consideration of it.

Figure 4.1

Legislative procedure: bill commencing in the House of Commons

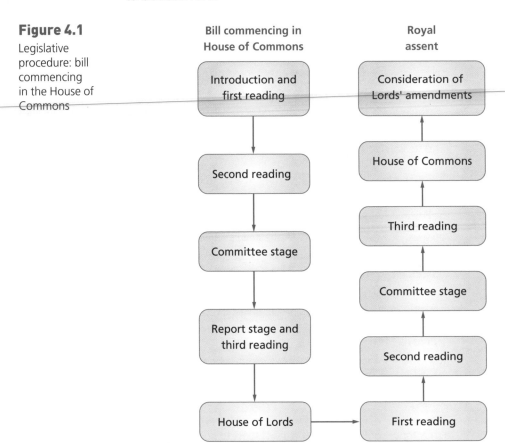

Generally, the debates at each stage of the proceedings can run their course. However, there is a danger of Members tactically prolonging debate in the hope that the bill will fall. Various procedural devices are available to limit the time available for debate. A **closure motion** may be moved at any time. If successful this curtails debate on the bill and a vote is taken. Another device allows for only certain amendments to be considered: this is sometimes known as the **kangaroo** as it involves taking certain amendments and then jumping over others to get to the next selected one. The most radical and controversial is what is generally known as the **guillotine**, though its technical name is the allocation of time motion. This provides for a set time for debate, after which the matter is again put to the vote.

Once the bill has completed its passage through the House of Commons, it commences its passage through the House of Lords. Here, it follows an equivalent procedure in terms of going through three readings with a committee stage after the second reading. One difference is that the committee stage is taken in the full House and not sent to a committee as is the practice in the House of Commons. The Lords may make amendments to the bill during its passage. These then go back to the House of Commons where they are considered. Once the final form of the bill is agreed it is presented for royal assent which is in practice carried out on behalf of the monarch by a parliamentary official. At this point the bill becomes an Act.

thinking point
How would you reform the legislative system?

Bills may also be introduced in the House of Lords, in which case the procedure follows the same pattern only in reverse, with the bill going through the House of Lords first and then being considered by the House of Commons.

85

Figure 4.2
Legislative procedure: bill commencing in House of Lords

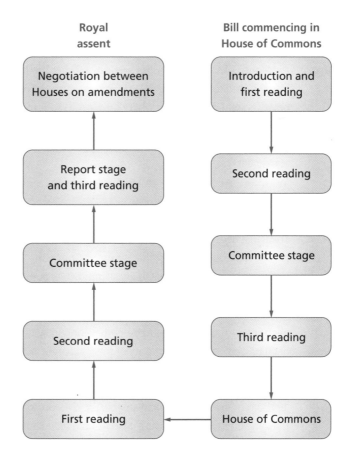

Disagreements between the House of Commons and House of Lords

A question arises as to what happens if the House of Lords or the House of Commons will not pass a measure passed by the other House. In practice, as in many other areas of British constitutional practice, the reality is not always reflected in the model. The formal procedural steps through which legislation passes are easily described, but the reality is that there is much dialogue between the two Houses during the passage of legislation with the object of smoothing the passage of bills through Parliament. However, where this breaks down, then we need to look at the relationship between the Houses. The House of Commons, as the elected chamber, has the greater claim to enforce its will. This is recognized in the Salisbury agreement, a convention whereby the House of Lords agrees not to block a bill that has been passed by the House of Commons implementing a manifesto commitment on the part of the government. There may be some debate as to whether the part of the bill to which objection is being taken is in fact a manifesto commitment thus triggering the convention, but where it is recognized that this is the case, then the Lords should give way and pass the measure as approved by the House of Commons. The superiority of the House of Commons is thus recognised and reinforced.

If all else fails then the Parliament Acts 1911 and 1949 may be invoked. These provide for a bill to be presented for the royal assent notwithstanding that it has not been passed by the House of Lords. In order for this to occur, by virtue of s.2 (as amended) the bill must have been passed by the House of Commons in two successive sessions and been rejected by the House of Lords in each of those sessions. A year must elapse between the second reading in the House of Commons in the first session and it passing through the House of Commons in the second session. The powers of the House of Lords are thus reduced to a power of delay over bills which will eventually pass into legislation. The power is limited still further where the bill is a **Money Bill** (s.1). Here, the bill is delayed for only one month before being presented for the royal assent.

....

Money Bill

a bill which in the opinion of the speaker of the House of Commons is concerned solely with taxation and other matters related to public money (s.1(2))

....

The Parliament Acts have been little used in practice, as using them almost amounts to an acknowledgement that the House of Commons has been unable to persuade the House of Lords of the desirability of the bill in question. A recent example of its use was the Hunting Act 2004. In *R(Jackson) v Attorney General* [2006] 1 AC 262, one of the arguments put to the House of Lords was that the Parliament Act 1949, which had been used to secure the passage of the Hunting Act, was not a valid Act as it had itself been passed under the authority of the Parliament Act 1911. On this basis it was argued that all legislation passed under the terms of the 1949 Act was invalid. The House of Lords rejected this argument holding that there was no limitation in the Parliament Act 1911 which prevented the Parliament Act 1949 being passed in the way it was; and that the Parliament Act 1949 was a valid Act of Parliament. It therefore followed that as the

thinking point
If the Parliament Acts are not used very often, why are they needed at all?

cross reference
This is considered further in Chapter 3.

Hunting Act 2004 was passed in accordance with its terms that, too, was a valid Act, at least on that ground.

The use of delegated legislation

One issue that has become more prominent in recent times has been the practice of creating legislation that comprises a framework, leaving the details to be filled in by means of delegated legislation. Delegated legislation is subject to much less formal scrutiny than primary legislation, and the fear is that the government will be able to make significant and, in some cases, fundamental changes to the detail of legislation by this without it being the subject of proper parliamentary debate. The potential danger of this practice is heightened when the power contained in the Act is a power to repeal primary legislation by means of delegated legislation. Such a power appears in s.10 of the Human Rights Act 1998, the justification here being that this power is only used where legislation has been found to be incompatible and swift amendment is needed to enable the public authorities affected by the problem to be able to adjust their practice as swiftly as possible to prevent further breaches of the human rights of affected individuals.

cross reference
See further Chapters 5 and 10

thinking point
Is giving the government the power to make delegated legislation an abuse of power?

Although Parliament can insert safeguards into the Act creating the power to make delegated legislation, the power of the government to secure the passage of its measures may mean that this ability is more apparent than real. It is worth bearing in mind, however, that delegated legislation, unlike Acts of Parliament, is subject to review by the courts who may declare it to be invalid. There is thus, at least potentially, the possibility of scrutiny even after delegated legislation has been passed. We will return to this issue later when discussing judicial review.

Scrutiny of the executive

The legislative process

One of the features of the British constitution is that the executive is part of the legislature and the legislature has as one of its functions holding the government to account. One way in which this occurs is through the legislative process. At each stage in the passage of legislation there is a debate and a vote. In debates, the government can be asked to explain and justify its proposals and in votes, the government may be defeated though given that it has a majority this is an unlikely event, unless some back bench Members of Parliament on the government side vote against their own party.

Parliamentary questions

There are other devices that provide opportunities for the government to be held to account. One of the more public of these is Question Time, when the Prime Minister and other Ministers answer questions in the House. One of the privileges of being a Member of Parliament is having the right to ask questions of government Ministers in the House. Questions may be written or oral and may require a written or oral answer. The general wisdom is that political points may be made more easily by requiring an oral answer but that written answers often elicit more actual information. In asking a question requiring an oral answer, the Member of Parliament, if from one of the opposition parties, may seek to try to show government policy in a bad light whilst at the same time promoting the policies of the opposition party.

Equally, back bench Members on the government side may seek to ask questions designed to show government policy in a good light. Part of the skill is to ask an innocuous question which is then followed up by something more difficult to which the Minister has to make an instant response. There is a certain theatrical quality to these encounters and they are often viewed rather light-heartedly in the media. However, as many Ministers have made clear, they are not to be taken lightly (see e.g. Nigel Lawson *The View from No. 11* (Bantam Press, 1999) p.12). Ministers are normally expected to answer questions that are put to them. There are, however, circumstances in which a Minister is not required to answer a question; examples might be day-to-day operational matters, matters where the public interest would not be served by an answer and answers where the cost of providing an answer would be disproportionate.

activity

Watch or listen to Question Time with either the Prime Minister or other Ministers. What do you think is the point of it?

Debates

Various forms of debate also provide the opportunity for government Ministers and their policies to be subjected to scrutiny, such as Adjournment Debates and debates on Early Day Motions. There are, at various times during the parliamentary year, set piece debates such as the debate on the Queen's Speech, which traditionally opens the annual parliamentary session, and the Budget. The ultimate debate holding the government to account is a debate on a motion of no confidence. These are occasionally moved by the opposition parties, but in recent times the only example of such a motion being passed was in 1979, following which the Prime Minister, Mr. Callaghan, resigned and called a general election.

Committees

Less public than the activities that take place in the House of Commons itself, but extremely important in terms of holding the government to account, are the various committees. We have already seen that once a bill has received its second reading it is sent to a standing committee for detailed scrutiny. There are also a number of other committees that scrutinise various aspects of governmental activity. The most powerful of these is the Public Accounts Committee which scrutinizes the government accounts to ensure that the government is spending money properly and responsibly. A series of Select Committees oversee particular aspects of the work of the government. Some are related to particular departments, such as the Defence Committee, whilst others cut across departmental boundaries, such as the Public Accounts Committee itself or the Broadcasting Committee. These committees produce influential reports and can, in the course of the sessions they hold, subject Ministers and their officials to extensive questioning.

Control of finance

The constitutional settlement established the primacy of Parliament in matters of national finance. Article 4 of the Bill of Rights 1689 established that the levying of taxation is a matter for Parliament and not for the monarch. Gradually, it became established that the House of Commons was the body within Parliament that had control over taxation. The events leading up to the passing of the Parliament Act 1911 illustrate the assertion of this by the House of Commons and ultimately this was enshrined in law by s.1 of the Parliament Act 1911, discussed above. All bills relating to finance start in the House of Commons and the Chancellor of the Exchequer is always a Member of the House of Commons. So too is the Prime Minister, who also holds the nominal title of First Lord of the Treasury. The work of the Public Accounts Committee has already been mentioned. This is supplemented by the Comptroller and Auditor General, who is an officer of the House and is responsible for scrutiny of government expenditure, though not the government's financial policies.

Redress of grievances

One of the earliest functions of Parliament was to redress grievances and it retains this function today. There are a number of ways, both formal and informal, that a Member of Parliament can seek to deal with grievances raised by constituents. Members of Parliament have access to Ministers and may write to the Minister or ask a question in the House on behalf of a constituent. The Member may also write on the constituent's behalf to a body or organization outside Parliament. Members of Parliament are also able to refer complaints about failures of government departments to act properly to the Parliamentary Commissioner for Administration, or ombudsman. The ombudsman is only able to act where there is evidence of maladministration.

A more collective form of grievance resolution may be in the form of the passing of a bill to remedy an injustice that has been brought to light. By passing an Act of Parliament, issues that are affecting society as a whole or any part of it may be addressed.

 # 4.3 The House of Lords

Historically, the seat of the most important landowners in society, the House of Lords has in modern times become something of an anachronism with regard to its composition. It was only in the 20th century that any real attempt was made to reform its composition to reflect more modern notions of the qualifications necessary to entitle a person to a seat in the legislature. More recently, the Labour government of 1997 onwards has embarked on some more fundamental reforms which, at the time of writing, are still incomplete. Changes to the composition of the House of Lords have, however, raised fresh questions about its powers, as the two issues are seemingly intertwined.

4.3.1 **Membership**

Historically, membership of the House of Lords depended on the holding of a peerage, which was passed on to the heirs of the deceased peer. Thus, membership of the House of Lords passed through families by accident of birth rather than any other qualification. New peerages were created carrying with them the right to membership of the House, but no real attempts were made to widen the membership base. The creation of life peerages for the Lords of Appeal in Ordinary, created in 1873–6 reforms of the court system (Appellate Jurisdiction Act 1876), did little to alter the nature of the membership of the House, as they were not expected to participate in its legislative work. The only other group represented in the House of Lords were the Archbishops and certain bishops of the Church of England, who again remain in the House today.

It was not until 1958 that a serious attempt was made to widen the composition of the House of Lords. The Life Peerages Act 1958 provided for the creation of life peerages (s.1), which would not descend to heirs on the death of the holder. Part of the thinking behind this was to extend the range of expertise amongst members of the House by drawing on those who had made significant contributions to society, including former members of the House of Commons. It was also designed to make the House more professional in its operations by creating peers who would be expected to sit regularly and contribute to the business of the House, thereby ensuring that the House conducted its operations more efficiently. The effect of this was to increase the membership of the House in terms of numbers and also in terms of those attending its sittings. An additional effect was to change the political composition of the House, which had always had an inbuilt Conservative majority. The landed classes that made up the membership were either formally members of the Conservative Party or at least Conservative sympathizers. This was particularly problematic when a Labour government was in office. A further reform was effected in 1963 by the Peerage Act of that year, s.1 of which enabled hereditary peers to disclaim their peerages and thereby remove the disqualification from membership of the House of Commons that this carried. This is less significant now owing to changes in the composition of the House of Lords discussed below.

Despite many proposals, both official and otherwise, for reform of the House of Lords it has only been since 1997 that any serious changes have been considered and made. In all its documents on this the Labour government has been clear that the role of the House of Lords is subservient to the House of Commons, and that it is essentially a revising chamber. The House of Lords Reform Act 1999 made a significant change to the composition of the House by excluding all bar 90 hereditary peers from membership of the House of Lords (ss.1, 2). This was essentially a compromise designed to secure support for this particular reform. Reform of the system of appointing peers is also under way, as the power of appointment of life peers has been felt to confer too much power on the Prime Minister.

A further set of changes has been effected by the Constitutional Reform Act 2005, which came into force in 2006. The Lord Chancellor has long been the subject of criticism due to his position as a member of the executive, the legislature and the judiciary. The 2005 Act removes the Lord Chancellor from his position as head of the judiciary, giving that role instead to the Lord Chief Justice (s.7). It makes provision for the election of a Speaker of the House of Lords to relieve the Lord Chancellor of that role also (s.10; Sch.6). The present incumbent, Mr. Straw, is the first Lord Chancellor to be a member of the House of Commons as well as being Secretary of State for Justice, and, although he has legal qualifications, this is not now a necessary requirement for the role (s.2).

At the time of writing the reforms are incomplete. The final decision as to how membership will be determined has not yet been taken, with some members of Parliament being unhappy about the prospect of a House that is appointed by the Prime Minister. A white paper in July 2008 (*An elected Second Chamber: further reform of the House of Lords* Cm 7438 (2008)) seeks to address these concerns by proposing a second chamber that would be predominantly elected, though smaller than the House of Commons. The position of the bishops is also subject to discussion, with some favouring the removal of religion as a criterion for membership, whilst others argue that the opportunity should be taken to extend religious representation to all religions, not just the Church of England. The white paper favours the retention of the bishops, though in numbers proportionate to the reformed House. It seems clear that reform will not occur until after the next general election which will probably be in 2010.

thinking point
Who do you think should be eligible for membership of the House of Lords?

Under the terms of the Constitutional Reform Act 2005 (Part 3) the Law Lords will relocate to the new Supreme Court when that body is established and the link between the highest court and the legislature will be formally severed.

4.3.2 **Functions of the House of Lords**

The functions of the House of Lords to a degree mirror those of the House of Commons. The House of Lords is, as we have seen, part of the legislative process. Its functions here are to revise legislation sent from the House of Commons. This allows for amendments to be made where appropriate. Some bills begin their passage through Parliament in the House of Lords. Bills are thus proceeding both from the House of Lords to the House of Commons and vice versa. This enables more legislation to be passed, and by this division of work Parliament as a whole runs more effectively. The House of Lords does a great deal of useful work in scrutinizing delegated legislation. It also debates matters of public importance. In pursuance of these activities, it engages in scrutiny of the executive. The location in the House of Lords of the highest court in the system is an historical anomaly which will be corrected by the establishment of the Supreme Court.

The major problem for the House of Lords is that, despite its reformed membership, it will not experience any gains in power. The possibility of the House of Lords rivalling the House of Commons in terms of powers has always been dismissed on account of the composition of the House of Lords as an unelected House. Now that the composition is being reformed, there may be arguments that the House of Lords should exercise greater

thinking point
As the membership of the House of Lords has been reformed, should it be given more power?

power, if necessary blocking measures passed in the House of Commons. This seems very unlikely even if the House of Lords ultimately becomes an elected chamber, as the House of Commons would not sanction any enhancement of powers on the part of the House of Lords that would weaken its own position. The issue appears resolved for the time being in that the whole framework of the House of Lords reforms being promoted by the present government locates the House of Lords firmly as a subservient chamber with powers of revision only.

? Questions

If you answer the following questions, you will have appreciated the main issues raised in this chapter. Check your answers against the notes provided at the back of the book.

1 How does the present electoral system operate?

2 Is the present electoral system in need of reform?

3 What are the functions of Parliament?

4 How successfully do you think it carries out these functions?

5 What functions does the present House of Lords perform and how successfully do you think it carries them out?

6 Would a reformed House of Lords improve the working of Parliament or are the present arrangements satisfactory?

Further reading

To further your understanding of the topics covered in this chapter, have a look at the reading materials mentioned below. Useful web links are also provided on the Online Resource Centre.

Rodney Brazier, *Constitutional Reform* (Oxford University Press, 3rd ed., 2008) ch.4
This provides you with a critical review of the current and possible future voting systems.

Rodney Brazier, *Constitutional Reform* (Oxford University Press, 3rd ed., 2008) ch.5
This subjects the House of Lords to critical scrutiny in a succinct but informative way.

Jeffrey Jowell and Dawn Oliver (eds), *The Changing Constitution* (Oxford University Press, 6th ed., 2007) ch.7
This will give you a critical overview of the way Parliament is currently composed, how it functions and how it might be improved.

The executive

Introduction

This chapter examines the executive and considers how people become members of it and what they do as part of it. A particular concern is to identify the sources of the powers exercised by the executive and how the legislature and judiciary provide mechanisms for accountability, or checks and balances, to prevent the executive abusing its power. The word 'government' is used in this chapter and elsewhere in two distinct senses. First, it means the whole system of government of the state, which is the sense in which it is used when discussing separation of powers theory. Secondly, it is used to mean the government in the sense of the executive. The executive consists of those whose function is to initiate and execute policy, and so includes both the government in the political sense as well as the civil service and other agencies carrying into effect the policies of the government.

5.1 The executive

cross reference
You may wish to refresh your memory by re-reading the section on the separation of powers in Chapter 2.

The constitutional role of the executive is to formulate policy and to bring about its implementation. It will be immediately apparent that part of the executive function is concerned with the development of policy. This function is carried out by the government at central and local levels: we'll concentrate here on central government. The implementation of policy is divided between a number of bodies including the civil service, local government officials and the police. In order to give effect to policy decisions, however, powers need to be given to, or duties imposed on, those involved in this activity. As we will see later, such powers may come from the royal prerogative or, more commonly, from statute.

Thinking back to the idea of the separation of powers, we can see that, in order to have the power to implement its policies, the executive needs to rely on the legislature to pass laws and on the courts to interpret them in a way that allows the executive to carry out its wishes. This is where, in separation of powers theory, the idea of checks and balances comes in, for the legislature and the judges may take a different view from that of the executive as to what its powers are or should be.

However, the legislature and judges stand in different relationships with the executive. As we have seen, under the separation of powers idea we would expect each of these functions to be separate. With regard to the judges, this is the case. The overlap of functions formerly exercised by the Lord Chancellor has been gradually dismantled by the Constitutional Reform Act 2005. The head of the Judiciary is now the Lord Chief Justice, whilst the Lord Chancellor now exercises purely executive functions as head of the Ministry of Justice. Even before this, however, Lord Falconer, the last traditional Lord Chancellor, had indicated that he would not sit as a judge. It is sometimes said that the Law Officers—the Attorney General and Solicitor General—combine executive and judicial functions, but this is not really the case. They exercise functions connected with the legal system, such as making decisions to prosecute in cases where consent is required, but these are not really judicial functions. They are, rather, functions of an executive nature. The result of all this is that a structural separation between the executive and the judiciary now exists in a way that it did not previously.

5.2 Executive and legislature

If we turn to the relationship between the executive and the legislature, a wholly different picture emerges. As we have seen, a peculiarity of the British constitution is an overlap between that part of the executive that is concerned with policy formulation—the government—and the legislature—Parliament.

> Ministers are:
>
> 1. Members of Parliament (House of Commons or House of Lords).
> 2. Normally attached to a particular department.
> 3. Senior Ministers sit in the Cabinet.

By convention, in order to be a member of the government a person also has to be a Member of one or other House. One of the consequences of the 'first past the post' system of elections is that the party that ultimately becomes the government cannot guarantee that its leading members, those it has lined up to become Ministers, will be elected. In the event that such people are not elected, the government has to try to secure a place in the legislature for them by some means or other, either by getting them selected for a safe seat or by means of a peerage. Neither is satisfactory politically, for rejection of the individual by the voters in the first place is not a situation easily redeemable. Also, given the primacy of the House of Commons, putting the person in the House of Lords may weaken the government and also its accountability to the elected house. The problems were graphically illustrated by the experience of Patrick Gordon Walker.

> ### *Patrick Gordon Walker*
> . . . .
> He was a leading member of the Labour Party that was elected to office in 1964. However, he lost his seat in the election. Nonetheless, the Prime Minister, Harold Wilson, appointed him as Secretary of State for Foreign Affairs in the anticipation that he would acquire a seat elsewhere. He was not the only member of the 1964 government without a seat, for Mr. Wilson had also appointed Frank Cousins, a leading trade unionist, as Minister of Technology. Seats had to be found for them, so 2 Labour MPs in apparently safe seats were persuaded to accept peerages, creating by-elections in their former constituencies, Nuneaton and Leyton. Mr. Cousins and Mr. Gordon Walker were nominated for these seats. Mr. Cousins was

elected and thus able to continue in government, but Mr. Gordon Walker managed again to fail to be elected and had to leave the government, temporarily as it turned out: he later won the seat in Leyton in the 1966 election and returned to government office.

However, there have been examples of individuals being given peerages to enable them to join the government, most recently when Peter Mandelson rejoined the government as Secretary of State for Business, Enterprise and Regulatory Reform in October 2008.

The overlap between legislature and executive means, therefore, that Ministers must undertake a dual role as Members of Parliament and as Ministers. In the case of Members of the House of Commons, it means that they must carry out their function as representatives for their constituency and constituents as well as acting as members of the government. It might be thought that being a Member of the House of Commons is a full time activity, but, as we have seen, membership of Parliament is structured so that members can do other things as well.

thinking point

If an MP is also a Minister, does it make a difference to her ability to represent her constituents?

Given the priority that has to be given to running the country, it might be expected that the constituency might suffer from having a Minister as its representative, quite simply because the Minister will not have time to devote to constituency duties. Even accounts from Ministers concede that this is the case. However, the presence of members of the government in Parliament does mean that they can readily be subjected to scrutiny and held to account in a more direct way than might be possible under other arrangements.

By limiting the number of Ministers who can sit in the House of Commons to 95, s.2(1) of the House of Commons (Disqualification) Act 1975 ensures that not all Ministers will be drawn from the House of Commons. Indeed, some ministerial posts are tied to the House of Lords, such as the Lord Privy Seal, though the Lord Chancellor is no longer necessarily a member of the House of Lords: Mr. Straw recently became the first holder of the office to be a member of the House of Commons. The division of Ministers between the two Houses is subject to some important conventions. Both the Prime Minister and the Chancellor of the Exchequer must be members of the House of Commons, which reflects the primacy of that House with regard to financial matters. It is also generally thought that the heads of the other main government departments should be members of the House of Commons. Some controversy was caused by the appointment of Lord Carrington as Foreign Secretary in the Conservative government of 1979. It was argued that it deprived the House of Commons of the ability to question the Foreign Secretary about matters of foreign policy. The argument that other Ministers from the Foreign Office were members of the House of Commons did not persuade everyone, as it was felt to be important that the head of that ministry was personally subject to scrutiny, especially during the Falklands War in 1982.

5.3 The Queen's government

In her speech at the State Opening of Parliament, the Queen always refers to 'My Government'. This might sound odd, but we must remember that, prior to the development of cabinet government as we know it, the monarch actually governed the country and had powers across the full range of government functions. Gradually, as more modern notions of democracy came to influence the political complexion of the state, the power of Parliament, and particularly the House of Commons, was asserted, and a shift of power from the monarch and to Parliament occurred. However, the tradition has been that government continues to be carried out by Her Majesty's Government (and opposed by Her Majesty's Opposition). The Queen's Government exercises powers in her name and on her behalf though to all intents and purposes she has nothing to do with the running of the country. So the question is: what role does she play in what is described as the constitutional monarchy? To answer this we need to look a bit more closely at some commonly used terms.

5.3.1 Crown, sovereign and monarchy

The terms most commonly encountered in connection with the Queen are the Crown, the Sovereign and the Monarch. Put simply, the terms Sovereign and Monarch refer to the Queen in her personal capacity as head of state and the Crown refers to her symbolic position as representing the government of the state. In *Town Investments Ltd v Department of the Environment* [1978] AC 359 at 381 Lord Diplock explains:

> ...instead of speaking of 'the Crown' we [should] speak of 'the government'—a term appropriate to embrace both collectively and individually all the Ministers of the Crown and parliamentary secretaries under whose direction the administrative work of government is carried on by the civil servants employed in the various government departments...Executive acts of government that are done by them are acts done by 'the Crown' in the fictional sense in which that expression is now used in English public law.

So, according to Lord Diplock, when people talk of the Crown they really mean the government. The issue is not as clear cut as Lord Diplock suggests, but for the present, it will suffice.

thinking point
Is the idea of the government acting in the name of the Queen an unnecessary and artificial one?

5.3.2 The Queen as sovereign

If we turn to the Queen as sovereign, an initial question is: how is the succession determined? This was regularized by the Act of Settlement 1700 which provides, in s.3, that the monarch must 'joyn in communion with the Church of England'. This remains the law: a recent example of its potency was provided by Peter Phillips, son of the Princess Royal, who, on marrying, could only retain his position in succession to the throne by

thinking point
Should the monarch retire at a certain age?

virtue of his wife renouncing her catholic faith. There has been some controversy about the link with the Church of England, especially with regard to the possibility that Prince Charles, the current heir to the throne, is a divorcee and is now married to a divorcee, yet may become head of the Church of England, one of whose fundamental doctrines is upholding the sanctity of marriage. He has also expressed an interest in taking a more inclusive view of other faiths, which again has generated controversy.

The sovereign traditionally dies in office. A seamless succession follows with the heir to the throne assuming the monarchy in law the moment the pervious monarch dies. This is summed up in the phrase 'the king is dead, long live the king' signifying the seamless end of one reign and commencement of another. There are, however, precedents for the monarch stepping down (abdicating). In 1936, King Edward VIII abdicated in order to marry a divorcee, which, at the time, was not permissible for the king, not least in his role as head of the Church of England. An Act of Parliament (His Majesty's Declaration of Abdication Act 1936) was passed to amend the Act of Settlement to deal with this unforeseen event. More recently, it has been suggested that the present Queen, aged 80 at the time of writing, might consider 'retiring' but there are no signs of this occurring. The succession favours male heirs of the sovereign, so that the precedence of heirs to the throne shows Prince Charles and his children followed by the Duke of York and the Earl of Wessex and their children ahead of the Princess Royal, who is the Queen's second child.

thinking point
Does anything to do with the royal family matter given their largely ceremonial role in modern Britain?

5.3.3 **The monarchy**

The monarchy is financed by the **Civil List**. This is under parliamentary control and is governed by a series of Acts of Parliament. What does the Queen do to justify the not inconsiderable sums paid to her and her family by way of the Civil List? The Queen, of course, represents the UK, as head of state, abroad. This is not only symbolic but also practical. The separation between the functions of head of state and head of government means that the Prime Minister is saved from having to undertake a number of ceremonial and other duties to focus on his function as head of government, which itself involves, in an increasingly globalized world, large amounts of foreign travel. Internally, the Queen again has symbolic functions. She embodies the nation and serves as a figurehead for her subjects. The monarch also has certain rights, duties, powers and immunities, to which we will return more fully later.

thinking point
Should the division between head of state and head of government remain?

Civil List

the name given to the money allocated, on an annual basis, to the royal family to enable them to perform their official duties

5.3.4 **Personal powers of the monarch**

One of the powers attaching to the monarch is that of appointment of the Prime Minister and Ministers. In theory, she could choose whoever she wished as Prime

Minister. However, all of the powers exercisable by the monarch are subject to well developed conventions as to how they should be exercised. This is the case with the power of appointment of Prime Minister, where the convention is that the Queen appoints as Prime Minister the leader of the party with a majority of seats in the House of Commons following a general election. So, following the 2005 election, the Queen simply reappointed Mr. Blair once it became clear that the Labour Party commanded the highest number of seats. The decision was in practice automatic.

The only circumstances where the Queen would have to exercise some form of judgement would be where there was a 'hung' parliament: that is, where no single party had a majority. She would have a duty to act in these circumstances because, in Sir Ivor Jennings' memorable phrase (*The Queen's Government* (Pelican, 1965) p.35), although she does not steer the ship, she has to make certain that there is someone at the wheel. It has been argued that with the advent of a significant third party (now the Liberal Democrats) in the traditional two party scheme, there has become the possibility of no one party holding an overall majority. The nearest an election result has come to requiring the Queen to do something other than make an automatic decision was, ironically, before the present situation of having three large parties.

The 1974 general election

. . . .

In 1974, the dominance of the Labour and Conservative Parties over the British political system meant that an election would ordinarily be decisively won by one or other of those parties. However, the general election in February of that year produced a result that gave the Labour Party 301 of the 635 seats and the Conservative Party 297, the rest of the seats being divided unevenly between smaller parties. Mr. Heath, the Prime Minister prior to the election held discussions with the smaller parties as did his counterpart in the Labour Party, Mr. Wilson. In the event, Mr. Heath resolved the matter by resigning, having satisfied himself that he could not form a workable government, and Mr. Wilson duly became Prime Minister. A further election in October of the same year resulted in Labour taking 319 seats thus gaining an overall majority. (See Mr. Wilson's own account of this: *Final Term* (Weidenfeld & Nicolson, 1979) ch.1.)

5.3.5 **Formal powers of the monarch**

thinking point
Should decisions as important as the appointment of the Prime Minister and Ministers be regulated by law?

Throughout the 1980s and beyond, commentators argued for electoral reform, bringing with it the possibility that no single party would have an overall majority, thus raising the possibility of having to involve the Queen in decision making and possibly also rethinking the conventions that surround the exercise of the prerogative of choice of the Prime Minister. Such possibilities aside, the actual role of the Queen in the government of the country is one that is formal and symbolic rather than real. Government is, however, carried on in her name by the Prime Minister and other Ministers. The latter are technically appointed by the Queen but on the advice of the Prime Minister, who effectively decides who will become Ministers and how long they will remain in office. In theory the Queen could refuse to endorse the choice of the Prime Minister, but this would never happen in practice.

One of the factors that ensures that the Queen does not become embroiled in political controversy is that she is aware of her constitutional position and acts accordingly. What happens behind the scenes in the working relationship between the Queen and her government we do not know. The 19th century writer, Walter Bagehot (*The English Constitution* (revised ed., Fontana, 1963) p.111) said that the monarch had the right to be consulted, the right to encourage and the right to warn. As with many other features of the British constitution, the way in which relationships play out in practice are dependent in part on the personalities involved and what they make of their roles. Thus the position of the present Queen, who has vast experience of working with Prime Ministers over more than 50 years, may differ from that of a new monarch and may vary according to the nature of the Prime Minister of the day. But like so many other features of the unseen working of the constitution, we do not know.

5.4 Prime Minister and other Ministers

Turning to the roles of the Prime Minister and other Ministers, we have seen that, following the election, the Queen will appoint the Prime Minister, the 'appointment' being a mere formality. She will then appoint as Ministers those whom the Prime Minister has chosen. They all become members of the Privy Council, to which they are sworn in if they are not already members. The continued existence of the Privy Council is really a historical legacy from its time as the body comprising the sovereign's closest advisers, but continues to perform judicial and some formal executive functions. Just as there is no statutory framework for the role of the monarch, so there is none for the Prime Minister and other Ministers. Indeed, the structure of modern cabinet government is largely the creation of convention rather than any statutory framework. Most Ministers have a dual role as members of the Cabinet and as head of a government department, in addition, of course, to their role as a constituency Member of Parliament. The Cabinet comprises the leading ministerial figures in the government and tends to be around 24 strong. Its size and the ministries represented in it are fluid, there being no set membership, but in practice the large ministries—such as the Treasury, Home Office, Foreign Office, Education, Defence etc.—are always represented. Departments may be created or abolished; some ministries are not always represented in Cabinet. All depends on the Prime Minister of the day.

5.5 The Cabinet

The Cabinet meets regularly on a weekly basis and is the forum for the formulation of government policy. Proceedings of the Cabinet are secret. The idea is that Ministers can speak freely in the interests of allowing full and frank discussion of issues before a policy emerges. Once a policy has been agreed by Cabinet, Ministers are expected to support it outside the Cabinet room. This is the basis of the idea of collective responsibility. Ministers can voice their disagreement of a proposal in the confines of the Cabinet room but once a policy is agreed they should support it publicly. This accords with popular notions that the government should speak with one voice and present a united front to Parliament and the wider public.

thinking point

Should the Crossman Diaries have been published?

The viability of collective responsibility depends on the continuance of Cabinet secrecy for its credibility: the idea that 20+ people will all agree to a proposed policy is clearly unrealistic. It is, however, possible to accept that Ministers will support something they do not necessarily agree with as a matter of political expediency. The matter came before the courts in *Attorney General v Jonathan Cape* [1976] QB 752.

case close-up

Attorney General v Jonathan Cape **[1976] QB 752**

The case concerned the publication of the diaries of Richard Crossman. He had been a member of the 1964 Labour government and had kept a diary during his time as a Minister in which he had recorded not only his thoughts on the public aspects of his work but also descriptions of the business of the Cabinet and his reflections on that. After his death, extracts from the diaries were published. The Attorney General sought an injunction to prevent further publication of the diaries, arguing that they were in breach of Mr. Crossman's oath of secrecy and that, if published, they would destroy the notion of cabinet secrecy and with it the freedom of Ministers to debate issues fully and frankly. Ministers might not express themselves freely if they knew that their views would later be publicly available. This, he argued would be contrary to the public interest. The Court of Appeal rejected this view and held that, whilst there was a public interest in preserving the secrecy of cabinet deliberations, this did not apply indefinitely. As the events described in the diaries had occurred ten or more years previously, the need for secrecy to continue had not been demonstrated, and there would be no harm to the pubic interest or the integrity of cabinet discussions by allowing publication of the diaries. Since this time, ministerial diaries have been published at regular intervals and the court's view that their publication would not harm either the cabinet or the public interest seems to have been vindicated.

5.6 Ministers and departments

The Crossman Diaries also reveal the other side of the work of a Minister, that of being the head of a government department. The political heads of the major government departments are called Secretary of State. They are one of a team of Ministers of various rankings. Below the Secretary of State there may be one or more Ministers of State, and below them Parliamentary Under Secretaries of State. Ministers of State and Parliamentary Under Secretaries of State are often referred to collectively as junior Ministers. Those heading lower ranking departments are simply called Minister. Ministers represent the department in both Cabinet discussions and in Parliament. In order to understand these relationships, it is necessary to look at the position of the civil service.

Figure 5.1

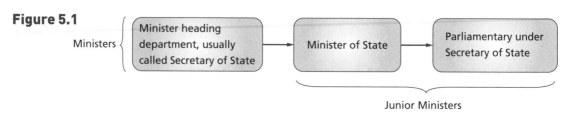

Junior Ministers

5.7 The civil service

The role of the civil service is to carry out the policy of the government of the day. The civil service is said to be 'politically neutral'. This conveys a number of ideas. First, the civil service does not change when the political complexion of the government changes. It serves governments of all political persuasions and implements their policies. Thus, civil servants are required to give effect to the policy of the government of the day even if it is diametrically opposed to that of the previous government. It also means that, however much civil servants might be personally opposed to the policies of the government of the day, they are still bound to give effect to it if they are to remain in post.

Civil servants also 'sign the Official Secrets Act'. The phrase is rather misleading, as civil servants are by virtue of their employment bound by the Official Secrets Acts and thus cannot disclose matters learned within the course of their employment. This has caused problems of conscience for some civil servants in circumstances where they have felt that the government is suppressing information or misleading the public. Thus, in the 1980s, Clive Ponting felt that the government was suppressing information concerning the sinking of the ship the General Belgrano during the Falklands War. He passed the information on to a Member of Parliament who raised questions in the House of Commons. Mr. Ponting was charged under s.2 Official Secrets Act 1991 which, as it stood at the time, made unauthorized disclosure of official information an offence (*R v Ponting* [1985] Crim LR 318). Mr. Ponting put forward a defence that the disclosure was in the public interest. The judge ruled that this was no defence and, in effect, the jury was invited to convict Mr. Ponting. In fact, they acquitted him. As the deliberations of the jury are confidential we do not know the reasons for this. Following the case, however, measures were put in place to try to prevent the problem recurring.

However, in the late 1990s, a member of the Security Service (M15), David Shayler, admitted that he had passed documents relating to matters of security to a national newspaper. He was charged with making unauthorized disclosures under the Official

Secrets Act 1989, which had amended the 1911 Act to distinguish between authorized and unauthorized disclosures, removing the absolute prohibition on disclosure that was contained in s.2 Official Secrets Act 1911. Mr. Shayler argued that in disclosing the material he was acting in the public interest and that any restriction preventing him from doing so was contrary to his right to free speech under Article 10 of the European Convention on Human Rights, which had become part of English law by virtue of the Human Rights Act 1998. The House of Lords held (*R v Shayler* [2003] 1 AC 247) that the 1989 Act, in creating a distinction between authorized and unauthorized disclosures had not created a general defence of disclosure in the public interest. Further, the scheme of the Official Secrets Act 1989 was not an excessive restriction on the right to free speech bearing in mind the interests that the state was seeking to protect. These cases illustrate that the duty of the civil servant is one of loyalty to the Minister and to the government.

5.7.1 Relationship between Minister and civil service

Civil servants are Crown servants. They work under contracts regulated by the royal prerogative (see below) and are subject to a different employment regime from other workers. Their contracts can, for example be changed unilaterally by the Crown (i.e. the government) as the CCSU case (*Council of Civil Service Unions v Minister for the Civil Service* [1985] AC 374), discussed later, illustrates. In theory, civil servants remain anonymous in the political process, any issues relating to them remaining within the department. The Minister accounts for the activities of the department in the public domain. Thus, as far as the public is concerned, if civil servants have done something well, the Minister gets the credit, and if they have done something badly the Minister takes the blame. In each case it will be for the Minister to decide how to deal with the matter internally. This convention has been gradually breaking down over the years. An extreme example of a Minister protecting civil servants occurred in what became known as the Crichel Down affair in the 1950s.

The Crichel Down affair

Land had been requisitioned during World War II. When the previous owner, the Crichel Estate, tried to buy it back, the Ministry of Agriculture refused, essentially because some civil servants did not like Lieutenant-Commander Marten, the main protagonist on behalf of the estate. Despite the fact that the civil servants in question were pursuing their own personal agenda rather than following departmental policy, and the Minister, Mr. Dugdale, was not directly at fault for the events that occurred, he nevertheless resigned over the affair. At most, he was guilty of not ensuring that civil servants were properly supervised or having policies to prevent this type of occurrence. (See further Geoffrey Wilson, *Cases and Materials on Constitutional and Administrative Law* (Cambridge University Press, 2nd ed., 1976) pp.155–64; J.A.G. Griffith, 'The Crichel Down Affair' [1955] 18 MLR 557).

There have been far worse cases of ministerial culpability that have not resulted in resignation, as illustrated below.

From this example of a Minister going to extreme lengths to take responsibility for the acts of his civil servants, the position of civil servants has become less anonymous as the years have gone by. By 1972, we find a civil servant being named in the report on the collapse of the Vehicle and General insurance company. The company had collapsed following a leak from a government department. The report into this laid the main blames for the leak on a named civil servant who had failed to take proper steps to prevent the information being disclosed (See Geoffrey Wilson, *Cases and Materials on Constitutional and Administrative Law* (Cambridge University Press, 2nd ed., 1976) pp.165–72) Since then, there has been a move to isolate those instances where the Minister has some personal blame attached and to distinguish these from circumstances where the blame lies with the civil servants. This is considered further below.

thinking point
Why should civil servants not be identified and held responsible when they have made mistakes?

5.7.2 **Civil servants acting on behalf of Ministers**

When the government is given a power by statute, it is usually designated as being given to 'the Secretary of State'. This formula is useful as it means that when government departments are reorganized the legislation does not have to be amended. It also reflects the theory that there is only one Secretary of State, though the modern practice is to have several. In practice, the decision as to which powers are exercisable by which Secretary of State is made administratively. In this way, government is able to exercise the powers it has been given by Parliament within a suitable framework.

However, given the number of powers exercisable by Ministers, it would, in practical terms, be impossible for the Minister personally to exercise every power nominally given to her. The question therefore arises as to whether civil servants can act on behalf of Ministers in the exercise of their statutory powers. The issue of whether this practice was lawful arose in the case of *Carltona Ltd v Commissioner for Works* [1943] 2 All ER 560.

case close-up

Carltona Ltd v Commissioner for Works
....

The company challenged the validity of an order requisitioning their premises on the ground that it had been made by officials on behalf of the Commissioners of Works. It was held that the order was valid and that senior civil servants were able to act on behalf of the Minister. Lord Greene MR said:

> In the administration of government in this country the functions which are given to Ministers (and constitutionally properly given to Ministers because they are constitutionally responsible) are functions so multifarious that no Minister could ever personally attend to them. To take the example of the present case no doubt there have been thousands of requisitions in this country by individual Ministers. It cannot be supposed that this regulation meant that, in each case, the Minister in person should direct his mind to

the matter. The duties imposed upon Ministers and the powers given to Ministers are normally exercised under the authority of the Ministers by responsible officials of the department. Public business could not be carried on if that were not the case. Constitutionally, the decision of such an official is, of course the decision of the Minister. The Minister is responsible. It is he who must answer to Parliament for anything that his officials have done under his authority…

In this passage, Lord Greene recognizes, in a very practical way, that government depends on civil servants taking decisions or making orders on behalf of Ministers, as Ministers cannot personally do everything. He also recognizes that ultimately the Minister is responsible for the conduct of his or her department, including the decisions of civil servants in cases such as this. However, implicit in what he says is also a recognition that there may be some decisions which have to be taken by the Minister personally, and that ultimately it is a matter of interpretation of the regulation in question. But the *Carltona* principle provides a workable solution to addressing the practicalities of government action, and the need for such a principle has increased in the years following the decision. Actions of civil servants acting on behalf of the Minister have been upheld in many subsequent cases with regard to matters such as tax demands (*Commissioners of Customs and Excise v Cure & Deeley Ltd* [1962] 1 QB 340) or the making of delegated legislation (*R v Skinner* [1968] 2 QB 700).

(5.8) **Ministerial responsibility**

The idea that civil servants can take actions for which the Minister ultimately bears the responsibility leads into a consideration of the responsibility of Ministers. When thinking about this we need to consider what is meant by talking of ministerial responsibility. For what are Ministers responsible, to whom and for whom? Keeping these questions in mind we can explore ministerial responsibility in its individual and collective dimensions. As Geoffrey Marshall says (*Constitutional Conventions* (Clarendon Press, 1984) p.54), '…collective and individual responsibility are two doctrines, not one, and each divides in turn into a series of disparate topics'. The idea of individual responsibility, put simply, is that the Minister is responsible for the conduct of his department and for his own personal conduct. Collective responsibility reflects the notion, discussed earlier, of the public expression of support for government policy once it has been agreed by the Cabinet. In both cases, Ministers are, as the passage from Lord Greene quoted above makes clear, responsible to Parliament.

cross reference
See Chapter 4 on the accountability of the executive to parliament generally.

5.8.1 **Individual responsibility of Ministers**

Turning first to individual responsibility. As indicated above, it seems natural, under the notion of the relationship between Parliament and the executive, that Ministers should account for the conduct of their departments to Parliament. This preserves the non-political nature of the civil service by leaving the Minister as the link between Parliament and government departments. The Minister is responsible for the conduct of the department, both where it succeeds and where it falls short. As we saw in the previous chapter, there are a number of mechanisms by which Ministers can be called to account for the conduct of their department, including debates, questions and committees. It needs to be borne in mind that the parliamentary scrutiny of the government is not immune from politics. Opposition members are as much concerned with discrediting the government as they are with examining the conduct of government business through the departments. Thus, Question Time not only enables MPs to criticize performance of the Minister's department but to link this to criticisms of government policy or the Minister personally.

Departmental failings

The next question that arises is what happens where departmental performance has been shown to be deficient. The ultimate sanction for the Minister is resignation. As well as recognizing the responsibility of the Minister for the failings of the department, this also has a political impact which is potentially or actually damaging to the government. There have been resignations where the department has been incompetent. In 1982, the invasion of the Falkland Islands was not anticipated by either the Foreign Office or the Ministry of Defence. The respective Ministers, Lord Carrington and John Nott, offered their resignations in recognition of these failings. The Prime Minister, Mrs. Thatcher, accepted the resignation of Lord Carrington but not that of Mr. Nott. (See her own account in *The Downing Street Years* (HarperCollins, 1993) pp.178–94). It may be that part of the thinking here was that in the event of a conflict (which is what happened) it would not be advisable to enter into it with new individuals in post in two of the key ministries. But what this episode also illustrates is that the Prime Minister is a key figure in determining whether or not a Minister should resign. We should not underestimate what occurs behind the scenes in these situations, of which we have no knowledge. We have seen an extreme example in the Crichel Down affair of a Minister resigning in the face of actions taken by civil servants acting for their own reasons, with no culpability on the part of the Minister.

thinking point
Should Ministers be responsible for every paper clip the department uses?

The breadth of ministerial responsibility has narrowed in recent years with Ministers increasingly drawing distinctions between activities for which they can be held responsible and where resignation remains a possibility, and those where, effectively, there was an operational or administrative failure for which the Minister cannot be said to be at fault.

A controversial example occurred in following events in 1983 when a number of prisoners escaped from the Maze Prison in Northern Ireland. The Northern Ireland Secretary, James Prior, refuted calls for his resignation by arguing first that an inquiry was to be conducted and that he would consider his position in the light of its findings. When the report of the inquiry appeared, Mr. Prior argued that as it had not found any fault on his part, he was under no obligation to resign. This is a contentious area, as different views as to ministerial culpability might be held. What this debate does illustrate is the flexibility and changeable nature of conventions. With legal rules, the changes would be formal and apparent. Because conventions are not written but evolve with changing practices the changes are less immediately apparent.

Personal conduct of Ministers

The notion of fault extends to the Minister's personal conduct. We have seen that there is some debate as to the circumstances in which a Minister should resign where the department has been at fault. The question Mr. Prior and others have asked is whether they were personally at fault with regard to departmental policy or practice. There have, however, been examples where the Minister has misused his position and has required the department to act in inappropriate ways. Recent examples include Peter Mandelson, who resigned (again: he had previously resigned in 1998 over his financial dealings: see below) in 2001 following allegations that he had helped two Labour supporters to acquire British passports and David Blunkett, who resigned as Home Secretary in December 2004 when it emerged that he had fast tracked a visa application for the nanny of his former lover (see Bamforth [2005] PL 229). Mr. Blunkett was already attracting criticism over his personal life, and his resignation perhaps also illustrates that often there is not one single issue that leads to a ministerial resignation but rather a collection of issues.

The same might be said of one of the most notorious resignations of the 20th century, that of John Profumo in 1963.

John Profumo

Mr. Profumo, who was a married man, became involved with a young woman, Christine Keeler, who worked in cabaret clubs and was also engaged in a relationship with Eugene Ivanov, a Soviet Attaché at the embassy in London. Later, in the face of rumours and allegations about the nature of his relationship with Ms Keeler, Mr. Profumo made a statement to the House of Commons in which he said that there was 'no impropriety' in his relationship with her. He was later forced to admit that he had lied to the House and subsequently resigned. Cumulatively, the various problems surrounding Mr. Profumo, and it must be remembered that the Cold War between the West and the Soviet block was at a particularly tense stage in its relationship, were such that he had to resign. (See further Alan Doig, *Westminster Babylon* (W.H. Allen, 1990) pp.73–90).

It might also be asked why a Minister's private life has anything to do with their work if there is no complaint about their performance in office. The traditional view is that a Minister should resign if there is something about his conduct that suggests he is unfit to hold ministerial office. This may be in the form of financial dealings that reveal a lack of integrity, as occurred with regard to Mr. Mandelson, who resigned in 1998 after taking out a secret loan, or a failure to comply with the Ministerial Code as occurred with Mr. Blunkett when he was Secretary of State for Work and Pensions and led to his second resignation from the government in 2005.

Allegations of improper conduct in the field of personal morality may produce different results depending on the current concerns and how closely they touch on current government policy. Thus, Ministers engaged in extramarital affairs might be expected to resign when government policy is explicitly upholding traditional moral values as was the case with the Conservative governments under both Mrs. Thatcher and Mr. Major, but not where this is not part of the government's agenda, as occurred with regard to Mr. Prescott in 2006. Mr. Prescott resisted attempts to force him to resign when the nature of his relationship with a civil servant in his department became public.

thinking point
Does a Minister's private conduct really have anything to do with her ability to do the job?

5.8.2 Does the Minister always resign?

The resignation of a Minister is thus not inevitable. It depends on a range of factors. In an article written in 1956 but still instructive today, 'The Individual Responsibility of Ministers' (1956) 34 *Public Administration* 377–96), Professor Finer identified four alternatives to resignation and a future outside the government. These were:

- reliance on party support through collective responsibility to remain in office;
- being moved in a reshuffle;
- reliance on personal standing to remain in office; and
- resignation and reinstatement.

The relationship between individual responsibility and collective responsibility

The first is the link between individual responsibility and collective responsibility, or, as Finer describes it, the counter convention of collective responsibility. He sees the two conventions working together with the tendency to resignation being countered by the collective tendency of the other convention. As a member of the government a Minister can ordinarily rely on the support of colleagues when there is a suggestion that (s)he should resign. The relationship between the two doctrines was explained by Mr. Winston Churchill, who, speaking in 1952, said (500 H.C. Deb., 5s. Col. 188, 6 May 1952: see Geoffrey Wilson, *Cases and Materials on Constitutional and Administrative Law* (Cambridge University Press, 2nd ed., 1976) p.43):

> Every Departmental Minister is responsible to Parliament for the policy and administration of his department. This is a fundamental principle in our system of Parliamentary democracy. But it is an equally respectable and necessary principle that Ministers as a whole are collectively responsible for government policy as a whole. This means that a Minister's personal responsibility must be exercised in harmony with the views of his ministerial colleagues.

As Mr. Churchill makes clear, the Minister's standing within his party can have an impact on the decision as to whether or not he resigns, coupled with the likely impact of that decision on the rest of the government.

Reshuffle

The second alternative is for the Prime Minister to reshuffle the government, moving the Minister elsewhere within government or out of government on a temporary or permanent basis. The advantage politically is that the government remains in control of its own composition. A recent example involved the removal of Charles Clarke from the Home Office following his admission that he did not know, nor did his department know, how many foreign prisoners were at large having been released without being considered for deportation.

Stay in office

A third possibility is what Professor Finer calls the 'Fair cop' approach whereby the Minister in question concedes the alleged problem but relies on his personal standing to survive in office.

Resignation and reinstatement

The final possibility is for the Minister to resign and be reinstated at a later date. That is what happened to both Mr. Mandelson and Mr. Blunkett, who both resumed ministerial office after a suitable period only to resign again over different issues. In Mr. Mandelson's case, appointment as EU Trade Commissioner was followed by restoration to a position as Secretary of State for Business, Enterprise and Regulatory Reform in the British government in October 2008 and a peerage. Another option might be that illustrated by the Maze escapes, namely to set up an inquiry. This at least delays a decision and may, as in that instance, exonerate the Minister.

thinking point
If a Minister has made an error, should this automatically lead to resignation?

5.8.3 **Collective responsibility**

Returning to collective responsibility, the idea was originally a defensive mechanism to protect the government against the monarch. Now, as Professor Wilson indicates, it has more to do with notions of strong government and a show of strength when presenting matters to Parliament. In purely practical terms, it also means that the government can rely on a significant support in any vote in the house. As the Crossman Diaries case (*AG v Jonathan Cape*) makes clear, though, it is not applied consistently and internal divisions are from time to time openly acknowledged. As suggested earlier, the idea that 20+ people will agree on the substance of a proposed policy is less readily acceptable than the idea that they will support it once it has been agreed.

A Minister who cannot support an agreed policy effectively has two choices. One is to stifle the dissent and to support the policy in public. A second is to resign from the government which then enables the individual to argue against the policy. A recent example

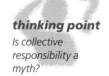
of this occurred in 2003, when Robin Cook, John Denham, Lord Hunt and Clare Short all resigned as Ministers because they could not support government policy over the invasion of Iraq.

Leaks and briefings

A third way has been for Ministers to brief journalists on an unofficial basis and for the dissenting views to appear without a personal attribution with a formula such as 'sources close to the government'. These leaks act as a form of 'safety valve' and have been recognized and tolerated by Prime Ministers. As Mr. Callaghan, Prime Minister from 1976–1979, said to his Ministers: 'Briefing is what I do and leaking is what you do' (quoted in de Smith & Brazier *Constitutional and Administrative Law* (Penguin books, 8th ed., 1998) p.199). The distinction he was alluding to was that between the official and unofficial revelations of government information.

Indeed, he was also clear that the operation of collective responsibility was under the control of the Prime Minister, for he also said: 'I certainly think the doctrine [of collective responsibility] should apply except in cases where I announce that it does not' (quoted in de Smith & Brazier, *op cit.*, at p.198). A good example of this occurred in 1975 during the referendum on whether the UK should continue its membership of the European Communities on the terms negotiated by the Labour government, or leave. Opinion was divided over this issue, and the Prime Minister, Mr. Wilson, said that he would suspend the operation of collective responsibility over this issue for the duration of the campaign and allow Ministers to speak against government policy, which was to retain membership on the renegotiated terms. This would only apply, however, outside Parliament. Within Parliament collective responsibility applied and Ministers could not speak against government policy. (For the text, see Wilson *The Governance of Britain* (Sphere, 1977) pp.235–7). A junior Minister in the Department of Industry, Eric Heffer, spoke out against the government's view in the House of Commons and was forced to resign. This episode shows that both the operation of the doctrine and the terms of its operation are under the control of the Prime Minister.

The framework within which the government operates is thus very flexible, which, as we saw at the outset, is one of the characteristics of the British constitution, and in this instance is largely brought about by changes to conventions. This may be seen as an advantage as it means that the structures and operation of government can accommodate changing demands and requirements. On the other hand, the absence of clear and fixed principles means that there is limited guidance as to how government should be constructed or run.

 ## 5.9 **Executive power**

In order to carry out its policies, at least where these affect others or involve the expenditure of money, the executive needs legal powers. This is in line with the rule of law. One of the features of the rule of law is the idea that government is carried out according to law rather than by sheer force. Accepting the principle of the rule of law means that the government has to operate within a legal framework. In a strict separation of powers, the legal framework would be created by the legislature and its limits would be decided by the courts. However, in the United Kingdom, the historical development of the constitution has meant that the picture is not so clear. The British government has powers deriving not only from Parliament but also from the common law, in other words, from the courts. These common law powers are called the royal prerogative. They occupy, however, only a small, but nevertheless significant, part of the powers modern governments enjoy. All powers these days given to the executive come from Parliament. The position is different with regard to local government. As local government is the creation of statute it is only able to exercise powers given to it by Parliament.

We will begin by looking at the nature of the royal prerogative, before going on to consider its current state. This will involve looking at the development of the prerogative in order to be able to understand its current peculiar position in British constitutional arrangements.

5.9.1 **The royal prerogative**

The characteristics of the royal prerogative

A glance at some traditional definitions of the royal prerogative will help to indicate some of its characteristics. Blackstone, in his *Commentaries on the Laws of England*, described the prerogative in this way (I, p.239):

> By the word prerogative we usually understand that special pre-eminence which the king hath over and above all other persons....it can only be applied to those rights and capacities which the king enjoys alone, in contradistinction to others and not those which he enjoys in common with any of his subjects; for if once any one prerogative of the Crown could be held in common with the subject, it would cease to be prerogative any longer...

Whilst Dicey said (*An Introduction to the Study of the Law of the Constitution* (10th ed., 1959 ed. E.C.S. Wade) p.424) it was:

> ...the residue of discretionary or arbitrary authority which at any given time is legally left in the hands of the Crown.

Both descriptions are helpful in drawing attention to particular characteristics of the prerogative. First, they emphasize that the prerogative is something which is only available to the Crown. We saw in the previous chapter that, in modern times, that means the government, although there are some prerogatives still exercisable by the Queen. Blackstone makes the point that powers exercisable by anyone other then the Crown are not prerogative powers. Both also hint at the importance of the historical development of the prerogative. The prerogative is a legacy of the time when the monarch ruled the country exercising almost absolute, and certainly, as Dicey says, discretionary or arbitrary powers. The changes in the nature of government in Britain have meant that power has devolved elsewhere, and as the position of the monarch has dwindled, and along with it the power of the common law to create laws, the creation of any new powers for the Crown is solely a matter for Parliament. As Diplock LJ said in *BBC v Johns* [1965] Ch 32, 79:

> It is 350 years and a civil war too late for the Queen's courts to broaden the prerogative. The limits within which the executive government may impose obligations or restraints on citizens of the United Kingdom without any statutory authority are well settled and incapable of extension.

Further, the principle of the sovereignty of Parliament and its dominance over the common law means that prerogative powers may be abolished or reduced. This is what Dicey means when he talks of the prerogative as the residue of discretionary or arbitrary authority. It is what is left after the previous powers of the Crown have been removed or limited by Parliament.

The content of the royal prerogative

It might seem odd that these powers have survived into the 21st century given their origins, though this may be soon to change (see House of Commons Public Administration Select Committee, *Taming the Prerogative: Strengthening Ministerial Accountability to Parliament* HC 422 (2004)). In order to understand why they have survived, we can undertake a brief examination of the content of the prerogative. The prerogative had, as we have seen, its origins in the powers exercised by the monarch before the development of more modern notions of democratic governance. Some of the prerogatives are still exercised by the sovereign. Examples are the power to appoint the Prime Minister and other Ministers, to give the Royal Assent to legislation and to dissolve Parliament. The exercise of all these prerogatives is, however, governed by convention, as indicated below. Most other prerogatives are exercised by Ministers in the name of the Crown. These include a number relating to foreign affairs, including the making of treaties and declarations of war and peace. Within the United Kingdom they include the regulation of the civil service, the making of certain appointments and the granting of honours, the issuing of passports and prerogative in the criminal justice system such as the discontinuance of prosecutions and the granting of pardons.

The prerogative does not consist solely of powers to do things, however. Two very significant rights that the Crown enjoys are freedom from being bound by statutes unless the statute requires this either expressly or by implication, and the immunity from legal action expressed in the maxim 'The king can do no wrong'. The immunity from legal action has been severely limited by the effect of the Crown Proceedings Act 1947, but the principle remains at common law.

Objections to the prerogative

Prerogative powers have been regarded as objectionable for a number of reasons, but two in particular stand out. First, as part of the common law they lack the precision of definition that statutory provisions have. This gives them a flexibility which, as the cases below show, can lead to disagreements as to their scope, which ultimately the courts have to sort out. Secondly, their exercise is not subject to parliamentary control. If, for example, the government wishes to enter into a treaty with another country it does not have to seek parliamentary approval to do so. The only circumstance in which parliamentary support is needed is if the exercise of the prerogative involves additional expenditure of money. This is, however, only an indirect form of parliamentary accountability and will not be necessary if the government already has sufficient funds available to allocate without the need to ask Parliament for more.

It is, of course, always open to the government to seek parliamentary approval for its actions. The present government did this with regard to its decision to invade Iraq in 2003, and secured parliamentary support. This did not prevent continuing controversy over the legality of that action, but at least the government could argue that it had put the matter to Parliament and had its decision endorsed there. There is an argument for this course of action being followed on every occasion. The Select Committee on the Constitution of the House of Lords has argued for this position with regard to declarations of war (*Waging war: Parliament's role and responsibility* HL 51 (2007)). A further argument for subjecting government decisions under the prerogative to parliamentary scrutiny is that it goes some way to meeting arguments based on the uncertainty of the prerogative, whilst retaining the flexibility that the prerogative currently has. This would be lost if the more radical position, of replacing all prerogative powers with statutory powers, was adopted.

thinking point
Should a government be able to exercise its powers without parliamentary support?

Prerogative and convention

The use of the prerogative may also be limited by convention, which goes some way to lessening the potential for its misuse. Virtually all of the prerogatives which have some involvement of the Queen herself have conventions governing their use. Thus, for example, the Queen appoints as Prime Minister the leader of the party with a majority of seats in the House of Commons; the Queen appoints as Ministers those chosen by the Prime Minister; the Queen always gives the Royal Assent to measures passed by Parliament; the Queen dissolves Parliament when requested to do so by the Prime Minister. The fact that the Queen always acts in accordance with those conventions means that controversy is avoided. However, as we have seen, the prerogatives exercised by the government on behalf of the Crown are not so closely controlled.

thinking point
If the Queen has to exercise her legal powers according to established conventions, why not replace the prerogative with clear rules?

The prerogative and the courts

As it came to be accepted that even the Crown was subject to the rule of law, it followed that the courts could determine whether a claimed prerogative power was one which was recognized by the common law. A critical period in the development of the prerogative occurred in the early 17th century when the common law courts, under

Coke CJ asserted their right to limit royal power in the face of claims made by James I. In a series of cases, the courts either refused to recognize claimed prerogatives or placed severe limits on their exercise. In doing so the courts were not only asserting their own power as custodians of the common law but were also recognizing the growing claims of Parliament as law maker. Thus, in the *Case of Proclamations* (1611) 12 Co Rep 74; 77 ER 1352, it was held that the King could not change the law by proclamation. The constitutional settlement under the Bill of Rights 1689 placed the monarchy under parliamentary control, and effectively prevented the expansion of Crown powers by anything other than parliamentary enactment.

The powers of the courts with regard to the prerogative came to enable them first to determine whether or not a claimed prerogative existed. A prerogative might not exist because the courts had never recognized it. In *BBC v Johns* [1965] Ch. 32 it was held that a prerogative in broadcasting, claimed by the BBC, did not exist. We might expect that if a claimed prerogative existed there would be some evidence of it, perhaps in previous cases, or in books of authority such as Bracton, Coke or Blackstone.

However, in *R v Secretary of State for the Home Department ex p Northumbria Police* [1989] QB 349, Nourse LJ decided that previous authority was not a necessary evidential requirement for a claimed prerogative. He argued that the absence of evidence for a prerogative might be because it was so obvious that it did not need to be evidenced in any document. On this basis, he held that a prerogative allowing the Home Secretary to act to prevent breaches of the peace did exist notwithstanding the absence of any evidence pointing to its existence. An alternative issue relating to the existence of a prerogative is the question whether it has been superseded by statute. This is essentially a matter of statutory interpretation. In the *Northumbria Police* case, it was held that nothing in the relevant legislation had removed the prerogative claimed by the Home Secretary and therefore that did not eliminate the possibility of the existence of the prerogative.

Where a prerogative has been completely superseded by statute, the Crown can only act by using the statutory power. It cannot choose which power it exercises. In *AG v de Keyser's Royal Hotel* [1920] AC 508, the Crown had requisitioned a hotel during World War I. It claimed to have done so under the royal prerogative, thereby avoiding the need to pay compensation. It was held that the Defence of the Realm Regulations had superseded the prerogative and therefore any question of compensation had to be determined according to the Regulations.

If a prerogative was found to exist, the courts were able to determine its limits. This may be to decide what scope the common law had allowed to the particular prerogative. This was the issue in *Burmah Oil v Lord Advocate* [1965] AC 75.

case close-up

Burmah Oil v Lord Advocate [1965] AC 75

British forces had destroyed oil installations in Burma during World War II. The company claimed compensation for this loss. Burmah Oil was not arguing about the lawfulness of the acts, but only whether such actions gave rise to a right to compensation. The Crown denied that compensation was payable on the basis, it argued, that the royal prerogative gave a right to destroy property in order to prevent it falling into enemy hands and that such action did not give rise to a claim for compensation. The House of Lords held, however, by a majority, that compensation was payable. The prerogative did not extend to carrying out such acts without the payment of compensation, as the Crown had not established that this was part of the prerogative.

thinking point

Was the passing of the War Damage Act 1965 an abuse of power?

The sequel to this case, however, illustrates the significance of parliamentary sovereignty. The government introduced, and Parliament passed, a measure that became the War Damage Act 1965 This reversed the decision of the House of Lords and provided that compensation was not payable in these circumstances. It even made this operate retrospectively.

The courts may have to determine the extent of the prerogative where a statute has not abolished the prerogative but has limited its scope. Again this is a matter of statutory interpretation. So, for example, in *Universities of Oxford and Cambridge v Eyre and Spottiswoode* [1964] Ch 736, Plowman J held that the Copyright Act had limited the prerogative so that the right to print or authorize printing no longer extended to material that would constitute a breach of copyright. So, in that case the Crown's rights over the printing of editions of the Bible only covered the King James Version of 1611 and not the New English Bible.

There may be circumstances where the prerogative has not been limited by statute but where the prerogative operates alongside a statutory power. An example of this arose in the case of *Laker Airways v Department of Trade* [1977] QB 643.

case close-up

Laker Airways v Department of Trade [1977] QB 643

. . . .

Under the Civil Aviation Act 1971, a person wishing to run an airline flying between the United Kingdom and the United States of America had to apply to the Civil Aviation Authority (CAA), a statutory body, for a licence. Additionally, a carrier had to be designated by the UK government under the terms of a treaty between the United Kingdom and the United States of America in order to obtain landing rights. A carrier thus needed both in order to operate on the transatlantic route. Laker Airways applied to fly between the United Kingdom and the United States of America and were granted a licence by the CAA. The United Kingdom government also designated Laker Airways under the treaty. The designation had to be countersigned by the American government in order to be valid. Before the document had been signed, there was a change of government in the United Kingdom. The new government withdrew Laker Airways' designation under the Treaty. Without the designation under the Treaty, Laker Airways would not be able to land in America, making their licence from the CAA effectively useless. Laker Airways challenged the decision of the UK government to withdraw the designation. The Court of Appeal held that the government was acting unlawfully. It could not use the prerogative to undermine the licence Laker had received under the Civil Aviation Act. Where the exercise of a statutory power depended on a prerogative power, the prerogative power must be exercised in accordance with the statutory power.

This may be seen as an assertion of the sovereignty of Parliament and recognition that the prerogative is subordinate to the will of Parliament.

The courts have now taken the view, following the decision of the House of Lords in *Council of Civil Service Unions v Minister for the Civil Service* [1985] AC 374, that prerogative powers are subject to judicial review in the same way as statutory powers, as long as the subject matter raises a justiciable issue. Thus, the courts have held that they can consider issues such as the issue of a passport (*R v Secretary of State for Foreign and Commonwealth Affairs ex p Everett* [1989] QB 8110) though not areas of the prerogative concerned with executive policy such as the making of treaties (see *R v Secretary of State for Foreign and Commonwealth a Affairs ex p Rees-Mogg* [1994] QB 552).

cross reference
This is considered further in Chapter 11.

Although the prerogative continues to excite controversy and questions continue to be asked about its future, it seems likely that the very flexibility of the key prerogatives—especially those governing international relations and defence—will ensure that their conversion into statutory powers is resisted. Some other, less contentious prerogatives, such as the issuing of passports, could perhaps more readily be put on a statutory footing.

5.9.2 **Statutory powers**

Following World War II, there was, and continues to be, a vast expansion in the extent of the activities of government, at both central and local level. In order to carry out its various tasks, government needs powers, as many of its functions involve regulating the lives of individuals. The rule of law demands that any interference with the autonomy of individuals is either with consent or with some legal justification. Modern notions of democracy require that any powers to interfere with the lives of citizens given to government are given by Parliament as representatives of the people. In any event, the decline in the creative powers of the common law coincided with the growth in both government and statute law. Thus, the powers of modern governments derive exclusively from Parliament. The idea of separation of powers suggests that Parliament acts as a check against giving the government too much power by the contents of legislation it agrees to, and that it will scrutinize carefully the legislative proposals brought forward by government. There are, as we saw when looking at Parliament, a variety of mechanisms whereby the proposals and activities of the government can be subjected to scrutiny. However, the majority that the government has in Parliament means that it can generally secure the passage of its measures into law, unless there is a major revolt on the government's back benches. Thus, despite the theory, in real terms the government is able to create the framework within which it operates, which is not quite what the idea of the rule of law envisages.

thinking point

Is it an abuse of power for the government to use its majority in Parliament to ensure that the legislation it wants is passed?

Delegated legislation

The above is concerned with powers to carry out executive acts granted by Acts of Parliament. The picture is, however, more complex. The modern tendency in legislation, particularly that creating powers for government, and indeed in imposing duties on local authorities and other public bodies, is to create a framework in the Act of Parliament and then to fill out the detail by means of delegated legislation. The power to make delegated legislation is potentially wide ranging, handing government Ministers the ability to legislate in significant ways without submitting the matter to detailed parliamentary scrutiny as would be the case with primary legislation. There are several potential safeguards against abuses of this law making power. First, the parent Act can contain limitations on the power. This may, for example, take the form of limiting the subject matter on which the Minister may make legislation, or the circumstances in which legislation may be made, or by providing for consultation prior to legislating. Secondly, the parent Act may build in safeguards relating to the procedure by which any delegated legislation is passed.

There are two general parliamentary procedures for delegated legislation. The first, the positive resolution procedure, requires that before any piece of delegated legislation comes into force a resolution must be passed to this effect. The other, the negative resolution procedure, is much less onerous. Here, delegated legislation is before the House for 40 days and if a resolution has not been passed preventing it from coming into force, it will be valid once the 40 days have expired. There is so much delegated legislation that where this procedure is followed it requires vigilant Members of Parliament to be aware of what is before the House and to raise objection to it. Given the amount of delegated legislation that goes through Parliament, this is a significant task. It is for these reasons that delegated legislation is regarded with suspicion. Once delegated legislation has been passed, a further set of controls are available through the courts, who may rule that delegated legislation is unlawful if it is outside the scope the parent Act, for example that the Minister has legislated in areas in which he has no authority, or has failed to consult as required.

cross reference
Delegated legislation is subject to judicial review: see Chapters 11 and 12.

It will be clear from this that the government will want to keep its powers of making delegated legislation as broad as possible. A further power that governments may want is the power to amend primary legislation by means of delegated legislation, as again this avoids the need for detailed parliamentary scrutiny, though governments would argue that it is more administratively efficient. The Legislative and Regulatory Reform Act 2006 has been particularly controversial on this score. It allows for the amendment of a large amount of legislation by means of delegated legislation. During the debates on the Bill, the Opposition objected that this is giving the government too much power. The government argues that the powers under the Act will provide it with a more efficient mechanism for reducing bureaucracy by allowing it to alter things quickly without the need for following the full legislative process.

There are precedents for allowing the alteration of primary legislation by means of delegated legislation. A particularly striking one is in the Human Rights Act 1998. Where a declaration of incompatibility has been made by a court under s.4, the government may use its power under s.10 to amend, by means of delegated legislation, the offending provision. A significant difference between the power in s.10 and the proposed powers under the 2006 Act is that the latter are much more wide ranging and therefore potentially carry a greater chance of being abused. Provisions which allow the government wide ranging powers to amend or pass legislation are sometimes called Henry VIII clauses, as he is seen as embodying autocratic government. Whether this charge can properly be levelled against governments relying on the powers in the 2006 Act will, to a large extent, depend on how the powers under the Act are exercised.

thinking point
Is the extensive use of delegated legislation desirable or necessary?

 # Questions

If you answer the following questions, you will have appreciated the main issues raised in this chapter. Check your answers against the notes provided at the back of the book.

1   Who are the members of the executive?

2   What mechanisms exist to prevent abuses of power by the executive?

3   What is the nature of the relationship between Ministers and their civil servants?

4   In what ways are Ministers accountable for what they do?

5   What powers are available to the executive?

Further reading

To further your understanding of the topics covered in this chapter, have a look at the reading materials mentioned below. Useful web links are also provided on the Online Resource Centre.

A.W. Bradley and K.D. Ewing, *Constitutional and Administrative Law* (Pearson Longman, 14th ed., 2007) ch.13
This gives you a detailed account of the composition and functions of central government.

Colin Turpin and Adam Tomkins, *British Government and the Constitution* (Cambridge University Press, 6th ed., 2007) chs. 6 and 7
This gives you access to edited extracts from primary sources together with commentary.

Dawn Oliver, *Constitutional Reform in the United Kingdom* (Oxford University, Press 2003) chs.11 & 12
These give you some ideas as to how the government and civil service might be reformed.

The judiciary

Learning Objectives

While reading this chapter you should aim to understand:

- how judges are appointed;

- how the judiciary is organized;

- the reasons for securing the independence of the judges from political interference and how this is achieved under the British constitution;

- the powers the judges have and the sources of those powers; and

- what limitations there are on judicial power.

Introduction

The judiciary constitutes the third branch of the government of the state, along with the executive and the legislature. The members of the judiciary, the judges, are a constant within the constitution: rather than changing following a general election or change of government, they remain, like the monarchy and the civil service, in post. Judges generally only leave office when they retire. Their position is protected from political interference, whether by the government or by Parliament. This is seen as necessary to preserve the independence of decision making that is seen as an essential hallmark of their position. The idea is that judges should be able to make decisions without fear or favour; that is, that they should decide cases purely on the legal merits rather than be influenced by political or other factors, including their job security. To that extent, the judges are said to be politically neutral.

However, as we shall see, judges are not completely immune from political controversy. Every decision a judge makes, especially in cases involving the state or central or local government, has political implications in deciding whether the state can or cannot do something. The judges thus hold a key position within the constitution in holding the balance between the various organs of government within the state and between the state and the individual. If judges are to exercise such potentially extensive powers, then two things appear to follow. First, the position of the judges needs to be protected against political interference and their independence safeguarded; and, secondly, the judges need to be carefully chosen. Both of these aspects of the judicial function have been reformed in recent years. The issues of who the judges are, their protection from interference and their political neutrality are all important because of the powers they exercise. However, preserving the independence of the judiciary poses a threat to notions of accountability by insulating them from external forces. However, as judges exercise power on behalf of the state in its widest sense they should, it might be argued, be accountable for the power they exercise, though to whom and in what ways becomes a legitimate matter to debate.

6.1 Judicial appointments

One of the characteristics of the reforms brought about by the Labour government in the years after 1997 has been to move to a more transparent appointments system for key public roles, in line with its equality agenda. Notions of equality of opportunity support the idea that appointments should be made on the basis of application and selection by an independent body working to published criteria which reflect what are felt to be the necessary attributes of the job. Such a process is preferable to a secret system whereby individuals are chosen by a member of the government on the basis of information that is not subject to any form of scrutiny.

6.1.1 **Appointment by the Lord Chancellor**

What happened previously for appointments to the higher judiciary, was that the Lord Chancellor would keep records on barristers, who, for consideration for the higher judiciary would normally be Queen's Counsel, drawn from information provided by judges and other high ranking lawyers, and would then decide on the basis of this information whether to approach a person and offer him (and it would usually be men who were the beneficiaries of this process) a position as a judge. The system was said to work on the basis that the number of eligible candidates (QCs) was essentially small and finite; that the Bar was sufficiently small that everyone knew the abilities of its leading practitioners; that the judges and others were hearing these people arguing cases on a regular basis and could gauge their ability; and that the system had worked well in the past in securing the best candidates for the bench.

thinking point

What personal and professional qualities do you think a judge should have?

This last assertion in particular is open to question, as it throws open the whole question of what qualities are needed in a judge. Confining appointments to barristers not only contained the assumption that being a barrister was the best qualification for being a judge but also thereby excluded solicitors from the higher ranks of the judiciary. Solicitors could become circuit judges and then be promoted from the circuit bench to the High Court bench and beyond, but this did not offer solicitors the direct route to the bench that was open to barristers. Whilst it does not necessarily follow that practice at the Bar provides the best preparation for the bench, it equally does not follow that it does not produce good judges: the argument was rather that the system was ignoring other talents who had not followed that particular route. The system also tended to self perpetuate, producing a higher judiciary that was almost exclusively male and white.

thinking point

Does it matter whether judges are generally white and male as long as they are competent and have integrity?

6.1.2 **The Judicial Appointments Commission**

The creation of the Judicial Appointments Commission, by virtue of Part 4 of the Constitutional Reform Act 2005, seeks to address a number of issues relating to the nature and composition of the judiciary. By taking the power of appointment away from the Lord Chancellor, it seeks to buttress the independence of the judiciary and create a structural separation of powers with regard to this matter by removing any appearance of political interference in the process and, in particular, any impression of government control. It also seeks to create greater transparency by replacing the old system of soundings and secret files with a more open system whereby published criteria govern the appointment of judges and decisions are made by a body that is independent of both government and Parliament. Individuals will be invited to apply for posts rather than being approached to be asked whether they wished to be appointed. A wider range of individuals will be eligible for judicial appointment, a tendency taken further by the Tribunals, Courts and Enforcement Act 2007. This extends eligibility for the bench to holders of legal qualifications not previously recognized as providing a basis for judicial office, such as those qualified as legal executives.

thinking point
Is a judiciary that is representative of society as a whole a desirable goal? Is it achievable?

By creating a new framework, it is hoped that the composition of the judiciary will be broadened and become more representative of society as a whole. It is too early in the operation of this new system to evaluate whether it has achieved, or is moving toward achieving, these objectives and, perhaps more importantly whether they have changed the nature and quality of the judiciary and judicial decision making.

6.2 Organization of the judiciary

The recent reorganization of the judiciary is also part of the Labour government's programme to restructure the constitution so that it secures the separation of powers. As we have seen, one of the criticisms of the previous constitutional arrangements centred on the role of the Lord Chancellor. The Constitutional Reform Act 2005, in altering the constitutional status and roles of the Lord Chancellor, removed the Lord Chancellor from being head of the judiciary, giving that role instead to the Lord Chief Justice. The objections to the Lord Chancellor, as a member of the government, sitting as a judge had already been addressed by Lord Irvine, who had indicated that he would not sit as a judge, although he had done so earlier in his period of office (see, for example, *DPP v Jones* [1999] 2 AC 240).

His role as head of the judiciary was also changed because of the constitutional objections to having the judges, and judicial appointments, under the control of the Lord Chancellor, who was, and remains, a member of the government and, as such, a political appointment. In line with the theory of the separation of powers, it was felt necessary to secure the independence of the judiciary from potential political interference. There was no suggestion that the Lord Chancellor had actually interfered with the impartiality of the judges, but rather that the change was necessary in order to restructure relations between the government and the judiciary and that it was better to secure this through a reorganization rather than leaving its effective running to be dependent on personalities.

These changes emphasize the independence of the judiciary from the government. However, the effect may not be totally positive. In losing the Lord Chancellor as head of the judiciary, the judges have lost a voice in the Cabinet, as one of the many roles undertaken by the Lord Chancellor involved speaking for the judges in a variety of situations. Whether this means that the views of the judiciary will cease to be represented to the government as effectively as before remains to be seen: it is again too early to judge.

6.3 A Supreme Court

The other major change affecting the judiciary brought about by the Constitutional Reform Act 2005 was the creation of a Supreme Court to replace the House of Lords as the final appeal court. The dual function of the House of Lords, as both a court and the second chamber of the legislature, has always been an historical anomaly and one of the peculiarities of the British constitution. It dates back to the time when the earliest Parliaments served as a general forum for the redress of grievances and devised a number of ways of dealing with them. Parliament could try to resolve matters brought to them by passing laws to remedy the situation or by acting as a court to conduct a trial to resolve the matter. Ultimately, the legislative function came to predominate, but this residual judicial function remained. In a series of events in the 19th century, changes were made to the way in which the House of Lords carried out its various functions. Thus, by convention, judicial proceedings of the House came only to involve those peers who were legally qualified. In the reforms of the judicial system in 1873–6, the original plan was to abolish the judicial functions of the House of Lords and establish a new supreme court.

6.3.1 Lords of Appeal in Ordinary

However, these plans did not come to fruition, the judicial function survived and a new type of peer was created: the Lord of Appeal in Ordinary. This carried a membership of the House for life only. Those appointed as Lords of Appeal in Ordinary, or Law Lords as they came to be known, continued to be promoted from the lower courts as before.

This situation continued to the present day and will continue until the 2005 Act is brought fully into effect. An enduring question concerns the dual role potentially exercisable by the Law Lords by virtue of their membership of the House of Lords as both judges and legislators. This has not been an issue for judges who are not peers, for, as long ago as the Act of Settlement 1700, judges were prohibited from membership of the House of Commons, which was a condition for securing their independence under that Act.

The convention that only those who were legally qualified sat as judges has as its counterpart the convention that the Law Lords do not take part in debates on bills that are politically controversial. It was during the 19th century that the convention arose whereby only those peers who were legally qualified sat when the House of Lords was acting in its judicial capacity: Professor Hudson (*O. Hood Phillips' First Book of English Law* (Sweet & Maxwell, 8th ed., 1988) p.97) dates this convention from the case of *O'Donnell v R* (1844) 11 Cl. & Fin. 155.

thinking point

Can members of the judiciary perform a dual role as legislators and judges? Why might this be problematic?

It might be thought undesirable that judges should take part in debates on any bills whatsoever, as ultimately they may have to rule on the meaning or effect of legislation, and, if they have already expressed a view during the legislative proceedings, they are unable to approach the interpretation of the Act with an open mind. It might equally be argued, however, that it is a waste to deprive the House of Lords of the expertise the Law Lords can bring to its deliberations, and, in particular, how they could, by contributing to the debates before a measure is enacted, anticipate some of the potential difficulties caused by the drafting of the measures and suggest amendments which might, in the future, prevent the need for litigation by improving the final version of the Act.

In the event, a form of compromise was arrived at in the form of a convention whereby the Law Lords would be able to speak in debates on measures that were not matters of political controversy; in other words, essentially matters of technical law on which their advice might be invaluable in improving the finished Act. However, deciding what is a measure on which it is appropriate for a Law Lord to speak and what is not, is not an easy task.

A good example of the controversies that can arise here was the debates on a series of criminal justice measures introduced first by the Conservative government in the 1980s and early 1990s and then by the Labour government from 1997 onwards. A particular issue was the extent to which the judges had discretion over the type and length of sentence that should be imposed in any individual criminal case. The government was keen to restrict the powers of the judges in this regard by providing for particular kinds of sentence to be imposed automatically if certain preconditions were met. The judges, not surprisingly, opposed this and argued that they needed to have some discretion in order to pass a sentence that was appropriate to the individual circumstances of the case taking into account both the nature of the offence and the nature of the offender. They further argued that the fixing of an individual sentence was a matter for the judiciary. Some criticisms were voiced by Ministers that the intervention of the judges in this matter was inappropriate and amounted to a breach of convention as it was a matter for the government of the day to determine overall policy, and that the matter was not one of purely legal technicality. Such controversies will not disappear when the judges take up their posts as Justices of the Supreme Court and cease to be Members of the House of Lords. What will happen is that the venue of these controversies will shift from Parliament to the Supreme Court and the context will move from the political to the legal.

thinking point

Who do you think ought to decide what is an appropriate sentence in any particular criminal case?

6.4 Judicial independence

One of the many battles of the 17th century was to secure the independence of the judiciary, primarily from royal control. As Professor Shetreet points out (*Judges on Trial* (North-Holland Publishing Co., 1976) p.17), the notion of independence of the judiciary in modern times needs to be considered in two particular contexts, namely the independence of individual judges and the independence of the judiciary as a whole. As to the first, this carries with it the idea that judges should be able to make decisions which are not subject to outside interference and that their tenure should be protected to enable them to do this. As to the second, the judiciary as a whole should be free from interference by either the executive or the legislature.

thinking point

Why is the independence of the judiciary regarded as so important?

This has only recently been secured. The system whereby judges were appointed by, in effect, the Lord Chancellor did not satisfy the requirement of independence. However, the alterations to the role of the Lord Chancellor under the Constitutional Reform Act 2005 and the creation of a new structure for the judiciary headed by the Lord Chief Justice attempt to meet this concern. The change was in any event necessary because

Article 6 of the European Convention on Human Rights requires a fair trial by an independent and impartial tribunal. This last requirement has been interpreted to mean that the judge must be free from executive or legislative interference and must thus have security of tenure to secure this.

Formally, independence was finally established by the Act of Settlement 1700, which provides that judges of the higher courts hold office during good behaviour and can only be dismissed following an address supported by both Houses of Parliament. The judges were thus, formally at least, freed from executive interference, though not taken outside the control of Parliament. However, the powers available to Parliament under the Act of Settlement have never been used in modern times (Shetreet *op cit.*, p.99). They are further supported by conventions that prevent Members of Parliament from criticizing individual judges, though, like all conventions, there may be some evidence in recent times that this convention is undergoing change. Government Ministers in particular have taken to criticizing judges whose decisions they do not like.

6.5 Judicial impartiality

One of the reasons that the independence of the judges is so strenuously preserved is to protect them from being influenced by government or Parliament in order to preserve their neutrality. Equally, judges are not expected to let their own political or other beliefs influence their decisions, which should be made solely on legal considerations. That, at least, is the theory. It is felt to be necessary in the interests of maintaining public confidence in the judicial system. In *R v Gough* [1993] AC 646, Lord Goff said (at p.659): 'there is an overriding public interest that there should be confidence in the integrity of the administration of justice'. Speaking extrajudicially, Lord Denning said: 'it is of the utmost importance that every person should be able to feel that his case has been tried by an upright and impartial judge' ('The Independence and Impartiality of the Judges' (1954) 71 SALJ 345 at 355). These two quotations illustrate two aspects of this issue. First, that individual litigants need to feel confidence in the impartiality of the judge hearing their claim; and secondly that, in order to encourage individuals to use the courts in order to settle disputes, the public as a whole needs to have confidence that the courts will offer a fair hearing.

thinking point
Can judges, as human beings, ever be completely impartial?

The idea of the administration of justice without bias is at the heart of Article 6 of the European Convention on Human Rights. In practice, it is impossible to be totally objective and immune from the influence of factors other than the purely legal. Judges would be criticized for being out of touch if they were to ignore entirely the context in which the law operates and the world outside the courtroom. As Professor Griffith points out (*Politics of the Judiciary,* Fontana, 4th ed., 1991 pp.18–19):

> If the judicial function were wholly automatic, then not only would the making of decisions in the courts be of little interest but it would not be necessary to recruit highly trained and intellectually able men and women to serve as judges and to pay them handsome salaries.

In the technological age, a computer could be programmed to decide disputes. The judicial function, however, involves the exercise of judgement, weighing factors, interpreting words, deciding what is relevant and what is not, and so on. This necessarily involves the interpolation of the human characteristics of the judge.

This has particular significance in relation to the question of which judge hears which cases, and which combination of judges hear appeal cases, as their particular approach to the case can determine its outcome. This is not only a case of their inclinations as human beings but also of their legal personalities. The two do not necessarily coincide: judges may be liberal in person but judicially conservative. The matter becomes significant in relation to the appeal courts where the composition of the bench can have an impact not only on the outcome of the individual case but also on the development of the law. The Court of Appeal generally sits in benches of three, while the House of Lords normally sits in panels of five. One of the questions surrounding the Supreme Court has been whether it should always sit with all the judges forming the panel in each case, as is the situation in some countries such as the United States of America where all the Supreme Court Justices sit in every case, or whether, as at present, only some of the judges should sit in each case. It has been decided that the current practice of having a selection of judges for each case will remain and thus the question of personalities will continue to be a factor in the way in which the court operates. One of the reasons for this is operational efficiency in that more than one court may be sitting at any given time, and some judges may be involved in other activities such as chairing inquiries.

thinking point
Should it matter which judge hears a case?

6.6 Judicial bias

cross reference
See Chapter 12.

Given that a human being can never be wholly objective, the question thus becomes one of deciding which biases are permissible and which are not. The position of the judges is the same as that of any other decision maker, and is subject to the rules of natural justice. These rules, which are discussed more fully in Chapter 12, require that a decision maker is not tainted by bias and that an individual is given a fair hearing. The rules were formulated and developed with a judicial context in mind, as their earliest application was to judicial proceedings in the lower courts and tribunals.

> Bias affects the judge in one of three ways:
>
> 1. Actual bias—automatic disqualification or quashing of decision
> 2. Apparent bias—automatic disqualification or quashing of decision
> 3. Apparent bias—discretionary disqualification or quashing of decision

6.6.1 **Actual bias**

If we consider first the application of these rules to judicial proceedings, the governing principle is that, in the famous phrase of Lord Hewart in *R v Sussex Justices ex p McCarthy* ([1924] 1 KB 256 at 259), 'justice must not only be done but must manifestly and undoubtedly be seen to be done'. The implications of this in terms of legal principle have been, first, that actual bias will either disqualify a person from acting in a judicial capacity or will operate to quash a decision made by a person who is in fact biased. In practice, given the integrity of the judges, it is hardly surprising that cases of actual bias are difficult to find, especially in modern times.

6.6.2 **Apparent bias**

Automatic disqualification

Secondly, the mere appearance of bias may disqualify a judge from sitting or lead to his decision being quashed. It has long been established that where a judge has a financial or proprietary interest in the outcome of the case, that will either disqualify him or invalidate any decision he has made. Further, even if he is sitting with others, his apparent bias will taint the decision, even though he is only one party to it, with the result that the decision will be quashed.

The leading case on financial and proprietary interests is *Dimes v Grand Junction Canal Co* (1852) 3 HLC 759; 10 ER 301.

case close-up

Dimes v Grand Junction Canal Co (1852) 3 HLC 759; 10 ER 301
. . . .
Here, the Lord Chancellor heard a case involving the Canal Company, in which he held shares. Whilst the court took great pains to emphasize that this shareholding had in no way influenced the Lord Chancellor's decision, and that he had reached the decision wholly impartially, nevertheless the decision could not stand. He could not be seen to be impartial, given his financial interest in the outcome, which would inevitably affect the value of his shares, and that was sufficient to invalidate his decision. In such cases, disqualification of the judge or invalidity of his decision is automatic.

thinking point

Does the principle in Dimes *cast doubt on the integrity of the judges? Should we be able to expect a professional judge to put aside any influences of this type and reach a decision objectively on its merits?*

For many years it remained the case that this was the only circumstance in which a judge was automatically disqualified for apparent bias. However, the category of automatic disqualification for apparent bias was extended by the House of Lords in 2000 in the case of *R v Bow Street Metropolitan Stipendiary Magistrate ex p. Pinochet Ugarte (No 2)* [2000] 1 AC 119.

R v Bow Street Metropolitan Stipendiary Magistrate ex p. Pinochet Ugarte (No 2) [2000] 1 AC 119

The House of Lords had ruled in favour of allowing the extradition of General Pinochet, the former Chilean ruler (*R v Bow Street Metropolitan Stipendiary Magistrate ex p. Pinochet Ugarte* [2000] 1 AC 61). In these proceedings, the organization Amnesty International had been allowed to make submissions before the House of Lords supporting the extradition of General Pinochet. One of the Law Lords hearing the case was Lord Hoffmann. He had previously been a director of Amnesty International, and his wife remained connected to the organization. This information only came to light after the House of Lords had announced its decision, and General Pinochet's lawyers argued that the decision of the House of Lords should be set aside as it was tainted by the presence of Lord Hoffmann as one of the judges and his connection with one of the parties: where an individual is tainted with bias, that bias infects the other members of the panel and affects their decision. This challenge went to the House of Lords and was heard by a panel of judges, none of whom had sat in the original proceedings. They found in favour of General Pinochet on the ground that Lord Hoffmann's connection with Amnesty International affected the original decision as this caused it not to appear impartial, and that it must be set aside. The result was that the extradition proceedings had to be heard afresh before a third, and different, panel of judges in the House of Lords, comprising judges who had not been involved in the previous two sets of proceedings.

thinking point

Why should the apparent bias of one member of the court affect the others who are sitting with him?

Discretionary disqualification

The test for bias: a real danger of bias?

A further set of circumstances exists where a judge may be disqualified or a decision invalidated because of apparent bias. Apparent bias can occur in many different ways: the judge may, for example, know one of the parties to the case, or have had business dealings with them, or have expressed views about the subject matter of the dispute or one of the parties to it. It is thus necessary to formulate a general test to apply across the board. In *R v Gough*, the House of Lords stated the test in terms of asking whether there was a real danger of bias on the part of the judge. As Lord Goff explained ([1993] AC at 670):

> I think it unnecessary in formulating the appropriate test to require that the court should look at the matter through the eyes of the reasonable man because the court in cases such as these personifies the reasonable man; and in any event the court has first to ascertain the relevant circumstances from the available evidence, knowledge of which would not necessarily be available

to an observer in court at the relevant time. Finally, for the avoidance of doubt, I prefer to state the test in terms of real danger rather than real likelihood, to ensure that the court is thinking in terms of possibility rather than probability of bias. Accordingly, having ascertained the relevant circumstances, the court should ask itself whether having regard to those circumstances, there was a real danger of bias on the part of the relevant member of the tribunal in question, in the sense that he might unfairly regard (or have unfairly regarded) with favour or disfavour the case of a party to the issues under consideration by him . . .

The test for bias reformulated: the perspective of the 'fair-minded and informed observer'

Lord Goff emphasizes that bias can operate both positively, by favouring one party, or negatively by being disposed against a party. *Gough* was, however, decided prior to the enactment of the Human Rights Act 1998, and the impact of Article 6 in particular needed to be considered when some suitable opportunity arose. That occurred in the case of *Re Medicaments and Related Classes of Goods (No 2)* [2001] 1 WLR 700.

case close-up

***Re Medicaments and Related Classes of Goods (No 2)* [2001] 1 WLR 700**

. . . .

Here, in a case in the Restrictive Practices Court, a question arose as to the impartiality of one of the lay members of the court, R. It transpired that she had applied for employment with a firm for whom an expert witness in the case was a director. However, it became clear that the firm was not planning to employ her, and, on that basis, the court decided that it could proceed with the hearing as there was no likelihood of bias either on the part of R or, by association, on the other members of the judicial panel. In considering the question whether the court was correct in its view, the Court of Appeal took the opportunity to reconsider the test for bias formulated in *Gough* in the light of the requirements of Article 6 and its interpretation by the European Court of Human Rights.

The Court of Appeal held that the test for bias was basically satisfactory but that it needed to be adjusted to reflect the objectivity stressed by the European Court. In *Gough*, Lord Goff had said that the court personified the reasonable man for the purpose of a standpoint from which the possibility of bias could be assessed. However, as Lord Phillips pointed out in *Re Medicaments*, this poses some difficulty when the question is whether the court (i.e. the judge) appears to be tainted by bias. To achieve the necessary degree of objectivity it was necessary to look at the matter from the standpoint not of the judge but of the objective onlooker. Given that the matter is concerned essentially with appearance, this seems a better standpoint from which to judge the matter. Following this line of reasoning, Lord Phillips reformulated the test as follows ([2001] 1 WLR at 727):

> The court must first ascertain all the circumstances which have a bearing on the suggestion that the judge was biased. It must then ask whether those circumstances would lead a fair-minded and informed observer to conclude that there was a real possibility, or a real danger, the two being the same, that the tribunal was biased.

Applying this test, the Court of Appeal decided that a fair-minded observer would conclude that R would be unable to be objective with regard to the evidence of the expert witness from the firm she had contacted, despite her assertion that she was unaffected by this association and had retained her objectivity as a member of the court. The potential bias on her part also affected the other two members of the judicial panel and they too were disqualified from hearing the case.

Extrajudicial activities

One area where judges may be vulnerable to claims of impartiality is in respect of their activities off the Bench. We have already seen that the argument about Lord Hoffmann's objectivity was based not on his conduct when sitting as a judge but on his associations while not sitting as a judge with an organization that later became a party to a case in which he was involved in his judicial capacity. Judges engage in a number of activities when they are not involved in court proceedings. They write, they make speeches, which lead to their views becoming known. There is a long tradition of judges conducting public inquiries, where their skills in extracting, managing and evaluating evidence as well as conducting proceedings are particularly sought. However, these activities may disclose views on issues that might come before them in their judicial capacity and may disqualify them from hearing particular cases.

Bearing in mind the remarks of Lord Phillips in *Re Medicaments* that judges should take a robust view to claims of bias whilst at the same time recognizing the overall requirement that proceedings should not only be conducted fairly but also seen to be conducted fairly, there is again a line to be drawn between those activities, associations, writings and speeches that can properly lead to a claim of apparent bias and those where a claim of bias is merely fanciful. In *Lockabail Ltd v Bayfield Properties* [2000] QB 451, the Court of Appeal heard a number of cases together in which a claim of bias on the part of the judges had arisen.

case close-up

Lockabail Ltd v Bayfield Properties [2000] QB 451

In one of these cases, a part-time judge who was a partner in a large firm of solicitors sat on a case where the firm had acted against one of the parties in litigation. The partner in question had not been involved in that litigation, nor was he aware of it. It was held that this did not invalidate his decision. Another case involved a complaint by an employee of the Inland Revenue (now HM Revenue and Customs) heard by a chairman of an Employment Tribunal who had worked for the Inland Revenue 35 years previously. It was again held that he was not disqualified from hearing the case on account of that association. In a third case, a judge was a non-executive director and shareholder in a company which had one of the parties, a large national company, as one of its tenants. Again, this did not bar the judge from sitting as his connection was felt to be too remote. However, in a fourth case, involving a claim for personal injury, a recorder, who had a large practice in personal injury and had previously written articles in legal professional journals expressing what the court described as a pro-claimant anti-insurer view, was open to challenge on grounds of apparent bias.

The last of these illustrates the potential difficulties a judge may meet when speaking in a non-judicial capacity and the care needed to avoid subsequent accusations of having effectively prejudged an issue. Yet we would expect judges to have views about a range of matters and to express them forcefully. There is clearly a fine line to be drawn in this area. More recently, for example, Lord Steyn was not able to sit on the panel of judges in the House of Lords to hear the case of *A v Secretary of State for the Home Department* [2005] 2 AC 68 because of a perception of bias based on a lecture he had previously delivered expressing a view about the effect of Article 5 of the European Convention on Human Rights on the position of those detained without trial (see '2000–2005: Laying the Foundations of Human Rights Law in the United Kingdom' [2005] EHRLR at 350).

The matter is not just confined to comments made extrajudicially. For example, Lord Denning (*ex p Church of Scientology of California, The Times,* 20 February, 1978) and Lord Lane (*The Guardian*, 16 November, 1984) both stood down from cases on the basis of statements that they had made in previous cases which were felt to cast doubt on their impartiality.

thinking point

If judges reveal their views, then an evaluation of potential bias can be made on the basis of their expressed views; if they do not express their views, no such evaluation can be made because their views are not known: they may have views that might suggest potential bias or they might not. Is it preferable to know what their views are or is it better not to know?

6.6.3 **What should a judge do when infected with bias?**

In *Re Medicaments*, the issue as to bias arose in respect of R who was a lay member of the Restrictive Practices Court. It is perhaps understandable that she was confident of her ability to remain objective despite her involvement with the firm from which the expert witness came. She would not be expected to be familiar with the line of case law establishing the principles of natural justice and, in particular, the development of the law relating to the rule against bias as it applies to judges. The same cannot be said for professional judges who not only ought to be familiar with the relevant legal principles but have, in many cases, themselves applied them to cases involving others.

The question of whether a judge in any given case is tainted by bias is perhaps more easily dealt with after a decision is made, in which case the decision either stands or is quashed depending on the outcome of the appeal. This was the situation in the *Pinochet* case, where Lord Hoffmann's involvement with Amnesty International was not raised until after judgment had been given. This is, however, less satisfactory as time, effort and expense will have been expended.

It is more desirable to deal with the matter at the outset, or even beforehand, and we might expect judges to be robustly self critical and to consider the question of their own possible bias objectively and, if necessary, to decide that they cannot sit in that particular case. It may be more difficult to deal with where, before the case has even been heard, the judge's impartiality is questioned in circumstances where the judge himself has seen no objection. It may be a delicate matter for counsel to suggest to the judge in question that something to do with that judge leads to a perception of bias.

thinking point

If judges are able to tell others when there is a perception of bias, should we expect them to apply the same principles to themselves?

In *Re Medicaments*, Lord Phillips suggested that, while judges should be sensitive to suggestions of potential bias, they should also be robust in considering any such claim on its merits and not simply accede to the merest suggestion of potential bias. In other words, it requires the judge to make a realistic and objective assessment of the evidence, looking at the matter not from the standpoint of the court but from that of the informed observer, as indicated by the court in *Re Medicaments*. Further, depending on how far the case has progressed, there is the potential delay, cost and disruption caused by having to allocate a new judge. Where a judge decides that the evidence suggests that he is tainted by actual (unlikely) or apparent bias, then he should **recuse** himself from hearing the case.

recuse

where a judge disqualifies himself from sitting in a particular case

A recent example of the difficulties faced by individual judges in the face of claims of apparent bias is provided by *AWG Group Ltd v Morrison* [2006] 1 WLR 1163.

AWG Group Ltd v Morrison [2006] 1 WLR 1163

Here, at the outset of what was listed to be a six month hearing, the defendants argued that the listed judge should recuse himself on grounds of apparent bias. J, one of the witnesses whom the claimants proposed to call and who was a director of the claimant company, had been personally known to the judge for a number of years. The judge drew attention to this relationship, and the claimants said that they would not call J as a witness as they recognized that it would be problematic. However, the defendants argued that J's evidence could be relevant and he had in fact already made a witness statement. The trial judge ruled that he did not think that his involvement with J would affect his decision with regard to AWG and that removing J as a witness would not affect the conduct of the trial. He therefore refused to recuse himself, bearing in mind both the nature of the issues involved and the effects of having to recommence the proceedings with a new judge. The defendants challenged that refusal. The Court of Appeal held that the judge should have recused himself. Even removing J as a witness would not remedy the potential bias as the trial would have necessarily involved consideration of matters to which J had been a party and therefore there was still a risk of potential bias on the part of the judge in relation to J's involvement. Further, the paramount consideration was that justice should be administered impartially and be seen to be so.

Two features of the law in this area are of particular interest. First, as Lord Phillips emphasizes in *Re Medicaments*, issues of bias are not confined to the individual proceedings in which a claim arises. There is a wider public interest in the impartiality of the judicial system. This is reflected in the test developed in that case, whereby the matter is regarded not from the standpoint of the judge in question but from the position of the fair minded and objective observer. Justice must be seen to be done by the public and not simply by the court, or, in other words, the judge. Judges are required to look at the allegation of bias from this public standpoint and think how the matter might appear to the onlooker.

thinking point

Is it possible to draw a clear line between apparent biases that might affect fairness and those which do not?

Secondly, the law is concerned with actual or potential bias on the part of an individual judge in particular proceedings. The factors that might give rise to a possibility of bias are specific, such as personal knowledge of a party or witness, as in *Gough* and *Re Medicaments*. The law does not concern itself with general characteristics of the judges. Professor Griffith (*op cit.*) has argued that judges tend to uphold conservative values, to defend property rights, to side with the state, the police, employers, or what might be termed the establishment generally against challenges by individuals or minority groups, especially where those groups espouse unpopular causes. This argument may have lost some of its force in recent years, as, especially following the Human Rights Act 1998, the courts have taken a robust view of individual rights that has not always found favour with the government, and which has upheld the rights of unpopular groups such as asylum seekers and terrorism suspects.

thinking point

See the cases discussed in Chapter 7.

(6.7) Judicial power

The question of how effectively the judges can act to prevent abuses of executive and legislative power depends on the powers they, as judges, exercise. However, the powers exercised by the judges need to be seen in the context of other forces in the constitution. Thus for example, we need to consider the role of the judges in preventing abuses of power by the executive alongside the role of the legislature in doing so.

Judicial power comes from:

1. Parliament
2. The judges themselves determining their powers by developing the common law

Judges get their powers from two sources: from Parliament and from the courts themselves exercising their inherent jurisdiction—in other words, their power to create law. Each of these may be examined in turn.

6.7.1 **Acts of Parliament**

Excluding the courts completely

Parliament can, by the way it frames legislation, determine the scope within which judges can operate. This may range from attempting to exclude the judges altogether to placing limits on their power to interfere in executive decisions. As to the first of these, the judges do not readily accept that Parliament has excluded them from being able to determine whether the executive has acted lawfully. Such provisions are termed **ouster clauses**; that is, they seek to oust the jurisdiction of the courts. The courts have, on occasions, employed ingenious lines of reasoning to overcome their apparent exclusion from being able to adjudicate. A good example is provided by *Anisminic v Foreign Compensation Commission* [1969] 2 AC 147.

thinking point
If Parliament wishes to exclude the courts, why should the courts try to resist this?

. . . .

ouster clause

a provision in an Act of Parliament that seeks to exclude the courts from exercising jurisdiction over any or all of the subject matter of the Act

. . . .

case close-up

Anisminic v Foreign Compensation Commission [1969] 2 AC 147
. . . .

The Foreign Compensation Act 1950 provided that a determination of the Foreign Compensation Commission could not be questioned in a court of law. The House of Lords held that Parliament could not have meant that the courts should be excluded completely, otherwise a person who had been subject to an incorrect or unlawful determination of the Foreign Compensation Commission would have no way of seeking an independent review of the decision. For this reason if no other, as Lord Reid points out (at p.170), any such exclusion should be construed narrowly:

> It is a well established principle that a provision ousting the ordinary jurisdiction of the court must be construed strictly—meaning, I think, that, if such a provision is reasonably capable of having two meanings, that meaning shall be taken which preserves the ordinary jurisdiction of the court.

Following this line of reasoning, the House of Lords held that the provision in question should be read so that it only applied to correct determinations of the Foreign Compensation Commission but not to incorrect determinations. This effectively undermined the prohibition on judicial scrutiny as the courts would have to determine whether the determination was correct or not in order to determine whether they had jurisdiction or not.

cross reference
See Chapter 3.

Similarly creative reasoning enabled the courts to get round the apparent prohibition in Article 9 Bill of Rights 1689 with regard to parliamentary proceedings. Article 9 provides that the 'freedom of speech and debates or proceedings in Parliament should not be impeached or questioned in any court or place out of Parliament'. As we have seen, this effectively prevents the courts from considering remarks made in Parliament. However, in *Pepper v Hart* [1993] AC 593, the House of Lords was invited to allow recourse to **Hansard** in order to assist courts to determine the true meaning of Acts of Parliament. This has always been a contentious issue, not least because so many things are said in the course of a debate on a bill that it might be difficult to disentangle those views that provide a helpful guide to meaning and those that do not. There is also an issue of the effect on litigation with regard to the extra research that recourse to Hansard would entail, and the consequent extra cost, as well as the additional length it would add to arguments before the courts if not carefully checked, again something carrying cost implications.

. . . .

Hansard

this is the name given to the verbatim published record of what is said in Parliament

. . . .

The House of Lords held that this could be done, though limited the circumstances when courts would be able to exercise this power. The provision in question had to be ambiguous and there had to be a clear statement of the intent behind the provision, usually from a sponsoring Minister. This decision appeared to contradict the prohibition in Article 9 quoted above. The House of Lords dismissed this argument on the basis that merely looking to see what had been said in Parliament did not involve questioning what was said and therefore did not violate Article 9.

activity

Hansard is available on the web site for Parliament: select a day when Parliament has been debating a bill and read some of the transcript. What does it tell you about the bill in question?

thinking point

Having read Hansard, do you think that looking at what is said in Parliament would help to clarify or confuse the meaning of terms used in an Act of Parliament?

Excluding the courts from considering particular matters

Parliament may, in enacting legislation, use words which seem to exclude the courts from intervening in particular aspects of the operation of the statute. Here again, the inherent ambiguity of language means that it is open to interpretation, and it then becomes a matter for the courts to determine whether they are going to interpret terms in such a way as to permit their intervention or to reach an interpretation that excludes them from interfering with an executive decision. It is not, however, just a matter of interpretation: the subject matter has also to be taken into consideration.

Most obviously the courts will not intervene where the matter concerns issues of executive policy. This includes areas such as national security and foreign policy and is most likely to arise in the context of the royal prerogative, though not exclusively so, as the following case illustrates.

case close-up

Chandler v DPP [1964] AC 763
....

A group of protesters had demonstrated by sitting on a runway at an airbase. They were charged, amongst other offences, under s.2 of the Official Secrets Act 1911 with engaging in acts that were prejudicial to the safety or interests of the state. They claimed that their actions, far from being prejudicial to the safety or interests of the state, were in fact beneficial to the state as they would prevent the possibility of nuclear war. The House of Lords held that this was a debate into which the courts could not enter. What was in the interests of the state was purely a matter for the government of the day and could not be questioned in the courts. In part, this decision is explicable in terms of the separation of powers in that the judges are recognising what they regard as the proper territory of the executive and the courts.

thinking point

Does it seem right to allow the government to determine the interests of the state and to exclude other views? See also R v Ponting [1985] Crim LR 318.

cross reference
See Chapter 12.

The courts have, however, intervened to interpret statutes to enable them to question executive acts even in circumstances where the statute, at face value, does not seem to permit this. Thus, in *Roberts v Hopwood* [1925] AC 578, a local authority was empowered to pay such wages as it should think fit. It decided, amongst other things, to pay a minimum wage and to pay men and women at the same rate. The House of Lords held, however, that the authority could not simply pay its employees at whatever rate it thought was appropriate: it had failed to take proper account of the interests of the ratepayers, the decline in the value of money, the going rate for the job and the fact that no other authority paid men and women at the same rates. There are plenty of other examples of cases showing the courts either intervening or refusing to do so in Chapter 12 where the issues are discussed more fully.

6.7.2 Powers arising from the development of the common law

Judiciary and legislature

Turning to the development of the common law, the judges have shown equally varied approaches. Although much of the power to develop new law has diminished as statute has replaced the common law as the dominant form of law, a development that characterized the 20th century, the courts are still able to develop aspects of the law through their decisions, though developments tend to be incremental rather than dramatic. Despite these more general trends, it is still possible to point to major legal developments that are almost entirely judge made. The growth of administrative law in the second half of the 20th century and the development of the tort of negligence

cross reference
See Chapter 3.

provide two examples. Here, the courts have developed principles of law which have a profound impact on the state and individuals. It is, however, interesting to contrast the approach taken by the courts to relations with the legislature with their approach to the executive. As Chapter 3 illustrated, the courts have decided that they have no power to declare legislation to be invalid. Even the Human Rights Act 1998 has not given them this power, nor have they used the impetus to judicial activity granted by that statute as a basis for reconsidering their position. Thus, even with their enhanced powers of interpretation under s.3 of the Human Rights Act, the most they can do, formally at least, is to issue a declaration of incompatibility under s.4. It might be argued that the duty under s.3 to arrive at an interpretation of legislation to ensure its compatibility with the convention rights leaves open the possibility for judicial creativity but even here the courts have made clear that s.3 does not authorizes the courts to rewrite legislation: the task is simply one of interpretation to which there are limits.

cross reference
See Chapter 7.

Thus, in *Re S* [2002] 2 AC 291, where the Court of Appeal introduced a series of administrative requirements into the operation of a Care Order under the Children Act 1989 that were not sanctioned by the Act but were felt to be appropriate in order to make the order comply with the convention rights, the House of Lords held that this was an impermissible extension of the courts' powers. The furthest the courts have been able to go is under EU law, in order to give effect to the principle of community sovereignty. In recognition of this principle, it has been held that the courts can disapply legislation that is not compatible with the requirements of EU law.

cross reference
See Chapter 3.

As we have seen in Chapter 3, this was starkly illustrated in the leading case of *R v Secretary of State for Transport ex p Factortame* [1990] 2 AC 85; where the House of Lords had to consider what to do in a case where a piece of British legislation, the Merchant Shipping Act 1988, appeared to be in conflict with the requirements of EC law. The House of Lords could not find an interpretation of the legislation that made it compatible with the requirements of EC law, and referred the matter to the European Court of Justice which ruled that the Merchant Shipping Act was indeed incompatible and that EC law must be given effect in preference to it. The House of Lords had ultimately to disapply the 1988 Act. It has used this power subsequently, for example, to disapply parts of UK employment law in *R v Secretary of State for Employment ex p Equal Opportunities Commission* [1995] 1 AC 1, and this, in many ways, remains the courts' most potent power as against the legislature.

The judiciary and the executive

cross reference
See Chapter 10.

Turning to relations with the executive, the courts have developed the principles of administrative law which govern the exercise of powers, both statutory and common law, by the state or by emanations of the state such as local authorities or the police. These powers that the courts enjoy have again received a boost from the enactment of the Human Rights Act 1998 which, as we have seen, has further enhanced the judicial role and provided new concepts for the courts to work with.

In this regard, the courts have, firstly, developed principles which decision makers are required to observe and, secondly, decided what the limits of their own powers are when applying those principles. Thus, in *Associated Provincial Picture Houses v Wednesbury Corporation* [1948] 1 KB 223, Lord Greene crystallized the principles forming the framework within which decision makers were required to operate when exercising statutory powers. Decision makers should ensure:

- that they have directed themselves correctly as to their legal powers;

- that they have identified the proper purpose for which those powers had been given and had exercised them in accordance with that purpose;

- that they had taken into account relevant considerations and not taken into account irrelevant considerations; and

- that they had not acted in a way that no reasonable authority would have acted.

cross reference

This case is discussed further in Chapter 12.

This was taken further by the House of Lords in *Council of Civil Service Unions v Minister for the Civil Service* [1985] AC 374 (sometimes called the *GCHQ* case as it concerned civil servants working at GCHQ, the government's communications monitoring centre). Here the House stated that these principles should apply also to the royal prerogative. Lord Diplock reorganized the principles laid down by Lord Greene under three headings of illegality, irrationality and procedural impropriety. He also noted that the European doctrine of proportionality might become a fourth head of review. This last rose in prominence once the Human Rights Act 1998 came into force and has become an important feature of judicial scrutiny.

The House of Lords in the *GCHQ* case identified as the key to judicial intervention the notion of justiciability. This is the idea that, in order for the judges to adjudicate on a matter, that matter must be something on which the court is competent to pronounce. It involves recognition of the separation of powers and the idea that there are areas exclusively within the jurisdiction of the executive or the legislature. This is particularly relevant to exercises of the prerogative given its subject matter, dealing with issues of defence and foreign policy. But it is equally applicable to review of the exercise of statutory powers. Essentially the matter of the powers the courts exercise is largely within their own control. They can find principles on which to intervene or they can recognize, in a self-denying way, that there are areas into which they do not wish to venture. This is part of the balance within the constitution based on ideas of the separation of powers. The powers of the court have changed significantly since the enactment of the Human Rights Act 1998. It seems unlikely, given the framework created by the Constitutional Reform Act 2005, that their powers will change significantly when the Supreme Court becomes operational.

thinking point

Should we know more about the judges? How many of the leading judges would you recognize?

One thing that is unlikely to change is that, as compared to politicians, the judges remain generally unknown to the public at large. Following the discussion earlier in this chapter, it is perhaps helpful to keep it this way, as it means that the impartiality of judges does not come under scrutiny, something essential to preserving the integrity of justice as a whole. Perhaps it is that politicians and judges, despite the fact that they play vital roles within the constitution, need to have different public profiles in order to be able to carry out their different functions.

Questions

If you answer the following questions, you will have appreciated the main issues raised in this chapter. Check your answers against the notes provided at the back of the book.

1 How are judges appointed? Do you think the present system is an improvement on the previous system?

2 How is the judiciary organized? Is the removal of the Lord Chancellor from his role as head of the judiciary making a difference to the judges?

3 Why is judicial independence from political interference regarded as so important?

4 What is the test for bias? Why is it so important that judges should be seen to be impartial when trying cases? Can judges ever be totally impartial?

5 What powers do the judges have? Where do these powers come from?

6 What limitations are there on the powers exercised by the judges?

Further reading

To further your understanding of the topics covered in this chapter, have a look at the reading materials mentioned below. Useful web links are also provided on the Online Resource Centre.

A.W. Bradley and K.D. Ewing, *Constitutional and Administrative Law* (Pearson Longman, 14th ed., 2007) ch. 18
This gives you a detailed account of the judges and the courts from a constitutional perspective.

Gary Slapper and David Kelly, *The English Legal System* (Routledge Cavendish, 9th ed., 2008) ch.6
This provides you with an account of the judiciary which examines their function in the English legal system.

Penny Darbyshire, 'Where do English and Welsh Judges Come From?' [2007] CLJ 365
This gives you some insight into the characteristics of judges at all levels in the judicial hierarchy.

The Human Rights Act 1998

Learning Objectives

When reading this chapter, you should aim to understand:

- why the Human Rights Act 1998 was passed;
- how the Human Rights Act has incorporated the European Convention on Human Rights into English law;
- which rights have been incorporated into English law and in what circumstances they can be limited; and
- the potential impact of the Human Rights Act on public authorities and the courts.

Introduction

The Human Rights Act 1998 came into force on 2 October 2000, which ranks as one of the most important dates in English legal history. In this chapter, we look at the way in which English law has developed protection for individual rights. An historical introduction explains the transition from civil liberties to human rights and why it is important. The Human Rights Act 1998 is then examined and the key Articles from the European Convention on Human Rights, which the Human Rights Act brings into English law, are identified. It is worth bearing in mind at the outset that the Human Rights Act has only been in force for a few years, so that there are relatively few decisions of the highest courts to consider: the human rights regime is still in its early stages and the cases that have been decided are indicative of initial trends rather than representing definite standpoints. As Lord Steyn put it in a recent article ('2000–2005: Laying the Foundations of Human Rights Law in the United Kingdom' [2005] EHRLR 349), the courts have so far been laying the foundations of human rights law, on which subsequent cases will build.

7.1 From civil liberties to human rights?

7.1.1 Shortcomings of the common law

One of the deficiencies of the common law is that it does not recognize any fundamental rights, still less has it taken a systematic approach to the protection of individuals against the exercise of state power. The absence of a written constitution meant that the courts were working in a context in which there were no fundamental principles, and therefore little to guide the courts when cases came before them. The common law can only develop on the basis of cases brought before the courts, and this haphazard process accounted for the piecemeal development of the law. The common law operated by means of providing remedies for wrongs rather than positive rights that the individual could assert. The consequence of this was that if, say, a person was physically restrained by a police officer or state official, the individual would have to bring an action for trespass to the person, for which the law recognized the existence of a remedy. The impetus for such action would lie with the individual who would have to prove that the ingredients of the tort were satisfied in order to succeed.

As the common law recognizes no fundamental rights, the principle of the sovereignty of Parliament operates to allow Parliament to legislate to remove or restrict even the most fundamental of freedoms with no possibility of challenge in the courts. The position of individual freedom was therefore precarious. However, as well as having the potential to remove individual freedom, Parliament also has the potential to enhance it. In both respects, though, Parliament, like the courts, acts in a haphazard way, legislating on matters that reflect the political agenda but ignoring areas that do not. The result of these developments has been that individuals have only had at best a patchy series of common law rules and statutory provisions to rely on against incursions by the state. Such protection as has been secured has often been incomplete and often inadequate.

The result of the situation described above was that civil liberties were said to be residual: that is, a person could do as he wished as long as there were no laws prohibiting him from doing it. Equally, however, state officials could only stop somebody doing something if a law existed to prohibit it but not otherwise. This is illustrated in *Entick v Carrington* (1765) 19 St Tr.1029; 2 Wils. 275; 95 ER 807.

case close-up

Entick v Carrington (1765) 19 St Tr.1029; 2 Wils. 275; 95 ER 807

State officials entered the premises of the plaintiff and conducted a search for seditious material, arguing state necessity by way of justification, or, alternatively, relying on the terms of a general warrant issued by the Home Secretary. It was held that their actions were unlawful, as the law did not recognize any power available to the Home Secretary to issue a general warrant, nor did it recognize state necessity as a ground legitimizing the search of a person's premises. In giving the judgment of the court, Lord Camden CJ said:

> By the laws of England, every invasion of private property...is a trespass. No man can set his foot upon my ground without my licence, but he is liable to an action, though the damage be nothing...If he admits the fact, he is bound to shew by way of justification that some positive law has empowered or excused him. The justification is submitted to the judges, who are to look into the books; and see if such a justification can be maintained by the text of the statute law or by the principles of common law. If no such excuse can be found or produced, the silence of the books is an authority against the defendant and the plaintiff must have judgment.

(This passage only appears in the State Trials version of the report from which an extract appears in Michael Allen and Brian Thompson, *Cases and Materials on Constitutional and Administrative Law* (Oxford University Press, 9th ed., 2008) ch.4 at p.158.)

cross reference
It might be useful to re-read the section in Chapter 2 on the rule of law at this point.

Although the language is archaic, the underlying principles Lord Camden outlines remain valid as an expression of notions of the rule of law which requires that state action has to be justified in law. As he also indicates, of course, with regard to entry to premises, lawful entry may be made with the permission of the occupier, a matter to which we will return in due course.

The notion of the rule of law is, however, two edged. Whilst, as in *Entick v Carrington* it can be used to support the individual against the state, it can also work against the individual. At common law, if there is nothing in law to stop a particular activity carried out by or on behalf of the state, then that activity remains lawful even if it operates to the detriment of the individual. An example is provided by *Malone v Metropolitan Police Commissioner* [1979] Ch 344. The plaintiff in this case alleged that his telephone was being tapped and that such activity was unlawful. Unfortunately for him, English law, because of its piecemeal development had not developed, either through the common law or Parliament, a law of privacy making such activity unlawful. It was held, therefore, that, as there was no law preventing it, tapping Mr. Malone's telephone was lawful.

The common law position was thus deficient in a number of respects. It provided remedies rather than rights, placing the onus squarely on the individual to challenge state action as unlawful rather than on the state to justify its actions. Coupled with this was the uncertainty of the common law as developed by the courts. In many areas of law there was no definitive wording for those laws that did exist, as different judges used different forms of words to express the same ideas. This compounds the difficulties for the individual wishing to challenge state action. The principle of parliamentary sovereignty meant that Parliament could override the common law, perhaps to the advantage of the individual or perhaps to his detriment. Indeed, Parliament could simply legislate to take away even the most apparently fundamental freedoms. Where Parliament had legislated, the courts could only interpret the statutory provisions; they could not challenge what Parliament had enacted. The unplanned development of law by both the judges and by Parliament meant that whilst some areas of individual freedom were heavily regulated, others were untouched: the example of privacy raised by *Malone* is but one example of the latter.

thinking point

Given the uncertainties of the position at common law, and the absence of any statement of fundamental rights or freedoms, were people in the UK oppressed prior to the enactment of the Human Rights Act?

7.1.2 International obligations

A further issue related to the UK's international obligations. The United Kingdom had been a signatory to the European Convention on Human Rights since 1951, and indeed had been actively involved in drafting it. Yet, until the implementation of the Human Rights Act 1998 on 2 October 2000, its provisions were not part of domestic law and were thus unenforceable in the English courts. This created the odd looking situation that the UK was a signatory to something its citizens could not enforce in the domestic courts. A citizen could take a case against the United Kingdom to the European Court of Human Rights. But the UK only granted its citizens the right of individual petition in 1966. So for the 15 years from 1951 to 1966, individual citizens did not even have the possibility of redress through the European mechanisms: during this period only another state could bring a case against the UK. The difficulty of taking a case to the European Court of Human Rights should not be underestimated. In the first place, the individual had to have exhausted domestic remedies before taking the case to the European Court of Human Rights. The time, expense and persistence just to exhaust domestic remedies are considerable. To go further and take the case to the European Court of Human Rights required even more persistence and expense. The time taken by this process was also considerable: an average of five years was needed to bring a case to its conclusion. Notwithstanding these formidable difficulties, however, a steady stream of cases were taken by citizens of the UK in the years following 1966, many of them (in excess of 50) resulting in a decision in favour of the applicant.

Additionally, until the Human Rights Act 1998 came into force, the domestic courts were, officially, unable to take the European Convention on Human Rights into account in their decisions as it was not part of English law. In practice, courts did look at the European Convention and it informed decision making, though often by enabling the courts to hold that a decision they had made on the interpretation of English law also conformed to the UK's obligations, thus giving it extra credibility. But the Convention could not be used to fill gaps in English law. In *Malone*, for example, Megarry V-C was invited to use Article 8 of the European Convention in the absence of an English law of privacy. He declined to do so, on the ground that he had no power to do so as the Convention was not part of domestic law.

7.1.3 A home grown Bill of Rights?

The apparently logical argument that, as the United Kingdom had signed the European Convention on Human Rights, it should give expression to those rights by incorporating them into English law was not universally accepted. Two other arguments were dominant in debates about whether the United Kingdom should enact a Bill of Rights. (The history of the debates is charted in detail in M. Zander, *A Bill of Rights?* (Sweet & Maxwell, 4th ed., 1997).) The first was opposed to any such development. Proponents argued that Parliament could provide better protection for individual rights. Acts of Parliament could provide more detailed protection for individuals than a collection of general principles such as the European Convention on Human Rights or any other similar instrument. Parliament could also enact specific measures to deal with the needs of the UK and its citizens rather than the pan-European regime under the European Convention on Human Rights. Further, as Parliament, notably the House of Commons, was elected by and answerable to the citizens of the United Kingdom, it was uniquely placed to enact measures appropriate to the present needs of the country and its population rather than relying on principles drawn up in the 1950s on a cross Europe basis. Opponents of a Bill of Rights also pointed out that enactment of such a document would involve a considerable power shift away from Parliament and the government and to the judges. Government by the judges, as an extreme form of the argument had it, was undesirable in principle as the judges were not accountable in the ways that Members of Parliament and of the government were. This represented a powerful set of arguments that prevailed until the late 1990s. A further explanation is also provided by a lack of political will to take the step of enacting a Bill of Rights, whatever the logic of the arguments.

thinking point

What do you think of the argument that Parliament is better able to provide protection for individual rights than having a charter of rights?

A variation on this came from those who, whilst supporting the enactment of a Bill of Rights, felt that the European Convention on Human Rights was not what was needed and would prefer a Bill of Rights drafted in, by and for the United Kingdom. This argument strengthened as the century progressed, as the European Convention, which reflected the concerns of the European states in the aftermath of World War II, became less of a reflection of the current concerns of the United Kingdom. Whilst this position had its attractions, not least in its desire to enact something that was tailored to the present needs of the United Kingdom, there were also some drawbacks to this position. Firstly, it would have created a paradox in that the United Kingdom would be a signatory to one Bill of Rights, the European Convention, yet have its own home-grown Bill of Rights for domestic purposes. Secondly, any Bill of Rights drawn up solely in the United Kingdom would run up against the problem of credibility unless there was a strong political consensus surrounding it. The European Convention has the advantage of having been drawn up internationally, so that internal political differences were not reflected and it had a credibility based on its international nature.

thinking point

Would it have been better to develop a set of rights relevant to Britain in the late 20th century?

145

7.1.4 **Bringing rights home**

Notwithstanding these arguments, the incoming Labour government in 1997 was elected with a commitment to incorporate the European Convention on Human Rights into English law. A party document in 1996, entitled *Bringing Rights Home: A Consultation Paper* (Labour Party, 1996) outlined the arguments for taking this step. Many of these were reiterated when the Labour government published its White Paper *Rights Brought Home: The Human Rights Bill* (Cm 3782 (1997)) and in the debates on the Bill that ultimately became the Human Rights Act 1998. Two particular arguments persuaded the Labour Party to take this step. The first was the view that it was wrong that British citizens had to go to the European Court of Human Rights to vindicate their rights rather than having them adjudicated upon in the domestic courts. Secondly, it felt that the argument that incorporation of the European Convention on Human Rights was not necessary because UK legislation complied with the European Convention had been discredited by the number of cases where the UK was found to have violated such rights. Legislation was, therefore, necessary to make the Convention rights accessible to citizens and to do so via the domestic courts.

7.2 The Human Rights Act 1998

The Human Rights Act 1998 was not brought into force until 2000 in order to enable public authorities to consider and, if necessary, adjust their working practices to ensure that they were compliant with the new regime. An extensive programme of training for judges was also necessary so that they would be fully conversant with the implications of the Act from the day it came into force. Although a fundamental change brought about by the Act is the incorporation of the Convention rights into domestic law and adjudication over them by the domestic courts, the right of an individual to take a case to the European Court of Human Rights has not been abolished. The same conditions apply, in that the possibilities through the domestic courts must have been exhausted, and thus none of the barriers to adjudication by that court identified earlier—cost, time, persistence—has disappeared. However, it might be anticipated that the number of cases following this route will decline, largely as a result of such matters being dealt with by courts in the UK. It might also be anticipated that the number of successful applications against the UK will fall as the UK becomes more consciously human rights compliant, having positive duties to uphold the Convention rights rather than the situation under the previous common law regime which did not require compliance in the same explicit way.

However, the Human Rights Act has not completely replaced the former regime. The Act only comes into play when a public authority is doing something, or had failed to do something, which, it is claimed, infringes a person's Convention rights. Many claims against the state and its agencies will not involve a human rights issue and will thus remain untouched by the 1998 Act. It follows that not all of the defects of the previous common law regime have been eradicated. Further, the Human Rights Act is parasitic in that it depends on the public authority doing something it already had power to do and, at one level, simply provides a new set of principles against which the action of the public authority may be judged. As with any other legal action in the courts, academic issues cannot form the basis of a claim: the public authority must be doing something or neglecting to do something in order to engage the Convention rights. The Human Rights Act does not, therefore, provide a complete break with the past but, rather, adds to the previous legal framework. What it does provide, in cases where a human rights issue is involved, is a set of principles against which the law or the conduct of the public authority can be judged, which was not, save for a few broad generalities, the position prior to 2 October 2000.

We can consider the Human Rights Act in two parts. Firstly, by looking at the structure of the Act and then at the rights incorporated into English law by the Act. It is worth remembering at the outset that the Human Rights Act affects not only rules of law, whether statutory or common law, but also the way in which such rules are administered. So, for example, it will apply to the statutes such as the Police and Criminal Evidence Act 1984 which sets out a range of powers available to police officers and will also apply to the way in which individual police officers use these powers in particular situations such as when making an arrest. It is also worth noting that s.11 of the Human Rights Act provides that reliance on a Convention right does not restrict any other right conferred by English law. The object in implementing the Convention is to expand protection of human rights, not restrict it.

7.2.1 The structure of the Human Rights Act

Public authority

Bearing in mind the circumstances in which the European Convention on Human Rights was drawn up, it is not surprising that its focus is to protect individuals against abuses of state power. The idea of an agency exercising state power is expressed in the Act by the term 'public authority'. The rights are thus said to have vertical effect and are enforceable against a public authority.

Figure 7.1
Vertical effect

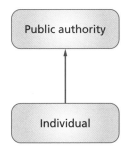

They do not generally apply to disputes between individuals, and so are said not to have horizontal effect. This view is not universally accepted, however, and is discussed further below.

Figure 7.2
Horizontal effect

Identifying a body as a public authority is crucial because of the duties and responsibilities placed on such bodies by the Act. The fundamental duty is outlined in s.6(1).

statute

Human Rights Act 1998, s.6 (1)

It is unlawful for a public authority to act in a way which is incompatible with a Convention right.

As this duty only applies to public authorities, a key issue in the scope and operation of the Act is to identify those bodies that fall within this description. This is partially explained in s.6(3).

statute

Human Rights Act 1998, s.6 (3)

(3) In this section 'public authority' includes—

(a) a court or tribunal, and

(b) any person certain of whose functions are functions of a public nature,

but does not include either House of Parliament or a person exercising functions in connection with proceedings in Parliament.

This does not include the House of Lords acting in its judicial capacity (s.6(4)), which is, as are all other courts, a public authority for the purposes of the Act. The term 'public authority' will cover central and local government together with others exercising executive power such as the police.

A body is not a public authority if the nature of the function it is performing is private in nature. This means that if a body which is otherwise a public authority is acting in a private law matter, for example, in relation to an individual employment contract or a contract with a supplier, then it is not acting as a public authority for the purposes of s.6. Although the Act is generally not thought to apply to disputes between private individuals or to matters of private law, it should be noted that in the event of any dispute between private parties the court adjudicating on the matter is still acting as a public authority and is still under a duty to uphold the Convention rights by virtue of s.6(1). This has led some commentators (such as H.W.R. Wade, 'Horizons of Horizontality' (2000) 116 LQR 217; M. Hunt, 'The "Horizontal Effect" of the Human Rights Act' [1998] PL 423) to suggest that the Human Rights Act does apply to private disputes, not through obligations attaching to the parties but due to the duties placed on the court, though this view is not universally accepted.

Whether a body is or is not a public authority has implications for that body in terms of the requirements under the Human Rights Act. There has, as a result, been litigation on the question of whether particular bodies are or are not public authorities. In the leading case of *Aston Cantlow etc Parochial Church Council v Wallbank* [2004] 1 AC 546, a dispute about liability to pay for church repairs, it was held that a parochial church council was not a public authority, as it was not an emanation of government. This may seem surprising given that the Church of England is the state church, but the House of Lords looked particularly at the functions of parochial church councils and concluded that they were not exercising powers that were analogous to those exercised by central or local (secular) government.

thinking point

Does it matter whether a body is a public authority for the purposes of the Human Rights Act? Wouldn't any organization want to uphold human rights?

This is not an easy issue to resolve, with particular difficulty created where the public and private sectors overlap. This may be illustrated with reference to two cases concerning the question of whether private residential care homes looking after residents who were there as a result of statutory duties on local authorities to provide accommodation under Part III of the National Assistance Act 1948, and who were being paid for out of public funds, were public authorities for the purposes of the Human Rights Act.

case close-up

R(Heather) v Leonard Cheshire Foundation [2002] 2 All ER 936

The Foundation ran a number of residential homes for older people who had been in the armed services, and received money from public funds toward the care of some of the residents. It was held that the running of homes was not a public function, but rather a private arrangement between the residents and the Foundation and that the receipt of public money did not alter this nor change the character of the Foundation's activities.

case close-up

L v Birmingham City Council [2008] 1 AC 95

A similar issue arose in this case. Residents of a private care home for older people were there as a result of arrangements with the local authority to accommodate them in satisfaction of the local authority's duties to provide accommodation under Part III of the National Assistance Act 1948. The House of Lords held, 3:2, that the home was not exercising function of a public nature under s.6(3)(b) and therefore was not a public authority for the purposes of the Human Rights Act. The fact that the House of Lords was divided on this issue indicates the difficulty in drawing the line between public authorities and private bodies. The House of Lords divided on a number of issues, but a key issue for the majority was the fact that the care home provider was a private body whose relationships with its residents were governed by contract, and further that it would be incongruous to differentiate between the rights of residents depending on whether they were privately or publicly funded. The minority laid particular emphasis on the nature of the function of providing residential accommodation for those unable to care for themselves at home.

Parliament, however, has taken a different view from the House of Lords on this issue. Section 145 of the Health and Social Care Act 2008 reverses the decision in *YL v Birmingham City Council* and provides that, in the circumstances of that case, private care homes are public authorities for the purposes of the Human Rights Act.

In *R(Beer) v Hampshire Farmers' Markets Ltd* [2004] 1 WLR 233, the company which ran farmers' markets was held to be a public authority notwithstanding that it was a private company. This was because the licensing functions it exercised had been delegated by a local authority, and so Hampshire Farmers' Markets Ltd was exercising a function that would otherwise have been exercised by the local authority and was therefore a public authority on the basis of exercising governmental functions. In the end, where bodies are not obviously public authorities, much will depend on the weight given to the relevant factors by a court determining its status. The cases suggest that the functions carried out by the body will be a major consideration in determining this issue, which, as *Wallbank* suggests, must be of a governmental nature if the body is to be considered a public authority. However, as they also illustrate, this can lead to conflicting views as to what the nature of any given function might be.

thinking point

Is the public/private divide helpful here? Should, for example, large companies be regarded as public authorities in view of the power they exercise?

7.2.2 **The Convention rights**

The recognition of a body as a public authority has implications, as we have seen, in that a public authority has to uphold the Convention rights. As s.1 makes clear, this phrase is used to mean the rights set out in Schedule 1 to the Human Rights Act 1998. It might have been thought that, in deciding to bring the European Convention into English law, the government and Parliament would have implemented the Convention in its entirety. This is not, however, the case, and the relevant parts that have been incorporated are set out in Schedule 1, which reproduces Articles 2–12 of the Convention, Articles 1–3 of the First Protocol and Articles 1–2 of the Sixth Protocol all of which need to be read with Articles 16–18 of the Convention.

Article 1, which effectively provides that the contracting parties shall observe the provisions and give citizens the benefit of them, was felt to have been satisfied by enacting the Human Rights Act and therefore including that Article was an unnecessary duplication. Article 13 provides in effect that states should make available to citizens an effective range of remedies. The view taken here was that, following reforms of the civil process, Article 13 was satisfied and that again its inclusion would lead to unnecessary duplication. The Convention allows for individual states to enter reservations from the effect of particular articles of derogations form the provisions of the Convention for particular purposes. The British government has entered a reservation with regard to part of Article 2 of the First Protocol, restricting the right of parental choice with regard to education in accordance with their religious or philosophical beliefs. The UK only respects this in so far as it is compatible with the provision of efficient instruction and training and the avoidance of unreasonable public expenditure. There is also a general derogation with regard to terrorism, which was secured in the 1970s when the issue of terrorism emanating from Ireland was a major concern.

thinking point

If the UK is committed to the promotion of human rights, should it simply have adopted all the European Convention with no omissions, reservations or derogations?

Examples from the Articles that have been incorporated into English law are considered below (They are considered more fully in Howard Davis, *Human Rights Law* (Oxford University Press, 2009)). Most are structured in a similar way. Article 8 will serve as an example.

statute

Human Rights Act 1998, Article 8

1. Everyone has the right to respect for his private and family life, his home and his correspondence.
2. There shall be no interference by a public authority with the exercise of this right except such as is in accordance with the law and is necessary in a democratic society in the interests of national security, public safety or the economic well-being of the country, for the prevention of disorder or crime, for the protection of health or morals, or for the protection of the rights and freedoms of others.

It will be immediately apparent that the right that is stated with apparent clarity in Article 8(1) is then qualified by Article 8(2). This structure is common to many of the incorporated Articles of the Convention: a right is stated and then subjected to qualifications, setting out circumstances in which the state can limit, or even curtail, that right. Such circumstances are commonly stated to require, first, that any such limitation must be brought about by law, rather than by any other means. Secondly, such limitations must be on the stated grounds—in this particular instance, national security, public safety, economic well-being of the country, prevention of disorder or crime, protection of health or morals or for the protection of the rights and freedoms of others—which represents a formidable list both in breadth and scope whereby law makers can reduce the protection apparently guaranteed in Article 8(1). Some restriction on this power is, however, provided by the further requirement that such limitations must be necessary in a democratic society: the key word here is necessary. It means that the state will have to justify the interference with the right, rather than requiring the individual to argue that the interference is excessive, an important change of emphasis from the position prior to the Human Rights Act as summarized above. Thirdly, any such limitations must be effected by law, a requirement that upholds the idea of the rule of law.

7.3 The courts

7.3.1 The duty under s.3

As we have seen the courts have their own duty under s.6 to uphold the Convention rights. Additionally, they have specific powers and duties placed on them by other parts of the Human Rights Act. In particular, ss.2, 3 and 4 need to be read together to see what courts are required to do when faced with an issue of interpretation of laws. Their duty under s.6 also requires them to uphold the Convention rights when considering whether laws themselves are compatible or how laws have been used by the executive. The primary duty placed on a court faced with an issue of the interpretation of rules of law is found in s.3(1), which provides the following:

statute

Human Rights Act 1998, s.3 (1)

So far as it is possible to do so, primary legislation and subordinate legislation must be read and given effect in a way which is compatible with the Convention rights.

An early consideration of the implications of s.3 came in *R v A* [2002] 1 AC 45.

case close-up

R v A [2002] 1 AC 45

The defendant had been charged with rape and sought to bring evidence of his previous consensual sexual relationship with the complainant as evidence to support his contention that the sexual relations that occurred on the occasion in question were with the complainant's consent. He argued that the effect of s.41 Youth Justice and Criminal Evidence Act 1999, which excluded such evidence in all but a limited set of circumstances, operated to deny him a fair trial as required by Article 6 of the European Convention on Human Rights.

The question for the House of Lords was whether s.41 of the Youth Justice and Criminal Evidence Act 1999 could be **read down** so as to comply with Article 6 in accordance with the duty imposed by s.3 of the Human Rights Act 1998. It held that s.41 should be read so that the test of whether such evidence was admissible should depend on whether it was so relevant to the issue of consent that it would involve a denial of a fair trial to exclude it. In reaching this conclusion, the House of Lords considered the effect of s.41 on the complainant, and, recognizing that it was designed to offer protection to the complainant, this had to be balanced against the possible prejudice to a fair trial.

read down

where a statutory provision has a range of possible meanings, a court must, in pursuance of its duty under s.3, give it a meaning that is compatible with the Convention: so where a court reads down a provision it is giving it the meaning that complies with the Convention right.

Members of the House of Lords considered the effect of s.3 and were clear that it represented a departure from the previous rules of statutory interpretation. Lord Hope of Craighead put the matter starkly (at p.87):

The rule of construction which section 3 lays down is quite unlike any previous rule of statutory interpretation. There is no need to identify any ambiguity or absurdity. Compatibility with the Convention rights is the sole guiding principle.

Lord Steyn was equally emphatic (at p.68):

It is a general principle of the interpretation of legal instruments that the text is the primary source of interpretation: other sources are subordinated to it ... Section 3 qualifies this general principle because it requires a court to find an interpretation compatible with Convention rights if it is possible to do so.

Both judges were clear (Lord Steyn at p.68; Lord Hope at p.87) that s.3 applied to all cases, even to those where there was no ambiguity to be resolved. All legislation needs now to be interpreted so as to be compatible, and where a range of meanings is possible, courts will need to adopt the one that is compatible with the Convention rights. The words 'so far as it is possible to do so' allow the courts to stretch the meanings of words to try to find a meaning that will enable compatibility with the Convention to be achieved. As Lord Steyn observed (*ibid.*), this may involve the adoption of an interpretation which linguistically may appear strained.

However, whilst the courts are given considerable scope to explore in an expansive way the possible range of meanings of words used in a statute or statutory instrument in order to satisfy the requirements of s.3, there are limits within which the courts must remain. They cannot rewrite the Act. The duty is one of interpretation of what Parliament has set down rather than rewriting what they think Parliament should have said or adding requirements that Parliament has not laid down.

thinking point
What is the difference between interpretation and rewriting?

This is illustrated by *Re S* [2002] 2 AC 291, where the House of Lords held that the Court of Appeal had gone beyond the permissible scope of interpretation and strayed into the impermissible realms of redrafting.

case close-up

Re S [2002] 2 AC 291

The case concerned a care order made under the Children Act 1989. The Court of Appeal sought to supervise the operation of the order to safeguard the rights of the child to whom it related by inserting a number of what it referred to as starred stages, by which time certain things had to be done. They envisaged that if the order was not administered in accordance with the court's requirements, then the matter would be brought back to the court which would take over supervision of the administration of the order. The House of Lords held that the Court of Appeal, in inserting the starred stages into the operation of the order had gone beyond its powers of interpretation under s.3 Human Rights Act and was adding requirements to the Act that had no statutory justification.

7.3.2 **The duty under s.2**

The European Court of Human Rights has emphasized that the interpretation of the Convention should produce results that give individuals protection that is real and effective rather than theoretical. Further, that the Convention should be regarded as a living instrument to be interpreted in the light of modern conditions which are not necessarily those pertaining at the time the Convention was drafted. Given that the European Court of Human Rights takes a more flexible approach to the notion of precedent, this means that decisions of the European Court may have to be reinterpreted as times change. The same is true of the courts in the UK, who must also seek to keep the interpretation of the

Convention rights relevant to changing conditions. The ability of the domestic courts to do this has been built into the framework surrounding the incorporation of the European Convention into English law by s.2.

When engaging in the interpretation of legislation in the context of s.3, a court must also observe the requirements of s.2. This obliges courts, when determining a question relating to Convention rights, to take into account a number of matters, the most important of which are the decisions of the European Court of Human Rights. This duty to take into account the decisions of the European Court of Human Rights imposed by s.2 also brings with it a duty to take account of doctrines developed by that court, which are also relevant to the interpretation of statutory provisions in the light of s.3. Three in particular may be identified:

• **Margin of appreciation**

• **Proportionality**

• **Judicial deference**

These are considered further below.

. . . .

margin of appreciation

a doctrine developed by the European Court of Human Rights which recognizes that certain matters may be decided by individual countries in the light of local conditions

proportionality

the idea that any interference with a Convention right must be no more than is necessary to achieve the legitimate objects of the state

judicial deference

this recognizes that some matters are so policy laden that they are best determined by the legislature or government rather than by the courts

. . . .

It will be noted that the duty is only one to 'take into account' rather than to follow unquestioningly. Further, s.2 only obliges a court to take such matters into account if in the opinion of the court they are relevant to the issue under consideration. The consequence of this is that a court need not follow the decisions of the European Court of Human Rights if the judge believes it would not be appropriate to do so.

thinking point

Should the English courts be bound to follow decisions of the European Court of Human Rights? What do you think might happen if the English courts took a different view from that of the European Court of Human Rights?

7.3.3 **Margin of appreciation**

The idea of margin of appreciation involves recognition by the European Court of Human Rights that some matters are more appropriately decided by states at national level rather than in an across-the-board way by the European Court. This has been particularly applied to areas involving considerations of religious observance or personal morality. It allows national courts and other bodies to take account of the needs and requirements of local conditions.

7.3.4 **Proportionality**

The second is the idea of proportionality. This holds that any interference with a Convention right should not be any greater than is necessary to achieve the state's legitimate objectives. It will always be a question of evaluation as to whether a particular law or exercise of a legal power is disproportionate and this in turn will depend on the court's evaluation of the purposes of the provision in question and the objects to be achieved by it. Two contrasting cases illustrate the point. In *R(Daly) v Secretary of State for the Home Department* [2001] 2 AC 532 a policy of requiring all prisoners to remain outside their cells while they were searched was challenged on the basis that it breached their rights under Article 8, especially in relation to the right to privacy of correspondence. It was held that, whilst it might be appropriate to refuse to allow prisoners to remain in their cells in some instances, a universal policy to this effect was disproportionate and unlawful.

By contrast, in *Brown v Stott* [2003] 1 AC 681, a provision in an Act required a person who had been subject to a breath test on suspicion of driving whilst over the legal limit to answer a question as to whether they had been driving a particular vehicle. It was objected to as this could incriminate the individual in question and was disproportionate. It was held that, bearing in mind that the person had to have been shown to be in excess of the legal limit and that the object of the statute in question was to prevent loss of life and accidents through drunken driving, the provision was lawful and was not disproportionate to the attainment of these objectives.

The difficulties posed by trying to implement the requirement to act proportionately is illustrated by *A v Secretary of State for the Home Department* [2005] 2 AC 68.

thinking point

How could the Home Secretary have acted lawfully in these circumstances?

case close-up

A v Secretary of State for the Home Department **[2005] 2 AC 68**

Here, the policy of detaining suspected terrorists without trial was challenged. It was argued by the Home Secretary that as the provisions only applied to foreign nationals they were proportionate. However, it was held that even this restriction was disproportionate, as it was not necessary to include all foreign nationals. Further, by limiting the provisions to foreign nationals the Home Secretary's actions were also discriminatory, contrary to Article 14 of the Convention, as they discriminated against individuals on grounds of nationality. The case illustrates that where public authorities seek to act proportionately by limiting the individuals to whom a particular prohibition or provision applies, the ground they choose to effect that limitation needs to be carefully chosen so as to avoid falling foul of Article 14.

7.3.5 **Judicial deference**

A third doctrine developed by the European Court and adopted by the English courts is that of judicial deference. This essentially involves recognition by the judges that certain matters raise considerations that the court is not able to consider or evaluate and, indeed, which are better considered by Parliament or the executive. This is, in part, driven by considerations relating to the separation of powers, whereby the courts recognize their relationship with the other organs of government and the limits this imposes.

An example is provided by *Bellinger v Bellinger* [2003] 2 AC 467. Under s.10 Matrimonial Causes Act 1973, the parties to a marriage must be respectively male and female. The parties were a male and a male female transsexual who argued that, as English law determines a person's gender at birth, the law was in breach of the couple's Article 12 rights. The House of Lords held that the relevant provisions in the Matrimonial Causes Act were incompatible with the couple's rights. However, the question of whether changes of gender should be recognized for this purpose or whether transsexuals should be regarded according to the gender they were currently rather than the gender they were at birth were issues raising wide-ranging questions that were more appropriately considered by Parliament which would have access to a wider range of information about the issues raised. Parliament ultimately changed the law in the Gender Recognition Act 2004.

thinking point

What other kinds of issue do you think are more appropriate to be considered by Parliament rather than the courts?

7.3.6 **Declaration of Incompatibility**

If, having gone through the process required under ss.2 and 3, a court cannot reach an interpretation of a provision that accords with the Convention rights, then s.4 allows a Declaration of Incompatibility to be made. Before doing so, s.5 gives the Crown a right to be joined to the proceedings and to make submissions. If, however, the court is satisfied that the provision is incompatible it may make a declaration to that effect. This is entirely at the discretion of the court and, given the latitude given to the courts under s.3, and in the light of the comments made about the application of s.3 in *R v A* (above), it is unlikely that Declarations of Incompatibility will be frequently issued.

However, courts may be forced into the position that there is no possible interpretation of a statutory provision that is compatible with the Convention rights and that a Declaration of Incompatibility should be issued. For example, parts of the Mental Health Act 1983 have been found to be incompatible. In *R(H) v London North and East Region Mental Health Tribunal* [2002] QB 1, provisions in ss.72 and 73 of the Mental Health Act were held to be incompatible with Article 5 (the right to liberty) on the ground that they put the burden of proof on a patient seeking discharge from detention in hospital to show why he should be discharged rather than putting the onus on the hospital to show why he should continue to be detained. As the court was unable to stretch the meaning of ss.72 and 73 to achieve this result, it made a Declaration of Incompatibility. Further examples of Declarations of Incompatibility are provided by the cases of *Bellinger v Bellinger* and *A v Secretary of State for the Home Department* discussed earlier.

Where a court does issue a Declaration of Incompatibility, the law in question remains valid and in force unless and until it is changed. This preserves parliamentary sovereignty by giving the power of altering incompatible legislation to Parliament rather than to the courts. This is potentially given to the government rather than Parliament by virtue of s.10 which provides a fast track procedure for altering primary legislation by means of a statutory instrument which is not subject to the same procedural safeguards as an amending bill would be. It has the advantage, however, of speeding up the process of amending legislation found to be incompatible, a matter of practical significance to those affected by it. This process was used in the aftermath of *R(H) v London North and East Region Mental Health Tribunal*, discussed above, when the Mental Health Act 1983 (Remedial) Order 2001 (SI 2001/3712) was passed to effect the necessary amendment.

thinking point
Would it be easier and less protracted simply to let the courts change legislation?

Declarations of Incompatibility can only be made by the higher courts; that is, by the House of Lords, Court of Appeal or High Court. Courts below these, such as the county court and magistrates' courts, are not allowed to make a declaration under s.4. All they can do is to indicate their view that provisions are incompatible. However, they must follow the legislation rather than the Convention, though it might be anticipated that this would form a ground for an appeal.

In order to prevent incompatible legislation being passed in the future, s.19 provides that a Minister or sponsor of a bill should make a statement, during the passage of a bill through Parliament to the effect that the provisions of the bill in question are compatible with the Convention rights. This is not, however, binding on a court which may still find in subsequent proceedings that notwithstanding the statement by the Minister or sponsor, particular provisions are incompatible.

(7.4) **Proceedings under the Human Rights Act**

Perhaps surprisingly, enforcement of the Human Rights Act requires action by individuals. No formal enforcement mechanism was built into the Act, despite calls for a Human Rights Commission, or something similar, with powers of enforcement. This has been partially remedied by the creation, under s.9 of the Equality Act 2006, of a Commission for Equality and Human Rights, which came into effect in 2007. This will combine the various commissions under the antidiscrimination legislation and add an explicit human

thinking point
Should enforcement of the Human Rights Act be left largely to individuals?

rights dimension to its activities. The Commission, like those under the antidiscrimination legislation, will not be a body charged with enforcing the law: that will remain a matter of individual activity. It will, however, have a role in educating and disseminating information to promote awareness and understanding of the importance of human rights and encouraging compliance by public authorities.

7.4.1 **Victims**

The position therefore remains that, under s.7 Human Rights Act, proceedings against public authorities alleging violations of the Convention rights may only be brought by a victim, a term which is explained in s.7(7) to mean a person who would be regarded as a victim for the purpose of Article 34 of the Convention. This does not define the word 'victim' but does indicate that the European Court of Human Rights can receive applications from any person, non-governmental organization or group of individuals claiming to be a victim of a violation of a Convention right by a member state. This may seem unduly onerous, particularly for disadvantaged individuals who may have experienced violations of Convention rights under legislation dealing with, say, health (physical or mental) or social care, welfare, etc. and links to the point made earlier that enforcement of the Human rights Act will be left largely to individuals.

7.4.2 **Time limits**

Proceedings must be brought within one year, beginning with the date on which the act complained of took place, which is quite a stringent limit when compared with other forms of legal action. However, as with judicial review proceedings, the wider public interest requires that the matter needs to be resolved swiftly to enable public authorities to make necessary adjustments as soon as it becomes apparent that they are acting unlawfully. In any event, s.7(5) allows for an extension of the time limit if the court considers it to be equitable in all the circumstances. If a person is out of time for a claim under the Human Rights Act, a non-Human Rights Act claim will still require the court to uphold the Convention rights by virtue of its duty under s.6.

7.4.3 **Remedies**

If the claimant is successful, s.8 gives a court the power to grant such relief or remedy or to make such order within its powers as it considers just and appropriate. This leaves the court with considerable discretion to do justice in individual cases as well as having the flexibility to choose from the range of remedies available to it. However, it is a defence for a public authority to show that it had to act in a way that is incompatible with the Convention rights because it was required to do so by an Act of Parliament.

The defence is essentially one of parliamentary compulsion. Here the authority must be forced to this conclusion in order to rely on the defence: if there is, for example, a choice between competing interpretations of the provision(s) in question, then the pubic authority must choose the interpretation that is compatible.

7.5 The Convention rights

The rights appear in Schedule 1 to the Human Rights Act 1998. They are largely drafted in the same way, as indicated earlier. The right is stated but is then followed by a series of grounds on which that right might be limited, together with a statement that restrictions must be 'prescribed by law' and be 'necessary in a democratic society'. The general idea is that any restrictions on the right should not be excessive and it will be for the state to justify any restrictions it imposes. Two issues not dealt with directly in the Convention itself are whether there is any hierarchy of rights and how conflicts between rights are to be resolved. As to the first of these, the right to life in Article 2 is clearly the most fundamental, but after that it becomes less easy to evaluate one right against another in terms of importance, and this is an exercise that the European Court of Human Rights has not pursued.

7.5.1 Conflicts of rights

In terms of resolving conflicts between rights, the Human Rights Act itself seeks to provide some limited guidance. Under s.12, when dealing with matters involving freedom of expression, courts are directed to have 'particular regard to the importance of the Convention right to freedom of expression'. Further, where the proceedings relate to material which appears or is claimed to be journalistic, literary or artistic material, courts must also have particular regard to the extent to which the material is in the public domain and the public interest in publication, but considering also any privacy code. This provision has obvious relevance to issues where the right to free expression in Article 10 comes into conflict with the right to privacy under Article 8.

The importance of Article 9 is emphasized in s.13, which provides that court should have particular regard to the importance of exercise by members of religious organizations of the right to freedom of thought, conscience and religion. Other than these two provisions, courts have to reach their own decisions between competing rights.

cross reference
See Schedule 1 of the Human Rights Act 1998 in Appendix X, p.297.

7.5.2 The rights themselves

The rights may be briefly identified, though relevant Articles are discussed further in the context of the areas to which they relate in other chapters. The first three rights in

Schedule 1 are fundamental:

Article 2: the right to life;

Article 3: the prohibition on torture and inhuman or degrading treatment; and

Article 4: the prohibition on slavery and forced labour.

Article 5 deals with the right to individual liberty, and protects personal autonomy and security: it has a particular relevance to aspects of the criminal justice system and police powers, but also applies to other forms of detention such as that under the Mental Health Act 1983.

The right to a fair trial is contained in **Article 6**, which also safeguards the presumption of innocence in criminal proceedings as well as securing certain minimum rights in connection with criminal proceedings.

Further provision in relation to the criminal law is made in **Article 7** which outlaws any form of retrospective criminal law.

Art 8 provides for the rights to respect for privacy, family life and the home together with protection for correspondence, which impact on matters such as publication of individual information, entry to premises and the breaking up of families through the criminal justice or social care systems.

Article 9 protects the right to freedom of thought, religion and conscience, including the right to exercise religious observance.

Article 10 is the important right to free expression which is expressed as including the right to receive and impart information.

Article 11 provides for the rights of free assembly and association, particularly securing the right to establish trade unions.

The right to marry is secured by **Article 12**.

Article 14 prohibits discrimination on a variety of grounds, though it should be noted that this is not a free-standing right to protection from discrimination, but refers to a prohibition on discrimination in the enjoyment of the rights under the Convention.

Articles 16–18 set out to clarify and emphasize certain features of the preceding rights. **Article 16** provides that Articles 10, 11 and 12 cannot be used to prevent states from restricting the political activity of aliens. **Article 17** seeks to prevent any reductions in the rights set out in the Convention other than as permitted under the Convention, whilst **Article 18** limits the restriction of Convention rights to the purposes specified.

The First Protocol secures the right to the enjoyment of property (**Article 1**) and education (**Article 2**). The right to education includes the right of parents to ensure that it is in conformity with their religious or philosophical convictions. The UK has entered a reservation with regard to this right, accepting this only insofar as it is compatible with the provision of efficient instruction and training and the avoidance of unreasonable public expenditure. **Article 3** provides for the right to free elections, including a stipulation that this must be by secret ballot. **The Sixth Protocol** provides for the abolition of the death penalty though does allow the death penalty to be used in times of war.

thinking point

Are the rights identified in Schedule 1 all that are needed in a modern democratic society? Are there any rights you can think of that should be included but are not?

7.5.3 **Protection of rights**

The way in which the courts approach the interpretation of the legislation will be critical to the way in which individual rights are recognized and protected. Now that there is a definite starting point for the consideration of individual rights, the argument will not be, as it was under the traditional common law system, whether a particular right exists. Although it is theoretically possible for the rights guaranteed under the Human Rights Act to be removed wholesale, it would be unlikely to occur without replacement: if a future government were to seek to repeal the Human Rights Act or parts of it, it would be politically difficult to secure support for such a move unless the existing protections were to be replaced with something comparable. The Conservative Party has suggested that it will repeal the Human Rights Act but proposes to replace it with a British Bill of Rights.

In any event, attacks on human rights are rarely full frontal. This is graphically described in Lord Lane's memorable phrase, 'Oppression does not stand on the doorstep with a toothbrush moustache and a swastika armband. It creeps up insidiously; it creeps up step by step; and all of a sudden the unfortunate citizen realises that it has gone.' (Hansard 7 April 1989 col. 1331)

In dealing with creeping encroachments on individual rights, the courts are often confronted with test cases involving unpopular causes or individuals. In a characteristically robust judgment, Scrutton LJ, in *R v Secretary of State for Home Affairs ex p O'Brien* [1923] 2 KB 361 at 382, a case concerning a member of the Irish Republican Army whom the government wanted to intern and then deport to Dublin, recognized the significance of this phenomenon:

> This appeal raises questions of great importance regarding the liberty of the subject, a matter on which English law is anxiously careful, and which English judges are keen to uphold … This care is not to be exercised less vigilantly, because the subject whose liberty is in question may not

be particularly meritorious. It is indeed one test of belief in principles if you apply them to cases with which you have no sympathy at all. You really believe in freedom of speech, if you are willing to allow it to men whose opinions seem to you wrong and even dangerous; and the subject is entitled only to be deprived of his liberty by due process of law, although that due process if taken will probably send him to prison. A man undoubtedly guilty of murder must yet be released if due forms of law have not been followed in his conviction. It is quite possible, even probable, that the subject in this case is guilty of high treason; he is still entitled only to be deprived of his liberty by a due process of law.

More recently, cases involving terrorist suspects, such as *A v Secretary of State for the Home Department*, discussed above, have provided an example of the same phenomenon, with the courts having to decide between the competing claims of state and individual.

The Human Rights Act has already had a considerable impact on the legal regime in the UK. It is still too early to provide a measured assessment of its effects, not only on the substantive areas of law that is relates to but also in terms of the relationship between the courts, the government and Parliament.

? Questions

If you answer the following questions, you will have appreciated the main issues raised in this chapter. Check your answers against the notes provided at the back of the book.

1   Why was the Human Rights Act 1998 passed?

2   How has the Human Rights Act incorporated the European Convention on Human Rights into English law?

3   Which rights have been incorporated into English Law and in what circumstances can they be limited?

4   What impact might the Human Rights Act have on public authorities and the courts?

Further reading

A.W. Bradley and K.D. Ewing, *Constitutional and Administrative Law* (Pearson Longman, 14th ed., 2007) ch.19
This gives you a more detailed account of the issues discussed here.

Lord Steyn, '2000–2005: Laying the Foundations of Human Rights Law in the United Kingdom' [2005] EHRLR 349
This gives you a useful survey of the first five years of the Human Rights Act by one of the more liberal judges in the House of Lords

Michael Allen and Brian Thompson, *Cases and Materials on Constitutional and Administrative Law* (Oxford University Press, 9th ed., 2008) ch.9
This provides you with a selection of primary source material together with commentary.

Individual freedom and police powers

Learning Objectives

While reading this chapter you should aim to understand:

- which human rights are protected;
- what limitations are permissible on those rights;
- what powers the police have to interfere with individual freedom; and
- whether an appropriate balance has been achieved between giving the police enough power to do their job and giving individuals sufficient safeguards to uphold their human rights and prevent abuses of power.

Introduction

One of the key areas where the state and the individual interact is through the actions of the police. Individuals may approach the police for help in the detection of crime, or the police may initiate contact with an individual, perhaps where that person is suspected of committing a criminal offence. Creating the right balance between preserving individual freedom and giving the police adequate powers to carry out their functions effectively has been a constant feature in debates on police powers, and is not easily resolved, as opinions vary widely on where that balance properly lies.

A selection of police powers is examined here: powers of stop and search, arrest, entry and search of premises, seizure of items that might be used as evidence, and the more general question of the admissibility of illegally obtained evidence are considered. Finally, we identify the remedies available for unlawful police action. The use of police powers in relation to terrorism raises particular questions going beyond the scope of this chapter, which focuses on the role of the police in the investigation of crime generally. The legal response to terrorism is considered in Howard Davis *Human Rights Law* (Oxford University Press, 2009) ch.23.

 ## **Principles and rights**

A number of Articles in the European Convention on Human Rights have potential relevance to the exercise of police powers:

- Article 3, the prohibition of torture and inhuman or degrading treatment could impact on ways in which the police treat suspects, particularly in the context of questioning, search of the person or premises, and detention.

- Article 5, the right to liberty and security of the person, has obvious relevance to powers of arrest, search and detention.

- Article 6, the right to a fair trial, has implications for the gathering of evidence during an investigation and its admissibility at trial; the presumption of innocence, laid down in Article 6.2, is at the heart of the criminal justice system.

- Article 8, the right to respect for privacy, family life, home and correspondence could be relevant to the question of powers of entry to premises, to the gathering of evidence and to situations where families are separated where a person is taken into police custody.

- Article 1 of the First Protocol, which guarantees the right to enjoyment of property and possessions, may again be relevant in respect of entry to premises by police officers and seizure of items as evidence.

Most of these will impact on the way in which police powers are exercised rather than on the question of whether the powers themselves are consistent with the convention rights.

Even before the Human Rights Act, English law had recognized that interference with the autonomy of an individual or the integrity of their property was only possible in two situations:

- where the individual consents to the activity in question; and

- where the state, in this context, in the form of the police, has some legal justification for acting in the particular way.

These principles have long formed part of English law, and find a clear and powerful statement in early cases such as *Entick v Carrington* 1765 19 St Tr.1029; 2 Wils 275; 95 ER 807.

---

case close-up

Entick v Carrington 1765 19 St Tr.1029; 2 Wils 275; 95 ER 807

Here, state officials entered the plaintiff's house, without his permission, and conducted a search. When challenged, in an action for trespass, it was argued that the actions of the officials were justified in law because they had a warrant from the Home Secretary authorizing them to search for seditious material. This justification was rejected: the Home Secretary had no power to issue such a warrant. Secondly, it was argued that the actions were justified on the ground of state necessity. The court rejected this argument also. No such justification was known to the law. It was held therefore that the actions of the state were unlawful and that judgment would be entered for the plaintiff. In a robust judgment, Lord Camden CJ said:

> By the laws of England, every invasion of private property ... is a trespass. No man can set his foot upon my ground without my licence, but he is liable to an action, though the damage be nothing . . . If he admits the fact, he is bound to shew by way of justification that some positive law has empowered or excused him. The justification is submitted to the judges, who are to look into the books; and see if such a justification can be maintained by the text of the statute law or by the principles of common law. If no such excuse can be found or produced, the silence of the books is an authority against the defendant and the plaintiff must have judgment.

(This passage only appears in the State Trials version of the report from which an extract appears in Michael Allen and Brian Thompson, *Cases and Materials on Constitutional and Administrative Law* (Oxford University Press, 9th ed., 2008) ch.4 at p.158.)

8.1.1 Emergence of the present regime

The current regime governing police powers and individual rights had its origins in the *Report of the Royal Commission on Criminal Procedure* (Cmnd. 8092; the Phillips Report) published in 1981. This put forward a large number of recommendations for improving the criminal process. Particularly relevant in the present context was the recommendation that police powers should be put on a statutory footing. This may sound surprising, but police powers, at the time that the Royal Commission was sitting, were largely governed by the common law. The courts can only consider issues and make rulings on cases which are brought before them: they have no power to develop the law otherwise. The law had consequently developed in a haphazard fashion on the basis of litigation that had come before the courts rather than on any overall scheme. Consequently, there were cases covering some issues but not others and there were gaps in the law. What was needed, the Phillips Committee recommended, was a systematic approach to reform of the law in this area to provide a coherent set of powers for the police. There should, however, be a proper balance between the powers given to the police and the provision of safeguards for suspects. This has remained a contentious issue, if not *the* contentious issue in this area: views on whether a 'proper' balance has been achieved differ according to individual views as to what is 'proper' in this context.

thinking point
Why is it felt to be desirable to separate investigation from the decision to prosecute?

A further recommendation was that there should be separation of the functions of investigation of crime and the decision whether or not to prosecute: under the regime operating at the time of the Royal Commission, the police did both. This was felt to be unsatisfactory. It was felt that there was a need for an objective view of the strength of the evidence and the policy factors that might affect the decision to prosecute which those investigating the offence could not bring. It was therefore proposed to create a new body to make decisions about whether or not to prosecute.

The government accepted many of the recommendations of the Royal Commission and those relevant in the present context were implemented in two stages. The Police and Criminal Evidence Act 1984, almost universally abbreviated to PACE, created a new regime for police powers and related matters. This was followed in 1985 by the Prosecution of Offences Act, which created the Crown Prosecution Service (CPS) which is now responsible for decisions relating to prosecutions. These Acts still form the basis of the current law, although they have been amended subsequently. Significant amendments have been made by a number of statutes, especially the Criminal Justice and Public Order Act 1994 and the Serious Organised Crime and Police Act 2005. The Human Rights Act 1998 has, of course, also affected this whole area of law and its operation.

167

REMINDER Remember that the Human Rights Act affects not only the law itself but the way in which the law is used.

8.2 The Police and Criminal Evidence Act 1984

The Police and Criminal Evidence Act is supplemented by Codes of Practice, which, as explained below, provide important guidance as to how the legislation should operate, and it is worth briefly identifying these, in general terms, at the outset: their more detailed application is considered as appropriate alongside the particular provisions to which they relate.

8.2.1 Codes of Practice

Under ss.60 and 66 of the Police and Criminal Evidence Act 1984, the Home Secretary is given power to make Codes of Practice, which provide an important supplement to the provisions of the Act. Whilst the Act sets out the powers, duties and rights of the police, suspects and others, the Codes explain how the powers should be used. The Codes do not have the force of law, so that a breach of one of the provisions of the Code does not amount to an illegal act. However, a police officer breaching a provision in the Code can be subject to disciplinary proceedings. Breach of the provisions of one of the Codes may also provide evidence to support a claim that the police have acted unlawfully. Six Codes have been issued and are regularly revised to reflect changes to the law: the latest amendments became effective on 1 February 2008. The Codes relate to:

- Stop and Search (Code A)
- Search of Premises and Seizure of Property (Code B)
- The Detention Treatment and Questioning of Suspects (Code C)
- Identification (Code D)
- Tape Recording of Interviews (Code E)
- Video Recording of Interviews (Code F)
- Arrest (Code G)
- Terrorist suspects (Code H)

A key principle underlying the exercise of powers under PACE is that, wherever possible, the police should seek voluntary cooperation from the public and only use coercive powers as a last resort, unless the circumstances are such that formal powers need to be used immediately. This accords, in principle at least, with notions of proportionality required by the human rights regime.

8.2.2 Stop and search

The general principles underlying the powers of the police to stop and search individuals without first making an arrest are those identified in *Entick v Carrington*: in the absence of consent or legal justification the police cannot stop a person in a public place, search that person or require that person to answer questions. This is illustrated by *Kenlin v Gardiner* [1967] 2 QB 510.

case close-up

Kenlin v Gardiner [1967] 2 QB 510

Here, two schoolboys were going house to house to remind members of a rugby team about an upcoming match. Police officers asked what they were doing, whereupon one of the boys ran away, but was grabbed by one of the officers, whereupon the boy kicked the officer. He was charged with assaulting a police officer in the execution of his duty. Clearly, a key question was whether the officer was acting in execution of his duty, or in other words doing something he was entitled in law to do. It was held that the boy had been entitled to refuse to answer questions as the officer had no legal power to require him to answer questions or to grab hold of him. The boy was therefore entitled to act in self defence. Thus, in the absence of consent or legal justification, any such action by the police will be unlawful.

The power of stop and search

There has never been a general power of stop and search. This remains true. The present power, contained in s.1 Police and Criminal Evidence Act 1984, only authorizes stop and search where the officer has reasonable grounds for suspecting that a person has stolen or prohibited objects. Prohibited objects fall into a number of categories:

1. offensive weapons:
   under the Prevention of Crime Act 1953, three categories of item constitute offensive weapons

   • those which are offensive in themselves, in the sense that they have no other purpose, such as swords, truncheons or flick knives;

   • those which have been adapted to cause injury such as a sock full of marbles or a potato studded with razor blades; and

   • those which are carried with the intention of being used offensively, which could cover a huge range of everyday items. What turns them into offensive weapons is that they are being carried with the intention of causing personal injury.

   This categorization has been adopted in a guidance note in Code A (A GN 22).

2. Bladed or sharply pointed objects (s.139 Criminal Justice Act 1988).

3. Articles made or adapted for use in burglary, theft, fraud or offences under s.12 Theft Act 1968 (taking motor vehicle without consent).

4. Fireworks prohibited under fireworks regulations (Fireworks Act 2003).

The power under s.1 exists in addition to other specific statutory rights of stop and search such as that contained in s.23 Misuse of Drugs Act 1971. The power is one that can only be exercised in public places: s.1 does not authorize entry to private premises. A police officer can only stop and search someone if he has reasonable grounds for suspicion. The suspicion must be formed by the officer in relation to the particular individual before him. However, there must be some objective basis giving rise to the suspicion. As both Code A (paras.2.2–2.5) and *Lodwick v Sanders* [1985] 1 WLR 382 make clear, this cannot be on the basis of stereotypical assumptions based on factors such as age, race, dress or similar factors. The use of powers under s.1 is on the basis of individualized decision making: the factors that give rise to the suspicion will depend on the circumstances of each case. The only exception is where certain groups are habitually known to carry weapons and can be identified by their common dress (Code A, para.2.6). This is an area that has attracted considerable controversy. As the *Report of*

thinking point
What might lead an officer to suspect that a person has stolen or prohibited objects about his/her person?

169

the *Stephen Lawrence Inquiry* (1999, Cm.4262; often known as the Macpherson Report after its chairman Sir William Macpherson of Cluny) indicates, a major issue with regard to the powers of stop and search has been the way in which those powers have been used. The Macpherson Report makes clear they have been disproportionately used with regard to young black males. The powers are so wide ranging that it is hardly surprising that the main issue has been the way they are used, for they give individual officers a very broad discretion.

Code A

What Code A in particular emphasizes is that a 'sixth sense' approach is not justified. There must be some evidence relating to the particular individual that gives rise to reasonable grounds for the individual officer concerned to suspect that he has about his person stolen or prohibited items. There is no power to stop or detain a person to find out whether there may be grounds for a search: the grounds must exist, or be reasonably thought to exist, at the time the officer stops the person (Code A, para.2.11). Nor is there any power to question in order to find out whether such grounds exist. However, once the person has been stopped, the officer may ask questions with a view to discovering whether a search is necessary: as Code A (para.2.9) indicates, the explanation put forward in response to the officer's question may satisfy the officer that a search is not necessary.

thinking point
Why do you think certain groups are more likely to be stopped and searched than others?

The power to stop and search is a coercive power. In keeping with the general tenor of the powers under Police and Criminal Evidence Act and their use, the power in s.1 does not affect the situation where an officer stops and searches an individual with that person's consent. However, to prevent abuse of this power, such actions must be recorded at the time (ss.2, 3 PACE; Code A paras.4.12–4.20). Recording requirements also apply to searches made under the formal powers in s.1, and a copy of the record must be given to the person searched (*ibid.*).

The Act (s.2) and Code A (paras.3.1–3.7) also provide guidance as to how the search is to be conducted. It should be carried out at or near the place where the person has been stopped. It must be carried out in such a way as to cause the minimum embarrassment. Given that any public search is going to cause embarrassment to the person who is subjected to it, this requirement simply reminds officers that they should act in such a way as to reduce the inevitable embarrassment as far as possible. The requirement that it should take no longer than is reasonably necessary reinforces this notion, as does the provision that it should not involve removal of clothing in public other than an outer coat, jacket or gloves. Further, wherever possible the search should be carried out with the cooperation of the person concerned, though reasonable force may, as with other powers under the Police and Criminal Evidence Act, be used where it is necessary. All of these requirements, whilst seeking to minimize the discomfort caused to the person who has been stopped and searched, also serve to remind officers that the rights of the individual, especially those under Article 5, can only be subject to a legally authorized and proportionate interference.

s.60 Criminal Justice and Public Order Act 1994

In addition to the specific powers under s.1 of Police and Criminal Evidence Act, there is a wide-ranging power under s.60 Criminal Justice and Public Order Act 1994 enabling a senior officer (that is, a person of the rank of inspector or above) to authorize the stopping and searching of persons and vehicles in a particular locality where he reasonably anticipates that incidents involving serious violence may take place and that persons may be carrying dangerous instruments or offensive weapons without good reason. Whilst the power contained in s.1 Police and Criminal Evidence Act is given to individual officers to exercise in an individualized way by forming judgements about people they encounter, this is a much more generalized provision, and the order made by the senior officer in effect removes the need for officers to make individual judgements, as they can stop and search anyone or any vehicle within the designated area. The order in effect supplies the reasonable grounds for suspicion and individual officers do not need to justify their actions with regard to individuals. It is thus a wide-ranging power, and, in recognition of this, only lasts for 24 hours.

8.2.3 **Arrest**

So far, we have been examining powers that can be exercised without making an arrest. **Arrest** is a significant act in the exercise of police powers because it triggers a number of ancillary powers of search (of both the person and premises) and detention. It also needs to be considered in the light of Article 5 of the European Convention on Human Rights, which permits the deprivation of liberty by means of a lawful arrest in order to bring a person before a competent authority on suspicion of having committed a criminal offence. However, as Code G emphasizes (Code G para.1.2) the power of arrest represents 'an obvious and significant interference with that right' and, as such, use of the power of arrest must be a proportionate and necessary response to the particular situation. The requirement of proportionality means that the officer should consider whether action short of arrest may be appropriate (see Code G para.1.3), and the current s.24 of the Police and Criminal Evidence Act (as substituted by s.110 of the Serious Organised Crime and Police Act 2005) makes clear, as will be seen, that a person may only be arrested where it is necessary to do so. If arrest is an excessive response, then this can be a ground for regarding it as unlawful.

. . . .

arrest

arrest occurs when one person deprives another person of his liberty and continues for as long as that deprivation of liberty continues

. . . .

A question of fact

Whether a person has been arrested is, first of all, a question of fact. As explained in *Lewis v Chief Constable of South Wales* [1991] 1 All ER 206 an arrest occurs when one person deprives another person of his liberty and continues for as long as that deprivation of liberty continues. Having established that an arrest has occurred, the issue that must then be considered is whether the arrest is lawful or not. As *Entick v Carrington* indicates, that lawful authority must be found in either statute or common law. Where an arrest cannot be justified by reference to some legal authority, it is unlawful and the person arrested has a remedy in tort for a trespass to the person, such as false imprisonment or assault and battery. Other possible outcomes of an unlawful arrest, and for unlawful police action generally, are considered more fully later. Further grounds for arguing that an arrest is unlawful may relate to the way in which it is carried out. As with other police powers under the Police and Criminal Evidence Act, reasonable force may be used in executing an arrest, and it will be a matter of judgement on individual facts whether or not the force used was reasonable in the circumstances.

Reason for arrest

Where a person is arrested, s.28 of the Police and Criminal Evidence Act requires that he must be told that he has in fact been arrested and also why he has been arrested (and see Code G paras.2.2, 3.3). The real reason for the arrest must be given—a person cannot be arrested for one thing and told he has been arrested for another. In order to make sense of the requirement that he must be told the reason for his arrest, the courts have said that the person arrested should be told the reason in non-technical language that he can understand. Whilst the merits of this approach are self evident, in that it is no use telling somebody something if the language used has no meaning for that person, the practical application of this principle will always be open to question by examining how individual officers have fulfilled this requirement with regard to individual arrestees. Thus, in *Taylor v Chief Constable of Thames Valley Police* [2004] 1 WLR 315, the Court of Appeal was prepared to accept that telling a ten year old that he had been arrested for violent disorder (a technical term describing the offence under s.2 Public Order Act 1986) was sufficient to satisfy the obligation imposed on the officer by s.28 Police and Criminal Evidence Act. This conclusion was by no means inevitable, but whether the reason given by the officer and the language used to describe it were adequate for the purposes of s.28 will be essentially a matter for the trial court, and so an appeal court will be reluctant to interfere with a finding at first instance.

Warrant

. . . .
warrant

a warrant is a document issued by a court authorizing the person to whom it is issued to do something
. . . .

Arrest may be with or without a **warrant**. There is a general power to issue arrest warrants under s.1 Magistrates Courts Act 1980, and specific powers exist under other legislation. Where a warrant is issued, the arresting officer must comply with its requirements. However, the vast majority of arrests are carried out without warrant.

Arrest without a warrant

There is a general power of arrest contained in ss.24 and 24A of the Police and Criminal Evidence Act and reinforced by Code G.

statute

Police and Criminal Evidence Act 1984, s.24(1)

…a **constable** may arrest without a warrant—

(a) anyone who is about to commit an offence;

(b) anyone who is in the act of committing an offence;

(c) anyone whom he has reasonable grounds for suspecting to be about to commit an offence;

(d) anyone whom he has reasonable grounds for suspecting to be committing an offence;

2. If a constable has reasonable grounds for suspecting that an offence has been committed he may arrest without warrant anyone whom he has reasonable grounds to suspect of being guilty of it.

3. If an offence has been committed, a constable may arrest without a warrant—

(a) anyone who is guilty of the offence;

(b) anyone whom he has reasonable grounds for suspecting to be guilty of it.

constable

the term 'constable' means any police officer, not just a person holding the rank of constable

The above provisions require the constable to make a judgement as to two particular matters. The first is with regard to the offence. Under s.24, the offence may have been committed, be in the process of being committed or be about to be committed. The first and last of these are the most difficult for the officer. As to the first, there must be evidence that the offence has in fact been committed in order for a constable to base his actions on this ground. As to the last, s.24(1) talks simply in terms of an offence about to be committed. There is no further explanation as to how imminent the commission of the offence must be, so it will be a matter of interpretation for the court on the facts of individual cases whether the degree of proximity is sufficient.

The second matter relates to the officer's perception that the particular individual he is arresting has committed, is committing or is about to commit an offence. This must be based on reasonable grounds. The two matters are interlinked, in that his suspicion about the first may be based on evidence relating to the second. So, for example, the fact that a person has blood on his hands might lead the officer to suspect, in the particular circumstances, that the person in question has committed an offence involving the shedding of blood by the victim.

However, the presence of one of the matters contained in s.24(1) is not of itself sufficient to justify the use of the power of arrest by the officer. The officer must believe that the arrest is necessary for one of the reasons listed in s.24(5).

statute

Police and Criminal Evidence Act 1984, s.24(5)

(a) to enable the name of the person in question to be ascertained (in the case where the constable does not know, and cannot readily ascertain, the person's name, or has reasonable grounds for doubting whether a name given by a person as his name or address is his real name);

(b) correspondingly as regards the person's address;

(c) to prevent the person in question—

    (i) causing physical injury to himself or any other person;

    (ii) suffering physical injury;

    (iii) causing loss of or damage to property;

    (iv) committing an offence against public decency . . . ;

    (v) causing an unlawful obstruction of the highway;

(d) to protect a child or other vulnerable person from the person in question;

(e) to allow the prompt and effective investigation of the offence or of the conduct of the person in question;

(f) to prevent any prosecution for the offence from being hindered by the disappearance of the person in question.

It will be apparent that the powers given to the officer are again dependent on the officer's perception of the situation. It is inevitable, as we have seen with regard to the powers of stop and search, that officers have a wide discretion in order to exercise their powers on an individualized basis by requiring them to assess the situation with which they are confronted rather than act in any pre-planned and/or generalized way. Thus, creating the framework for individualized decision making may appear desirable. Courts are, however, reluctant to interfere with the exercise of powers by police officers in these situations because the court, considering the matter in the cold light of day some months after the event, is in a very different position from that of the officer on the spot having to make an almost instantaneous decision as to whether or not to use his powers.

thinking point

Why do you think the courts are reluctant to interfere with decisions made by the police acting on the spot in the heat of the moment?

There is, in language which, as we have seen, is used in this context, a need to strike a proper balance between, on the one hand, giving the police the powers they need to do the job society expects of them and, on the other hand, to provide a sufficiently tight framework to protect suspects by reducing the risk of abuse of those powers. It is a difficult balance to achieve and opinions will legitimately differ as to whether the Police and Criminal Evidence Act (as amended) succeeds in this regard. Responses to this will be conditioned by the standpoint of the analyst.

It is one thing to define powers clearly, but, in an area where some discretion is inevitable, there is the ancillary question of whether the exercise of those powers is capable of challenge. The police, like any other individual or body, are governed by the rule of law. One aspect of this lies in ensuring that this is meaningful by making, in this particular instance, the police accountable for the way they exercise their powers.

'Citizen's arrest'

A further set of powers of arrest appear in s.24A(1). Only constables may exercise the power of arrest contained in s.24(1). The powers in s.24A(1) apply to any person, whether a constable or not, and provide the circumstances in which a so-called citizen's arrest can take place.

statute

Police and Criminal Evidence Act 1984, s.24A(1)

a person other than a constable may arrest without a warrant—
   (a) anyone who is in the act of committing an indictable offence;
   (b) anyone whom he has reasonable grounds for suspecting to be committing an indictable offence.
(2) Where an indictable offence has been committed, a person other than a constable may arrest without a warrant—
   (a) anyone who is guilty of the offence;
   (b) anyone whom he has reasonable grounds for suspecting to be guilty of it.

It will be immediately apparent that the list of circumstances is much shorter than that applicable to constables. First, the offences must be an indictable offence for the purpose of s.24A(1) whereas the power given to constables under s.24(1) applies to any offence. This immediately presents a very practical problem for any citizen thinking of making an arrest of being able to identify that the offence in question is an indictable offence. This is not knowledge that many citizens are likely to have and thus there is the potential for citizens, acting from the best of motives, to fall foul of the law by making a wrongful arrest. This may be because they do not know the law, as, for example, where the offence for which they exercise the power of arrest is not an indictable offence. Or it may be a mistake of fact, for example, where an offence has not been committed. Further restrictions appear in the requirement that the offence must in fact have been committed or be in the process of being committed before the power can be exercised. There is no power to arrest before the commission of the offence has begun. With regard to the person arrested, there are parallels in that the person making the arrest must

thinking point

Why do you think constables are given wider powers of arrest than ordinary citizens?

either know or reasonably believe that the person he arrests is the person committing or having committed the offence.

As with the powers given to constables, there are further restrictions on the power to arrest. Under s.24A(3), a power of arrest under s.24A(1) and (2) (above) can only be exercised under the following circumstances.

statute

Police and Criminal Evidence Act 1984, s.24A(3)

(a) the person making the arrest has reasonable grounds for believing that for one of the reasons mentioned in subsection (4) it is necessary to arrest the person in question; and

(b) it appears to the person making the arrest that it is not reasonably practicable for a constable to make it instead.

(4) The reasons are to prevent the person in question—

(a) causing physical injury to himself or any other person;

(b) suffering physical injury;

(c) causing loss of or damage to property; or

(d) making off before a constable can assume responsibility for him.

Determining the lawfulness of an arrest

With regard to both forms of arrest described above, there are three components that need to be considered when determining the lawfulness of an arrest whether made by a constable or by an ordinary member of the public, namely that there are facts on which the decision to arrest is based; that these facts have led him to form a suspicion that the person in front of him has committed, is committing or is about to commit an offence (in other words, he must have formed a suspicion relating to both the offence and the individual); and that the suspicion must be based on reasonable grounds:

Facts

First, there is a need to ascertain the facts which form the objective basis—the reasonable grounds—for the execution of the power. It was emphasized in *Castorina v Chief Constable of Surrey* (1988) 138 NLJ (Reports) 180 that the court must look objectively at the information available to the officer.

Suspicion

Secondly, there is a need to consider the constable's evaluation of the available information which leads him to form the requisite suspicion. In *O'Hara v Chief Constable of the Royal Ulster Constabulary* [1997] AC 286, the House of Lords pointed out that, in forming the suspicion as to the offence or as to the possible involvement of the individual in it, the information leading to this suspicion could be drawn from a variety of sources, of which what the officer sees is only one.

Reasonable grounds

Thirdly, having formed a suspicion as to the offence and the person, the House of Lords continued in *O'Hara*, the officer's conduct in arresting the person then becomes subject to scrutiny by the court. In deciding whether the constable's conduct is lawful, the court will ask whether a reasonable person would regard the suspicion that the officer formed as a reasonable one. If it is, the arrest is lawful. If not, it is unlawful and, again, the person wrongly arrested has a remedy in, say, tort.

8.2.4 **Breach of the peace**

cross reference
Breach of the peace *is more fully considered in Chapter 9.*

breach of peace

'...there is a breach of the peace whenever harm is actually done or is likely to be done to a person or in his presence to his property' (Watkins LJ in *R v Howell* [1982] QB 416 at 427)

In addition to the power to arrest without warrant contained in ss.24 and 24A, there remains at common law the power to arrest without warrant in connection with a breach of the peace. The position was summarized by Lord Bingham in *R(Laporte) v Chief Constable of Gloucestershire* [2007] 2 WLR 46 at para. [29]:

> Every constable, and also every citizen, enjoys the power and is subject to a duty to seek to prevent, by arrest or other action short of arrest, any breach of the peace occurring in his presence, or any breach of the peace which (having occurred) is likely to be renewed, or any breach of the peace which is about to occur.

cross reference
We will examine more specific applications in Chapter 9.

The concept of breach of the peace is an anomaly in English law. Breach of the peace is not a criminal offence (see *Williamson v Chief Constable of the West Midlands Police* [2004] 1 WLR 14), yet a power of arrest exists in relation to it. The powers available in connection with breach of the peace are essentially preventive.

The courts have had to focus on two main questions. First, what constitutes a breach of the peace; and secondly, in what circumstances can an arrest lawfully be made. As to the first, the generally accepted definition is that provided by Watkins LJ in *R v Howell* [1982] QB 416 at 427:

> We are emboldened to say that there is a breach of the peace whenever harm is actually done or is likely to be done to a person or in his presence to his property.

The hallmark of a breach of the peace is thus violence or the threat of it. The first of these is self evidently easier to assess than the second which involves some form of speculation on the part of the officer as to future events. This leads to consideration of when an arrest might lawfully be made in connection with an actual or anticipated breach of the peace. Again, it is easier to deal with when a breach of the peace is occurring. The contentious issue here will be whether arrest is a necessary and proportionate response to the situation. With regard to the future, the courts have been trying to identify the point at which it becomes appropriate to exercise a power of arrest once the officer is satisfied that a breach of the peace is likely to occur. After much discussion, the House of Lords in *R(Laporte) v Chief Constable of Gloucestershire* has concluded that the anticipated breach of the peace must be imminent. The court must further be satisfied that the officer's view that a breach of the peace was imminent was one based on reasonable grounds, both as to the occurrence of the breach of the peace and its imminence. Unless all these elements are present, the arrest will be unlawful.

8.2.5 **Detention and questioning**

Once a person has been arrested, he must be taken to a designated police station as soon as practicable. The principles on which he may be detained are the same as for those who have attended a police station voluntarily. A person may not be detained other than by consent or with legal justification. In the absence of consent or legal justification, the detention is unlawful and the person wrongfully detained has a remedy in tort for false imprisonment. A person may use the ancient action of **habeas corpus** to challenge the legality of his detention. This requires the person detaining him to justify to a court the detention. If no such justification can be found, the court will order the person to be released.

....

habeas corpus

this is a form of proceedings directed to a person who is detaining another requiring him to produce that other person before a court and to show some legal justification for the detention

....

One phrase often used (and often misunderstood) in this context is where somebody is said to be 'helping the police with their inquiries' at the police station. In *R v Lemsatef* [1977] WLR 712 Lawton LJ said clearly that in law there was no right to detain a person for the purpose of getting help with inquiries. The position in law is thus that any person who is at a police station voluntarily can leave at any time unless placed under arrest (see Code C para.3.21).

Given that a person has the right to personal freedom, guaranteed by Article 5 of the European Convention on Human Rights, and the general principle of proportionality, it follows that any detention of an individual must be for the shortest period necessary to satisfy the purpose for which that person is detained. This principle finds expression in s.34 of the Police and Criminal Evidence Act and Code C (para.1.1), which together state that a person in custody must be dealt with expeditiously and released as soon as the need for detention ceases.

Custody officer

Where a person is detained at a police station, he becomes the responsibility of a custody officer. A custody officer must be a police officer of the rank of at least sergeant (s.36 PACE) or be a staff custody officer (ss.120, 121 Serious Organised Crime and Police Act 2005). This officer becomes responsible for, amongst other things, the following:

- ensuring that the provisions of the Police and Criminal Evidence Act and the Codes of Practice are complied with (s.39 PACE);
- deciding whether to charge, detain for questioning or release the individual (s.37 PACE);
- advising him of his right to contact a friend or relative (s.56 PACE; Code C para. 3.1);
- advising him of his right of access to a solicitor (s.58 PACE; Code C paras. 3.1, 6.1–6.17; Article 6(3)(c) European Convention on Human Rights);
- advising him of his rights under the Codes of Practice (Code C para. 3.1); and
- opening and maintaining a custody record (Code C paras.2.1A–2.7), which, apart from its general evidential value, is also significant in demonstrating that the individual's human rights have been respected during his detention.

'Detention clock'

The Police and Criminal Evidence Act limits the amount of time that a person can be detained, with what is sometimes referred to as the 'detention clock' identifying times during the period of detention when the detention must be reviewed and renewed, and setting out maximum periods of time during which a person can be detained. The safeguards become more stringent as time passes. The maximum period for which a person can be detained is 96 hours for an indictable offence and 24 hours for all other offences.

Figure 8.1
Detention clock

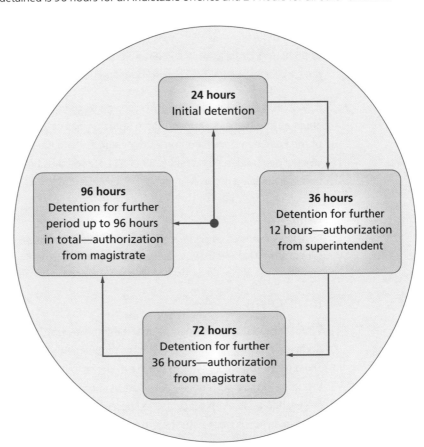

There is thus an initial period of detention for 24 hours for all offences (s.41 PACE). The purpose of detaining the person is in order to question him, which in turn informs the decision whether to charge the person, seek to detain him for further questioning, or release him without charge.

For indictable offences, the 96 hour period is broken up into a series of stages, each with its own procedural hurdles which the police must surmount if they wish to detain the suspect further. These hurdles become more stringent as time progresses. It must be remembered that this whole process operates against the background of Article 5 of the European Convention on Human Rights: the police are thus arguing for the removal, albeit temporary, of this freedom in the interests of the detection of crime, and it will be for the police to show why the suspect should be detained rather than for the suspect to show why he should be released.

After the initial 24 hour period, an officer of the rank of superintendent can authorize detention, in relation to an indictable offence, for a further 12 hours if this is considered necessary to secure or preserve evidence (s.42 PACE). The key word here is 'necessary'. Whilst it may be desirable for the police to detain the suspect or they may wish to do so, they are only able to do so where the superintendent is satisfied that it is necessary. To detain the suspect further, an application has to be made to a magistrate for a warrant of further detention (s.43 PACE). If granted, this authorizes detention for a further 36 hours.

The police may make a final application, again to a magistrate, for an extension of the warrant of further detention, which can only authorise detention for up to a maximum of 96 hours in total (s.44 PACE). After 96 hours from the initial detention have expired, the suspect must be either charged or released.

If, following investigation, the police decide to charge the suspect, a further decision arises as to whether to remand the suspect on bail or in custody. Under the influence of the European Convention on Human Rights, there is a presumption in favour of the suspect being released on **bail** (s.38 PACE). He will thus be released on bail unless it is necessary to keep him in custody.

. . . .

bail

This is where a person is released from police custody pending further stages in the criminal process. Courts can also decide whether to release a person on bail or detain him in custody following court hearings

. . . .

Interviews

Whilst the person is detained he may be interviewed. The procedure is governed by Codes C and E, the latter dealing with the requirements for tape recording of interviews. The object of the interview is to acquire evidence to assist in the decision whether or not to charge the suspect, and interviews must end when the police have obtained enough evidence to enable a prosecution to succeed, though may continue until that point is reached, in accordance with the provisions in the Police and Criminal Evidence Act on detention, outlined above, and on interviews. Interviews must take place under caution (Code C paras.10.1, 10.5, 10.8), and the caution must be renewed whenever there is a break in the interview. Suspects also have a right to legal advice and the presence of a legal adviser (Code C part 6), and where the suspect is a child or a vulnerable adult, to the presence of an appropriate adult (Code C paras.6.5A, 11.15–11.17). The role of the appropriate adult is not to act as a second legal adviser but rather to protect and support the suspect during the interview. The appropriate adult may be a family member or perhaps a social worker.

Confessions

....

confession

a statement made by a suspect in which he admits that he committed the offence in question

....

The police may hope that during the course of an interview, the suspect will confess to having committed the offence that they are investigating. A **confession** makes subsequent proceedings much simpler from the point of view of the prosecution as it does not have to gather evidence or rely on inferences being drawn from the available evidence. A confession also vindicates the decision to arrest the individual and completes the investigation, as it will be assumed that the suspect who has confessed will plead guilty when the matter comes to court. Historically, the temptation to persuade the suspect to confess has led to attempts from less scrupulous public officials to employ inducements, whether in the form of rewards or, in extreme cases, torture, to extract a confession. The legal framework surrounding confessions has thus emphasized that any confession, to be admissible as evidence, must have been freely given. This is an aspect of the right to a fair trial guaranteed by Article 6 of the European Convention on Human Rights.

181

Any inducements, whether positive or negative, will invalidate the confession as evidence. Thus, s.76 Police and Criminal Evidence Act provides that a confession must be excluded if it has been obtained by oppression or in circumstances which make it unreliable. Two aspects of this provision should be noted. First, that if there is anything that prevents the confession being regarded as reliable, then it *must* be excluded: there is no discretion. Secondly, that a confession may be regarded as unreliable where there is evidence of oppression or of some other form of inducement. In *R v Fulling* [1987] QB 426, it was held that the word 'oppression' has its ordinary everyday meaning to cover, in the court's description, exercises of power in a burdensome, harsh or wrongful manner, or unjust or cruel treatment of the suspect. Thus, under s.76, both 'sticks' and 'carrots' are covered.

thinking point
Why do you think the law places restrictions on the admissibility of confessions?

Admissibility of evidence other than confessions

It is worth mentioning the position with regard to the admissibility of evidence other than confessions. The general common law position is that illegally obtained evidence is generally admissible, though this has to be read in the light of Article 6 of the European Convention on Human Rights and s.78 Police and Criminal Evidence Act. Underlying s.78 is that notion that illegally obtained evidence may be admitted. However, s.78 gives the judge a direction to exclude evidence where it has been improperly obtained and its admission would have such an adverse effect on the fairness of the proceedings that the court ought not to admit it. In effect, the judge has to balance the value of the evidence to the case against the unfairness of the circumstances in which it was obtained. We will return to this later when considering the circumstances in which the police can remove items from premises they have entered.

8.2.6 **Entry, search and seizure**

Obtaining evidence from the individual suspect is one aspect of the investigative process. Another is to search premises for evidence and to take away items that may ultimately be produced in court. In order to conduct a search or seize items, the police will have to gain entry to the premises. Thus, we need to look at the legal framework governing these issues. The general principles underlying this area of law start with the European Convention on Human Rights, which guarantees the integrity of property (Article 1 Protocol 1) and the right to respect for privacy (Article 8). This has long been a principle recognized in English Law. The phrase 'an Englishman's home is his castle' was uttered by the courts many centuries ago (see, for example, *Semayne's Case* (1604) 5 Co Rep 91a; 77 ER 194).

The position in law is that a person may only enter the premises of another with the consent of the owner or occupier or with legal authority. We saw earlier how, in *Entick v Carrington*, the defendants sought to justify their entry to the plaintiff's premises on the grounds of a general warrant issued by the Home Secretary or alternatively on grounds of state interests. The court rejected both of those grounds as they had no basis in law, and awarded the plaintiff damages for trespass. These principles remain good law today.

Entry and search with consent

Where a person enters with the consent of the occupier, three particular issues arise.

- first, it must be clear that the occupier has freely given consent to the other person to enter the premises: any form of force or persuasion may vitiate the consent;

- secondly, the consent to enter may be general, allowing access to the whole of the premises, or it may be more restricted. This is often problematic in that occupiers do not always specify with precision which parts of the premises the visitor may enter; and

- thirdly, consent must continue for the whole of the time the person is on the premises in order for the person's presence on the premises to remain lawful. Consent may, however, be withdrawn at any time by the owner or occupier. Where this occurs, the visitor must leave the premises or show some legal justification entitling him to remain. In the absence of such legal justification, the visitor becomes a

thinking point
When you allow someone onto your premises, do you specify what parts of the premises your visitor may enter?

trespasser and the owner or occupier can use reasonable force to eject him from the premises.

Where this occurs, the matter may come to court as a charge of assaulting a police officer in the execution of his duty (s.89 Police Act 1996), in which case the court must determine whether the police officer was acting in execution of his duty. Two contrasting cases illustrate the point.

case close-up

Davis v Lisle [1936] 2 KB 434

Police officers entered a garage to enquire about a vehicle. The garage proprietor asked them to leave. The officers asserted that they had a right to remain on the premises in order to ask questions. The garage proprietor then assaulted one of the officers and was subsequently charged with assaulting a police officer in the execution of his duty. It was held that he was not guilty of this offence as the officers were not acting in execution of their duty, as there was no legal right to remain on premises in order to ask questions.

This may be contrasted with *Robson v Hallett* [1967] 2 QB 939.

case close-up

Robson v Hallett [1967] 2 QB 939

Here, police officers had been allowed to enter the defendant's house. They had then been asked to leave. They were making their way to the front door when they were assaulted by one of the occupants. It was held that an offence of assaulting a police officer in the execution of his duty was made out as the officers were leaving the premises and should be given a reasonable opportunity to do so before the occupier exercised the right to forcibly eject them.

Entry with consent does, of course, depend on permission to enter having been given by someone who has authority to do so. Further, as Code B (paras.5.1–5.4) makes clear, where the police are seeking to enter and search premises with consent they must make clear to the occupier their purposes in seeking entry. They must also not exceed the permission that is given to them to enter the premises. This is an area of potential uncertainty. When a person is given permission to enter premises, the occupier does not usually state the precise terms upon which the person may enter or the activities in which they may engage whilst on the premises. A degree of interpretation and inference may be needed if the matter is challenged in court. Similarly, where an occupier withdraws consent for a visitor to remain on the premises, this is rarely couched in terms that are legally precise, and again this requires a court to engage in inference and interpretation (see, for example, *Snook v Mannion* [1982] RTR 321).

thinking point

If you allowed someone into your home, what would you expect that permission to cover (if you have not specified the extent of the permission)? Would it include going into every room? Or looking in cupboards?

Where the police are unable to gain entry to premises with the consent of the owner or occupier, or it would be inappropriate or impracticable to do so, they may only enter with legal authority. Various statutory provisions authorise entry to premises for a variety of individuals exercising official functions. The present discussion is, however, limited to the position of the police. The police must comply with the particular provisions of the statute under which they enter premises. This may require a warrant or be without warrant.

Entry and search with a warrant

A warrant is a document giving legal authority for a particular activity. It also provides protection to the police against any legal action as long as they are acting within its terms. There is a general power to obtain a warrant in accordance with ss.8–16 of the Police and Criminal Evidence Act, considered below. There are also specific powers which enable the police to apply for a warrant: commonly used examples are s.26 Theft Act 1968 and s.23 Misuse of Drugs Act 1971.

Where a warrant authorizing entry and search of premises is sought under the Police and Criminal Evidence Act, an application must ordinarily be made to a magistrate. The application is made by the police without notifying the person whose premises it is intended to search, as clearly this would defeat the object of obtaining the warrant. It thus falls to the magistrate to scrutinize the police application carefully and ask the questions that would otherwise be asked by a representative opposing the application. Before issuing the warrant, s.8 of the Police and Criminal Evidence Act requires that the magistrate must be satisfied that the grounds under s.8 have been made out on the basis of the evidence presented by the police.

statute

Police and Criminal Evidence Act 1984, s.8

(1) If on an application made by a constable a justice of the peace is satisfied that there are reasonable grounds for believing—

(a) that an indictable offence has been committed; and

(b) that there is material on [the specified] premises . . . which is likely to be of substantial value (whether by itself or together with other material) to the investigation of the offence; and

(c) that the material is likely to be relevant evidence; and

(d) that it does not consist of items subject to legal privilege, excluded material or special procedure material;

The terms 'items subject to legal privilege', 'excluded material' and 'special procedure material' are explained in the box below. In addition to the requirements in s.8(1), there is a further series of conditions to the effect that the issue of a warrant is necessary in order to gain access to the premises.

Items subject to legal professional privilege

. . . .

The reference to items subject to legal privilege, excluded material and special procedure material in s.8 relates to categories of material to which different regimes apply. Under s.10, items subject to legal professional privilege are defined as communications between professional legal advisers and clients in connection with legal advice or legal proceedings. This will cover items such as letters from a solicitor to a client which gives legal advice or from a client to a solicitor requesting it. Such material is unobtainable under the Police and Criminal Evidence Act.

Excluded material

Excluded material is defined in s.11 as personal records acquired or created in the course of a trade, business, profession or other occupation and held in confidence; human tissue or tissue fluid taken for the purposes of diagnosis or medical treatment and held in confidence; or journalistic material held in confidence. The hallmark of such material is that it is material held in confidence.

Special procedure material

Special procedure material is defined in s.14 as material held in confidence other than excluded material; and journalistic material not held in confidence. There is no particular logical reason for the classification of particular types of material as excluded material or special procedure material; both are the result of pragmatic political decisions taken during the drafting and passage of the Police and Criminal Evidence Act.

Whilst items subject to legal professional privilege cannot be obtained under the Police and Criminal Evidence Act, by virtue of s.9, excluded material and special procedure material may be the subject of a warrant obtained from a circuit judge or district judge under the procedures set out in Schedule 1.

Returning to the situation of an application for a warrant to search for material not in one of these special categories, if the magistrate is satisfied of the matters set out in s.8 (listed above) then a warrant may be issued, specifying the name of the person who applied for it, the date of issue, the enactment under which it is issued, the premises to be searched and, so far as is practicable, the articles sought.

Execution of a search warrant

When it comes to executing the warrant, the Police and Criminal Evidence Act and Code B attach a number of requirements and guidelines.

The warrant must ordinarily be executed at a reasonable hour (s.16(4) PACE and Code B para.6.2). What constitutes a reasonable hour will depend on the individual circumstances and, like other guidelines in this area, need not be observed where it may, for example, lead to the object of the search being defeated.

On arriving at the premises, the officer should identify himself and produce the warrant (s.16(5) PACE). Again, this procedure need not be followed where it might lead to the object of the search being defeated. For example, if it was likely that, whilst the officers were knocking on the door and reading the warrant etc the goods for which they were about to search would be disposed of, then this would provide a reason for dispensing with this requirement. Equally, where observing the formalities would expose the officers to the danger of harm, then again the formalities need not be observed. Whether it was appropriate to dispense with formalities where violence was feared was considered in *R v Longman* [1988] 1 WLR 619, where the police used an imaginative, if perhaps devious, ploy to secure access to premises.

case close-up

R v Longman [1988] 1 WLR 619

In this case, the police feared that they would be assaulted when they arrived to execute a warrant to search for prohibited drugs. They devised a plan whereby an officer in disguise pretended to be delivering a bunch of flowers. While she knocked on the door, other officers were hiding nearby behind hedges and bushes. When the door was opened officers surged forward and entered the premises. It was held that this action was lawful.

The Court of Appeal said that a departure from the normal formalities may be appropriate, especially in drugs cases, to prevent the disposal of evidence or in cases where the officers feared that they would be in danger if they executed the warrant observing the normal procedural steps. In the last resort, reasonable force may be used to gain entry to the premises and indeed in the conduct of the search (Code B para.6.6 and s.117 PACE).

It seems also that reasonable force may be used against people as well as things.

case close-up

DPP v Meaden [2004] 1 WLR 945

The police had obtained a search warrant which they executed by searching one room initially and then confining the occupants of the premises to that room whilst they searched the rest of the property. It was held that the use of reasonable force sanctioned by s.117 extended to people as well as the premises and that therefore confining the occupants in that way was lawful.

The key issue is whether the force used is reasonable. What degree of force is reasonable will again depend on the particular circumstances in question.

Extent of the search

An important requirement is that the police may only enter and search to the extent permitted by the warrant (s.16(8) PACE and Code B para.6.9). This means that the parts of the premises entered and searched, and the way in which that search is conducted, must bear a relationship to the items sought. Thus, a different type of search will be appropriate for small items capable of being concealed in drawers or under floorboards from a search for a large and indivisible object. This restriction may not be as stringent as it at first appears. A certain degree of creativity may be permissible: a large object may be dismantled into its component parts and thus reduced to a number of smaller items, rendering a more extensive search reasonable than would be the case if it were in its original undivided form. A large bronze sculpture, for example, can be melted down into smaller ingots and hidden in small spaces. The limitation is significant, however, in that a search that is excessive when considered against the objects being sought will be unlawful.

thinking point

Think of various objects for which the police might search: What sort of search would be justifiable for each of the objects you have identified?

Also, the police must make sure that they carry out the search fully on the occasion that they execute the warrant, for a warrant may only be used once (s.15(5) PACE). The police may not go back to search again on the basis of the original warrant. To return for another search they must obtain a fresh warrant.

Seizure of items

Where the police are searching under the authority of a search warrant, they may seize and retain anything for which the search is authorized (s.8(2) PACE). A question arises as to the position if they come upon other items that might have evidential value in the course of their search. Under s.19, a constable who is lawfully on the premises may seize anything if he has reasonable grounds for believing that it has been obtained in consequence of the commission of an offence and needs to be seized to prevent its loss or destruction, unless it is an item subject to legal professional privilege. A key requirement here is that the officer must be lawfully on the premises. In a search with a warrant, the warrant satisfies that requirement as it gives lawful authority for the officer to be on the premises, and, as long as the search falls within the requirements of s.16(8), that part of s.19 will be satisfied and any objects the officer comes upon in the course of a search for the items specified in the warrant may lawfully be seized if the other requirements in s.19 are satisfied.

Entry without warrant

Under s.17(1), a constable may enter and search premises for a number of purposes:

- to execute an arrest warrant;
- to arrest for an indictable offence;
- to arrest under certain statutory provisions;
- to recapture someone; and
- to save life or limb or to prevent serious damage to property.

In all cases, there must be evidence to support the particular ground relied on. The last of these is potentially wide ranging, especially when coupled with the powers of entry in connection with breach of the peace. By virtue of ss.17(5) and (6), a constable may also

enter premises under common law powers where a breach of the peace is occurring or to prevent a reasonably apprehended breach of the peace.

Entry following arrest

Where a person has been arrested, powers of entry and search are triggered. Under s.32, a constable may enter and search the premises in which a person has been arrested or where he was immediately before he was arrested in order to search for evidence of the indictable offence for which he was arrested. In *R v Badham* [1987] Crim LR 202, it was observed that the power under s.32, although not subject to time limits, was envisaged as being used immediately after the person was arrested.

The reason for the use of s.32 in these circumstances becomes apparent when s.18 is examined. This provides that a senior officer, of the rank of inspector or above, may authorize a constable to enter and search premises occupied or controlled by the person who has been arrested. The search may be for items relating to the indictable offence for which he was arrested or relating to some other indictable offence connected to or similar to that offence. The power is limited to circumstances where there has been an arrest for an indictable offence, which is a justifiable limitation given that the power involves entry to premises. Extensions to the power come from the ability of officers to search for items relating to indictable offences connected with or similar to the offence for which he was arrested. The latter is particularly vague, as s.18 does not qualify the degree of similarity required.

In connection with search following arrest, the provisions in ss.32, 18 and 19 need to be read together to gain a fuller picture. The limitations imposed by ss.18 and 32 may be rendered minimal given the wide-ranging nature of the power of seizure under s.19. The critical issue will be whether, when seizing the items under the authority of s.19, the officer is lawfully on the premises, which involves doing something he is legally entitled to do. As long as that threshold requirement is satisfied, then items the officer comes upon may be seized without being subject to the limitations in ss.32 and 18.

8.3 Consequences of unlawful police action

Police officers are not immune from legal action if they exceed their powers and act unlawfully. If police officers act unlawfully, a number of possible consequences arise. Indeed, one of the issues for a person aggrieved by the actions of the police is to decide which is the most appropriate course of action to follow. Without being exhaustive, the following may be possible:

8.3.1 **Habeas corpus**

Article 5 of the European Convention on Human Rights requires that states must ensure that a person who has been deprived of his liberty is entitled to bring proceedings to determine the lawfulness of his detention (Article 5(4)). Where a person claims to be unlawfully detained, an application for habeas corpus requires the person detaining the individual to produce that individual in court and to justify the detention by reference to some legal power authorizing it. The onus is on the person detaining to show that there is a power allowing it rather than on the detained individual to show why he should be freed. A successful application has the result of freeing the individual, and doing so speedily, as habeas corpus applications are prioritized for hearing.

8.3.2 **Action for damages**

For definitions of all the terms which appear in bold below, see the Glossary on p.301

A number of torts cover possible instances of misconduct and would provide a remedy in damages. Where a person has been arrested and the officer has taken hold of him or otherwise physically restrained him, then if the arrest is unlawful, a trespass to the person, **assault** or **battery**, has been committed. An alternative might be a claim for **false imprisonment** where his freedom of movement has been restricted. A claim for **trespass to land** may follow an unlawful search of premises, and a claim for **trespass to goods** might follow unlawful seizure of items. If the individual was being proceeded against falsely, then an action for **malicious prosecution** might follow. Under s.88 Police Act 1996, the chief constable is **vicariously liable** for torts committed by police officers in the execution or purported execution of their duty.

8.3.3 **Prosecution for a criminal offence**

Officers acting unlawfully are not immune from prosecution if their conduct amounts to a criminal offence. Relevant criminal offences might include offences under the Offences against the Person Act 1861 such as **assault occasioning actual bodily harm** (s.47) or **malicious wounding** or causing **grievous bodily harm** (s.20). In extreme cases, officers may be prosecuted for **murder** or **manslaughter** at common law. If officers were acting in a way that distorted or suppressed evidence they may be liable for the common law offence of perverting the course of justice.

8.3.4 **Complaint**

The Police Act 1996 (Part IV) provides for a system whereby complaints about the conduct of police officers may be brought. This would cover not only conduct that amounts to unlawful action but also conduct not involving illegality, such as officers being rude or acting oppressively.

8.3.5 Disciplinary proceedings

One possible outcome of a complaint might be that the officer in question is subjected to disciplinary proceedings. If the disciplinary allegation is proved, the officer may be subject to a range of penalties, from warnings to dismissal from the force. A range of conduct can form the subject matter of a disciplinary charge, notably, in the present context, failing to observe the requirements of the Codes of Practice under the Police and Criminal Evidence Act.

8.3.6 Exclusion of evidence

As we have seen, ss.76 and 78 provide for the exclusion of evidence in certain circumstances. Under s.76, confessions must be excluded if obtained by oppression or in circumstances that make them unreliable. Under s.78, illegally obtained evidence may be excluded at the court's discretion if its probative value is outweighed by the unfairness of the way it was obtained, always subject to the overriding effect of Article 6 of the European Convention on Human Rights.

Thus, there exists a range of possibilities following unlawful activity on the part of the police. The question in each individual case will be, in circumstances where the individual has any degree of choice, what is the most appropriate course of action to pursue. In part, this will be conditioned by a number of considerations, including finance and the determination of the individual to pursue the matter to its conclusion.

thinking point
Given the range of possibilities when the police act unlawfully, how does a wronged individual decide which to pursue?

Questions

If you answer the following questions, you will have appreciated the main issues raised in this chapter. Check your answers against the notes provided at the back of the book.

1   Which human rights, protected by the European Convention on Human Rights, are
    relevant in this area?

2   What limitations on those rights are permissible?

3   What powers do the police have to interfere with individual freedom?

4   Has an appropriate balance been achieved between giving the police enough
    power to do their job and giving individuals sufficient safeguards to uphold their
    human rights and prevent abuses of power?

Further reading

To further your understanding of the topics covered in this chapter, have a look at the
reading materials mentioned below. Useful web links are also provided on the Online
Resource Centre.

Gary Slapper and David Kelly, *The English Legal System* (Routledge Cavendish, 9th ed.,
2008) ch.10
This will provide you with a more detailed account of the investigation of crime.

Michael Zander, *Cases and Materials on the English Legal System* (Cambridge University Press,
10th ed., 2007) ch. 3
This gives you the edited text of a selection of primary materials in an accessible form
together with commentary and further references.

Tim Newburn and Robert Reiner, 'From PC Dixon to Dixon PLC: Policing and Police Powers since
1954' [2004] Crim LR 601
This gives you a brief history of changes in policing in the second half of the 20th century

Freedom of expression and assembly and public order

Learning Objectives

While reading this chapter, you should aim to understand:

- which human rights are protected;

- what limitations on those rights are permissible;

- what form such limitations take in public order law;

- what powers are given to the police to prevent disorder; and

- whether an adequate balance has been achieved between giving the police sufficient powers to prevent disorder whilst upholding the right to free expression.

Introduction

The right to free expression is one of the most fundamental in any democracy, not least because it enables political debate to be conducted in an open and critical way. The right to assemble to express a common viewpoint is an important associated right. As with all other fundamental freedoms, however, the common law did not recognise either a right to free expression or the right to assemble. These freedoms could be, and were, reduced by Act of Parliament or judicial decision. The law consisted, and still consists, of a series of restrictions on these freedoms. These restrictions were, as they are now, largely in the form of criminal offences, backed by powers given to the police to maintain order with a further set of criminal sanctions for disobedience to police instructions. The position at common law was thus that people could assemble and express their views as long as they were not acting unlawfully, but could not assert a right to do these things.

The position is now modified as a result of the Human Rights Act 1998 and, in particular, by Article 10 (right to free expression) and Article 11 (right of assembly and association) of the European Convention on Human Rights. Additionally, the concept of proportionality has a particular impact here in restraining excessive use of police powers. The role of the police is critical to the operation of the law here. Police officers are under a common law duty to preserve the Queen's peace and enforce the law. The law in this area is structured so as to give the police powers to act to prevent disorder, backed up by a series of criminal offences prohibiting various forms of conduct both individual and collective. The Public Order Act 1986 remains a key statute, though it has been amended subsequently and exists alongside a number of other statutes which may be invoked in this context. The powers under the Police and Criminal Evidence Act 1984, discussed in Chapter 8 are also capable of being utilized.

cross reference

See the discussion of the Police and Criminal Evidence Act in Chapter 8.

In recent years, reducing anti-social behaviour has been a policy priority for the government and the law in this area increasingly reflects this concern. Indeed, much of the legislation is a response to, and consequently reflects, particular concerns. This has also been true of earlier legislation. The Public Order Act 1936 reflected concerns about the growth of fascist quasi-military organizations in the 1930s. However, the concerns are not merely governmental. Public order legislation needs to strike a balance between the rights of those who wish to express their views or gather together in public places and the rights of those who wish to be left alone. This is often difficult to achieve in practice, especially where the object of a protest is to draw the attention of the public to a particular cause or issue. A further feature of the way in which this legislation has developed is that the law increasingly applies to private as well as public space.

thinking point

As the internet provides a ready means for the communication and exchange of ideas and is subject to fewer restrictions than public assemblies, is the right to assemble or speak in public so important these days?

9.1 Offences

As with virtually all of the rights in the European Convention on Human Rights, the rights under Articles 10 and 11 are subject to limitations. These, in line with other permissible limitations under the Convention, must be prescribed by law and be necessary in a democratic society. One ground on which the state may limit these rights, which is common to both Articles 10 and 11, is the prevention of public disorder, a term which does not have a technical meaning in this context and is simply used and interpreted in its ordinary everyday sense. A key question, therefore, becomes whether the limitations are justified on this ground and whether any restrictions imposed are proportionate. The limitations on the rights of expression and assembly tend to be in the form of criminal offences. Some of these, such as those contained in the Public Order Act 1986, are specifically designed to deal with situations of public disorder. Others, such as the offences involving personal violence in the Offences against the Person Act 1861 (e.g. ss.18, 20 and 47), involve particular applications of more general offences. The law is thus found in a number of sources. In the following discussion, the focus will be on those offences that are specifically designed to deal with public disorder. A number of offences and additional police powers relate specifically to terrorism, and will not be discussed here as the focus of discussion will be the general law.

A wide range of offences thus exists to deal with outbreaks of public disorder. An issue is thus to identify which is the most appropriate in any given situation, as the conduct in question will often fit the requirements of more than one offence.

9.1.1 Offences under the Public Order Act 1936

Wearing a political uniform

Although the Public Order Act 1986 did much to modernize the law, it did not sweep away all of the previous public order legislation. Two provisions in the Public Order Act 1936 remain. Under s.1, it is an offence to wear a uniform signalling association with a political organization. This has, hardly surprisingly, given rise to very few prosecutions. Two questions arising under s.1 relate to what constitutes the wearing of a uniform and how a uniform is recognized as signifying association with a political organization. Both of these issues were considered in *O'Moran v DPP* [1975] QB 864.

case close-up

***O'Moran v DPP* [1975] QB 864**

. . . .

The defendants were attending a funeral in N. Ireland and were wearing black berets, dark glasses and black pullovers. They were convicted of wearing a political uniform contrary to s.1. The items, worn together, constituted a uniform which a number of people were deliberately adopting to signify their association with each other. Lord Widgery CJ, giving the judgment of the court, said that wearing involved the wearing of clothing as opposed to, say, sporting a badge. He went on: 'The simple fact that a number of men deliberately adopt an identical article of attire justifies in my judgment the view that that article is a uniform if it is adopted in such a way as to show that its adoption is for the purposes of showing association between the men in question.'

The key to this is the way in which the clothing is worn. If people just happen to wear similar items because they are the fashion of the day then it will not be a uniform. Similarly, the mere fact that something that can be regarded as a uniform is worn does not bring the wearer within s.1: the uniform must signify the political association and be worn as such. Badges or other items such as slogans on clothing may fall under ss.4 or 5 of the Public Order Act 1986, and are considered below.

Quasi-military organizations

An allied offence in s.2 of the Public Order Act 1936 is preserved. This is the offence of organizing or training or equipping members of an association either to take over the functions of the police or the armed forces or to use force in the promotion of any political object. Prosecutions under this provision are also rare. In one of the few cases brought under this provision, *R v Jordan and Tyndall* [1963] Crim LR 124, members of an organization called 'Spearhead' wore uniforms, performed military drill, carried out attack and defence exercises, used Nazi salutes and had bomb making equipment. In upholding their conviction under s.2, the Court of Criminal Appeal said that there did not have to be evidence of specific attacks being planned. Their activities were such as to give rise to a reasonable apprehension that they were being organized to use physical force in the promotion of a political object.

thinking point

Do uniformed quasi-military organizations still pose a threat as they did in the 1930s? Are the offences discussed above still necessary, especially as there have been so few prosecutions?

9.1.2 Offences under the Public Order Act 1986

One of the objects of the Public Order Act 1986 was to replace a number of common law offences and to update some existing statutory offences. A group of offences involving collective and individual conduct may be considered first.

> ### Offences under the Public Order Act 1986, ss. 1–5
>
> s.1 Riot
>
> s.2 Violent disorder
>
> s.3 Affray
>
> s.4 Fear or provocation of violence
>
> s.4A Intentionally causing harassment, alarm or distress
>
> s.5 Conduct likely to cause harassment, alarm or distress

Sections 1–5 create a series of offences, shown above in descending order of seriousness, covering certain manifestations of public disorder. Three points may be noted before discussing these. First, some of the concepts used appear in more than one offence. What differentiates the offences are the other requirements with which the common concept is coupled. Thus, each offence has its own particular blend of concepts common to other provisions and concepts unique to that particular offence. Secondly, the impact of numbers on the public is reflected in the offences of riot and violent disorder, which require a minimum number of people for their commission. A similar phenomenon is found in relation to the powers given to the police, some of which depend on the presence of a minimum number of individuals before they can be used. Thirdly, all the offences carry a power of arrest without warrant.

Riot

riot

see statute box for definition

The most serious public order offence is **riot**, which is only triable on indictment, (i.e. before a judge and jury in the Crown Court) and carries a maximum penalty of ten years' imprisonment or a fine or both. It is defined in s.1(1):

> **statute**
>
> Public Order Act 1986, s.1(1)
>
> Where 12 or more persons who are present together use or threaten unlawful violence for a common purpose and the conduct of them (taken together) is such as would cause a person of reasonable firmness present at the scene to fear for his personal safety, each of the persons using unlawful violence for the common purpose is guilty of riot.

A number of features of this offence may be noted:

- it requires at least 12 people, and is thus usually only likely to be used in respect of large scale gatherings;

- the term 'violence' is explained in s.8 as including violence against property, and, in a curious provision, it is also provided that 'it is not restricted to conduct causing or intended to cause injury or damage but includes any other violent conduct (for example, throwing at or towards another person a missile of a kind capable of causing injury which does not hit or falls short)'. It is unusual for statutory provisions to use examples in this way, but it serves to make the point that the concept of violence is intended to be wide ranging;

- the violence must be unlawful: this serves to exclude, for example, force used by way of self defence;

- although the people must be present together and must use or threaten unlawful violence, they need not use or threaten violence simultaneously. Each individual must, however, intend to use violence or at least be aware that his conduct may be violent;

- they must use or threaten violence for a common purpose. This is, perhaps, the most difficult element in the offence for the prosecution to prove, notwithstanding that s.1(3) provides that the common purpose may be inferred from conduct. The courts have, to some degree, loosened the rigour of this provision by taking a generous view of how this requirement might be met. In *R v Jefferson* [1994] 1 All ER 270 there was widespread disorder in the streets following a football match between England and Egypt, which the participants had been watching on television. The judge directed that the requirements of common purpose could be satisfied by the participants all engaging in football hooliganism, in the form of a violent celebration of the England victory. The subsequent conviction of the participants was upheld by the Court of Appeal, with the result that the common purpose does not have to be pre-planned nor specific;

- the conduct must cause a person of reasonable firmness to fear for his personal safety. The 'person of reasonable firmness' features in a number of the offences under the Act, and is essentially a hypothetical figure: the magistrates or jury need to imagine the impact of the conduct of an ordinary individual, who will be essentially someone like themselves. Clearly, evidence of the reaction of someone who actually witnessed the conduct in question will go some way to establishing this requirement, but, as s.1(4) makes clear, it is not necessary that such a person is present at the scene or is even likely to be present; and

- a final feature of the offence of riot that has echoes elsewhere in the legislation is that it may be committed in private as well as public places. The law on public order traditionally applied only to conduct occurring in public space. The privatization of public order law is a characteristic of the Public Order Act 1986, whose principal offences may be committed in both public and private space. Whilst this may be regarded as having changed the character of the law, it avoids the need to distinguish between public and private places, a distinction that has caused considerable difficulty in other areas of law where that distinction is drawn.

thinking point

If the object of the offence of riot is the effect on the public peace of large numbers acting violently, is 12 the right threshold for liability?

Violent disorder

violent disorder
see statute box for
definition

The next most serious offence is **violent disorder**, which is an either way offence, (i.e. one which may be tried either on indictment in the Crown Court or by summary procedure in a magistrates' court). This reflects the varying degrees of seriousness that it may entail. It is defined in s.2 (1):

Public Order Act 1986, s.2 (1)

Where 3 or more persons who are present together use or threaten unlawful violence and the conduct of them (taken together) is such as would cause a person of reasonable firmness present at the scene to fear for his personal safety, each of the persons using or threatening unlawful violence is guilty of violent disorder.

Again, the impact of numbers is recognized, but here the requirement is three or more people engaged in the conduct in question. The individuals involved must be using or threatening unlawful violence, 'violence' having the same meaning as for the offence of riot. It follows from the requirement that the violence must be unlawful that a person who is using or threatening lawful violence, such as force used by way of self defence, does not commit violent disorder. This can have an impact on the numbers and hence on whether the offence is made out. For example, in *R v Fleming* (1989) 153 JP 517, there was a street fight involving four individuals. However, of these, two were aggressors and two were acting in self defence. It was thus held by the Court of Appeal that the offence under s.2 was not made out as there were not three participants using or threatening unlawful violence: the two who were defending themselves were using lawful force.

The defendants must use or threaten unlawful violence though there is no requirement that they do so simultaneously. Each individual must, however, intend to use or threaten violence or at least be aware that that his conduct may be violent or threaten violence. As with riot, the person of reasonable firmness need not necessarily be present and the offence may be committed in public or private places.

affray
see statute box for
definition

Affray

Moving down the scale of seriousness, the offence in s.3 is **affray**.

Public Order Act 1986, s.3 (1)

A person is guilty of affray if he uses or threatens unlawful violence towards another and his conduct is such as would cause a person of reasonable firmness present at the scene to fear for his personal safety.

This offence may be committed by a single individual, unlike the two offences previously considered. There is also a more restricted definition of violence for the purposes of affray. It is clear from the wording of s.3(1) that violence against property will not be sufficient for affray: the violence must be used or threatened towards another person. Further, a threat cannot be made by words alone (s.3(3)); the requirement that there must be violence or a threat of violence must involve some conduct on the part of the defendant, though it may, of course, be accompanied by words. In *R v Dixon* [1993] Crim LR 579, for example, police officers were closing in on the defendant and his dog. The defendant said to the dog 'go on, go on'. The dog then ran toward the police officers and bit them. The defendant repeated the instruction to the dog, adding 'go on, kill'. He was charged with affray, and argued that as the offence could not be committed by words alone, he was not guilty as charged. The Court of Appeal upheld his conviction on the grounds that the dog was being used as a weapon and, in setting the dog on the police officers, the defendant was using the dog as he might have used any other weapon.

It is not, however, sufficient that the defendant is carrying something that could be used for violence but which has not yet, at the point at which the person is apprehended, been used in that way. Such a case was *I v DPP* [2002] AC 285. The defendants in this case were carrying petrol bombs which were primed but unlit. The House of Lords held that they were not guilty of the offence of affray as the mere possession of such items did not amount to a threat of violence directed towards another as required by s.3. As with the offences under ss.1 and 2, the person of reasonable firmness need not actually be or likely to be present at the scene, and affray may be committed in private as well as public places.

Threatening, abusive or insulting words or behaviour

The offences in ss.4, 4A and 5 introduce a new set of concepts. All three of these offences require that the words or conduct used are threatening, abusive or insulting. The interpretation of these words will be considered before examining the further individual requirements of the three offences. All the offences are structured in a similar way. They all have a requirement of threatening, abusive and insulting conduct which produces a particular result or is likely to do so.

The leading case on the interpretation of these words is still the decision of the House of Lords in *Brutus v Cozens* [1973] AC 854, a case decided under s.5 Public Order Act 1936 (threatening abusive or insulting words or behaviour likely to cause a breach of the peace). Although s.5 of the 1936 Act has been repealed, the 1986 Act uses the same words, ('threatening, abusive or insulting'), and thus *Brutus* remains good law on the interpretation of these terms.

case close-up

Brutus v Cozens [1973] AC 854
....

Protestors had staged a demonstration at the Wimbledon tennis tournament which involved invading the court during a match and handing out leaflets protesting about apartheid in South Africa. They were charged under s.5 of the Public Order Act 1936 (now repealed) with threatening, abusive or insulting words or behaviour likely to cause a breach of the peace. The magistrates found that their conduct was not insulting and they were discharged. The House of Lords held that the magistrates were entitled to come to this conclusion. The words 'threatening, abusive or insulting' were ordinary English words to be interpreted as such. Lord Reid observed (at p.862):

> ...vigorous and it may be distasteful or unmannerly speech or behaviour is permitted so long as it does not go beyond any one of three limits. It must not be threatening. It must not be abusive. It must not be insulting. I see no reason why any of these should be construed as having a specially wide or a specially narrow meaning. They are all limits easily recognisable by the ordinary man.

thinking point

How is a court to distinguish between language or conduct that is offensive, annoying or disgusting and language or conduct that is threatening, abusive or insulting?

One consequence of taking this approach and leaving the decision to the magistrates is that different benches of magistrates may reach different conclusions about certain types of conduct, leading to inconsistency in the application of these provisions. This is the inevitable result of taking the approach that the words are ordinary words capable of interpretation and application by lay justices.

thinking point

Is it desirable that different benches of magistrates can, potentially, come to different conclusions on essentially the same facts?

Whether words are threatening, abusive or insulting may need to be considered in the particular context in which they are used. Some expressions will fall within one of these descriptions irrespective of the context. Others may be more equivocal and their effect may only be judged by considering the circumstances in which they were used.

Considerations attaching to relevance of the audience in considering the impact of words were considered in *Jordan v Burgoyne* [1963] 2 QB 744.

case close-up

Jordan v Burgoyne [1963] 2 QB 744

Here, the defendant made a speech to an audience in Trafalgar Square in London. The speech had a strongly anti-Semitic pro-Nazi character, and this provoked disorder in sections of the audience, particularly anti-fascists and Jews. Jordan was charged under s.5 of the Public Order Act 1936. He argued that his words should be judged in the context of a reasonable audience, which, he claimed, would not be insulted by what he said. It was held, however, that he was rightly convicted under s.5. His words were deliberately insulting to people in the audience. The speaker must take his audience as he finds them and if necessary moderate his words accordingly.

The right to free speech and the impact of the Human Rights Act

Notwithstanding that, since *Jordan v Burgoyne* was decided, the passing of the Human Rights Act has led to the incorporation of the right to free speech (Article 10), it seems unlikely that the result in this case would, on this point, be different. Although the courts have said that the right to free speech must include the right to be controversial and the right to offend people, this does not include circumstances where the speaker deliberately insults his audience. Support for this view may be gained from *Hammond v DPP* [2004] Crim LR 851.

thinking point

Should there be any limits on the expression of religious beliefs?

> **case close-up**
>
> ### *Hammond v DPP* [2004] Crim LR 851
>
> Here, the defendant, an evangelical Christian, was preaching in the centre of Bournemouth backed by signs bearing the slogans 'Stop Immorality', 'Stop Homosexuality' and 'Stop Lesbianism'. A crowd gathered and was, on the evidence of the police officers who arrived at the scene, agitated, angry and insulted: there was evidence from individuals that they were insulted by the defendant's conduct. He refused to stop or remove the signs and was arrested for breach of the peace. He was subsequently charged under s.5 of the Public Order Act 1986. The magistrates convicted him, viewing his conduct as going beyond legitimate protest and insulting to the audience. They took the view that his right to free expression (Article 10) and to express his religious beliefs (Article 9) could be legitimately limited in such circumstances, providing such limitation was not disproportionate, which, in their view, it was not in this case. The defendant's appeal was dismissed, the Divisional Court holding that the magistrates were entitled to reach the conclusion they did, having taken account of the Convention rights and their application with regard to the defendant.

cross reference

Breach of the peace is considered below.

These are not easy issues to resolve. Courts have to consider the right to free speech against the need to preserve public order. Police officers on the spot have to decide how to manage the situation to prevent disorder breaking out or curbing it if it has already broken out. This issue is considered more fully in the context of breach of the peace, where many of the cases have had to address this issue squarely.

Fear or provocation of violence

> **statute**
>
> Public Order Act 1986, s.4 (1)
>
> (1) A person is guilty of an offence if he—
>
>   (a) uses towards another person threatening, abusive or insulting words or behaviour, or
>
>   (b) distributes or displays to another person any writing, sign or other visible representation which is threatening, abusive or insulting,
>
> with intent to cause that person to believe that immediate unlawful violence will be used against him or another by any person, or to provoke the immediate use of unlawful violence by that person or another, or whereby that person is likely to believe that such violence will be used or it is likely that such violence will be provoked.

In addition to the requirement that the conduct must be threatening, abusive or insulting, to which the considerations previously discussed apply, the offence in s.4 requires proof of a number of other elements. If the conduct consists of threatening, abusive or insulting words or behaviour, then that must be used 'towards another person'. This is a significant limitation. It means that, say, words spoken at large and not directed at any particular individual or group of individuals fall outside s.4.

case close-up

Atkin v DPP (1989) 89 Cr App R 199

Customs and Excise officers and a bailiff went to the defendant's farm to recover outstanding VAT payments. The Customs and Excise officers went into the farmhouse, while the bailiff stayed in the car outside. The officers told the defendant that if he did not pay the amount owed to them the bailiff would have to come and take some of his goods. The defendant said 'If the bailiff gets out of the car he is a dead 'un'. The officers noticed a gun in the corner of the room. One of the officers then went outside and told the bailiff of the threat. The defendant was charged under s.4, but it was held that the offence was not made out. The Divisional Court held that the words 'uses towards' required the physical presence of the person to whom they were directed, who must perceive them through his own senses. It was not sufficient that they were, as here, relayed to him.

Where the conduct consists of writing, sign or other visible representation then it must be distributed or displayed, a requirement that makes it wider than the corresponding provision relating to words or behaviour. The description 'writing, sign or other visible representation' in s.4(1)(b) could cover communication through a variety of media, including badges, flags, placards, clothing, tattoos and the like. Under both s.4(1)(a) and 4(1)(b), the defendant must intend his conduct to be threatening, abusive or insulting or at least be aware that this may be the case.

The second part of the definition of the offence in s.4(1) requires that the threatening, abusive or insulting conduct is used towards another 'with intent to cause that person to believe that immediate unlawful violence will be used against him or another by any person, or to provoke the immediate use of unlawful violence by that person or another, or whereby that person is likely to believe that such violence will be used or it is likely that such violence will be provoked'. This is a rather compressed provision disclosing a number of ways of committing an offence under s.4, assuming the conduct is threatening, abusive or insulting and is used towards another:

* the first is where the defendant intends to cause the person to whom the conduct is directed to believe that immediate unlawful violence will be used against him or against another person by the defendant or by any other person;

* secondly, where the defendant intends to provoke the immediate use of unlawful violence by the person to whom the conduct is directed or by another person;

* thirdly, where the conduct is used towards another person in such a way that he is likely to believe that immediate unlawful violence will be used; and

* fourthly, where the conduct is likely to provoke immediate unlawful violence.

In the first two situations, the intentions of the defendant are the crucial feature. In the third and fourth, it is the likelihood of the conduct to produce a particular result that is critical, and, ultimately, this is a matter of judgement for the court on the particular facts.

A requirement common to all of these is that the violence used or provoked will occur immediately ('immediate unlawful violence will be used . . .' etc.). This requirement was central to the decision in *R v Horseferry Road Metropolitan Stipendiary Magistrate ex p Siadatan* [1991] QB 260.

<table>
<tr><td>

case close-up

</td><td>

R v Horseferry Road Metropolitan Stipendiary Magistrate ex p Siadatan [1991] QB 260

· ·

This case concerned the publication of Salman Rushdie's novel *The Satanic Verses*. The magistrate was asked to issue a summons in respect of the book on the ground that its publication amounted to an offence under s.4 in that it contained abusive and insulting material that would provoke violence. The magistrate declined to do so, and the applicant sought to overturn this decision. The Divisional Court held that the magistrate had been correct in declining to issue a summons, as any violence the book might provoke would not be immediate. The court accepted that the word 'immediate' did not mean instantaneous, but said that it must be likely to occur within a relatively short period of time. Thus, an element of s.4 was missing and no offence under that section could be made out.

</td></tr>
</table>

Whilst the offence may, in common with other offences under the 1986 Act, be committed in private as well as public places, there is an exception in s.4(2): the offence is not committed where the conduct is carried out by a person who is inside a dwelling and the person to whom the conduct is directed is in that or another dwelling. The effect of this is, amongst other things, to exclude domestic situations which might otherwise be caught by the legislation. In *Atkin v DPP*, it was argued that s.4(2) applied to negate liability as the bailiff was not in the farmhouse at the time the defendant used the threatening words. It was held that the relevant person was the person to whom the conduct was directed—in that case, the Customs and Excise officers—rather than the person about whom the words were used, namely the bailiff. It followed therefore, that s.4(2) operated to exclude liability.

Causing harassment, alarm or distress

The offence in s.4A is more akin to the offence in s.5 than that in s.4 and will be considered after the discussion of s.5.

<table>
<tr><td>

statute

</td><td>

Public Order Act 1986, s.5

(1) A person is guilty of an offence if he—

    (a) uses threatening, abusive or insulting words or behaviour, or disorderly behaviour, or

</td></tr>
</table>

Offences

203

> (b) displays any writing, sign or other visible representation which is threatening, abusive or insulting,
>
> within the hearing or sight of a person likely to be caused harassment, alarm or distress thereby.

In keeping with the provisions previously discussed, the defendant must intend his conduct to be threatening, abusive or insulting or at least be aware that it may be threatening, abusive or insulting. There is, in s.5(1)(a), an additional type of behaviour specified: in addition to threatening, abusive or insulting conduct, the defendant may also come within s.5 if he engages in disorderly behaviour. The word 'disorderly' is not defined, and, in keeping with the approach to interpretation laid down in *Brutus v Cozens*, is interpreted as an ordinary English word. In the White Paper preceding the Public Order Act 1986, (*Review of Public Order Law* (Cmnd. 9510) (1985)) the government explained that it was concerned to include within the scope of the offence 'minor acts of hooliganism'. Examples given in the White Paper (para.3.22) included:

- groups of youths persistently shouting abuse and obscenities,
- rowdy behaviour in the street late at night,
- causing disturbances in the common parts of blocks of flats,
- banging on doors,
- knocking over dustbins, and
- throwing items down stairs.

What these examples demonstrate is that the threshold at which behaviour becomes categorized as criminal is quite low. The defendant must, however, be aware that his conduct may be disorderly. Seeking an anti-social behaviour order rather than prosecuting the individual for a criminal offence may be an alternative way of dealing with such conduct.

thinking point

What is the difference between people behaving boisterously or exuberantly and people behaving in a disorderly fashion?

Did someone see or hear the conduct in question?

As with s.4, the threatening, abusive or insulting words or behaviour must produce an effect. Here, it is that a person hearing or seeing them is likely to be caused harassment, alarm or distress. The conduct must actually be witnessed by someone for the offence in s.5 to be made out. This may be illustrated by *Holloway v DPP* (2005) 169 JP 14.

case close-up

Holloway v DPP (2005) 169 JP 14
· ·

Here, the defendant, from a vantage point overlooking a school, was filming children who were playing in the school grounds. At various points during the filming he removed his clothes and filmed himself naked. Whilst it was accepted that his nakedness could be insulting for the purposes of s.5, there was no evidence that anyone had actually seen him naked. The deputy district judge who tried the case initially convicted the defendant on the ground that anyone coming upon him in a state of undress would have been harassed, alarmed or distressed. The Divisional Court held, however, that the defendant must actually have been seen by someone in order to be convicted under s.5. It was not sufficient that a hypothetical person would have been harassed, alarmed or distressed had they come upon the defendant. In reaching this con-clusion, the Divisional Court contrasted the wording of s.3, where a conviction for affray could be secured without anyone actually witnessing the conduct as long as a notional person would have feared for his personal safety. This contrast in wording between s.3 and s.5 was significant and showed that different considerations applied. Thus in this case the finding that no-one had seen the defendant naked was critical to the outcome.

This was explained further by the Divisional Court in *Taylor v DPP* (2006) 170 JP 485.

case close-up

Taylor v DPP (2006) 170 JP 485
· ·

The defendant used language that was abusive. The district judge trying the case found that there were people near enough to hear the words who would be likely to be harassed, alarmed or distressed. The defendant argued that there must be evidence that someone did actually hear the words in order for the prosecution to succeed. It was held that as long as there was evidence that there were people at the scene who were near enough to hear the language used, then that would satisfy the requirement in s.5(1) that it must be 'within the hearing . . . of' someone.

This may be contrasted with *Holloway* in that in *Taylor* there was evidence of people on the scene being near enough to hear the words used, whereas in *Holloway* there was a finding that no-one had actually seen the defendant naked.

thinking point

Why do you think it is necessary for someone to have actually seen the conduct in relation to s.5 but not in relation to some of the other offences in the Public Order Act?

Was the person likely to have been harassed, alarmed or distressed?

Once it is established that there is someone within whose sight or hearing the conduct occurs, then the question is whether that person is likely to be harassed, alarmed or distressed. The words 'harassment', 'alarm' and 'distress' are not qualified, so it would appear that any amount of harassment alarm or distress will suffice. The courts have refused to accept as a matter of principle, that there are individuals who, perhaps by virtue of their work, are not capable of being harassed, alarmed or distressed. Each case has to be judged on its own facts.

This may be illustrated by *DPP v Orum* [1988] 3 All ER 449.

---

case close-up

DPP v Orum [1988] 3 All ER 44

The defendant was arguing with his girlfriend in the street late at night in a residential area. Police officers arrived and told him to be quiet and go home. He refused and abused the officers. It was accepted that the only people present were the defendant, his girlfriend and the officers. The defendant argued that the offence was not made out as police officers were incapable of being harassed, alarmed or distressed. This was based on the idea that the job that they did exposed them to frequent abuse that might simply be regarded as an occupational hazard. The Divisional Court rejected this argument and held that, notwithstanding the exposure to abuse in the course of their work, police officers were capable of being harassed, alarmed or distressed. The matter was to be determined on the facts in each case, and, as the magistrates had found as a fact that the officers were harassed, alarmed or distressed, the conviction was upheld.

Thus, for example, in *DPP v Clarke* (1992) 156 JP 267, anti-abortion demonstrators carrying placards showing aborted foetuses were convicted under s.5 where the evidence showed that they caused alarm and distress to police officers.

Unlike s.4, s.5 does not contain the phrase 'uses towards another', and so the conduct does not have to be directed at another person. In this respect s.5 is wider than s.4, as all that is required is that the defendant is engaging in the conduct and that it is within the sight or hearing of another person. There is, however, a provision parallel to that in s.4 where, by virtue of s.5(2), whereby, whilst the offence may be committed in public or private places, no offence is committed under s.5 where the conduct occurs within a dwelling and the other person is inside that or another dwelling. Thus, a person displaying an abusive placard in his front window which is only seen by someone across the road through his front window does not commit an offence under s.5.

thinking point

Why do you think that some offences, such as that under s.4 require that D uses conduct towards another person, whilst other offences, such as that under s.5, do not?

Reasonableness

statute

Public Order Act 1986, s.5(3)

It is a defence for the accused to prove:

(a) that he had no reason to believe that there was any person within hearing or sight who was likely to be caused harassment, alarm or distress, or

(b) that he was inside a dwelling and had no reason to believe that the words or behaviour used, or the writing, sign or visible representation displayed, would be heard or seen by a person outside that or any other dwelling, or

(c) that his conduct was reasonable.

In deciding whether the defendant has satisfied s.5(3)(a), the particular circumstances will need to be considered, including factors such as the nature of the defendant's conduct, the nature of the location, whether people frequent the area, and if so how often and so on. The defence in s.5(3)(b) expands the exemption in s.5(2) to cover situations where the matter is not covered by s.5(2). Potentially the most wide ranging defence is that in s.5(3)(c). However, that potential is limited by the requirement that whether the defendant's conduct is reasonable is judged objectively. It is not sufficient that the defendant thinks his conduct is reasonable, however sincerely he believes this to be the case; the decision is ultimately one for the court. Thus, in *Morrow, Geach and Thomas v DPP* [1994] Crim LR 58 anti-abortion protestors were causing distress to patients at an abortion clinic. They argued that their conduct was reasonable. The court held, however, that, given the nature of their conduct in shouting slogans, waving banners and trying to prevent people from entering the clinic, coupled with the evidence of the distress caused, the decision of the magistrates to convict could be justified. A similar conclusion was reached in *Hammond v DPP* [2004] Crim LR 851, discussed above.

Intentionally causing harassment, alarm or distress

The offence in s.4A is in the form of an aggravated version of that in s.5.

statute

Public Order Act 1986, s.4A

(1) A person is guilty of an offence if, with intent to cause a person harassment, alarm or distress, he—

(a) uses threatening, abusive or insulting words or behaviour, or disorderly behaviour, or

(b) displays any writing, sign or other visible representation which is threatening, abusive or insulting,

thereby causing that or another person harassment, alarm or distress.

In addition to the requirements of s.5, the defendant must have intended to cause harassment, alarm or distress and succeeded in doing so.

Racially aggravated offences

By virtue of s.31 Crime and Disorder Act 1998, the offences under s.5 and s.4A may also be racially or religiously aggravated, as also may the offence under s.4. This occurs where the defendant demonstrates hostility towards the victim's membership of a racial or religious group or the offence is motivated by hostility toward that group. Thus, in

R v Rogers [2007] 2 AC 62, the defendant addressed a group of Spanish women as 'bloody foreigners', telling them to 'go back to your own country'. The House of Lords upheld his conviction for using racially aggravated, abusive or insulting words with intent to cause fear or provoke violence, the use of the term 'foreigners' being sufficient to indicate that the comments referred to a racial group. The racial group must however be a group identified by national or ethnic or racial origins and not just a regional group. This is neatly illustrated in *DPP v Chippendale* [2004] Crim LR 755. The defendant was walking along a street singing a song with the words 'build a bonfire . . . put the scousers on the top'. He later changed this to 'put the Turks on the top'. It was held that, whilst the reference to the Turks constituted a racially aggravated form of a s.5 offence, the reference to scousers did not.

Stirring up racial hatred

A series of offences in ss.18–24 Public Order Act 1986 cover acts intended to stir up racial hatred against a group of persons in Great Britain defined by reference to colour, race, nationality or ethnic or national origins. These offences have common elements of conduct that is threatening, abusive or insulting and that the conduct is intended to stir up racial hatred or is likely to have this effect. In *Mandla v Dowell Lee* [1983] 2 AC 548 at 562, Lord Fraser explained what characteristics might identify a racial group. Whilst he was speaking in the context of a case where the issue was whether a Sikh boy who had been prevented from wearing his turban at school had been subjected to discrimination on racial grounds, his explanation has a wider application and would apply to the various offences of inciting racial hatred:

> For a group to constitute an ethnic group . . . it must, in my opinion, regard itself, and be regarded by others, as a distinct community by virtue of certain characteristics. Some of these characteristics are essential; others are not essential but one or more of them will commonly be found and will help to distinguish the group from the surrounding community. The conditions which appear to me to be essential are these: (1) a long shared history, of which the group is conscious as distinguishing it from other groups, and the memory of which it keeps alive; (2) a cultural tradition of its own, including family and social customs and manners, often but not necessarily associated with religious observance. In addition to those two essential characteristics the following characteristics are, in my opinion, relevant: (3) either a common geographical origin, or descent from a small number of common ancestors; (4) a common language, not necessarily peculiar to the group; (5) a common literature peculiar to the group; (6) a common religion different from that of the neighbouring groups or from the general community surrounding it; (7) being a minority or being an oppressed or a dominant group within a larger community, for example a conquered people (say, the inhabitants of England shortly after the Norman conquest) and their conquerors might both be ethnic groups.

Applying these criteria, he took the view that Sikhs constituted a racial group as their religion and race were inextricably intertwined.

Stirring up religious hatred

A gap in the law was revealed in that other groups, whose religious beliefs were not inextricably linked to common ethnic origins, were excluded from protection under the law. This was rectified by the Racial and Religious Hatred Act 2006, which inserted a new set of provisions into the Public Order Act 1986, as ss.29A–N, which broadly parallel those in ss.18–24. They create a series of offences whose common characteristic includes an intention to stir up religious hatred. 'Religious hatred' is explained in s.29A as hatred against a group of individuals defined by reference to religious belief or lack of religious belief.

9.1.3 **Other offences**

Obstruction of the highway

Two other offences of relevance may briefly be noted, both involving obstruction. The first is the offence of obstruction of the highway.

statute

> Highways Act 1980, s.137 (1)
>
> If a person, without lawful authority or excuse, in any way wilfully obstructs the free passage along a highway he is guilty of an offence . . .

The notion of wilful obstruction means that the defendant has acted intentionally. A question of interpretation arises here. Is it necessary for the defendant to intend to obstruct the highway or is it sufficient that the defendant intentionally does an act which causes an obstruction of the highway? The Divisional Court in *Arrowsmith v Jenkins* [1963] 2 QB 561 held that the second of these interpretations was correct, and upheld the conviction of the defendant in circumstances where she had addressed a public meeting which had caused a partial, and at times complete, blockage of the highway. She might not have intended to block the highway but that was the effect of her intentional act in addressing the meeting.

The traditional purpose of the highway is that it is to be used for passage and repassage—in other words, moving along it. It would appear that, on the face of it, anyone stopping on the highway potentially commits an obstruction. That is clearly too narrow a view, but the courts have had to provide some guidance as to the proper uses of the highway. They have done so around the notion of reasonableness. No offence will be committed by someone whose use of the highway is reasonable. In *Hirst v Chief Constable for West Yorkshire* (1986) 85 Cr App R 143, the Divisional Court identified some factors to be taken into consideration when deciding whether use of the highway was reasonable or not. Such factors included:

- the nature of the location where the alleged obstruction had taken place;
- the duration of the activity;
- whether an actual obstruction was caused;

and, more controversially; and

- the purpose of the activity.

The last is controversial because it may involve magistrates in making judgements as to the worth of particular activities, possibly even dragging them into political controversy.

The centrality of the notion of reasonableness as determining the lawfulness of use of the highway was reinforced by the House of Lords in *DPP v Jones* [1999] AC 240 where it was emphasized that use of the highway would only be unlawful if it was unreasonable.

thinking point

If you are walking along the street, should you be protected from people accosting you to hand out leaflets, or from demonstrators generally?

Obstructing a police officer in the execution of his duty

The other offence involving obstruction is that of obstructing a police officer in the exercise of his duty.

statute

Police Act 1996, s.89(2)

Any person who resists or wilfully obstructs a constable in the execution of his duty, or a person assisting a constable in the execution of his duty, shall be guilty of an offence...

As with the offence of obstructing the highway, a wilful obstruction will occur where a person does an intentional act which obstructs the officer in carrying out his duty rather than requiring that there should be an intention to obstruct the officer. Obstruction can take many forms including disobedience to an order or direction from a police officer, preventing an officer from doing something or deceiving an officer. If the conduct consists of physical contact with the officer, such as pushing an officer out of the way, then this becomes the more serious offence of assaulting a police officer in the execution of his duty. In order for either of these offences to be committed, the officer must be acting in the execution of his duty. Police officers, by virtue of holding the common law office of constable, are under a duty to uphold the law and preserve the Queen's peace. Many of the cases have involved a consideration of whether the officer is acting in execution of his duty when dealing with actual or apprehended breaches of the peace, which have raised some difficult questions of law. We will return to this issue when discussing police powers more generally.

9.2 Procedural requirements and police powers

cross reference

Other aspects of police powers are discussed in Chapter 8.

The police have a number of powers at their disposal to enable them to deal with public disorder, whether actual or potential. These may be summarized at the outset, in no particular order.

1. Arrest for breach of the peace, actual or imminent.

2. Action short of arrest to prevent an actual or imminent breach of the peace.

3. Arrest for a substantive offence.

4. Imposing conditions on an assembly under s.14 Public Order Act 1986.

5. Imposing conditions on a public procession under s.12 Public Order Act 1986.

6. Prohibiting processions under s.13.

7. Prohibiting trespassory assemblies under s.14A.

8. Requiring groups to disperse where there is an order in force under s.30 Anti-social Behaviour Act 2003.

activity

Revisit this list after reading the rest of this chapter and decide whether the various options should be in a particular order.

The powers under the Police and Criminal Evidence Act 1984 are as relevant here as in any other situation where the police take action with regard to an individual or group. The present discussion focuses on additional powers which are particularly relevant to the management of public gatherings and other forms of conduct in public space.

9.2.1 **Processions**

The law draws a distinction between processions and static assemblies, and different requirements apply to each. The requirements relating to processions are begun with s.11 Public Order Act 1986.

statute

Public Order Act 1986, s.11

(1) Written notice shall be given in accordance with this section of any proposal to hold a public procession intended—

(a) to demonstrate support for or opposition to the views or actions of any person or body of persons,

(b) to publicise a cause or campaign, or

(c) to mark or commemorate an event,

unless it is not reasonably practicable to give any advance notice of the procession.

(2) Subsection (1) does not apply where the procession is one commonly or customarily held in the police area (or areas) in which it is proposed to be held or is a funeral procession organised by a funeral director acting in the normal course of his business.

The word 'procession' is not defined in the Act, though it is clearly something more than simply a number of people who happen to be going in the same direction. In *Flockhart v Robinson* [1950] 2 KB 498, Lord Goddard said (at p.502) that a procession was not a mere body of persons, but was 'a body of persons moving along a route'. The requirement under s.11(1) is one of notification for any public procession falling within one of the designated descriptions. It is not a request for permission.

The requirements specified in s.11(1) do not apply to those processions described in s.11(2). In *Kay v Commissioner of Police of the Metropolis* [2008] 1 WLR 2723 the Court of Appeal held that monthly cycle rides, which followed a different and indeed random route, were not, as the Divisional Court had decided, processions commonly or customarily held, and thus s.11(2) had no application. The House of Lords took a different view and held that, notwithstanding the variation in route on each occasion the cycle rides took place, they constituted a procession customarily held within s.11(2) and were thus not required to give prior notice under s.11(1).

Power to issue directions

The police are given powers, under ss.12 and 13, to take steps to preserve public order, but only if the conditions for using those powers are satisfied.

statute

Public Order Act 1986, s.12

(1) If the senior police officer, having regard to the time or place at which and the circumstances in which any public procession is being held or is intended to be held and to its route or proposed route, reasonably believes that—

(a) it may result in serious public disorder, serious damage to property or serious disruption to the life of the community, or

(b) the purpose of the persons organising it is the intimidation of others with a view to compelling them not to do an act they have a right to do, or to do an act they have the right not to do,

he may give directions imposing on the persons organising or taking part in the procession such conditions as appear to him necessary to prevent such disorder, damage, disruption or intimidation, including conditions as to the route of the procession or prohibiting it from entering any public place specified in the directions.

Such conditions may be imposed in advance of the procession or at the time it is taking place. There is always a balance to be achieved between the rights of those wishing to exercise their rights to assembly and free expression and the rights of those who wish to be left alone. A third consideration is the preservation of public order, discussed further below. Further, the requirements of the Human Rights Act must also be considered. A procession passing through a busy town centre may inconvenience those using it, who may wish to avoid the procession or not wish to hear any message that those processing are sending out. Those marching or assembling have rights to freedom of expression which are also deserving of protection, as Article 12 of the European Convention on Human Rights makes clear, and any limitations on that right must be proportionate. The use of the word 'serious' in s.12(1)(a) makes clear that those processing should only be prevented from doing so in extreme circumstances. The use of the power to divert a procession from its original route may be controversial. A procession may wish to go past or through a particular location in order to get its message across, and a diversion from that route may defeat the very object of the procession itself. Imagine a procession outside a town hall to protest about council tax rises. Such a procession would lose much of its force if it were to be prevented from passing the town hall where those making decisions would be based. There is thus a delicate balance to be struck between the rights of those processing and the preservation of public order.

thinking point

How are the police to achieve a balance between the rights of protestors and the rights of those who want to be left alone without compromising the rights of either group?

Where the police do issue directions, it becomes an offence to disobey them, assuming, of course, that they are lawfully made.

case close-up

Police v Reid [1987] Crim LR 702

A demonstration was being held outside the South African Embassy at the same time as a reception was being held there. Demonstrators were shouting at guests as they arrived. The police, purporting to exercise powers under s.14 (which are in substantially the same terms as the powers contained in s.12 but applying to static assemblies) required the demonstrators to disperse as they believed that the purpose of the demonstrators was the intimidation of the guests. However, it transpired that the Chief Inspector who had given the directions had interpreted the word 'intimidation' to mean 'causing discomfort'. It was held that the term was stronger than simply causing someone discomfort. The conditions imposed by the police were therefore invalid and no offence was committed in disobeying them.

Banning processions

If the police feel that the powers under s.12 would be inadequate to prevent serious public disorder from occurring then, by virtue of s.13(1), the chief officer of police is required to apply to the local council for an order prohibiting all or a specified class of public processions. As a further check, the council is required, under s.13(2), to obtain the permission of the Home Secretary before acceding to the request. This is a power that was designed to be used sparingly and will be more so following the enactment of the Human Rights Act, for it will only be in wholly exceptional circumstances that an outright ban on processions would not be a disproportionate response.

9.2.2 Other public gatherings

There now exists a variety of provisions giving the police power, in a number of different situations, to direct or disperse public gatherings. There is no requirement of advance notice equivalent to s.11 in respect of other assemblies. There are, however, powers for dealing with static assemblies contained in s.14 which are the counterparts to those in s.12, and rely on essentially the same criteria. An assembly for this purpose is any gathering of two or more persons. Whilst this may appear excessively low as a threshold for the police to act it should be remembered that the conditions in s.14 are in substantially the same terms as those in s.12 and require either an intention to intimidate or pose a serious threat in one of the ways described in s.14(1)(a) (which corresponds to s.12(1)(a) above).

It ought, therefore, to be the case that in practice they will only be able to be used in respect of larger gatherings in places such as town or city centres. A recent case examining the use of such powers occurred in *R(Brehony) v Chief Constable of Greater Manchester Police* [2005] EWHC 640 (Admin).

case close-up

R(Brehony) v Chief Constable of Greater Manchester Police [2005] EWHC 640 (Admin)

Here, a group of pro-Palestinian demonstrators held regular protests outside a Marks and Spencer shop in Manchester city centre. They were opposed by a group of counter demonstrators. The Chief Constable imposed conditions prohibiting both groups from demonstrating in that location during the Christmas shopping period from the end of November until early January on the ground that he believed it would cause serious disruption to the life of the community. The groups were allowed to demonstrate at other locations during the specified period. These conditions were opposed, not least on the ground that they deprived the demonstrators of their rights under Articles 10 and 11 of the European Convention on Human Rights. Bean J held that the Chief Constable's directions were not unreasonable, bearing in mind the impact of the two demonstrations in the context of a busy city centre in the period around Christmas. Further, bearing in mind that it covered a limited time period and that alternative venues during that period were available, his actions were not disproportionate.

There are, however, other powers available to the police in respect of gatherings. The Criminal Justice and Public Order Act 1994 adds new provisions to s.14 which, in s.14A, allow the police to apply for a temporary order banning all **trespassory assemblies** from a specified area for up to four days.

trespassory assembly

a trespassory assembly though not explicitly defined, is essentially one that is held on land to which those assembling have no legal rights and that gathers in contravention of an order under s.14A

statute

Public Order Act 1986, s.14A

(1) If at any time the chief officer of police reasonably believes that an assembly is intended to be held in any district at a place on land to which the public has no right of access or only a limited right of access and that the assembly—

   (a) is likely to be held without the permission of the occupier of the land or to conduct itself in such a way as to exceed the limits of any permission of his or the limits of the public's right of access, and

   (b) may result
      (i) in serious disruption to the life of the community, or
      (ii) where the land, or a building or monument on it, is of historical, architectural, archaeological or scientific importance, in significant damage to the land, building or monument,

   he may apply to the council of the district for an order prohibiting for a specified period the holding of all trespassory assemblies in the district or part of it as specified.

An assembly for this purpose is a gathering of 20 or more, rather than the two to which the powers under s.14 apply. This is potentially a wide-ranging power, though it was restrictively interpreted in *DPP v Jones* [1999] 2 AC 240. Here, an order under s.14A had been made preventing trespassory assemblies from gathering in an area around Stonehenge. The defendant and others took part in a peaceful gathering on a highway within the area designated in the order. They were charged under s.14B with taking part in a trespassory assembly and were convicted of the offence by the magistrates. The case eventually reached the House of Lords where it was held (3:2) that no offence was committed. As long as the highway was being used in a reasonable manner, which was the case here, the assembly was not trespassory and therefore no offence was committed.

Anti-social behaviour

Further powers have been added by s.30 Anti-social Behaviour Act 2003. This allows a senior officer to make an order, which can remain in force for up to six months allowing a constable to disperse a group of two or more persons from a particular location if he has reasonable grounds for believing that their conduct is likely to result in members of the public being intimidated, harassed, alarmed or distressed. The effect of these powers was recently considered in *R(Singh) v Chief Constable of the West Midlands Police* [2006] 1 WLR 3374.

case close-up

R(Singh) v Chief Constable of the West Midlands Police [2006] 1 WLR 3374

The Birmingham Repertory Theatre had mounted a production of a play, *Behzti*, to which many Sikhs took exception and wished to protest about outside the theatre. There was in force an order under s.30 of the Anti-social Behaviour Act covering the Christmas period designed to deal with anti-social behaviour by revellers in the city centre during that period. The area covered in the order included the location of the theatre. A number of protesters turned up outside the theatre and were ordered to disperse, as the police on the scene feared that their actions would cause intimidation, harassment, alarm or distress to members of the public. The claimant sought to challenge this action, alleging that the order could not apply to those exercising their rights to free expression under Article 10 of the European Convention on Human Rights. The Court of Appeal held that the actions of the police were lawful. Whilst s.30 had to be read so as to be compatible with Article 10, a direction under s.30 was capable of being lawful. An order under s.30 could be used with regard to any form of anti-social behaviour, not just those that had prompted the original order, and, on the facts, the actions of the police in requiring the claimant and others to disperse was lawful.

9.2.3 Breach of the peace

'...there is a breach of the peace whenever harm is actually done or is likely to be done to a person or in his presence to his property' Watkins LJ in *R v Howell* [1982] QB 416 at 427

A further source of powers to control public gatherings and individuals in public (and also private) space is the common law. At common law, the police have a duty to preserve the Queen's peace and may exercise powers, including the power of arrest, to prevent actual or apprehended breaches of the peace. These powers are preserved by s.40(4) of the Public Order Act 1986 and, notwithstanding the statutory powers given to the police by that Act and others, they continue to be used in a range of situations. There is nothing in the Public Order Act that requires the police to use statutory powers rather than these common law powers, so the police therefore have a choice as to which powers they exercise, subject, of course, to the relevant criteria being present. There are certain advantages to using the common law powers as they have a degree of flexibility not enjoyed by those created by statute. However, in *R(Laporte) v Chief Constable of Gloucestershire* [2007] 2 WLR 46, discussed further below, the House of Lords indicated that the common law powers in relation to breach of the peace should only be used where it is necessary to do so and as a last resort, thus indicating that statutory powers should be used in preference to them.

Breach of the peace is also an anomalous concept in English law as it is not a criminal offence, yet there is a power of arrest in respect of it. The virtue of these powers has been explained primarily in terms of enabling the police to prevent disorder. Following this line of reasoning, the legality of an individual's conduct takes second place to the preservation of public order. As we will see, more recent cases, partly influenced by the Human Rights Act, have moved away from this idea to a position requiring fault on the part of anyone against whom the police act.

Where a person is arrested in connection with a breach of the peace, a number of options follow. Given the preventive nature of the powers, the person may be released with no further action. Alternatively, he may be brought before the magistrates under s.115 Magistrates Courts Act 1980 to be bound over to keep the peace. A third possibility is that he may be charged with a substantive criminal offence. As there is now a power of arrest attaching to all criminal offences, we may consequently expect a reduction in the number of arrests for breaches of the peace.

These common law powers may be exercised in one of three circumstances, which were summarized by Lord Bingham in *R(Laporte) v Chief Constable of Gloucestershire* [2007] 2 WLR 46 at [29]:

> Every constable, and also every citizen, enjoys the power and is subject to a duty to seek to prevent, by arrest or other action short of arrest, any breach of the peace occurring in his presence, or any breach of the peace which (having occurred) is likely to be renewed, or any breach of the peace which is about to occur.

What constitutes a breach of the peace?

The courts have had to focus on two main questions. First, what constitutes a breach of the peace; and secondly, in what circumstances can the police act with regard to an actual or apprehended breach of the peace. As to the first, the generally accepted definition is that provided by Watkins LJ in *R v Howell* ([1982] QB 416 at 427):

> We are emboldened to say that there is a breach of the peace whenever harm is actually done or is likely to be done to a person or in his presence to his property.

Although this appears rather vague, the European Court of Human Rights was prepared to accept, in *Steel v United Kingdom* [1999] 28 EHRR 603, that it was sufficiently precise to allow a restriction on free expression under Article 10. The hallmark of a breach of the peace is thus violence or the threat of it. It has been held that it follows from this that mere words, without a threat of violence, cannot amount to a breach of the peace. An example is provided by *R(Hawkes) v DPP* [2005] EWCA 3046 (Admin). Following the arrest of her son, the appellant sat in a police car, refused to get out and was abusive to police officers. It was held that this could not amount to a breach of the peace, as there was no threat of violence. This may be contrasted with *Howell*, where a noisy party had spilled out onto the street late at night and the police were called. It was held that the police had acted lawfully in arresting the defendant as they were entitled to conclude that there was a threat of violence, amounting to a breach of the peace, occurring if they did not act.

What can the police do with regard to a breach of the peace?

The question of when the police can act with respect to an actual or anticipated breach of the peace is more difficult to answer. There is a further and related question to consider: even accepting that the police can act in connection with a breach of the peace, what action can they take? These questions are easier to answer with regard to actual breaches of the peace than those which are anticipated. It has been long established that the police can act, indeed, are under a common law duty to act, including exercising the power of arrest, in respect of breaches of the peace that are occurring. This remains the position in law as long as arrest is not a disproportionate response to the situation.

It has been more difficult to resolve the issue of identifying the point at which the police may intervene where a breach of the peace is anticipated. After much discussion the House of Lords in *R(Laporte) v Chief Constable of Gloucestershire* has resolved a number of issues.

---

case close-up

R(Laporte) v Chief Constable of Gloucestershire [2007] 2 WLR 46

The House of Lords in *R(Laporte) v Chief Constable of Gloucestershire* concluded that the anticipated breach of the peace must be imminent. The court must further be satisfied that the officer's view that a breach of the peace was imminent was one based on reasonable grounds, both as to the occurrence of the breach of the peace and its imminence. Unless all these elements are present, the arrest will be unlawful. In that case, the claimant was travelling by coach from London to take part in a demonstration at RAF Fairford, an airbase in Gloucestershire. The chief constable believed that passengers on the three coaches that were travelling there were likely to cause a breach of the peace at that location, and instructed officers to intercept the coaches and, under an order made by virtue of s.60 Criminal Justice and Public Order Act 1994, to search them and the passengers they were carrying. The coaches were stopped some 5km from the airbase, and searches of both the coaches and the passengers were carried out. The coaches were then escorted back to London by the police, who did not allow them to stop until they had returned. The claimant challenged the legality of these actions. The House of Lords held that they were unlawful. Whilst the police did have powers to prevent actual or apprehended breaches of the peace, they had not used those powers lawfully in this instance: the police could only act with regard to an apprehended breach where it was imminent and there was no imminent breach of the peace at the point at which the coaches were stopped. Four of the judges were also of the view that the actions of the police were a disproportionate restriction on the rights of the claimant under Articles 10 and 11 in that they did not discriminate between those passengers who posed a threat to the peace and those, such as the claimant, who did not.

A number of features of this case may be noted. The first is the requirement that the anticipated breach of the peace must be imminent before any action by the police could be justified in law. The notion of imminence was explored in *Moss v McLachlan* [1985] IRLR 76. This was a case arising out of the miners' strike in 1984–5. Violence had occurred outside some pits involving pickets, the police and miners wishing to go to work. The police stopped cars which they believed to be carrying striking miners approximately a mile and a half from collieries in order to prevent them from proceeding to the collieries and joining a picket there. It was held that this action was lawful as the anticipated breach of the peace was imminent, given that it would only take a matter of minutes for the pickets to reach the colliery. On this basis, the House of Lords in *Laporte* distinguished between the situation in *Moss* and the situation in that case.

Secondly, in *Laporte*, the chief constable had instructed his officers not to arrest the passengers on the coaches because the anticipated breach of the peace was not imminent, but he believed that they could, in law, take action short of arrest. In this he was following previous case law. In *Moss*, the court seemed to envisage a sliding scale whereby the more imminent the breach of the peace, the more extensive the action the police could take. This was held to be incorrect in *Laporte*, where the House of Lords took the view that the police could only act when the breach of the peace was imminent and that if the circumstances did not justify the making of an arrest then they did not justify the taking of any other form of action. This has the effect of limiting the scope of the powers of the police, who now have a clearer threshold for action rather than the more elusive range of options left by cases such as *Moss*. The key judgement to be made is therefore the imminence of the breach of the peace.

A third feature is that the courts have moved to a position where the police can only act against those whose conduct is likely to be violent. In earlier cases, the courts had upheld the use of police powers against individuals whose conduct was otherwise lawful. Thus, in cases where a speaker was producing a hostile reaction from a crowd (other than in circumstances where the speaker was going out of his way to provoke it) one response from the police had been to require the speaker to desist. It seems clear now that the focus of the attention of the police ought to be toward the hostile factions in the audience, as to act otherwise would be to unjustifiably restrict the speaker's right of free expression under Article 10. In *Redmond-Bate v DPP* [2000] HRLR 249, a police officer, believing that a breach of the peace would occur if he did not prevent the defendant, an evangelical lay preacher speaking outside Wakefield cathedral, was held to have acted unlawfully.

Fourthly, there is the issue of the circumstances in which the judgement of the police officers on the scene may be challenged. The decisions of the police must be based on reasonable grounds, which allow them to be questioned by a court: the court does not simply defer to the police officer's judgement. Lord Bingham pointed out in *Laporte* that, while the judgement of police officers on the spot deserves respect, ultimately the court has to decide whether the police have acted lawfully, and can decide that, on the facts, they have not. More recent cases, such as *Redmond-Bate v DPP*, where it was held that the police could not reasonably have apprehended a breach of the peace, have shown a greater willingness on the part of the courts to challenge the judgement of the police.

thinking point

Do the powers the police have in relation to breach of the peace make up for a lack of flexibility in relation to their statutory powers?

The courts ultimately hold the balance between the police and the citizen in this complex area of law, and the more recent cases suggest that they are acting in a more robust manner to ensure that the rights of citizens are upheld than has been the case in the past, where they were more ready to simply defer to the police. However, the police have the difficult job of holding the balance between possibly competing claims of those taking part in and being affected by public gatherings in a situation where they have to act quickly.

thinking point

As the police have so many different powers available, how do they decide which one to use in any given situation?

 # Questions

If you answer the following questions, you will have appreciated the main issues raised in this chapter. Check your answers against the notes provided at the back of the book.

1 Which human rights are protected?

2 What limitations on those rights are permissible?

3 What form do such limitations take in public order law?

4 What powers are given to the police to prevent disorder?

5 Has an adequate balance been achieved between giving the police sufficient powers to prevent disorder whilst upholding the right to free expression?

 # Further reading

 To further your understanding of the topics covered in this chapter, have a look at the reading materials mentioned below. Useful web links are also provided on the Online Resource Centre.

Richard Card, *Card, Cross and Jones Criminal Law* (Oxford University Press, 17th ed., 2006) ch.13
This gives you a view of the subject matter from a criminal law perspective.

Richard Stone, *Textbook on Civil Liberties and Human Rights* (Oxford University Press, 7th ed., 2008) ch.7
This gives you a human rights perspective on the subject matter.

S.H. Bailey, D.J. Harris and D.C. Ormerod, *Bailey, Harris & Jones Civil Liberties Cases and Materials* (Oxford University Press, 5th ed., 2001) ch.4
This gives you access to a collection of edited primary materials together with commentary and copious references to other secondary sources.

Administrative law: an introduction

Learning Objectives

While reading this chapter, you should aim to understand:

- what administrative law is, what it relates to and what its purposes might be;

- the nature of judicial review and the differences between review and appeal; and

- what other mechanisms exist to resolve or avoid disputes relating to administrative matters.

Introduction

In accordance with the idea of the rule of law, the organs of the state—central government, local government, and bodies such as the police—operate within a legal framework. The law, usually statute but also common law in certain situations, may give them the power to do something or may place them under a duty to act in a particular way.

We saw earlier that, as a broad generalization, (and, as with all generalizations, not entirely accurate) constitutional law is concerned with the major structures of the state apparatus and with the creation of the legal framework within which the state operates. As with the scope and purpose of constitutional law, the nature and content of administrative law is subject to debate, but it is generally concerned with the regulation of decisions made and actions taken by the executive. The courts have a prominent role in ensuring that the executive acts within the scope of the powers it has been given and that it carries out any duties imposed by the law. The courts largely do this by means of judicial review. Judicial review is a process by which the court can determine whether a public body has acted lawfully or unlawfully in what it has done or, in some cases, is proposing to do in the exercise of statutory powers or the fulfilment of statutory duties, and, in the case of central government, in exercising the royal prerogative. It will be immediately apparent, given the scope of modern government and the predominant basis of its powers in statutory provisions that judicial review plays a hugely important role in the relationship between the courts and the executive. The impact of judicial review has grown significantly since the second half of the 20th century and continues to grow apace.

The courts are not the only bodies that seek to ensure that the executive stays within the limits of its power. Other mechanisms exist whereby the activities of the executive may be subject to scrutiny. We have seen that Parliament itself exercises this function with regard to the policies and legislative activities of the government. There is also a system of tribunals, which are specialist bodies, similar to but not identical with the courts in function, which resolve certain types of dispute between the individual and the state. Courts and tribunals can only deal with administrative failings that involve a breach of the law. Administrative failings which do not amount to unlawful action may fall within the jurisdiction of an ombudsman, whose jurisdiction deals with poor administration rather than illegality. There are several types of ombudsman in the public sector, each dealing with a different aspect of executive activity, such as central government (the Parliamentary ombudsman, formally known as the Parliamentary Commissioner for Administration), local government (Commissioners for Local Administration) and the National Health Service (Health Service Commissioners). Inquiries may look at issues prior to a decision being taken, as in a planning inquiry, or may examine an event or phenomenon with a view to finding out what has gone on has happened in order to promote better practice in the future: examples might relate to some form of disaster or scandal. These three forms of administrative adjudication are considered further below.

10.1 Purposes of administrative law

There is some disagreement as to the purposes of administrative law. Many accounts emphasize its function as a set of rules and procedures by which the executive can be held accountable for its actions and its power checked if it is being used outside its proper limits. On this view, the law has a generally negative impact on the executive, and is primarily designed to stop abuses of power. From a citizen's perspective, however, the idea that it is there to protect citizens and uphold their rights by curbing the power of the state, confining it within its legal limits, is very positive. Other accounts, whilst not denying this role, emphasize the function of the law in supporting good administration by creating a framework designed to promote appropriate decision making by public officials and bodies. This seeks to ensure a proper balance between the desire of the executive to act without undue restraint on its ability to do things that it believes are necessary or desirable, and the legitimate interests of citizens to have their rights and wishes considered.

> **thinking point**
>
> *Can the law operate both negatively to prevent abuses of power and positively to encourage good administration?*

cross reference
See Chapter 3.

Underpinning administrative law are some important constitutional principles, discussed earlier. The courts operate within the principle of parliamentary supremacy. They are not able to control the activities of Parliament and have held that they are unable to challenge the validity of an Act of Parliament (see *R(Jackson v Attorney General* [2006] 1 AC 262).

They can, however, ensure that those given statutory powers or duties by Parliament act in accordance with Parliament's intentions, which includes ensuring that legislation complies with the rights under the European Convention on Human Rights brought into English law by the Human Rights Act 1998. To this end, they interpret the legislation Parliament has passed. In doing so they have also developed a set of general principles that they assume Parliament intended to be part of all legislation. Amongst these are the principles of administrative law. These are rules developed by the judges and read into statutes affecting the executive unless Parliament has excluded them or has made express provision covering the same ground.

10.1.1 **Some distinctions**

Before considering these further, some important distinctions need to be drawn. Judicial review and the other mechanisms for resolving or avoiding disputes considered here lie in the field of public law, which can be distinguished from private law. Public law is concerned with the law that relates to matters in which the state, or some body exercising executive functions of the state, such as a local authority, exercises power. Private law, on the other hand, is concerned with the law that regulates dealings between private individuals. It is worth remembering that, in law, an organization such as a company or indeed a local authority is a 'person' capable of dealings in private law such as making contracts or committing torts. Administrative law is, therefore, not only concerned with the interpretation of legislation but is also concerned with the way in which government, local government and similar bodies act, largely in the exercise of statutory powers or the fulfilment of statutory duties. The implication of this is that judicial review is only available where a public body is exercising its public law functions. If it is acting as an ordinary individual, by, for example, making a contract with a supplier or acting as an employer with regard to its individual employees, then it is acting in a private law capacity. These distinctions will become clearer as we proceed to examine the law in this area.

A further distinction that needs to be drawn is between the functions of appeal and review. An appeal is usually by way of rehearing and is designed to consider the decision of the lower court and to see whether it was correct. By contrast, a review is concerned with a wider idea of legality—that is, whether the decision was within the range of decisions that a reasonable decision maker could properly have come to, rather than the question whether that decision is right or wrong. As long as a decision is within the range of acceptable decisions that could have been reached then it will be lawful. It follows that the court exercising its power of review is, on the whole, more concerned with the way in which the decision was reached rather than its merits. This idea is explored further in this section.

10.1.2 **Separation of powers**

cross reference

You may like to remind yourself of the principles involved by re-reading the relevant sections of Chapter 2.

An important underlying issue is the relationship between the courts, Parliament and the executive in relation to the exercise of power. The principles of the separation of powers and the rule of law are important theoretical bases here.

As we have seen, the courts have conceded that they have limited powers with regard to challenges to the validity of legislation. They can decide whether a particular instrument is an Act of Parliament. They can exercise powers of interpretation of it, especially with regard to ensuring that it complies with the requirements of the Human Rights Act which has the effect of giving the Act a wider or narrower application. They can disapply legislation which contravenes European Union law.

They have been more robust with regard to action taken by the executive in the exercise of statutory powers and, latterly, with exercises of the royal prerogative. It is of interest that Parliament has not sought to put the whole area of judicial review on a statutory footing but has largely left it to the courts to develop, especially with regard to the development of grounds of review. In part, this might be because the courts have exercised restraint in exercising their powers, recognizing the importance of maintaining a proper relationship between themselves and the government.

10.1.3 Limitations on judicial review

Judicial review is not the only mechanism for resolving disputes between individuals and the state. Courts have many good qualities as bodies for the resolution of certain types of dispute. However, they also have their limitations in providing appropriate forms of adjudication. It has not only been through recognition of this, but also the development of different and more appropriate forms of dispute resolution for certain types of disputes that have led to the development of other means. Before considering these it is worth examining other ways in which issues between individuals and the state may be dealt with. One possibility is to invoke the political process rather than legal channels by an individual contacting a Member of Parliament. One of the functions of Members of Parliament is to deal with matters brought to them by their constituents. This may be during surgeries held in the constituency or by an individual writing to a Member of Parliament about a particular issue.

To these informal mechanisms for resolving disputes must be added the more formal ways of dealing with them. Three such are tribunals, which provide a more appropriate forum for resolving particular types of disputes than the courts; inquiries, which are really concerned with the prevention of disputes by identifying the ways in which things have happened in the past with a view to preventing them happening in the future; and the ombudsman who is concerned with remedying failures in administration. Each of these may be considered in turn.

10.2 Tribunals

Tribunals are one way of resolving disputes outside the court system. Alternatives to the court system have grown up where it has been felt that the interests of justice are better served by resolving disputes outside that system. There have been two particular thrusts to the arguments relating to the desirability of tribunals, one positive and one negative. The negative aspect of the argument recognizes the limitations of the courts in dealing with particular types of dispute; for example, where the context of the dispute is an important factor in its successful resolution, as for example in relation to agriculture, health or industry, or matters involving economic or social arguments, rather than the matter simply being a question of the interpretation of legal provisions and their application to a set of facts. The positive argument in favour of tribunals lies in recognizing that, whilst the courts do a good job in resolving certain types of dispute, typically those involving complex questions of law, there may be a forum better equipped to resolve disputes in a more satisfactory way outside the courts system.

thinking point

As you read on, think about whether the development of a separate set of tribunals is a better solution than simply expanding the court system and changing the ways courts resolve disputes.

10.2.1 The development of tribunals

Expansion of the tribunal system

Tribunals grew up alongside the expansion in the functions of government following World War II and the development of the welfare state. These developments brought citizens into contact with the state in ways that had not occurred before, and there was a corresponding need to provide mechanisms for the resolution of the inevitable disputes that would arise, whether over welfare benefits, housing, health, or other aspects of social provision. Traditionally, these disputes would be expected to go to the courts, which were the only recognized means of resolving disputes about legal entitlement. However, disputes with the state over allocations and entitlements were likely to be characterized by a simple disagreement over the application of statutory requirements to the facts and thus the need for complex legal argument or procedures for the establishment of facts was not present. Equally, the volume of disputes this type of legislation would generate threatened to overwhelm the courts, making the establishment of other forms of dispute resolution imperative. Further, many of these disputes require swift resolution given the nature of the subject matter: deciding whether or not someone is entitled to welfare benefits cannot wait for years to be resolved.

All of these factors pointed toward the need for alternatives to the courts to enable such disputes to be dealt with in ways that were appropriate to their nature.

Features of the developing tribunal system

cross reference
The nature of a fair hearing is considered in Chapter 12.

A system of tribunals, therefore, grew up operating alongside the courts and subject to the supervisory jurisdiction of the High Court, as an important check on their activities and providing a mechanism by which their decisions could be reviewed. A significant feature of the system was its fragmentation. Each tribunal was attached to the government department to whose activities it related, as tribunals were seen as essentially administrative rather than judicial in character and thus an adjunct to the department in question. Further, each tribunal had its own jurisdiction and procedures, all generally based on the notion of a fair hearing but differing in detail.

The Franks Report

A major examination of the work of tribunals was undertaken in the Franks Report, published in 1957 (*Report of the Committee on Administrative Tribunals and Enquiries* Cmnd. 218). Whilst recognizing that tribunals were not courts (see para.40) the way tribunals are described in the report suggests they were seen as mini courts, with essentially similar adversarial processes. Franks identified openness, fairness and impartiality as the underlying principles for any system of tribunals (paras.23ff). This approach can be criticized for failing to recognize that tribunals are conceptually different from courts, being essentially directed to offering an alternative form of dispute resolution without the formalities of the ordinary courts, with an appreciation of the context in which disputes operate, and with speed and economy. It is also worth noting that tribunals are not conceived as an alternative to the courts in the sense of giving the litigant a choice as to which forum to use. Where tribunals are established to resolve disputes in particular contexts, they are the forum for resolving those disputes. The courts only become involved if the statute establishing the tribunal provides for an appeal against its decision or where a person seeks to challenge the decision of a tribunal by way of judicial review.

The Leggatt Review of Tribunals

The more recent Leggatt Review of Tribunals (*Tribunals for Users* 2001 <http://www.tribunals-review.org.uk/leggatthtm/leg-00.htm>) came closer to recognizing the significance of some of these matters. Its terms of reference were to recommend a system that was independent, coherent, professional, cost effective and user friendly. This last requirement recognized that one of the key features of tribunals was that people should, as far as possible, be able to use them unaided. Leggatt's recommendations were built upon by the White Paper *Transforming Public Services: Complaints Redress and Tribunals* (Cm 6243 (2004)) which, in turn, led to the establishment of the Tribunals Service in 2006 and the passing of the Tribunals Courts and Enforcement Act 2007, a wide-ranging measure which, amongst other things, creates a new structure for tribunals which began to become operational in November 2008. This essentially involves the creation of a single unified tribunal system rather than the previous fragmented system.

Independence from government

Tribunals have been divorced from their previous relationship with government departments, in which they were not independent adjudicatory bodies, as required by Article 6(1) of the European Convention on Human Rights. This provides, so far as is relevant for present purposes, that 'in the determination of his civil rights and obligations or of any criminal charge against him, everyone is entitled to a fair and public hearing within a reasonable time by an independent and impartial tribunal established by law'. The word 'tribunal' there is being used in its general sense of an institution whereby matters may be adjudicated rather than in the more limited and specialized sense in which it is used in the present context. Article 6(1) is thus satisfied by a court or similar form of institution. Given that tribunals in this narrower sense are involved in the determination of civil rights and obligations, they fall squarely within this provision and need, amongst other characteristics, to be independent of government.

10.2.2 Limitations of the courts and virtues of tribunals

The development of a range of tribunals was in part prompted by recognition of the limitations of the courts in their ability to resolve disputes in an appropriate way.

The context of a dispute

The courts are concerned with the resolution of disputes without putting that dispute into context. This is entirely appropriate when dealing with difficult points of law or when ascertaining complex facts but there are many disputes which would be more satisfactorily resolved by examining the subject matter in its context in order to appreciate what the matter is really about. Courts spend considerable amounts of time ascertaining the facts or adjudicating over complex arguments of law before reaching a decision.

There are many decisions however for which this process is not ideally suited. The development of tribunals recognizes not only the limitations of the courts but also, more positively, the virtues of deciding certain types of case in a different forum. Decisions in courts are made by judges who are experts in the law but have little professional understanding of the context in which the law operates, and are not, in any event, able to hear such argument, as arguments in courts of law are confined to matters of law. By bringing in people with expertise in the subject matter of the tribunal the decision making process is informed in a professional way by experts. Thus, the traditional composition of a tribunal will have a legally qualified chair, as matters of law are involved, with two other members skilled in the specialism involved. So, for example, an Employment Tribunal will have members drawn from the employers and the trade unions, whilst a tribunal dealing with mental health issues, now the First Tier Tribunal (Mental Health), will contain health and social care professionals. The object in expanding the membership of the tribunal is to broaden the basis on which decisions are made with a view to making better quality decisions in that particular field.

The adversarial approach

The adversarial approach to legal proceedings was also felt to be inappropriate to many types of dispute. The traditional legal hearing is conceived as two sides arguing their case before an impartial, and largely non-interventionist, judge who would then pronounce on the merits of the arguments that had been put. This may be appropriate where both sides are represented by lawyers, but there are implications for the fairness of the proceedings when parties are unrepresented.

thinking point
What do you think are the limitations of the courts as bodies for determining disputes?

thinking point

Are there better ways of determining disputes than the adversarial model? Do different types of dispute require a different approach?

Cost

Underlying these arguments about effectiveness of the adjudication process are issues of cost. By keeping lawyers out and by dealing with business more swiftly, cost is inevitably saved. As the terms of reference for the Leggatt Review recognize, the costs of justice are an important facet of its operation and much as we might like the budget to be open ended, the reality is that it is not, and pressures from the Treasury ensure that expenditure on the administration of justice is kept under control. Tribunals contribute to this by providing cheaper forms of dispute resolution. The budget for legal assistance has never been large enough to support representation in all cases, and in any event this may not always be suitable where the dispute is a relatively simple factual one.

Formality

Courts are very formal in everything they do, from the buildings in which they are housed to the procedures they adopt. Many disputes do not need to be resolved in these very formal surroundings, which can often be at least bewildering for litigants and at worst, intimidating. One of the guiding principles for tribunals was that they should be less formal than the ordinary courts. This may involve a relaxation of the normal rules of court procedure and also rules of evidence with a view to enabling a wider range of material to be discussed than is possible in an ordinary court. This has not always been achieved in all tribunals, some of which, to all intents and purposes, replicate most of the features of ordinary court procedure. Others, however, are noticeably different to the ordinary courts in dispensing with many of the formal trappings of the court room in terms of, for example, the nature of the premises, the layout of the room in which the hearing takes place, the clothes worn by the participants and the language used.

10.2.3 **Lawyers**

A key factor in the formality of proceedings relates to the presence of lawyers, who use formal language which is often unintelligible to the lay person. Lawyers are experts in interpretation of the law and in ascertaining facts, but, like judges, are not versed in the context in which particular disputes operate. Thus, on this argument, for tribunals to operate effectively lawyers might be discouraged. This was recognized by the Leggatt Review which, taking into account its terms of reference in establishing a system that is user friendly, concluded that this might lead to a reduction in legal representation. This has been a contentious issue throughout the history of discussions of tribunals, with two opposing views. One view is that lawyers should not be participants in the processes of tribunals unless their presence was necessary to secure fair procedure. For example, lawyers may be necessary to secure a fair hearing in situations where complex issues of law were involved or where the individual could not properly represent himself: again, tribunals dealing with issues of mental health would be an example where it would be appropriate to have legal representation. This is because they are concerned with the issue of whether a person should continue to be compulsorily detained under powers contained in the Mental Health Act 1983. In such cases, the individual may not be able to put the case adequately. Further, as the individual's livelihood is at stake it is imperative that the case is put as effectively as possible. These types of case apart, the argument would also be that lawyers would add unnecessarily to the costs and despatch of proceedings.

Objections as to whether evidence can be tested with sufficient rigour in the absence of lawyers could be met by a more interventionist approach on the part of the adjudicator(s), as long as the adjudicator's impartiality was maintained, which requires a delicate balance in the conduct of proceedings on the part of the adjudicator. The counter argument to this approach is that lawyers, properly briefed and representing the individual's interests are essential to ensure that matters are properly considered and evidence tested, both of which involve skills that the average lay person would not be expected to have and which do not put in jeopardy the impartiality of the adjudicator. Allied to this argument would be an argument that lawyers should be publicly funded to appear in tribunals as they are in the ordinary courts, an argument countered by opponents of lawyers in tribunal on the grounds that funding them to appear in tribunals is an unnecessary and ill advised drain on the resources which would be best targeted at ensuring representation in the courts. Given that the government is keen to keep the costs of the legal system under control, as with other aspects of public expenditure, especially in times of general economic hardship, it is unlikely that any activity involving an expansion in the funds needed by the system would find favour

thinking point
Are lawyers always necessary to ensure that disputes are effectively resolved?

10.2.4 **The Independent Tribunal Service**

A key feature of any form of dispute resolution, and one at the heart of the Leggatt recommendations, is the need for independence. This impacted at two levels in his report. First, tribunals had grown up to deal with particular disputes and had been located within the government department to which that dispute related. The advantage of this was that the specialism of the tribunal was preserved. Overall responsibility was given to the Council on Tribunals (now replaced by the Tribunals Service), an overarching body charged with supervising the running of tribunals. However, the system was not very efficient, for every department had to have its own administrative mechanisms to support those tribunals that existed under it. Leggatt recommended that in the interests of consistency and efficiency the tribunals should all come under one department with common administrative support.

The second aspect was securing independence in decision making. Where tribunals were linked to a government department and appointments were made by that department there was little appearance of independence. A particular impetus to achieve this came from the enactment of the Human Rights Act 1998, for, as seen above, Article 6 requires that the determination of civil rights has to be determined by an independent and impartial tribunal established by law. Both these objectives were, to a considerable degree, realized by the establishment of the independent tribunal service in 2006, and the trend has been continued by the Tribunals Courts and Enforcement Act 2007.

The procedures of tribunals

Where the new body can be expected to achieve some consistency is in respect of the procedures of tribunals. Each tribunal has its own rules of procedure which are all based on the principles of natural justice. They are more flexible than the rules of procedure for the ordinary courts, recognizing the greater informality of tribunal proceedings and the relaxation of some of the strict rules of evidence in the interests of proper resolution of the types of dispute with which they deal. However this cannot be pushed too far, as any relaxations of, for example, the rules of evidence must still conform to the requirements of natural justice.

10.2.5 The Tribunals, Courts and Enforcement Act 2007

The new system of tribunals is established under the Tribunals, Courts and Enforcement Act 2007 and is being phased in from 2008 onwards. It involves the creation of a two-tier system, with first tier tribunals and an Upper Tribunal. The former involve gathering into groups (called chambers) a set of tribunals with a certain commonality. So, for example, a health, education and social care chamber has been established which involves matters relating to mental health, care standards and special educational needs and will facilitate some pooling of expertise. The Upper Tribunal will effectively have an appellate and review function, which will, in part, mean that cases of judicial review will go there rather than to the Administrative court.

A further development involves changes to what were formerly the chairs of tribunals who have been upgraded to judges and become part of the judiciary, thus emphasizing their independence and adding gravitas to the tribunal system.

As with any new system, it will take time for the system to become fully established and for its operation to be evaluated.

thinking point
Do we need a system of tribunals? What do they add to the judicial system?

10.3 Inquiries

10.3.1 Two types of inquiry

Inquiries are really concerned with preventing disputes from arising in the future, rather than adjudicating over disputes that have arisen. They tend to be one of two kinds.

Informing the decision making process

First, there are inquiries which seek to contribute to the decision making process in relation to decisions that have yet to be taken. They seek to inform the decision making process by exploring issues that arise in respect of the decision and provide evidence which the decision maker can draw on in making the decision. The object of the exercise is to improve the quality of decision making. Such inquiries also have as part of the purpose to pre-empt any objections that might be raised about a decision by raising them before the decision is made rather than afterwards, so that account can be taken of them in the making of the decision. These are usually regular inquiries forming part of an established process. Planning inquiries would be a good example. The inquiry listens to a range of views about the proposal, tests those views by cross-examination and reaches a conclusion, drawing on the evidence that has been presented to the inquiry and making an assessment of that evidence. The results are then presented to the decision maker to help to inform the final decision.

Learning from events

The second type of inquiry is that which is held following an event. These are self evidently of an irregular nature. The object is to establish what happened and to learn from it in order to prevent a recurrence of the undesirable things that have happened. Recent examples include:

- the Shipman Inquiry, examining the circumstances surrounding the murders committed by Dr. Harold Shipman (six reports 2002–2005);
- the Victoria Climbie Inquiry (Cm 5730 (2003)); and
- the Hutton Inquiry into the death of Dr David Kelly, HC 247 (2004).

There is also the ongoing inquiry into the events of Bloody Sunday in Northern Ireland in 1972 which Lord Saville has been conducting since 1998 and which has not yet reported and shows no signs of doing so in the near future (see <http://www.bloody-sunday-inquiry.org.uk/index.htm>).

10.3.2 **Statutory and non-statutory inquiries**

Inquiries fall into two broad categories, statutory and non-statutory. The Inquiries Act 2005 rationalized the position regarding statutory inquiries by bringing all the powers for establishing an inquiry into one piece of legislation rather than being scattered across the statute book. The Act now gives Ministers the power to decide whether to hold an inquiry under that statutory framework. It leaves open the possibility of establishing a non-statutory inquiry which could, for example, be ordered by Parliament or established by way of a royal commission.

10.3.3 **Procedure**

The procedure at an inquiry is different from that in court proceedings in that it is not adversarial, though this might not always be apparent from the way it proceeds. As the object of the exercise is to gather and test information, the process involves a more inquisitorial approach, with the chair of the inquiry much more actively involved in the proceedings than a judge would be. Whilst the procedure of the inquiry will vary depending on the nature of it, the underlying principles remain those of natural justice. Thus, in principle, any objector or party to the inquiry must be given a fair hearing. Fairness needs to be seen in the context of the inquiry doing its job and arriving at a conclusion in a reasonable time, which may mean that not everyone who wishes to speak or cross-examine witnesses may be able to do so, as the multiplicity of parties may make this unworkable. Fairness is thus a question of balance between the various competing interests and parties. In *Bushell v Secretary of State for the Environment* [1980] 2 All ER 608, for example, an inspector at an inquiry was upheld in his decision not to allow every objector at the inquiry to cross-examine witnesses where this served no purpose and was consistent with the overall fairness of the proceedings.

In applying the principles of natural justice, however, it must be remembered that the inquiry is not actually making final and binding decisions. The ultimate decision is made by someone other than the chair of the inquiry, for example, a Minister. Thus in *R(Alconbury) v Secretary of State for the Environment*, [2003] 2 AC 29, proceedings under planning legislation at an inquiry were challenged on the basis that they breached Article 6 of the European Convention on Human Rights in not being conducted by an independent and impartial tribunal in that neither the inquiry nor the Minister, who was the eventual decision maker, satisfied those requirements. The House of Lords held that the proceedings did conform with Article 6, and by implication with the requirements of natural justice, in that, viewing the process as a whole, there were issues of policy involved which the Minister was entitled to take into account, and that sufficient independent and impartial determination was provided by the possibility of a review of the Minister's decision by the courts.

thinking point
Do you agree? Should every objector have an opportunity to put his view to the inquiry?

thinking point
If inquiries are not actually deciding anything, is there any point in having them?

10.4 Ombudsman

The ombudsman provides a different approach to the resolution of disputes with the state in being concerned with failures in administration. The courts can only adjudicate on disputes involving an allegation that the decision maker has acted unlawfully. The ombudsman has essentially two concerns. The first is to investigate individual complaints about failures in the administrative process. The second follows on from the first and is a concern to improve standards in public administration. In part this is achieved as a consequence of the first of the ombudsman's activities but additionally the ombudsman publishes reports which seek to improve standards in administration generally.

10.4.1 The parliamentary ombudsman

The ombudsman concept was imported from Sweden. The first ombudsman in the UK was the parliamentary ombudsman, or Parliamentary Commissioner for Administration (PCA), to give the full and proper title. This office was introduced under the Parliamentary

Ombudsman

233

Commissioner for Administration Act 1967. The idea was not universally accepted within Parliament. Members of Parliament felt that it was their role to investigate complaints about public administration and to take them up with Ministers thereby holding Ministers to account for their actions and those of their departments: there was thus a fundamental concern that the introduction of the ombudsman was undermining ministerial responsibility.

A compromise was reached whereby complaints could not be taken directly to the ombudsman, but had to be referred to a Member of Parliament in the first instance. The MP then has a discretion as to how to resolve the complaint, which may involve referring it to the ombudsman, though not necessarily. By this means MPs could, if they so wished, seek to resolve the complaint by whatever means they thought appropriate. One of these options is to refer the matter to the ombudsman. However, it is clear from *Re Fletcher's Application* [1970] 2 All ER 527 that an MP has a wide discretion as to whether or not to refer a matter to the ombudsman and that this discretion is difficult to challenge through the courts.

thinking point
Should members of the public be able to contact the ombudsman directly?

10.4.2 **The extension of the ombudsman system**

The ombudsman concept has developed from this initial version to provide for commissioners for local administration to exercise a similar function with regard to local government, and health service commissioners to oversee the National Health Service. The concept has also expanded into the private sector with an ombudsman for many aspects of financial services, banking, insurance and building societies.

10.4.3 **Jurisdiction**

The jurisdiction of the ombudsman is defined by the term maladministration. During the debates on the legislation, the term was explained by the sponsoring Minister, Richard Crossman, as meaning bias, neglect, inattention, delay, incompetence, inaptitude, perversity, turpitude or arbitrariness. This list was adopted judicially by Lord Denning in *R v Commissioner for Local Administration ex P Bradford Metropolitan City Council* [1979] 2 All ER 881. He went on to explain that this description covered the manner in which a decision was reached or discretion was exercised, but not the merits of the decision or the way in which discretion was exercised. It follows that if the decision has been properly taken or discretion properly exercised then it is not open to question by the ombudsman, notwithstanding that the citizen complaining about it is unhappy with it. This was taken further by Lord Donaldson in *R v Commissioner for Local Administration ex p Eastleigh Borough Council* [1988] 3 All ER 151, where he said that the notions of administration and maladministration were concerned with the manner in which decisions were reached and the manner in which they are or are not implemented, but have nothing to do with the nature, quality or reasonableness of the decision itself.

However, a major limitation on the effectiveness of the ombudsman relates to jurisdiction. A number of complaints, including those that reach the ombudsman, are rejected because they lie outside the jurisdiction of the ombudsman. For example, the ombudsman is unable to consider any matters that relate to the investigation of crime or national security, or matters which are or could be subject to the jurisdiction of a court. Further, there are limitations in what the ombudsman can do even if it is found that a complaint is justified, as there is no power to force the relevant body to act on the recommendations of the ombudsman. The ombudsman essentially relies on the good will and sense of responsibility of the body to which any decision relates to act on the ombudsman's decision in an appropriate way. However, it seems clear that it will be difficult for a person who is dissatisfied with the way in which the ombudsman has investigated a complaint to get redress through the courts. In *R v Parliamentary Commissioner for Administration ex p Dyer* [1994] 1 WLR 621, it was held that whilst the ombudsman is not immune from judicial review, he had a wide discretion in the way in which he investigated matters and with regard to any conclusion he might reach, and that a considerable measure of subjective judgement was involved in such decisions, making the whole process difficult to challenge, as the basis on which a court could intervene is very limited.

The problem that is left for any person who is aggrieved by the decision or actions of a public body is to decide which is the most appropriate way of challenging it. This may be borne in mind whilst reading the next two chapters on judicial review.

? Questions

If you answer the following questions, you will have appreciated the main issues raised in this chapter. Check your answers against the notes provided at the back of the book.

1 What is administrative law?

2 What matters does administrative law cover?

3 What are the purposes of administrative law?

4 What is judicial review? How does it differ from an appeal?

5 What other mechanisms exist to resolve or avoid disputes relating to administrative matters?

 # Further reading

 To further your understanding of the topics covered in this chapter, have a look at the reading materials mentioned below. Useful web links are also provided on the Online Resource Centre.

Justice—All Souls Committee, *Administrative Justice: Some Necessary Reforms* (Clarendon Press, 1988) ch.2
Although rather dated, this gives a useful account of the relationship between judicial review and other forms of administrative redress and the promotion of good administrative practices.

Lord Woolf, 'Public Law—Private Law: Why the Divide?' [1986] PL 231
This explores the implications of the division of English law into Public law and Private law.

Peter Cane, *Administrative Law* (Oxford University Press, 4th ed., 2004) ch.1
This gives you an introduction to the nature and purposes of administrative law.

Judicial review: procedure

Learning Objectives

While reading this chapter, you should aim to understand:

- the nature and availability of judicial review;
- who may bring a claim for judicial review and against whom a claim may be brought;
- the type of dispute that can be challenged by a claim for judicial review; and
- the main procedural requirements involved in a claim for judicial review.

Introduction

Law may be subdivided in many ways. One significant division, particularly relevant with regard to this chapter, is between substantive law and procedural law. Put simply, substantive law is concerned with *what* a person may or may not do, whilst the law relating to procedure is concerned with *how* a person may or may not act. A further distinction, of considerable relevance here, is between public and private law. Public law, as we have seen, is concerned with the law that regulates matters that involve the state whereas private law is concerned with the regulation of relations between individuals, (bearing in mind, as explained in the previous chapter, that an organization can be a person in law). This chapter and the next reflect these distinctions with regard to the court-based process of judicial review, with this chapter considering the procedural aspects of the process, whilst the next concerns the substantive grounds on which judicial review may be exercised. There have been significant changes to the process and terminology relating to judicial review over the years and it is necessary to be aware of the former terms when reading older cases.

As we saw in the previous chapter, judicial review is a process by which the court can determine whether a public body (a term explained more fully later) has acted lawfully or unlawfully in what it has done or, in some cases, is proposing to do. A claim for judicial review is heard by the Administrative Court, which is part of the High Court. The claim proceeds in two stages. First, the claimant has to seek permission to proceed. If successful, the case then proceeds to a full hearing where the merits of the claim are determined. If successful the claimant may be granted a remedy. This is all explored further below.

11.1 The decision making process

Traditionally, the focus of judicial review is on the process by which decisions are made and not on the substance of the actual decision. As Lord Brightman put it in *Chief Constable of the North Wales Police v Evans* [1982] 1 WLR 1155 at 1173, 'Judicial review is concerned, not with the decision, but with the decision-making process.' This is significant in that the function of the court has traditionally been conceived as deciding whether the decision was one that could legitimately have been reached. As long as the decision is within the range of decisions that a person or body could properly have come to, it will be unchallengeable. The courts are only concerned with overseeing due process and locating the decision within the scope of the powers given. They are not concerned with the question of whether it is 'right' or 'wrong': they are interested in legality rather than correctness. This is an important distinction, not least in relation to the aftermath of proceedings for judicial review.

thinking point
Why shouldn't a court consider whether a decision is right or wrong?

11.2 Remedies

If the claimant is successful, the court may issue one of a number of orders (see s.31 Supreme Court Act 1981, below). These are:

- Quashing Order (formerly certiorari)—this quashes a decision that has been made;
- Prohibiting Order (formerly prohibition)—this stops something from happening;
- Mandatory Order (formerly mandamus)—this requires someone to do something and is usually used in respect of duties;
- Injunction—this stops someone doing something;
- Declaration—this is the least coercive of the orders as it sets out the legal position of the parties and then leaves it to them to act lawfully in accordance with the position as identified by the court; and
- Damages—usually damages can only be obtained through judicial review proceedings when the unlawful activity of the decision maker gives rise to a cause of action e.g. a tort as well as being unlawful because it is an unlawful exercise of power. However, s.8 of the Human Rights Act 1998 allows a court to award an appropriate remedy, which may be damages, where there is a violation of the Convention rights by a public authority.

Remedies following successful judicial review proceedings are at the discretion of the court rather than automatic. Further, they generally leave open the possibility of the decision maker going back and making a fresh decision, only on the subsequent occasion doing so in a lawful manner. This may result in a favourable outcome for the claimant in that the decision maker may make a different decision, this time favourable to the claimant, second time round. However, it is also possible that the decision maker may make a fresh decision, but arrive at the same conclusion, unfavourable to the claimant. The decision maker may have adopted a different route to that decision which made it lawful.

An example is provided by the circumstances of *R v Gloucestershire County Council ex p Barry* [1997] AC 584.

thinking point
Is the response of Gloucestershire County Council unduly cynical?

case close-up

R v Gloucestershire County Council ex p Barry [1997] AC 584

Mr. Barry had been assessed by the council as needing community care services and services were provided for him. The council then became concerned about its financial situation and decided that it could not longer afford to provide services for Mr. Barry. It therefore told him that it was withdrawing the services, citing its lack of resources as the reason. Mr. Barry challenged this decision on two grounds. One was that the council was not entitled to take its resources into account when assessing need. On this point, Mr. Barry lost, though by the narrowest of margins. The House of Lords held, by 3: 2, that a council could take into account its resources when assessing need, even though the statute was silent on this point. However, at first instance, Mr. Barry won on his other point, which was that, once he had been assessed as needing services, those services could not be withdrawn without a further reassessment. This turned out to be a hollow victory, for Mr. Barry was subsequently reassessed by Gloucestershire County Council who decided that, taking its resources and his circumstances into account, he did not need the services that he had formerly been assessed as needing.

More recently, as will be seen, the courts have expanded the scope of their inquiry to look more closely at the substance of the decision as well as the process by which it has been reached. This is significant in that it extends the powers of the courts into areas hitherto largely left alone.

11.3 The framework for judicial review

As with many aspects of procedure, the rules relating to judicial review are governed by a mixture of statute, secondary legislation and case law. The statutory basis for judicial review is found in s.31 Supreme Court Act 1981, which provides that an application to the High Court for one or more of certain forms of relief (i.e. remedy, the terms are used interchangeably in this chapter)—a mandatory order, prohibiting order or quashing order and certain forms of injunction and declaration—'shall be made in accordance with rules of court by a procedure to be known as an application for judicial review'. This general statement is fleshed out by detailed rules in the form of the Civil Procedure Rules, which are regularly revised. Judicial Review is governed by Part 54 of these Rules, which refer to a claim for judicial review. It is unfortunate that, when s.31 was amended to reflect the new terminology for the remedies, it did not also replace the reference to an application for judicial review with a claim for judicial review, which is the term that will be used in this chapter.

11.3.1 When is judicial review used?

Building on s.31, r.54.1(2) provides that a claim for judicial review means 'a claim to review the lawfulness of an enactment or a decision action or failure to act in relation to the exercise of a public function'. As we saw in the previous chapter, judicial review is different in its nature and objectives from an appeal. Under Part 54, judicial review is subject to procedures that differ from those relating to an ordinary claim initiated in court in private law proceedings. This immediately raises a question as to when it is appropriate to use judicial review. From the point of view of the claimant, there are many advantages in bringing a claim under the normal civil process. In particular, the time limits are more generous, the rules of evidence are more liberal and there is no need to seek permission to proceed. The limitations on bringing a claim for judicial review, discussed below, exist to support the effective functioning of both the judicial and the administrative process.

It is not in the interests of either central or local government, for example, to be involved in proceedings that drag on, especially if they are going to have to change their practices as a result of the outcome of the case. It is of the essence of public law claims that they involve interests going beyond those of the immediate parties and those interests form a vital feature of any case. The judges have a duty to see that cases are heard fairly, fairness affecting not only the parties but the wider interests of justice.

thinking point

Are the interests of the government any different from those of any other individual or body with regard to litigation?

thinking point

Why should the court and not the claimant be able to choose which process to follow?

The question, therefore, is whether the clamant should be able to choose whether to proceed by way of an ordinary action or judicial review, or whether restrictions on that choice should be imposed. The courts have taken the latter course, and have limited the choices open to the claimant. This was made clear in a pair of cases decided in the House of Lords at around the same time. In *O'Reilly v Mackman* [1983] 2 AC 237, the House of Lords held that prisoners challenging the decision of a board of visitors must do so by means of a claim for judicial review and not by an ordinary writ. This was because their claim raised issues of public law and judicial review was the only procedure that could be followed where this was the case. In so deciding, the House of Lords drew a distinction between public law proceedings and those in private law as far as process was concerned. Those claimants bringing public law proceedings are, consequently, subject to the limitations indicated above that are part of the process of judicial review and which offer measures of protection for those bodies against whom a claim for judicial review is brought that are not available in ordinary civil proceedings. This is discussed further below.

This approach means that each decision will need to be scrutinized carefully to see whether it involves public law issues or private law issues, as the way in which the claim is characterized determines the process that must be used. However, cases do not always fall neatly into one or other category: they may contain elements of both public and private law. The difficulties and subtleties to which this can give rise were illustrated in the case decided alongside *O'Reilly v Mackman*, *Cocks v Thanet District Council* [1983] 2 AC 286. Here, the House of Lords had to consider the nature of decision making in relation to homelessness. They observed that a decision whether a person was or was not homeless within the meaning of the legislation was a matter of public law and could only be challenged by means of a claim for judicial review. However, if a council had decided that a particular individual was homeless and had failed to provide accommodation for him as required by the legislation, this was a matter of private law giving rise to a claim against the local authority that could be pursued by an ordinary action. The distinction is essentially between the general and the particular. Interpreting legislation is a public law function whilst denying an individual a right deriving from a decision in his favour is a matter of private law as it relates to him alone.

In one sense, the decision in *Cocks v Thanet DC* may be seen as recognizing the limits of judicial review and the distinction between public and private law, but the reality is that the effect of the decision in *O'Reilly* is to place limits on the use of ordinary claim procedure against public authorities. Limitations on the use of judicial review occur elsewhere however. Parliament may restrict the use of judicial review by either expressly excluding it or by placing limitations on the decision making process which have the effect of making any form of challenge difficult. The issue becomes important when it is borne in mind that there is no appeal against a decision unless Parliament provides for one. Where this is the case, judicial review takes on an added significance as possibly the only avenue through which the claimant can proceed in order to challenge a decision. The courts do not accept readily that Parliament has restricted the ability of an individual to challenge a decision through the courts even though, as *O'Reilly v Mackman* illustrates, they may place restrictions on the form that challenge takes.

11.3.2 Excluding judicial review

Clauses seeking to exclude the courts

Clauses seeking to exclude the jurisdiction of the courts are often referred to as ouster clauses, as they seek to oust the jurisdiction of the courts. Where Parliament seeks to exclude challenge completely, the courts have adopted a particularly robust stance and have sometimes employed very creative approaches to statutory interpretation. In *Anisminic v Foreign Compensation Commission* [1969] 2 AC 147, the Commission was established to determine claims to compensation by those suffering loss during the Suez crisis in 1956. It was provided that any determination of the Commission could not to be challenged in any court. The House of Lords held that the exclusion only applied where the Commission had made a correct determination of the matter, but did not apply where its determination was erroneous, because it had no jurisdiction to make erroneous determinations. Therefore, if it had made an erroneous determination the exclusion did not apply and the courts could intervene to quash the unlawful determination.

thinking point

If Parliament has decided to exclude the courts from determining certain matters, why should the courts not respect this?

The courts have sometimes been less robust in their approach to provisions where the jurisdiction of the courts is not ousted completely, but where challenge is difficult due to the wording of the governing legislation. The courts have had to scrutinize claims by the executive that they are unable to review decisions more carefully since the passing of the Human Rights Act, because Article 6 requires that an individual has the right to a fair trial, and excluding the courts from fully reviewing their claim may fall foul of this. As with virtually all rights under the European Convention on Human Rights, however,

Article 6 is qualified and there are restrictions that can be placed on this right, particularly in matters of high executive policy, which would cover matters such as international relations, national security or war.

Justiciability

cross reference

See Chapter 6 for discussion of the CCSU case (also known as GCHQ).

In *Council of Civil Service Unions v Minister for the Civil Service* [1985] AC 374, the House of Lords considered that the grounds upon which judicial review of the royal prerogative could be exercised should be those applicable to the exercise of statutory powers.

This was subject to the limitation that the subject matter must be justiciable. This means that the subject matter must be something a court is capable of trying, which is particularly relevant in the case of the royal prerogative, which deals with matters such as the making of treaties and declarations of war which relate to matters that the courts are not capable of deciding. The courts could not, for example, decide questions as to whether troops had been deployed in a reasonable way (see e.g. per Lord Roskill [1985] AC at 418), or whether entering into a particular treaty was a reasonable exercise of executive power (see e.g. *Blackburn v AG* [1971] 1 WLR 1037; *R v Secretary of State for Foreign Affairs ex p Rees-Mogg* [1994] QB 552). These matters are governed by policy considerations relating to international relations, the conduct of warfare, etc. which it is more appropriate for politicians, rather than judges, to decide. Such matters also involve recognition of the separation of powers in which each branch of government has its allotted sphere of work. The courts recognize the limitations of their powers in certain areas and defer to the executive. This is effectively the courts denying themselves jurisdiction because of the subject matter of the issue in question.

There are, however, limits to this self denial. In the *CCSU* case (also known as GCHQ), for example, whilst the courts recognized that they could not adjudicate in matters relating to national security, they reserved to themselves the right to determine whether any matter claimed by the executive to relate to national security did in fact involve security considerations. It was not sufficient for the Minister simply to claim that the matter was one of national security: the Minister would have to satisfy the court that this was the case. In the *CCSU* case itself, the House of Lords was satisfied that the matter did involve national security because of the nature of the work carried out by GCHQ, the government's communications monitoring centre, and the threat posed to national security should its operations in monitoring international communications be disrupted.

However, the matter is not determined simply because it relates to military or defence operations. In *R v Ministry of Defence ex p Smith* [1996] QB 517, the courts were prepared to consider the legality of discharging members of the armed forces because of their homosexuality, deciding, however, that the policy of discharging members of the armed services on the basis of their homosexuality and its application in that case were lawful.

The courts still defer to the executive in areas where such matters are involved, but earlier cases may need to be revisited in light of developments in the human rights era.

Thus, for example, in *Liversidge v Anderson* [1942] AC 206, the plaintiff was detained without trial under the Defence of the Realm Regulations. These provided that a person could be detained if the Secretary of State had reasonable grounds for believing him to be of hostile origins or associations. The courts had to consider whether this meant that the Secretary of State had to believe he had reasonable grounds for exercising his powers, or whether it meant that the grounds the Secretary of State put forward had to be objectively reasonable—in other words, whether the court believed them to be reasonable. The House of Lords held that it was sufficient that the Secretary of State was satisfied that he had reasonable grounds for acting as he did: his grounds did not have to be objectively reasonable. The effect of this was to make the executive decision immune from challenge through the courts. A powerful dissent from Lord Atkin, in which he castigated his fellow judges (at p.244) as being 'more executive minded than the executive', has since been recognized as indicating the better approach to the issues raised and the view that would be followed in modern times. The fact that the case was decided in the context of World War II may provide an explanation for the decision of the House of Lords but, given the doctrine of precedent, the decision stood as an authoritative decision on the interpretation of the regulations.

thinking point

Why are the courts not able to consider matters relating to national security?

It is virtually certain that the courts would not take such a view today, notwithstanding that considerations of national security necessarily have a limiting effect on the ability of the court to provide a remedy, given the focus on individual rights brought about since the implementation of the Human Rights Act 1998. In *A(FC) v Secretary of State for the Home Department* [2005] 2 AC 68, the question was whether the detention without trial of terrorist suspects was lawful. The House of Lords found that the legislation was in breach of obligations under the Human Rights Act, being an excessive restriction on the right to liberty under Article 5 of the European Convention on Human Rights.

Exhausting other remedies

The courts have been rather ambivalent as to whether a claimant needs to exhaust any other remedies that are available before bringing a claim for judicial review. The argument for insisting that a claimant should follow an appeal or other route laid down by Parliament is that in providing for an appeal Parliament had envisaged that the claimant would pursue that rather than bring a claim for judicial review and may have designed the particular form of such an appeal on the basis that it was particularly appropriate to the circumstances.

thinking point

Should the claimant be able to choose which process to follow or should the court determine this?

In *R v Inland Revenue Commissioners ex p Preston* [1985] AC 835 the House of Lords took the view that judicial review should not be available to a claimant where an alternative remedy exists, and that a claimant should exhaust such remedies before applying for judicial review. Lord Templeman (at p.862; see also Lord Scarman at p.852) pointed out that tax appeals had a system provided that recognized the importance of, for example, confidentiality when dealing with a person's tax affairs. That process should, therefore, normally be used. However, the House of Lords recognized that there might be circumstances where it might be appropriate to allow a claimant to proceed by way of judicial review rather than by a statutory appeals mechanism. The present case provided an example of such circumstances. The tax commissioners were acting unlawfully in initiating proceedings in respect of the taxpayer and this had the effect of making the appeals system unavailable to the taxpayer. He was, therefore, entitled to proceed by way of judicial review.

11.3.3 **Time limits**

Where judicial review is not excluded by statute, there are still the requirements of Part 54 to be satisfied. The time limits for bringing a claim require a degree of urgency on the part of the claimant. According to r.54.5, a claim must be filed:

* promptly;
* and in any event not later than three months after the grounds to make the claim first arose.

The wording of this is such that the overriding requirement is to act promptly. Even where a claim is brought within the three months period, it may still be ruled out if it does not display the characteristic of promptness, which is the overriding criterion. The reason for this, as we have seen, is to ensure that where a public body is acting unlawfully the error can be corrected at the earliest opportunity or where it is acting lawfully that its actions are vindicated and it can carry on acting in that way. The limits under r.54.5 may be compared with those in other actions: for example, one year in claims for defamation; three years in actions in tort for personal injury; six years for claims in contract or other actions in tort; and 12 years in actions for the recovery of land. This is why the issues raised in *O'Reilly v Mackman* are significant, for by denying the claimant the right to choose whether to proceed by judicial review or ordinary claim, the courts have denied the claimant the ability to use judicial proceedings tactically by using the form of action that is more advantageous to him as claimant. This is essentially designed to offer some measure of protection to defendant public bodies.

thinking point
Are you convinced by the argument that the needs of public administration demand that cases are dealt with quickly?

11.3.4 **Permission**

A second requirement is that the claimant must obtain permission to proceed. This was previously termed leave. The object here is to weed out unmeritorious claims at an early stage to prevent court time being wasted on something that has no chance of success. As such, it is only those cases that have no hope of success that will fall at this stage and consequently the hurdle presented here is not a particularly onerous one for the claimant. At this stage the court does not hear the full claim, and, as issues such as the standing of the claimant or the nature of the body against whom the claim is brought may be inextricably tied up with the substance of the claim, the House of Lords in *R v Inland Revenue Commissioners ex p National Federation of Self Employed and Small Businesses Ltd* [1982] AC 617, discussed further below, suggested that permission should only exceptionally be refused on these grounds. Where a claimant is successful in obtaining permission to proceed, it does not follow that the full claim will succeed when it is heard. This is because the permission stage only considers the claimant's case, and does not hear this in full. Further, it does not hear argument from the respondent. Thus, any view the judge forms of the merits of the case will only be a preliminary view which is then considered in detail at the full hearing.

thinking point
Does the permission stage serve any useful purpose given that few claims fail at that stage?

11.4 Parties

With regard to the parties to a claim for judicial review, there are limitations on the nature of the claimant and on the individual or body against whom a claim may be brought, which will be dealt with in turn.

11.4.1 The claimant

In order to bring a claim for judicial review, the claimant must have standing to do so. This was formerly termed '*locus standi*', but, with the abandonment of Latin terms brought about by the reforms in civil procedure, the English term is now used. The test, set out in s.31(3) Supreme Court Act 1981, is whether the claimant has 'sufficient interest' in the matter that forms the substance of the claim. This means that the claimant must have some interest in the matter over and above that of the public at large. It may be questioned why such a limitation is necessary. The judges have often spoken in terms of preventing busybodies and others with no genuine interest in the matter from clogging the courts with claims that have no legitimate purpose or are being pursued for perhaps political or capricious reasons rather than by virtue of being personally affected by the matter. There is a big difference between the notion of public interest as identified by the courts and something in which the public is interested. The difficulty lies in how to differentiate between the genuinely affected and the unmeritorious interferer. In *R v Inland Revenue Commissioners ex p National Federation of Self Employed and Small Businesses*, Lord Fraser captures the problem succinctly ([1982] AC 617 at 646):

> All are agreed that a direct financial or legal interest is not now required . . . There is also general agreement that a mere busybody does not have a sufficient interest. The difficulty is, in between those extremes, to distinguish between the desire of the busybody to interfere in other people's affairs and the interest of the person affected by or having a reasonable concern with the matter to which the application relates.

The effect of the requirement of standing is thus restrictive. The claimant must show an interest in the matter by demonstrating a connection with the matter in question. Often this will be easily satisfied: the claimant will be a person about whom a decision has been made and will thus have a personal interest in the final outcome. Matters become more difficult when the claimant is one of a number of people affected by the outcome of, say, a planning application. Here, the way in which the courts interpret this requirement can be critical in terms of access to the courts. A restrictive approach can severely limit the availability of judicial review; an expansive interpretation can undermine the notion of sufficient interest. It is clear that where something affects the public as a whole, remedies lie elsewhere through the political process. It is identifying the cut-off point between something of that nature and something affecting only a particular individual that is the task for the court, and they have not sought to generalize as to where that point lies.

thinking point

Why should anybody be excluded from asking the courts to overturn a decision taken by the government?

An additional factor to consider is the position of groups acting on behalf of individuals, or of groups such as pressure groups with an interest in a particular issue. Here, the courts have, in recent years, been relatively accommodating in admitting claims by groups with a demonstrable interest in the subject matter of the claim, especially where they are speaking on behalf of vulnerable or disadvantaged individuals, or indeed of phenomena such as environmental features, who or which might not otherwise have access to the courts. These points may now be illustrated with reference to some of the extensive case law.

An extensive discussion of a number of issues relating to the requirement of standing emerges from the decision of the House of Lords in *R v Inland Revenue Commissioners ex p National Federation of Self Employed and Small Businesses* [1982] AC 617.

case close-up

R v Inland Revenue Commissioners ex p National Federation of Self Employed and Small Businesses [1982] AC 617

The Federation wished to challenge a decision of the Inland Revenue. Casual workers for a number of national newspapers, then based in Fleet Street in London, had been working under obviously fictitious names such as 'Mickey Mouse', and had not been paying tax on their earnings. Following discussions with the employers, the Inland Revenue decided not to pursue back tax that was owed as a result of this practice in return for an undertaking by the newspapers that they would regularise the employment of such workers and ensure that they were properly registered for tax in future. The Federation was unhappy about this concession as, it argued, by not recovering unpaid tax the Inland Revenue would be imposing an additional burden on its members as taxpayers. A preliminary issue was whether the Federation had standing to bring such a claim. The Federation was given permission to bring the claim, pursuing it to the House of Lords on its substance. One of the points taken by the Inland Revenue was that the Federation did not have standing to bring the claim. The House of Lords held, first, that the Divisional Court had been correct to allow the claim to proceed to a full hearing. Matters of standing were often inextricably linked to the substance of the application and may not be capable of being determined at the permission stage. Courts hearing requests for permission should therefore only reject claims on this ground at this stage in exceptional cases. It held that one taxpayer did not have standing to bring a claim relating to the tax affairs of another taxpayer. A collection of taxpayers—which is in effect what the Federation was for this purpose—was in no better position than an individual taxpayer. It followed that the Federation did not have standing to challenge the decision of the Inland Revenue. The House of Lords indicated that it did not follow that there would never be circumstances when the decision of the Inland Revenue would be capable of challenge by a person other than the person to whom the decisions related, but, perhaps understandably, did not give instances of where this might be possible.

Groups and organizations

The notion that individuals who do not have standing cannot acquire it simply by banding together was reinforced in *R v Secretary of State for the Environment ex p Rose Theatre Trust Co* [1990] 1 QB 504.

case close-up

R v Secretary of State for the Environment ex p Rose Theatre Trust Co [1990] 1 QB 504

Here, the trust, which had been formed for the purpose of saving the site, wanted to challenge a decision of the Secretary of State in relation to a planning application with regard to the future of the site on which the Rose Theatre had stood, which was, argued the Trust, a site of historical significance that should be preserved. The Secretary of State argued that the Trust did not have standing to challenge decisions relating to the site as it did not have a greater interest than members of the general public. This view was upheld by Schiemann J. Individual members of the Trust did not have standing to bring a claim and merely by banding together into a trust could not acquire standing its individual members lacked: the trust had not greater claim to standing than the individuals who made up its membership.

thinking point

Do you agree? If a body has been formed to protect a particular interest, shouldn't the court allow it to represent that interest?

The courts have, however, accepted that organizations have standing to bring claims where the nature of the claim gives them a legitimate interest in doing so.

case close-up

R v Inspectorate of Pollution ex p Greenpeace [1994] 4 All ER 321

Greenpeace, an environmental campaigning organization, sought to challenge the inspectorate with regard to its alleged failure to prevent pollution by the discharge of radioactive waste from the British Nuclear Fuels processing plant at Sellafield in Cumbria. An initial question was whether Greenpeace had standing. Otton J held that it did. As a longstanding campaigning group which had demonstrated concern for the environment, Greenpeace had sufficient interest in the matter and consequently standing to bring a claim. He went on to argue that there were benefits from allowing Greenpeace to bring the case in that it had the expertise to argue the matter effectively and financial resources to meet any costs that might be awarded against them. He regarded this as an effective use of the court's resources, more so than in a situation where a challenge might come from a less well informed or financially secure applicant. Otton J's approach has much to commend it for the reasons he gives, as long as it does not serve to exclude other claimants from mounting a challenge.

This more expansive approach is seen in a number of other cases in which standing has been accorded to organizations such as:

- the World Development Movement in relation to the government's decisions in relation to the Pergau Dam in Malaysia (*R v Secretary of State for Foreign and Commonwealth Affairs ex p World Development Movement Ltd* [1995] 1 All ER 611);

- the Child Poverty Action Group in relation to benefit payments affecting parents (*R v Secretary of State for Social Security ex p Child Poverty Action Group* [1990] 2 QB 540);

- Help the Aged with regard to the proposed closure of a residential home (*R v Sefton Metropolitan Borough Council ex p Help the Aged* [1997] 4 All ER 532);

- the Joint Council for the Welfare of Immigrants in relation to the withdrawal of benefits from asylum seekers (*R v Secretary of State for Social Security ex p Joint Council for the Welfare of Immigrants* [1997] 1 WLR 275); and

- the Campaign for Nuclear Disarmament on the question whether the war in Iraq was legal (*R(Campaign for Nuclear Disarmament) v Prime Minister* [2002] EWHC 2759).

thinking point

In the last case, could any individual citizen wishing to challenge the legality of the war be able to do so?

Parties

249

Even where an organization has not brought a claim itself, the House of Lords has allowed submissions to be made on behalf of interested bodies, such as:

- Amnesty International in relation to the decision whether or not to extradite General Pinochet (*R v Bow Street Metropolitan Stipendiary Magistrate ex p Pinochet Ugarte (No 1)* [2000] 1 AC 61); and

- the Secretary of State for Health, the Mental Health Act Commission and the Registered Nursing Home Association on the question of the circumstances in which a patient could be treated informally under the Mental Health Act 1983 (*R v Bournewood Community and Mental Health NHS Trust ex p L* [1999] 1 AC 458).

Overall, these approaches enable the courts to hear argument from those perhaps best placed to marshal resources and expertise. This may be particularly important where the subject matter relates to something without an obvious representative, such as environmental phenomena or where the interest in question has implications going beyond the individual involved.

11.4.2 **The defendant**

Turning to the person against whom the claim might be brought, there are again limitations. The traditional formula is that judicial review may only be sought against a public body. The use of the word 'public' to qualify the word 'body' has a limiting effect and the contrast that is drawn is with private bodies. Thus, companies, no matter how large and influential, are excluded from the scope of judicial review. The phrase 'public body' obviously includes central government, including Ministers, local government and analogous bodies. The matter has become more complex with changes to the structure of government which have seen the establishment of bodies detached from the government yet exercising public functions. A whole range of agencies and other bodies exercising executive or advisory functions, such as the Benefits Agency, the Commission for Equality and Human Rights and The National Institute for Clinical Excellence, now exercise functions previously exercised by government departments. The question with regard to such bodies in the present context is how far they can be regarded as public bodies, against whom a claim for judicial review might be brought, when they have a degree of autonomy that would ordinarily lead them to be regarded as private bodies.

An extensive discussion of the issues appears in the judgment of the Court of Appeal in *R v Panel on Take-overs and Mergers ex p Datafin plc* [1987] QB 815.

case close-up

R v Panel on Take-overs and Mergers ex p Datafin plc [1987] QB 815

The issue was whether the Panel was a public body against whom a claim for judicial review might be brought. The Panel was not a body established by statute, which is often an indicator that it is a public body for this purpose, nor by common law nor contract, but was a voluntary body established within the financial sector to act as a watchdog to ensure proper conduct in dealings within the sector. The Court of Appeal held that it was a public body as it was performing public duties. A body would have had to have been created to exercise the functions performed by the Panel, for which there was a demonstrable need. The Panel was thus in fact a public body despite not being created in the same way as most public bodies, namely by statute, and despite its operations not being governed by statute. It was thus a public body in all but its legal form, and was thus capable of having its decisions challenged by way of judicial review.

Public v Private

The courts have contrasted public bodies with private bodies. As the law of contract governs private legal relationships it follows that bodies that are regulated by contract are private organizations, and thus outside the scope of judicial review. On this reasoning, the courts have, for example, held that the following are not public bodies and are therefore outside the scope of judicial review notwithstanding that they exercise a supervisory or disciplinary function in relation to their respective fields:

- the National Greyhound Racing Club (*Law v National Greyhound Racing Club Ltd.* [1983] 1 WLR 1302);

- the Jockey Club (*R v Disciplinary Committee of the Jockey Club ex p Aga Khan* [1993] 1 WLR 909); and

- the Football Association (*R v Football Association Ltd ex p Football League Ltd* [1993] 2 All ER 833) are all outside the scope of judicial review.

thinking point

Given the power and influence they exert, should public limited companies or other private organizations be within the scope of judicial review?

Public bodies and public authorities

The fact that something is a public body for the purposes of judicial review is not the same as saying it is a public authority for the purposes of the Human Rights Act. In *YL v Birmingham City Council* [2008] 1 AC 95, the House of Lords held that the fact that a body was a public body for the purposes of judicial review did not automatically determine the question of whether it was a public authority for the purposes of the Human Rights Act, even though it would often be the case that particular bodies fell under both definitions. What the House of Lords emphasizes is that the matter needs to be examined in its particular context. So, in that case, it was held that a care home accommodating residents who were living there by virtue of arrangements made with a local authority was not a public authority for the purposes of the Human Rights Act.

Public body exercising public law functions

Establishing that a body is a public body does not necessarily mean that it is open to judicial review. A claim for judicial review may only be brought where a public body is exercising public law functions. Again, the contrast is with a public body exercising private law functions. *Cocks v Thanet District Council*, discussed earlier, provides a good example. The House of Lords held that a decision whether or not a person was homeless under the relevant legislation was a matter of public law as it involved the exercise of a general statutory function. A failure by a local authority to provide accommodation for a person found to be homeless would be a matter of private law as that person had acquired an individual right following the council's decision as to the applicability of the legislation to his particular situation. Thus, a claim against a local authority for failing to identify a person as homeless would proceed by judicial review but a failure to provide accommodation would proceed by way of an ordinary claim. A claim involving both elements would be able to proceed by way of judicial review as it contained a public law claim.

On a similar basis it has been held, for example, that an employment law matter involving an individual employed by a public corporation was a matter of private law and thus not capable of challenge by way of judicial review (*R v BBC ex p Lavelle* [1983] 1 All ER 241) even though the body concerned is a public body. This is because, as we have seen, public bodies can exercise both public law and private law functions.

Sources of power

A public law issue can arise on the basis of the exercise of statutory powers or, in the case of central government, on the exercise of powers under the royal prerogative.

REMINDER the royal prerogative comprises the common law powers formerly enjoyed by the monarch but now largely exercised by central government: see Chapter 5.

The courts had, until comparatively recently, only exercised powers of judicial review in relation to statutory powers. Their position with regard to the royal prerogative had been that they would review the existence and exercise of the royal prerogative but not the way in which it was used. There were thus two regimes governing the exercise of executive power, and which one was employed depended on whether the power was exercised by virtue of statute or the royal prerogative. This was increasingly seen as anomalous, and, in the course of regrouping the grounds for judicial review in *Council of Civil Service Unions v Minister for the Civil Service* [1985] AC 374, Lord Diplock took the opportunity to make some observations about the reviewability of the royal prerogative.

case close-up

Council of Civil Service Unions v Minister for the Civil Service [1985] AC 374

The Minister had changed the contracts of civil servants working at GCHQ, the national communications monitoring station which, amongst other things, had an important intelligence gathering function that contributed to national defence, to prevent them from being members of a trade union. This was done without consultation with the trade unions. The union argued that this was unlawful because when changes had been made to employees' contracts previously, the unions had been consulted prior to any changes being made. The unions, therefore, argued that they had a right to be consulted prior to this change being made and that in the absence of consultation the change was invalid. As the civil servants were Crown servants, their terms of employment depended on the royal prerogative, and the changes to their contracts had been made by an **Order in Council**. One issue was, therefore, whether such an instrument was in principle reviewable. In an earlier case, *R v Criminal Injuries Compensation Board ex p Lain* [1967] 2 QB 864, it had been held that the decisions of the Board, which was established by virtue of the royal prerogative, were reviewable. The case was not dealing with the question of the review of the prerogative itself but only with the decisions of a board established under the prerogative. The same was true of the *CCSU* case, where the challenge related to an order made by virtue of the royal prerogative rather than the prerogative itself. The House of Lords held that, while the Order in Council was reviewable and notwithstanding that the unions had a legitimate expectation that they would be consulted prior to any change to their contracts of employment, the requirements of national security, which were established by the very nature of the work done by GCHQ, prevailed to make the change to the terms of their contracts lawful.

Order in Council

a form of delegated legislation made under the authority of the royal prerogative

The *CCSU* case was therefore not directly concerned with the question of whether the exercise of the royal prerogative was capable of being challenged by way of judicial review, and so any statements of the judges about this were strictly obiter. However, Lords Diplock, Scarman and Roskill all made statements expressing the view that, within limits, there was no reason in principle why the exercise of the royal prerogative should not be subject to judicial review. Lord Diplock based his argument on the view that the most important thing was not the source of the power but its nature (cf. Lord Reid in *Ridge v Baldwin* [1964] AC 40: see Chapter 10). Applying a test based on the nature of the power, it did not matter whether the basis of the power lay in statute or, like the royal prerogative, in common law. He recognized that, given the nature of the subject matter of the royal prerogative, some aspects of it would not be reviewable. He said that, to be reviewable, the subject matter must be justiciable; in other words it must be something capable of being determined by a court and not some matter of high executive policy. Lord Roskill took this notion a stage further and identified ([1985] AC 374 at 418) prerogatives that he did not think would be capable of being reviewed by a court, though his list was never meant to be exhaustive or binding but rather indicative of the sorts of matters that might be excluded:

> Prerogative powers such as those relating to the making of treaties, the defence of the realm, the prerogative of mercy, the grant of honours, the dissolution of Parliament and the appointment of ministers as well as others are not, I think, susceptible to judicial review because their nature and subject matter is such as not to be amenable to the judicial process.

thinking point
Why should the courts be excluded from considering such matters?

What both judges, and Lord Scarman also, were trying to do was to distinguish between those aspects of the prerogative that applied to matters not involving major issues of executive policy and which could be reviewed from those which were properly the preserve of the executive such as declarations of war or the making of treaties.

Subsequent case law has explored this distinction, as well as giving effect to the obiter statements in the *CCSU* case relating to the reviewability of the royal prerogative itself. Thus, in *R v Secretary of State for Foreign and Commonwealth Affairs ex p Everett* [1989] QB 811, it was held that the decision whether to grant a passport was capable of being reviewed. In *R v Secretary of State for the Home Department ex p Bentley* [1994] QB 349 it was held that a decision not to grant a pardon in respect of a person who had been executed was reviewable not as to the actual decision itself but because the Home Secretary had failed to recognize that the prerogative of mercy could be exercised by way of a conditional pardon as well as by a full pardon and that he should have considered the exercise of a conditional pardon in this case.

The position is thus that the courts can examine, by way of judicial review, a claim brought by a person with sufficient interest in the matter against a public body exercising public law functions, whether deriving from statute or, subject to the requirement that the matter is justiciable, the royal prerogative, as long as the claim has been brought in time and the claimant has been given permission to proceed to a full hearing. The grounds on which judicial review is exercised are considered in the next chapter.

Questions

If you answer the following questions, you will have appreciated the main issues raised in this chapter. Check your answers against the notes provided at the back of the book.

1   What is judicial review?

2   Who may bring a claim for judicial review and against whom may a claim be
    brought?

3   What type of dispute can be challenged by a claim for judicial review?

4   What are the main procedural requirements involved in a claim for judicial review?

 # Further reading

To further your understanding of the topics covered in this chapter, have a look at the
reading materials mentioned below. Useful web links are also provided on the Online
Resource Centre.

A.W. Bradley and K.D. Ewing, *Constitutional and Administrative Law* (Pearson Longman, 14th ed.,
2007) ch.31
This provides you with a detailed and wide-ranging discussion of the procedural issues
relating to judicial review.

Michael Allen and Brian Thompson, *Cases and Materials on Constitutional and Administrative
Law* (Oxford University Press, 9th ed., 2008) ch.11
This provides you with extracts from many of the primary sources mentioned in this chapter
together with commentary.

Peter Cane, *Administrative Law* (Oxford University Press, 4th ed., 2004) chs.2, 3 & 4
These chapters provide you with a different perspective and further detail on many of the
matters discussed in this chapter.

Judicial review: grounds

Learning Objectives

While reading this chapter, you should aim to understand:

- the grounds that might lead a court to declare a decision unlawful;
- how the courts apply those requirements in individual cases;
- whether the courts are consistent in the determination of cases of judicial review; and
- the impact of the Human Rights Act on judicial review.

Introduction

The substantive grounds on which judicial review can be exercised have been developed exclusively by the judges. In doing so, they have claimed to give effect to the will of Parliament, and at one level they are engaged in an exercise in statutory interpretation. But their function, as we have seen, goes much further than this. Traditionally, the underpinning notion has been the ultra vires principle: the judges have, as part of the checks and balances in the constitution, sought to prevent public bodies acting beyond the powers (which is what the term ultra vires means) that they have been given. In deference to the sovereignty of Parliament, they have not claimed powers to strike down legislation. Parliament did not give them this power under the Human Rights Act. Even where they have the power to disapply legislation that conflicts with EU law the courts have proceeded with caution, not wishing to trespass too far onto Parliament's sovereign territory.

cross reference
You might wish to refresh your memory by re-reading Chapter 3 before proceeding further.

12.1 **Wednesbury and beyond**

It is perhaps surprising that Parliament has not codified the principles on which judicial review is exercisable, not least in the interests of certainty and consistency. Nevertheless, it has been left to the judges to develop the grounds on which they themselves exercise judicial review: in effect, they have written their own rules.

thinking point

Would it be better for Parliament to lay down the grounds for judicial review rather than leaving it to the courts?

12.1.1 *Associated Provincial Picture Houses v Wednesbury Corporation*

The classic statement of this derives from the judgment of Lord Greene MR in *Associated Provincial Picture Houses v Wednesbury Corporation* [1948] 1 KB 223. The case concerned the question whether a local authority was acting lawfully in imposing conditions on a cinema licence that children should not be admitted to screenings on a Sunday. In explaining that public bodies such as local authorities should exercise their powers reasonably, Lord Greene went on to spell out in more detail what this meant. When he uses the term 'reasonably' he is not using it in its ordinary everyday sense but in the specific context of the exercise of statutory powers by public bodies. In the course of giving judgment, he identified four particular issues:

1. the decision maker must correctly identify what power has been given and must follow any statutory criteria;

2. the proper purpose of the power must be identified and the power only used for that purpose;

3. relevant considerations must be taken into account and irrelevant consideration must not be taken into account; and

4. the decision maker must act reasonably—a decision would be unreasonable where no reasonable authority or person could have come to it—this is the concept of '*Wednesbury* unreasonableness'.

thinking point

Why do you think Lord Greene gives the term 'unreasonable' a meaning that does not correspond with its everyday meaning?

Additionally, Lord Greene recognized that there were circumstances where decision makers would need to observe procedural requirements, most notably the rules of natural justice. The concept of natural justice, discussed more fully below, is traditionally expressed as two rules: the rule against bias, which represents the idea that a decision should be made by an impartial decision maker, and the right to a fair hearing. It is noticeable that Lord Greene identifies the requirements which decision makers must follow in order to act lawfully. Where decision makers fail to follow any of these criteria they will be acting unlawfully. The grounds can thus be expressed as a series of positive requirements which decision makers ought to follow or, negatively, as a set of criteria on which a decision might be made unlawfully and thus capable of being struck down by the courts.

At one level, he is stating a set of fairly obvious principles for decision making. We expect decision makers only to do things if they have the power to do them; to use powers for the purpose(s) for which they were given and for no other reasons; only to take into account those things that are relevant to the decision in question and to ignore anything that is irrelevant. And we would expect that if these basic principles were not followed that a decision maker would be acting improperly.

thinking point

Are the grounds for judicial review as stated by Lord Greene helpful in promoting good administrative practices by decision makers?

The only surprising one is *Wednesbury* unreasonableness, which is formulated in a singular fashion that does not accord with everyday usages. It is worth remembering that judicial review, certainly as conceived at the time Lord Greene was speaking, is traditionally concerned with the process by which decisions are made and not with the substance of the decision. As long as the decision is within the range of decisions that a person or body could have come to, it will be unchallengeable. The courts are only concerned with overseeing due process and locating the decision within the scope of the powers given. They are not concerned with the question of whether it is 'right' or 'wrong' and certainly, at that time, judges did not see their function as extending to questioning the merits of a decision. The concept of *Wednesbury* unreasonableness was as close as they came to doing this, and given the way in which it is formulated, it is only in very extreme and rare cases, some of which are discussed below, that a decision maker would be held to be acting in a way that is *Wednesbury* unreasonable. Given the nature of decision makers in this context—Ministers, public officials and the like—it would be surprising if they were to make decisions that could be said to be *Wednesbury* unreasonable, both because of the nature of the individuals or bodies themselves and also because they would in almost all cases be relying on legal advice before acting in ways that might be controversial.

12.1.2 *Council of Civil Service Unions v Minister for the Civil Service*

These grounds, as formulated by Lord Greene, remained the foundation of judicial review. In *Council of Civil Service Unions v Minister for the Civil Service* [1985] AC 374 (also known as the GCHQ case), Lord Diplock sought to rationalize them under three headings:

- Illegality
- Irrationality
- Procedural impropriety

Whilst this provides a more compact statement of the ideas at the heart of judicial review, it is simply shorthand for a number of ideas. The notion of illegality includes many of the ideas expounded by Lord Greene, but, whereas Lord Greene sought to emphasize the positive requirements on decision makers, Lord Diplock focused on the criteria by which decisions could be regarded as unlawful. Incorrect interpretation of legal powers, failure to follow statutory criteria, using powers for an improper purpose, not taking into account relevant considerations or taking into account irrelevant considerations would all fall under the notion of illegality. By irrationality Lord Diplock had in mind the notion of *Wednesbury* unreasonableness. By procedural impropriety he intended to cover not only the rules of natural justice but also any other procedural requirements.

Lord Diplock added a fourth possible ground of proportionality. This is the idea that there should be no greater interference with an individual than is necessary to achieve the government's legitimate objectives. Put colloquially, it expresses the idea that a person should not take a sledgehammer to crack a nut. This idea had been part of the law in the systems of continental Europe and had formed part of the principles developed by the European Court of Justice, but had not, at the time of Lord Diplock's judgment in *CCSU*, been accepted as part of English law. Lord Diplock acknowledged this. In this part of his judgment he was projecting forward and looking to the development of further grounds on which the courts could exercise their powers of review. The courts had been wary of incorporating the notion of proportionality for reasons similar to those on which the principle of *Wednesbury* unreasonableness was based, namely a reluctance to become involved with the substance of a decision, which such a principle could involve.

thinking point

Is it necessary to identify and categorize the grounds for judicial review? Should the courts simply be able to overturn a decision if they do not think it is right?

Whichever way they are described or categorized, it is clear that the courts have developed an extensive set of principles both to guide decision makers, using them in a positive sense, and to allow the courts to strike down decisions as being unlawful, using the principles in their negative sense. It is worth remembering at the outset that a decision may be deficient for more than one reason, and thus capable of being challenged on more than one ground. In the following discussion the grounds will be considered under the headings used by Lord Diplock in *CCSU*.

12.1.3 **Illegality**

Incorrect interpretation of law

In explaining what he meant by illegality, Lord Diplock observed that 'the decision maker must understand correctly the law that regulates his decision making and give effect to it'. A first issue, therefore, is whether the decision maker has correctly interpreted the law that applies to the particular decision. In part this is an aspect of statutory interpretation. However, it goes beyond merely interpreting the words that appear in the particular section of the particular Act in question, for the courts also require that the decision maker takes into account the principles of administrative law as described here. The words of the Act are, however, the starting point, and, as with all issues of interpretation, there is a degree of latitude involved. Words are inevitably ambiguous and many disputes relate to the question of whether a particular word covers a particular thing. Ultimately, it is for the courts to provide a ruling on the interpretation of the words in question, and the very fact that judges disagree as to issues of meaning illustrates the point that the conclusions in these cases are not inevitable: there is always scope for argument. Whether the courts will take a restrictive or an expansive approach is difficult to predict and may depend on the inclinations of the particular judges involved in deciding the case.

thinking point

As a public body will have taken legal advice as to whether its proposed course of action is lawful, how do legal advisers predict what conclusion the judges might come to? In the following cases, imagine you had been the legal adviser to the public body concerned: how might you have prevented the body from acting unlawfully?

These points can be illustrated with reference to a few examples where in each case the decision maker was held to be acting unlawfully because of the way in which they had interpreted the powers available to them.

case close-up

AG v Fulham Corporation [1921] 1 Ch 440

The Corporation was given a power to provide washhouses in its area. Using this power it provided laundries. It was held that this was unlawful. Washhouses were places which provided facilities for people to wash their clothes. Laundries were places where people brought their clothes to be washed by others. They were thus different types of facility and a power to provide washhouses did not therefore extend to the provision of laundries. This illustrates an important principle, that the power to do something only extends to that thing or to things of the same or a similar kind. It does not extend to activities that are conceptually different.

Many statutory provisions provide criteria which determine whether a power may be exercised. An example is provided by *Tameside Metropolitan Borough Council v Secretary of State for Education* [1977] AC 1014.

case close-up

Tameside Metropolitan Borough Council v Secretary of State for Education [1977] AC 1014

Section 68 of the Education Act 1944 provided that the Secretary of State could issue directions where a local education authority was acting or was proposing to act unreasonably. Tameside MBC had drawn up proposals for the reorganization of its schools as comprehensives. The Secretary of State had approved the plan. Following a local government election in May, the political complexion of the council changed and the new majority party wished to abandon the plans for comprehensive schools and reinstate a system of selection with grammar school places for the academically more able pupils. The Secretary of State exercised powers under s.68 to require the council to implement the previously approved comprehensive reorganization. Tameside MBC argued that the Secretary of State was acting unlawfully. As it believed that it was possible to operate a selective policy for school places which was capable of implementation for September entry, it could not be said to be acting unreasonably. If it was not acting unreasonably, the Secretary of State had no power to issue directions under s.68.

The House of Lords held that the Secretary of State was acting unlawfully. Tameside had a plan for selecting pupils which was capable of being implemented. Only if it was proposing to act in a way that was *Wednesbury* unreasonable could the Secretary of State intervene using powers under s.68. Here, the council was not acting in a way that was unreasonable in that sense and therefore the Secretary of State had no basis on which powers under s.68 could be exercised. The problem here was that the Secretary of State had misunderstood the basis on which his powers under s.68 could be exercised. It was not sufficient that the Secretary of State thought that Tameside were acting unreasonably; he could only use the powers under s.68 if a council was proposing to act in a way that no reasonable council could have acted. That test was ultimately one on which the court could arbitrate, as the word reasonable suggested an objective assessment.

It is clear that the decision in *Tameside* imposes a high threshold for the exercise of powers under that provision and consequently situations in which the powers could be used would be rare and extreme. This was not an inevitable conclusion, but depended on the view the courts took of the word 'unreasonably' in that context.

A more complex case of statutory interpretation, and the interaction of statute with other factors, was seen in *Bromley London Borough Council v Greater London Council* [1983] 1 AC 768.

case close-up

Bromley London Borough Council v Greater London Council [1983] 1 AC 768

Here, the ruling group on the GLC had been elected on a manifesto that included a commitment to reduce fares on buses and the underground by 25% across the board. The GLC was responsible for supporting the London Transport Board, and for subsidizing it in the provision of an 'integrated, efficient and economic' system of transport for London. The GLC implemented the 25% reduction in fares following the election. Bromley LBC argued that the reduction was unlawful in that the GLC was deliberately making a loss which then had to be recovered by an additional rate precept on the London boroughs, not all of whom would benefit from the fare reduction. As the GLC was spending ratepayers' money, it had to do so on a sound economic basis.

The GLC argued that its policy was lawful. By encouraging passengers to use public transport rather than other means, the amount of traffic in London would be reduced, thus enabling public transport to move across the capital more efficiently. There would be a reduction in traffic pollution due to fewer private cars using London's roads and the additional cost of supporting this policy was justifiable in promoting the greater integrity and efficiency of the system. Further, the voters of London had elected the ruling group on a manifesto promising to implement this policy, thus providing a mandate for it.

The House of Lords held that the policy was unlawful. The GLC had not placed enough emphasis upon the requirement that the transport system should be economic in addition to being integrated and efficient. Further, in spending ratepayers' money, the GLC had to use it responsibly and could not embark on policies that would inevitably result in a loss, necessitating an additional rate precept. The fact that the policy formed part of the manifesto of the ruling group on the GLC could not override its statutory obligations and could not therefore be regarded as binding.

thinking point

Where there are two terms in a piece of legislation, as here, how does a local authority decide what weight to give each of the requirements?

The *GLC* case is of interest in that there were various factors operating. As with the *Tameside* case there was a political dimension. In the *GLC* case, Bromley LBC was controlled by the Conservatives, whilst the GLC had a ruling Labour group. Tameside MBC was originally controlled by Labour but became Conservative controlled following the May election, whilst a Labour government was in power at national level. However, whilst many cases have a political dimension, the courts can only adjudicate where an issue of law is involved, though it is virtually impossible to separate out the legal from the political, as laws do not exist in a vacuum. The preferences expressed by courts are couched in terms of the law but there is a political undercurrent which is unavoidable when judges express preferences for one view as opposed to another.

thinking point
Is there a clear division between law and politics in cases such as these?

It is interesting to note that, whilst the restoration of grammar schools was part of the Tameside Conservative party's manifesto in the May election, this became a policy that was capable of implementation because it could be accommodated within the legal framework within which the council operated, whereas the manifesto commitment of the Labour group on the GLC was not capable of lawful implementation. The courts have consistently refused to accept manifesto commitments as binding commitments, an unsurprising conclusion perhaps, especially in the context of local government, given that councils exist within a statutory framework. Whether the ruling group on a local authority will be able to implement its manifesto commitments thus depends on whether those commitments are feasible within the statutory framework within which they operate.

Improper purpose

A second aspect of illegality is using powers for an improper purpose. When Parliament gives powers to, say, a Minister or to a local authority, it does so for a particular purpose or purposes. It does not usually say what these purposes are, but leaves this to be determined from the provisions in the Act as a matter of statutory interpretation. There may again be some measure of dispute as to what the true purposes of a particular statutory provision may be. An early example of such difficulties is provided by *Padfield v Minister of Agriculture* [1968] AC 997, where the statutory scheme included a procedure for resolving complaints by milk producers. The Minister had a discretion as to whether to refer a complaint or not, and in the instant case refused to refer Padfield's complaint. The Minister argued that it was for him to decide whether or not to refer a complaint and that he had exercised his discretion lawfully in refusing to do so in this instance. The House of Lords held, however, that his decision was unlawful. Although under the scheme the Minister could decide whether or not to refer a complaint, he could not exercise this power so as to defeat the purpose of the Act which was to provide a forum for the resolution of complaints.

thinking point
If a person is given a discretionary power by statute, why is it not left to him to choose whether or not to exercise that discretion?

A further example is provided by *Congreve v Home Secretary* [1976] QB 629, which concerned television licences.

Congreve v Home Secretary [1976] QB 629

The Home Secretary had announced an increase in the TV licence fee to take effect at a date in the future. Mr. Congreve and a number of like-minded individuals decided that, rather than wait for their current licence to expire and pay the increased fee for a new one, they would purchase a new licence before their old one had expired and thus pay the lower fee. The Home Secretary wrote to those who had done this stating that they could not purchase a new licence before their previous one had expired and demanding payment at the new higher rate. Mr. Congreve argued that the Home Secretary's demand was unlawful as there was nothing in the legislation that prevented people such as Mr. Congreve from acting as they had.

The Court of Appeal held that the Home Secretary's demand was illegal. The purpose of licensing was to regulate broadcasting, and not to make money. As there was nothing to prevent the licence holders from acting as they did, there was no basis on which the Home Secretary could demand the extra revenue. Moreover, he was in effect levying a tax, and not only was this not the purpose of the legislation, it was something that could not, according to Article 4 of the Bill of Rights 1689, be done without express parliamentary approval.

thinking point

If you had been advising the Home Secretary, how might you have prevented him from acting illegally?

A further complication arises when a statutory provision has more than one purpose. Apart from the exercise in interpretation in trying to discover what those purposes are, there is the question of what happens when a public body acts in a way that is lawful with regard to one of the Act's purposes but unlawful with regard to the other. This was the situation in *R v Inner London Education Authority ex p Westminster City Council* [1986] 1 WLR 28.

R v Inner London Education Authority ex p Westminster City Council [1986] 1 WLR 28

Here, ILEA was empowered to spend money in order to publish information relating to aspects of local government. ILEA organised a campaign to publicize awareness of the Council's views of the needs of the education service and to change the basis of public debate about the effect of government policies on education in London. Westminster City Council argued that this was unlawful as it was using the power for an improper purpose. Their view was upheld by the Court of Appeal. The court acknowledged that the ILEA campaign involved both the provision of information and an attempt to persuade readers to rethink the issues involved. Whilst the first of those activities was lawful, the second was not, as expenditure on propaganda was not authorized under the legislation. As long as the legislation was being used for one unlawful purpose then the whole decision was tainted and was unlawful notwithstanding that one of the other objectives was lawful.

Some uses of statutory powers for improper purposes are, however, more straightforward and, in some cases, blatant. In *Porter v Magill* [2002] 2 AC 357, for example, the ruling group on Westminster City Council used the power to sell council houses as a way of attracting more Conservative voters into the area. Using the power for such political purposes was not the purpose for which it was given, and the practice was held to be illegal. As indicated earlier, it is possible to bring a particular activity under more than one heading. This provides an example. Cases involving the use of a power for an improper purpose could equally be regarded as either the decision maker taking into account irrelevant considerations—the use of the power for something other than that for which it was given—or simply misinterpreting their power, and thus in either case acting illegally. These are not clinical divisions, and the outcomes of disputes of whether a decision maker has acted lawfully can often be explained on more than one ground.

thinking point

If Parliament does not indicate the purposes for which a particular power has been given, how are those using that power supposed to know what the purposes are?

Relevant and irrelevant considerations

Reverting to Lord Greene's explanation in *Wednesbury*, decision makers are required to take into account relevant considerations and not take into account irrelevant considerations. This is a principle that is simple to state and accords with common sense, but is difficult to apply in practice. A moment's thought will show that the list of relevant and irrelevant matters with regard to any particular decision is not easy to determine. First, the range of matters that could be included or might have to be excluded is extensive. Secondly, there may be disputes as to whether a particular factor is relevant or irrelevant: one person's relevance is another person's irrelevance. The judges are the ultimate arbiters here, and cases previously discussed provide examples. Thus, in *GLC*, it was held that taking into account a manifesto commitment prior to an election was not a relevant consideration in deciding to reduce fares on London Transport. In the *ILEA* case, a desire to change public views was equally regarded as irrelevant. Some examples are perhaps more obvious than others. In *R v Somerset County Council ex p Fewings* [1995] 1 WLR 1037, for example, the Council wished to implement a ban on stag hunting. They did so without reference to the relevant legislation. This was held to be unlawful: clearly the governing statutory provisions are relevant considerations that have to be taken into account. On the other hand, taking into account the moral views of those opposed to stag hunting was held to be an irrelevant consideration.

A good example of the difficulties that can arise in this area is provided by the case of *R v Gloucestershire County Council ex p Barry* [1997] AC 584.

case close-up

R v Gloucestershire County Council ex p Barry [1997] AC 584

Mr. Barry had been provided with services under community care legislation. Gloucestershire County Council found itself unable to continue to resource this assistance and withdrew the services it was providing, citing budgetary reasons for doing so. Mr. Barry challenged both the withdrawal of services and the decision of the Council in taking into account its resources in deciding whether to provide him with services, citing the relevant legislation (s.2 Chronically Sick and Disabled Persons Act 1970) which made no reference to resource. Mr. Barry argued that if the Council assessed him as having a need then they were legally obliged to provide services to meet that need irrespective of whether they had the resources to do so. The House of Lords held, by 3:2, that even though the statute was silent on the issue of resources, Parliament could not possibly have intended the assessment of need for services to be made without regard to the resources available to the Council. Resources were therefore relevant when it came to assessing need for services. The minority upheld Mr. Barry's argument and took the view that, as the statute was silent as to resources, the decision whether there was a need for services should be taken without regard to resources, which were irrelevant to that decision.

The case illustrates the difficulties in trying to predict in advance how the courts will regard such matters and the fact that the decision in *Barry* was a split 3:2 decision illustrates that such matters are not clear cut. Judicial preferences inevitably intrude into the decision making process here, though sometimes more subtly than others.

A robust statement as to relevance and irrelevance is provided by the decision of the House of Lords in *Roberts v Hopwood* [1925] AC 578.

case close-up

Roberts v Hopwood [1925] AC 578

Here, the local authority was authorized to pay 'such wages as it should think fit'. Poplar Council decided that it wanted to be a model employer, and adopted wages policies whereby there was a minimum wage payable to council workers, and that men and women should be paid at the same rate where they were doing the same job. The House of Lords held that the council was acting unlawfully. It had not taken into account a range of factors when fixing the minimum rate for its workers. These included a comparison of the going rate for the job with what was being paid elsewhere and changes in the value of money and the cost of living. As the council was not paying its workers the going rate for the job, but instead a higher sum, they were paying a gratuity rather than a wage. Further, no other council was paying men and women at the same rate, and this too should have been taken into account. In relation to both of these decisions, the council had failed to consider the interests of the ratepayers whose money was being used to make these payments.

thinking point

If a statute is silent with regard to something, what justification is there for the courts inserting words that Parliament has not used?

This last point raises an important issue. Lord Greene talks simply in terms of taking into account relevant considerations and not taking into account irrelevant considerations. Even after these have been identified, however, he gives no guidance as to the weight to be given to the factors that are to be taken into account. This is, in all instances, a problematic issue which will vary from decision to decision. It is a particular feature of matters

thinking point

How do decision makers decide how much weight to give to each matter they are required to consider?

involving local authorities that they are using money provided by, at the present day, council taxpayers. They are only able to spend money if they have statutory authority to do so and owe a duty to those taxpayers to spend money only in ways that are lawful. They are scrutinized by the auditor to ensure that money is being spent properly. How much weight to give to the interests of local taxpayers is a difficult issue, as both *Roberts v Hopwood* and the *GLC* case, discussed earlier, illustrate.

12.1.4 **Irrationality**

The second of Lord Diplock's broad grounds is irrationality. This is the idea expressed by Lord Greene and consequently known as *Wednesbury* unreasonableness, describing a decision that is so unreasonable that no reasonable person or authority would have come to it. Lord Diplock expressed the same notion ([1985] AC at p.410) as characterizing 'a decision so outrageous in its defiance of logic or of accepted moral standards that no sensible person who had applied his mind to the question to be decided could have arrived at it'. Two features of these statements stand out. First, that they are describing a situation that is unlikely to occur frequently. The level of unreasonableness is pitched at such a high level that few decisions are ever likely to be made that could be struck down by the application of this test. It is at the extreme margins and sets such a high threshold that its impact on decision making must necessarily be limited. This becomes all the more significant given that the decisions to which this test applies will have been made by public bodies, or individuals such as Ministers, almost inevitably on the basis of legal advice. To say that a Minister or local authority had made a decision that is so outrageous in its defiance of logic that no sensible person would have made it is an unlikely occurrence.

thinking point

If the public body has taken legal advice before acting and yet has been found to be acting irrationally, what does that mean as far as the legal advice is concerned?

Secondly, applying this test to a particular decision comes perilously close to scrutinizing the substance of the decision which, as we have seen, is something the courts have been reluctant to do. Judicial review, as traditionally conceived, is concerned with the decision making process rather than the substance of the decision itself. This may be seen as one justification for pitching the test of *Wednesbury* unreasonableness so high, so that instances of judicial interference on this ground are few and far between.

Nevertheless, there are examples of cases where the courts have held decisions of public bodies to be unlawful on this ground.

case close-up

Hall v Shoreham by Sea UDC [1964] 1 All ER 1

. . . .

This case concerned a planning application for permission to develop an industrial site. The Council granted permission subject to a condition that required the applicant to build an access road for the whole site which also gave rights of passage from similar roads on adjoining sites. These roads were to be provided at the applicant's own expense. It was held that the condition was unlawful. It was so onerous as to be completely unreasonable and, as such, was *Wednesbury* unreasonable.

A striking example was provided in *Backhouse v Lambeth LBC* [1972] *The Times* 14 October.

case close-up

Backhouse v Lambeth LBC [1972] The Times 14 October

. . . .

The council was given the power to make such reasonable charges for the tenancy of its houses as it should determine. The government had secured the passage of legislation (the Housing Finance Act 1972) which had as its object the raising of revenues from council tenancies in order to reduce reliance on central government grants. In order to evade the obligations to raise rents in order to meet financial targets, the council raised the rent of one house by £18,000, which was the sum necessary to meet its obligations. In fact, the house was empty and so the money was never going to be raised. It was held that this was a decision that no reasonable council could have reached and was consequently unlawful.

thinking point

Were these decisions really irrational or just decisions the courts did not like?

Wednesbury unreasonableness also provides an alternative way of looking at *Fewings*: it was *Wednesbury* unreasonable for the council to ignore the statute when considering the ban on stag hunting as no reasonable council would fail to consider its statutory powers and obligations.

The future of *Wednesbury* unreasonableness

The future of *Wednesbury* unreasonableness as a ground for review looks uncertain. The adoption of proportionality as a ground of review has made *Wednesbury* unreasonableness almost unnecessary, as anything which is *Wednesbury* unreasonable would automatically be disproportionate. Lord Slynn in *R(Alconbury Developments Ltd) v Secretary of State for the Environment Transport and the Regions* [2003] 2 AC 295 at 320–1 expressed a preference for proportionality over *Wednesbury* unreasonableness. This is unsurprising, as the use of the more broadly based concept of proportionality, discussed further below, gives the courts much greater scope to examine decisions and hold them to be unlawful, and to do so in a subtler way, rather than relying on the more blunt *Wednesbury* notion.

A sliding scale of scrutiny

The courts had, in any event, been moving in that direction by trying to distinguish between the application of the *Wednesbury* principles to different types of case, and, in doing so had anticipated the impact of a growing human rights culture in English law. The notion that the more important the impact of the executive decision the greater the degree of scrutiny to which it should be subjected is articulated by Lord Bridge in *R v Secretary of State for the Home Department ex p Bugdaycay* [1987] AC 514 at 531:

> within [the limitations on the scope of judicial review] the court must, I think, be entitled to subject an administrative decision to the more rigorous examination, to ensure that it is in no way flawed, according to the gravity of the issue which the decision determines. The most fundamental of all human rights is the individual's right to life and when an administrative decision under challenge is said to be one which may put the applicant's life at risk, the basis of the decision must surely call for the most anxious scrutiny.

The idea that there is, in effect, a sliding scale of scrutiny to which decisions should be subjected and that this depends on their subject matter has been taken up in subsequent cases, for example in *R v Ministry of Defence ex p Smith* [1996] QB 517.

case close-up

R v Ministry of Defence ex p Smith [1996] QB 517

Four people who had been discharged from the armed forces on the grounds of their homosexuality sought to challenge the decision to discharge them and the policy on which it was based, arguing, among other grounds that it was irrational. The Court of Appeal upheld the decision of the Divisional Court that the policy could not be said to be irrational, notwithstanding the impact of the decision on the applicants. Both courts hearing this case took the view that when dealing with a matter that involved consideration of human rights a greater degree of justification would be needed to uphold an administrative decision, but equally the courts should tread carefully when dealing with matters that were highly influenced by policy. Accordingly, the decision was one that could lawfully be taken and was thus valid.

12.1.5 **Procedural impropriety**

The third of Lord Diplock's formulations is procedural impropriety. By this phrase he means ([1985] AC at 411) 'failure to observe basic rules of natural justice or failure to act with procedural fairness towards the person who will be affected by the decision'. Statutes will frequently include procedural steps that have to be followed by decision makers and a failure to observe these, and to fulfil them in the spirit in which they are intended, will provide grounds for challenge. Thus, for example, a right to be consulted means that the decision maker must not only ensure that the person or body whom the statute requires to be consulted is given the opportunity to make representations to the decision maker but also that the decision maker will consider them with an open mind and take them into account when making the relevant decision.

However, as Lord Diplock makes clear, even where the statute is silent as to any procedural steps that have to be followed, the courts may still require the application of procedural rights deriving from the common law. These are essentially rooted in the ancient principles of natural justice. These were formulated originally in the context of courts proceedings and their origins are apparent in the traditional formulation into two rules:

- the rule against bias; and
- the right to a fair hearing.

These are sometimes expressed in Latin as the rule *nemo judex in sua causa* (or more briefly the *nemo judex* rule, roughly translated as 'no one should be a judge in his own cause'; it is also known as the rule against bias) and *audi alteram partem* (roughly translated as 'hear the other side'; this is the right to a fair hearing). These rules are considered more fully below, but, essentially, the rule against bias means that a person should be heard by an impartial decision maker or judge, whilst the right to a fair hearing contains, at its most basic, the right of an individual to know the case against him and to have the opportunity to answer that case.

Application of procedural requirements

The courts have, over the years, taken different stances with regard to the application of the rules of natural justice. In the 19th century, there was a fairly expansive approach to their application, prompted perhaps by the absence of statutory criteria in an age when the common law was still the predominant source of law. This is illustrated in the leading case of *Cooper v Wandsworth Board of Works* (1863) 14 CB(NS) 180; 143 ER 414.

case close-up

Cooper v Wandsworth Board of Works (1863) 14 CB(NS) 180; 143 ER 414

An Act provided that if a person began to build a new house without giving seven days' notice to the Board, then the Board could demolish the offending house. There was no provision in the Act for any steps to be taken by the Board prior to exercising this power and no opportunity for anyone to be consulted or make representations to the Board prior to demolition. Mr. Cooper began to build a house and, without warning, the Board demolished it. It was held that the Board was acting unlawfully. Even though the statute was silent as to any procedure to be followed prior to demolishing a house built in breach of the Act, the Board should have given Mr. Cooper notice of its intentions and given him an opportunity to respond before acting. The existence of the Board's power to demolish was not in question: what was at issue here was the way it should use its powers, and the court was filling a gap left by Parliament in this regard.

thinking point

Why should decision makers observe procedural requirements? If they want to do something, why should they not simply be able to do it without having to consult anyone else?

This seemed to open the way for the courts to intervene in a wide range of cases in order to give those affected by statutory powers some process rights and to prevent abuses of power by the executive. From an executive point of view, process rights can be very inconvenient. If the executive wishes, say, to build a new road or airport, or, perhaps in a more extreme case, do something controversial, then it would want to get on and do it. Consulting those affected by the development involves delay in beginning the work, and brings with it the danger of objections to the proposal: if a new motorway or airport is being built, those in the vicinity of it are unlikely to be pleased at the impact of it on their lives and are likely to raise quite legitimate objections to the proposal. The principles of natural justice seek to balance the wishes of the executive to get things done with minimal interference or delay against the rights of those affected to have the opportunity to put their views and try to influence the executive.

Judicial or administrative decisions

The courts developed a line of cases which drew increasingly fine distinctions between different types of decision, with the rules of natural justice applying or not applying according to how the decision in question was categorized. If a decision was judicial, then the rules of natural justice applied; if it was merely administrative in character then the rules did not apply. This distinction proved too blunt to be readily applicable to a wide range of decisions that fell somewhere in between, displaying both judicial and administrative characteristics, and so a further category of quasi-judicial decisions was developed, to which the principles of natural justice also applied. Much argument was generated as to how particular decisions could be characterized and a huge body of case law emerged.

A breakthrough was achieved by the House of Lords in *Ridge v Baldwin* [1964] AC 40.

case close-up

Ridge v Baldwin [1964] AC 40

A chief constable had been acquitted of charges alleging corruption. Notwithstanding his acquittal, the judge had made comments critical of the chief constable's conduct. The Watch Committee, which was at the time the body dealing with appointment and dismissal of chief constables, decided to dismiss him without any form of hearing, basing its decision on the court case and the judge's remarks. They later reconvened and allowed the chief constable to attend, but ended by confirming their original decision.

The House of Lords dismissed an argument that rules of natural justice did not apply to this particular decision. They held that, as a public office, this was not a dismissal from an ordinary employment, which would be a matter of private law and outside the scope of the rules of natural justice. They further held that it was not how the decision was characterized that determined whether the rules of natural justice applied but rather the nature of the power being exercised. This more flexible approach to the application of the rules of natural justice paved the way for the courts to apply them to a wider range of decisions than had previously been the case.

Despite the potentially liberating effect the decision in *Ridge v Baldwin* had for the application of the rules of natural justice to a range of decisions, and not just those resembling court proceedings; the courts proceeded with caution. They recognized that the application of the rules of natural justice could sometimes impose a disproportionate burden on decision makers and, indeed, frustrate the administrative process by causing delay and excessive cost, which benefit neither the administrator nor the person in respect of whom a decision is made.

> **thinking point**
>
> *Is it worth a decision maker listening to the views of those likely to be affected by decisions if he has already made his mind up?*

The position the courts had arrived at was that the rules of natural justice either applied or did not. If they did, then the courts would protect the right of the individual to a fair hearing before an unbiased decision maker. If they did not, then the individual to whom the decision related had no procedural rights unless the relevant statute provided any. In cases such as *Re HK* [1967] 2 QB 617, the courts sought to take a more subtle approach, recognized that, in cases where the rules of natural justice did not apply in a formal sense, the applicant could still enjoy some procedural rights though not the full range provided by the rules of natural justice.

case close-up

Re HK [1967] 2 QB 617

An immigration officer did not believe the declared age of a young person who was seeking entry as a dependant minor and refused him entry to the UK. Much argument ensured as to the nature of the immigration officer's decision and whether it was of a sufficiently judicial character for the rules of natural justice to apply. The Court of Appeal held that, post-*Ridge v Baldwin*, the important factor was the nature of the power being exercised. Even if the rules of natural justice did not apply, which, given the nature of the power being exercised by the immigration officer in this situation, they did not, the officer was, nevertheless, required to act fairly when making decisions as to whether to allow or refuse leave to enter the UK. This did not demand the full-blown hearing that the rules of natural justice might require, but should, in this situation, at least require the immigration officer to disclose his suspicions and give the would-be entrant an opportunity to address them.

This idea that there were procedural rights falling between the full application of natural justice and no procedural rights was developed further in subsequent cases. These suggested that there was, in effect, a sliding scale of procedural rights, depending on the nature of the decision in question, with greater procedural protection applying to more significant decisions. The notion was clearly articulated by Megarry VC in *McInnes v Onslow Fane* [1978] 1 WLR 1520.

case close-up

McInnes v Onslow Fane [1978] 1 WLR 1520

The case concerned an application for renewal of a boxing licence. The applicant had previously held a licence but had been refused a new one without being told why or being given any opportunity to explain why he should be given a licence. In the course of deciding that he should have been given this opportunity, Megarry VC distinguished between three types of applicant for a licence and sought to identify the different procedural rights each should have.

The lowest procedural rights would attach to what Megarry VC called the bare applicant, that is, the person who was applying for a licence for the first time. Such a person had only the right to have his application considered fairly. A person such as the applicant in the case itself, namely a person who had previously held a licence, had a right to be treated fairly when applying for renewal and, if refused a licence, to be given reasons as to why the application had been unsuccessful and an opportunity to challenge them. Finally, Megarry VC considered the position of the existing licence holder whose licence is forfeited by the licensing authority. Such a person would be entitled to the most extensive procedural rights under the rules of natural justice, not least because of the drastic effect such a decision would have on his livelihood.

thinking point

If different requirements apply to different decisions, how do decision makers decide how extensive procedural rights must be in any given instance?

Legitimate expectation

In the course of his discussion of the position of the applicant for a licence, Megarry VC considered that the applicants in his second and third categories—that is, the applicant for renewal and the existing holder whose licence is forfeited—would have a legitimate expectation that their licence would be renewed or would not be forfeited in the ordinary course of events. Only if something had happened to change the existing situation would such a decision be able to be justified. It followed that, if the situation remained unaltered, the licence would be renewed or would be allowed to continue during its currency. This notion of legitimate expectation has taken hold as a way of determining whether the rules of natural justice, or at the very least principles of fairness, would apply.

In cases such as *McInnes* the expectation would arise from the previous grant of a licence. This can be broadened to include, for example, previous practice, which enabled the House of Lords in the *CCSU* case (*Council of Civil Service Unions v Minister for the Civil Service*) to hold that, considerations of national security apart, the unions would have been entitled to be consulted over changes to their members' contractual arrangements: in the past consultation had always preceded alteration of contracts and so the unions had a legitimate expectation that they would also be consulted prior to this change.

thinking point

Why should a person expect that just because something has happened previously it should happen again? Does this mean that public bodies cannot change their minds?

Other circumstances in which a legitimate expectation could arise have been identified. An example is provided by *Attorney General for Hong Kong v Ng* [1983] 2 AC 629.

case close-up

***Attorney General for Hong Kong v Ng* [1983] 2 AC 629**

· ·

The applicant had entered Hong Kong illegally and had been deported. The authorities had previously given an undertaking that potential deportees would be interviewed and that each case would be decided on its merits. However, Ng had not been interviewed or given any opportunity to make representations as to why he should not be deported. The Privy Council held that he had a legitimate expectation of a fair hearing arising from the undertaking by the authorities that had not been honoured and therefore the decision to deport him was unlawful as it was in breach of this undertaking.

The flexibility of natural justice

The picture which emerges is that following *Ridge v Baldwin* the courts have moved away from a rigid set of rules relating to the circumstances in which the rules of natural justice do or do not apply to a more flexible situation where the court can decide whether or not the situation calls for the application of some form of procedural protection. If it decides that the situation does warrant the application of procedural rules, then the court has to go on to determine exactly what the requirements of natural justice or fairness are in the particular situation. This flexibility may, perhaps, solve the problems of the over rigid approach to the application or otherwise of natural justice but it brings with it a new issue relating to uncertainty as to precisely what is required in any given case. So, even if it is decided that some procedural steps should be involved in the decision making process, there is scope for argument as to exactly what is required.

thinking point

If the courts do not lay down the precise circumstances in which the rules of natural justice apply, how is a public body supposed to know what to do?

Even where the full application of the rules of natural justice is required, the precise configuration of procedural steps is not always clear. However, certain features of natural justice need to be considered in any situation and general principles applied. As indicated earlier, the two rules of natural justice are the rule against bias and the right to a fair hearing. As the rules were first developed by the superior courts in relation to the exercise of minor judicial functions by magistrates and the like, they retain the flavour of the judicial hearing and are conceived in essentially adversarial terms as a hearing between two sides over which a judge presides. It can be seen immediately that the difficulties described above in deciding when the rules applied were largely borne of trying to apply this model to processes that were not akin to a judicial hearing. Nevertheless, the model remains judicial, however much it has been adapted over the years. The rules may be considered in turn.

Bias

The notion that a decision maker should approach the decision in an objective way and without bias is an attractive and obvious one. But an immediate problem presents itself, which is that no person is completely objective. Individuals hold views on life deriving from their age, gender, ethnicity and political outlook, to name but a few. Some views may derive from the position a person holds, a particularly important consideration in the context of public bodies: a government Minister, for example, is going to want to decide matters in accordance with government policy, yet is also required by statute to make decisions. The law relating to bias is thus concerned not with achieving absolute objectivity, which is unattainable, but with removing those biases that the judges think affect the decision making process. As a result, part of the task for the courts is to decide not only what the nature of the allegation of bias involves, but also whether it is an allegation of substance as opposed to something spurious.

thinking point
Why are some biases apparently acceptable whilst others are not?

The question of bias can arise either before a decision is taken, where it is alleged that the person who has been charged with making the particular decision is tainted by bias. If this allegation is upheld then the effect is to disqualify that person from making the particular decision. Where bias is discovered after the decision has been taken, the decision will be quashed.

Disqualification for bias deals not only with cases where actual bias can be demonstrated but also those where there is apparent bias, for, as Lord Hewart famously observed, in the context of judicial proceedings (*R v Sussex JJ ex p McCarthy* [1924] 1 KB 256 at 259) 'justice should not only be done but should manifestly and undoubtedly be seen to be done'.

Actual bias

Cases where actual bias has been proved are said to be rare. This is unsurprising given that the law, as we have seen, relates to decisions made by Ministers, judges and the like and it might be expected that they would not only conduct themselves properly in this regard but would also refrain from making statements that might suggest a lack of impartiality. Where actual bias is present, the decision maker is automatically disqualified from making the decision or any decision made is tainted and automatically quashed.

Apparent bias: automatic disqualification

Turning to apparent bias, the courts have developed two categories. In the first, the decision maker is automatically disqualified or any decision taken automatically quashed. Decisions falling into this category are, first, those where the decision maker has a financial or proprietary interest in the outcome of the decision in question. A striking example is provided by the 19th century case of *Dimes v Proprietors of the Grand Junction Canal* (1852) 3 HLC 759. Here, the Lord Chancellor heard a case involving the canal company, in which he held shares. There was no suggestion that the Lord Chancellor was biased in deciding the case, and, indeed, the court was at pains to point out that there was no question of a lack of integrity on his part. Nevertheless, he had a clear interest in the outcome and could not appear to be impartial. As a result the decision was quashed, as a person cannot be a judge in his own cause.

A further category of case where a decision maker is automatically disqualified for apparent bias is where that person has an involvement with a particular cause and then is called upon to make a decision in connection with it. This was the outcome of *R v Bow Street Magistrate ex p Pinochet Ugate (No 2)* [2000] 1 AC 119.

R v Bow Street Magistrate ex p Pinochet Ugate (No 2) [2000] 1 AC 119

Proceedings had been commenced to extradite the former Chilean president, General Pinochet, to face serious criminal charges. The case ultimately reached the House of Lords, where the pressure group Amnesty International was allowed to make submissions. It was ultimately decided, by 3:2, that General Pinochet should be extradited (*R v Bow Street Magistrate ex p Pinochet Ugate* [2000] 1 AC 61).

It was subsequently discovered that one of the judges in the House of Lords, Lord Hoffmann, had been associated with Amnesty International. The question was whether this affected the decision of the House of Lords. It was held, by a differently constituted House of Lords, that the decision to extradite General Pinochet could not stand due to the apparent bias on the part of Lord Hoffmann, who should have been disqualified from sitting in the case. Further, that disqualification should have been automatic. It followed that any decision in which he was involved was tainted by the apparent bias on his part.

Where, as in this case, one member of a panel or committee is tainted with bias, then that affects all the other members and any decision made by a body including the person affected by bias cannot stand.

Apparent bias: non-automatic disqualification

In other cases where there is apparent bias, the decision maker is not automatically disqualified nor is any decision made by him automatically struck down. The matter is determined on the facts of each individual case. The task for the courts here has been to formulate a test by which it can be judged whether there is an unacceptable appearance of bias on the part of the decision maker which may seem to lead the decision maker to favour a particular individual or to be likely to find against that person. This may be because of a personal relationship or knowledge, or a particular standpoint with regard to that person, or some other form of interest or simply that the mind of the decision maker is closed as far as the particular individual or decision is concerned.

A lengthy series of cases sought to formulate a suitable test, which was finally achieved in the case of *Re Medicaments and Related Classes of Goods (No 2)* [2001] 1 WLR 700.

Re Medicaments and Related Classes of Goods (No 2) [2001] 1 WLR 700

The issue in this case was whether a lay member of a tribunal, R, should stand down in circumstances where she had sought employment with a firm, one of whose directors was an expert witness in the tribunal proceedings. The tribunal decided that she should continue to hear the case, and their decision was subsequently challenged. It was argued that R was tainted with an appearance of bias and that, if she was infected with bias, then this affected the other members of the tribunal also with the result that their collective decision could not stand. The Court of Appeal, in accepting this argument, held that the test for bias, which it formulated in judicial terms appropriate to the case being decided, was as follows ([2001] 1 WLR 700 at 727):

> The court must first ascertain all the circumstances which have a bearing on the suggestion that the judge was biased. It must then ask whether those circumstances would lead a fair minded and informed observer to conclude that there was a real possibility, or a real danger, the two being the same, that the tribunal was biased.

This test was subsequently endorsed by the House of Lords in *Porter v Magill* [2002] 2 AC 357. It will be noted that the test is formulated in terms of 'possibility' or 'real danger' rather than probability, and therefore provides for a lower threshold. As Lord Phillips noted in *Re Medicaments* (at p.710), the object is to secure public confidence in the integrity of, in this instance, the administration of justice. This is why the test is formulated in terms of how the matter would appear to a fair minded and informed observer rather than to a professional judge.

There are, of course, occasions where the only decision maker will be in some way tainted with bias. A government Minister, for example, may be the person designated by statute to make a particular decision but this may also involve implementing government policy. Clearly, the Minister is not going to be objective. The law here requires that the Minister approaches the matter in a spirit of fairness and makes the decision with as open a mind as is possible in the circumstances. The individuals concerned, or parties to a case, may also waive the potential bias and accept that the decision maker, whilst affected by apparent bias, is still capable of deciding the matter fairly, perhaps because there is no alternative. A neat example of this occurred in the case of *Bromley LBC v Greater London Council*, cited earlier. The point was taken explicitly in the Court of Appeal, where it was noted that all of the judges hearing the case stood to benefit from cheaper fares on London Transport, of which they were all users. As Lord Denning was of pensionable age, he also benefited from having a free pass. Notwithstanding these factors, the parties to the case accepted that the judges were capable of hearing it fairly and the case proceeded.

thinking point

Ministers are always going to favour government policy. Would it be better if they were simply excluded from making certain types of decisions where government policy is involved?

Fair hearing

What constitutes a fair hearing will depend on the particular circumstances in question. The more there is at stake, the more enhanced will be the requirements of a fair hearing. For example, if a person's livelihood is at stake, then a much more elaborate procedure is required than if the decision in question has less drastic consequences. Similarly, the subject matter of the decision will also be influential in determining what process needs to be followed to ensure fairness.

There must be a hearing

At its most basic, the courts are reluctant to accept that a person has no opportunity to a hearing to challenge a decision. *R v Secretary of State for the Home Department ex p Al Fayed* [1997] 1 All ER 228 concerned an application for British nationality by Mr. Al Fayed which was turned down by the Home Secretary. The legislation provided that there was no appeal against such a decision. However, the Court of Appeal followed the decision of the House of Lords in *Anisminic v Foreign Compensation Commission* [1969] 2 AC 147, discussed in Chapter 11, and held that this did not bar an application for judicial review, as the applicant had a right to be heard by the courts.

Once this initial hurdle of deciding that there is a right to be heard whether by the courts or any other body is surmounted, however, the precise ingredients of a fair hearing need to be determined. A number of elements constituting a fair hearing have been identified, but it is not necessary that they are all present in any given instance.

thinking point

If the content of natural justice is flexible, how do public bodies know what they are supposed to do in any given instance?

Knowing the case to be met

At its most basic however, a fair hearing will require the individual to know the case against him and to have an opportunity to put his case. *Cooper v Wandsworth Board of Works* provides an example of this most basic right. It will be recalled that the Board simply demolished Mr. Cooper's partially built house without giving him any notice of their intention to do so or of the reasons why they were proposing to act in that way. It was held that he was at least entitled to know why they were proposing to exercise their powers and to have an opportunity to respond to their proposals.

A significant feature of the right to know the case against an individual is the question of how much detail must be given. The simple answer to this question is that the individual must be given enough information to enable him to respond in a meaningful way. That is, he does not need to be given every detail as long as he is given sufficient to understand what it is that is being alleged.

There may, however, be good reasons for withholding certain information in particular circumstances. *R v Secretary of State for the Home Department ex p Hosenball* [1977] 1 WLR 766 provides an example.

case close-up

R v Secretary of State for the Home Department ex p Hosenball [1977] 1 WLR 766

The Home Secretary had issued an order requiring that the applicant, an American citizen, should be deported from the UK on the grounds that his presence in the UK was not conducive to the public good on grounds of national security. He was not told why the Home Secretary considered that this was the case, and the legislation in question (the Immigration Act 1971) did not provide for an appeal against such a decision. Here, the Court of Appeal held that the requirements of natural justice had to be modified in the interests of national security, and that, consequently, Mr. Hosenball did not have the right to any detailed information as to why he was being deported. Nor did he have the right to seek judicial review of the Home Secretary's decision, again for reasons of national security. In other words, the requirements of national security, which uphold the public interest, trump the individual's rights under the rules of natural justice, any individual injustice being regarded as subservient to the public interest in the security of the state.

Similar reasoning was used in *R v Gaming Board for Great Britain ex p Benaim* [1970] 2 QB 417.

case close-up

R v Gaming Board for Great Britain ex p Benaim [1970] 2 QB 417

Here, the applicant had applied for a gaming licence. The application was refused on the ground that the applicant was not a fit person to hold a licence as required by the legislation. This conclusion was reached on the basis of information received from the police relating to the applicant which cast doubt on his fitness to hold a licence. The applicant wanted to know what that information was in order that he could challenge it. The Court of Appeal held that disclosure of such information could prejudice police investigations and that, as long as the applicant was given sufficient information, in general terms, to alert him to the nature of the doubts as to his fitness to hold a licence, that was sufficient to satisfy the requirements of this aspect of natural justice. Again, the requirements of natural justice were modified to take account of a wider public interest in the investigation and prevention of crime.

thinking point

Is it ever justifiable to deny a person detailed knowledge of the case against him? How is he meant to respond to something when he does not know what it is?

Time to prepare response

Providing information as to the case to be met is of itself of little value without the corresponding right for the individual to respond to it, which in turn demands adequate time to prepare a response. The requirements are again flexible, as what constitutes an adequate time will vary according to factors such as the complexity of the matter and the significance of the outcome. A fairly extreme example occurred in *R v Thames*

Magistrates ex p Polemis [1974] 1 WLR 1371. A summons was served on the applicant requiring him to appear in court that afternoon to answer it. His subsequent conviction was quashed on the ground that he had not had a fair opportunity to prepare an answer to the summons.

Opportunity to be heard

Providing adequate time to prepare a response is again of little value without a suitable opportunity to present that response. The description of this aspect of the rules of natural justice as a right to a fair hearing is misleading insofar as it suggests an opportunity to put the case orally. As we have seen, whilst historically the rules developed in the context of court proceedings to which the notion of an oral hearing would be entirely appropriate, the application of the rules goes beyond this to cover situations where an oral hearing may not be necessary to satisfy the requirement that the person has had a fair opportunity to put his case. It may be, for example, that an exchange of correspondence provides a reasonable opportunity to put the case.

Opportunity to challenge evidence

Part of the provision of a reasonable opportunity to respond to the case must include the opportunity to correct errors or challenge assertions made. This has been recognized as a fundamental part of treating an individual fairly so that, even where the full requirements of natural justice are not applicable, this right attaches. Thus, in *Re Pergamon Press* [1971] 1 Ch 388, the Board of Trade had undertaken an inquiry into the running of a publishing company. It was held that, even though the rules of natural justice did not apply to such an inquiry, directors of the company should still be given the opportunity to challenge any view taken by the inspectors of the way the company conducted its affairs.

Additional and allied rights to see relevant documents, to call witnesses and to cross-examine those witnesses may also be necessary components of a fair hearing. Again, whether this is so is dependent upon factors such as the seriousness of the matter and also whether depriving the individual of the opportunity to do one or more of these things will render the hearing unfair. As the court pointed out in *R v Hull Board of Visitors ex p St Germain (No 2)* [1979] 1 WLR 1401, the right to a fair hearing is rather empty if the individual cannot bring forward evidence on his behalf. In that case, proceedings had been brought against inmates under the prison disciplinary rules, in the course of which the prisoners were not allowed to call witnesses. It was held that the right to a fair hearing in a case such as this included the right of prisoners charged with serious offences to bring evidence to establish facts, and where that required witnesses to do so then they should be allowed to call them. The court noted, however, that the right to call witnesses was not open ended: the chairman of the Board of Visitors, which was the body charged with hearing the allegations, might properly limit the number of witnesses called as long as this was consistent with the fairness of the proceedings.

Similarly, the right to cross-examine witnesses is not open ended. In *Bushell v Secretary of State for the Environment* [1980] 2 All ER 608, an inspector at an inquiry was upheld in his decision not to allow every objector at the inquiry to cross-examine witnesses where this served no purpose and was consistent with the overall fairness of the proceedings.

Legal representation

thinking point

In what sort of case might legal representation not be necessary?

It is equally the case that a hearing may be fair even though those involved do not have legal representation. As before, the issue depends on the same factors as were discussed earlier, the bottom line being whether the individual in question can be heard fairly without a legal representative or whether the matter is such that this is not necessary. The factors that might require legal representation were discussed in *R v Secretary of State for the Home Department ex p Tarrant* [1985] QB 251.

case close-up

R v Secretary of State for the Home Department ex p Tarrant [1985] QB 251

Here, prisoners were charged with offences against the prison rules and were found guilty following a hearing where they were unrepresented. They were sentenced to loss of remission. Under the relevant regulations, there was no right to legal representation though the Board of Visitors, which heard the charges, had discretion to provide it.

It was held that, given the serious consequences of an adverse finding, there had been a denial of natural justice in not making representation available in these circumstances. The court highlighted factors such as the seriousness of the consequences to the individual, whether any difficult points of law were involved and the capacity of the person to put over his case as factors that might point to a need for legal representation if there was any doubt about these matters. In this case, there were doubts regarding each of these factors and it could not therefore be said that the hearing had been fair.

Reasons

A related issue is whether a decision maker needs to give reasons for the decision that has been made. At common law, there is no general duty to give reasons, but, if a hearing to challenge a decision is to be fair and meaningful, then clearly the individual concerned must have some idea of the reasons for which the decision has been reached. This was raised earlier as an aspect of knowing the case to be met and was seen to be an important part of a fair hearing. It might also suggest that the giving of reasons should be the norm rather than the exception. The courts, however, have held to the view that cases where reasons should be routinely given are the exception to the general common law rule that they should not.

As a consequence of this, there generally has to be something that triggers a right to reasons and the courts have sought to identify occasions when this might occur. Thus, in *R v Secretary of State for the Home Department ex p Doody* [1994] 1 AC 531, the Home Secretary had departed from the tariff recommended by the judge under the system that then operated with regard to determining the length of a life sentence. The applicant wanted to know why the Home Secretary had deviated from the recommendation of the judge. The House of Lords held that fairness required that he should be given reasons for this change.

thinking point

Should reasons for decisions always be given as a matter of good administration?

An attempt to articulate broad categories where reasons might be necessary appears in the judgment of Sedley J in *R v Universities Funding Council ex p Institute of Dental Surgery* [1994] 1 WLR 242.

R v Universities Funding Council ex p Institute of Dental Surgery [1994] 1 WLR 242

The Institute wished to challenge the research rating given to it by the Council. The Council had given no reasons for its decision and part of the Institute's case was to argue that reasons should have been given. In considering this argument, Sedley J said that the situations requiring reasons for decisions fell into two broad categories. First, there were those where the nature of the process required reasons, the judicial process being an obvious example. The second category was where there was something aberrant about the decision itself that triggers the right to reasons; for example, a decision made seemingly against the evidence. The decision in the present case fell into neither category, as the nature of academic judgement was not such as to require reasons to be given routinely and therefore the Council was not required to give reasons for its decision.

12.1.6 Proportionality

A fourth broad ground on which the courts could review a decision that Lord Diplock identified in the *CCSU* case was proportionality. This is a European doctrine used by both the European Court of Justice and the European Court of Human Rights. Put simply, it is the idea that any interference with an individual's rights should be no greater than is necessary to satisfy some legitimate objective. At the time the *CCSU* case was decided, this idea had not been recognized as a ground for judicial review in English law and Lord Diplock was simply identifying it as a possible future development. The idea was not taken up readily by the courts. There were concerns that the notion of proportionality would take the courts beyond the traditional function of judicial review of examining the process by which decisions were reached toward a consideration of the merits of decisions, which they did not regard as their function. Although the idea of *Wednesbury* unreasonableness did take the courts to the point of considering the merits of a decision, this only affected a very small number of decisions in extreme circumstances. Utilizing the concept of proportionality would affect a much broader range of decisions and bring examination of decisions themselves into the mainstream, rather than remaining on the margins, of judicial review. It would also give the judges greater power to overturn decisions of public bodies.

These views are clearly articulated by members of the House of Lords in *R v Secretary of State for the Home Department ex p Brind* [1991] 1 AC 696.

R v Secretary of State for the Home Department ex p Brind [1991] 1 AC 696

The government had imposed a ban on broadcasts by or involving terrorists. The legality of this was challenged on a number of grounds, one of which was that a ban on all broadcasts by or involving terrorists was disproportionate and that a selective ban would be more appropriate. In the event, the House of Lords did not have to address the issue of proportionality directly. It held that the ban was lawful and that, given the issues involved, the Secretary of State had exercised his powers lawfully. The Law Lords did, however, comment on proportionality, displaying differing degrees of enthusiasm for using it as a ground for judicial review. The idea that this was moving beyond the supervisory function toward a more interventionist approach was a significant reason for acting cautiously.

In the result, the possibility of proportionality becoming a ground for review was left open as a possibility for the future. Given the way in which the House of Lords decided the case, they did not need to decide the matter. It is perhaps significant that they did not shut out the possibility, as this was subsequently taken up, receiving a considerable impetus with the passing of the Human Rights Act 1998. Proportionality has now become a potent tool for the courts in exercising the power of review.

Of course, the Human Rights Act, as we have seen in Chapter 7, is a wide-ranging measure and the rights it brings into English law, both substantive and procedural, will impact on many types of decision. A useful discussion of the relationship between the traditional approaches of the common law grounds and the Human Rights Act occurs in *R(Daly) v Secretary of State for the Home Department* [2001] 2 AC 532.

case close-up

R(Daly) v Secretary of State for the Home Department **[2001] 2 AC 532**

A policy had been adopted whereby prisoners were not allowed to remain in their cells while their cells were being searched. Part of the search involved officers looking at documents and prisoners argued that this infringed the right to respect for their correspondence contrary to legal professional privilege and Article 8 of the European Convention on Human Rights. Lord Bingham posed the question (at p.543) for the courts to answer in terms of whether this policy was justifiable as a 'necessary and proper response to the acknowledged need to maintain security, order and discipline in prisons'. Looking at the considerations involved, he concluded (at p.543):

The policy cannot in my opinion be justified in its present blanket form. The infringement of prisoners' rights to maintain the confidentiality of their privileged legal correspondence is greater than is shown to be necessary to serve . . . legitimate public objectives.

In reaching this conclusion, the House of Lords conceded that it may be necessary to conduct some searches of cells without the inmate being in the cell at the time. However, this was not necessary in all cases, and hence the blanket policy was unlawful.

The notion of proportionality has enabled the courts to take a more subtle approach to review. The courts can apply different levels of review appropriate to different situations, reflecting in some ways the differing approaches to the application of principles of procedural fairness. It has also enabled the courts to discriminate between differing types of executive response. As Lord Bingham put it in *Daly* [2001] 2 AC at 541:

The more substantial the interference with fundamental rights, the more the court would require by way of justification before it could be satisfied that the interference was reasonable in a public law sense.

So, whilst the action in *Daly* was regarded as disproportionate, the courts could take a different view in *Brown v Stott* [2003] 1 AC 681. Here, statute required a person who was found to be over the legal limit for alcohol to declare whether she had been driving a vehicle. It was argued that this infringed the right to a fair trial, contrary to Article 6, as it infringed the right against self incrimination and thus the presumption of innocence. It was held that, in the context of the various aspects of the investigation of possible drink-driving offences, this was not a disproportionate response, bearing in mind the needs of road safety.

However, the executive, and indeed the legislature, needs to have more than just the principles of proportionality in mind when acting and must, as we have seen, not infringe the Convention rights (s.6).

case close-up

> ### *A(FC) v Secretary of State for the Home Department* [2005] 2 AC 68
> ....
> The question was whether the detention without trial of terrorist suspects was lawful. Amongst many arguments it put forward, the government claimed that it had acted proportionately in that it had only detained foreign nationals and not all terrorist suspects. The House of Lords dismissed this argument, on the basis that, if the government could deal with terrorist suspects who were UK nationals without detaining them without charge, then it was disproportionate to deal with all foreign nationals in this way. Further, by only applying these measures to foreign nationals the government was acting in a way that infringed Article 14, as it was discriminating against them on grounds of nationality.

The courts thus have at their disposal a range of tools for scrutinizing the legality of executive action. It remains unpredictable in any given case what emphasis or weight they will give to the various factors involved in any decision that is questioned, or how they will interpret any particular statutory provision. This is what makes judicial review such an endlessly dynamic subject.

❓ Questions

If you answer the following questions, you will have appreciated the main issues raised in this chapter. Check your answers against the notes provided at the back of the book.

1 On what grounds might a court declare a decision of a public body unlawful?

2 How do the courts apply those requirements in individual cases?

3 Are the courts consistent in the determination of cases of judicial review?

4 What is the impact of the Human Rights Act on judicial review?

Further reading

To further your understanding of the topics covered in this chapter, have a look at the reading materials mentioned below. Useful web links are also provided on the Online Resource Centre.

A.W. Bradley and K.D. Ewing, *Constitutional and Administrative Law* (Pearson Longman, 14th ed., 2007) ch.30
This provides a full and detailed account of the grounds on which a decision may be challenged.

Michael Allen and Brian Thompson, *Cases and Materials on Constitutional and Administrative Law* (Oxford University Press, 9th ed., 2008) ch. 10
This provides you with extracts from many of the cases mentioned in this chapter together with commentary.

Guidance on answering the end-of-chapter questions

Chapter 1

1. What are the main characteristics of the British constitution?

   You should be able to identify a number of characteristics – it is unwritten, flexible, has a constitutional monarchy etc, but the key point is to understand what these terms mean and being able to explain them. Some are also contentious – following the devolution of government to Scotland and Wales, is the UK moving from being a unitary state to being a federal state? Some would argue it is, whilst others might say that given the limitations imposed on the Scottish Parliament and the Welsh Assembly this has not gone far enough to create a federal state. Less tangible characteristics such as the historical development of the constitution and the parallel characteristics of continuity and change are also important ways in which the constitution can be characterised.

2. How does the British constitution differ from constitutions of other countries?

   The British constitution differs from almost all others in that it is unwritten – this does not mean nothing is written down but rather that there is no single document or collection of documents that form the constitution in the sense of forming the fundamental basis of the government of the country. Instead of a written constitution the UK has the sovereignty of Parliament at its centre. Think about the implications of this for the way in which the constitution develops, and why it is difficult to compare the UK with other countries as its arrangements are not replicated elsewhere – even so called Westminster model constitutions are generally written and thus operate in a different way. In any event, the idea of modelling a constitution is especially difficult with regard to the British constitution given its constantly changing nature and lack of formal structure.

3. Describe the structure of British government, both national and local

   In answering this it is important to differentiate between the central, devolved and local government structures. What they all have in common is that the political members are, with the exception of members of the House of Lords, elected. They also have in common that they are divided between the political members and the administrative members. The political part of the central government is located in Parliament whilst the administrative part comprises the civil service. Both are divided into Departments. Government in Scotland revolves round the Scottish Parliament and the Executive contained within it, rather like the situation with regard to the British government. The same is true of the Welsh Assembly. Both get their power from statute, which impose limits on their ability to act. This is unlike the central government which has some inherent powers such as those exercisable under the royal prerogative. The system of local government is wholly based on statute and only enables councils to exercise limited powers.

4. What is the impact of British membership of the European Union?

In thinking about this, differentiate between the political implications and the legal impact. Our concern is with the legal impact and this requires consideration of the way in which membership has been given effect. Have a look at the European Communities Act 1972, especially s.2 and think about the implications of this for Parliament, the courts and citizens. One important consequence has been that the hierarchy of laws has altered in that Acts of Parliament that are incompatible with European Union law have to give way in order to implement the principle of European sovereignty which is necessary to enable the law to be uniformly applied across the various member states. Have a look at the *Factortame* litigation for an example.

Chapter 2

1. Explain the theory of the separation of powers

It is important to remember that the theory of the separation of powers is essentially a political theory concerned with the distribution of power within a state, the object being to prevent abuses of power by an excessive concentration of power in any one individual. The theory provides for the distribution of powers across different bodies, identified as the legislature, executive and judiciary, in order to provide a balance of power between these institutions, each acting as a check on the other two. As with all theories, the real question relates to whether it works in practice. The real danger with the theory is that if it works effectively, it can prevent each of the institutions actually doing anything.

2. To what extent does the separation of powers apply to the British constitution?

This is a question of degree rather than something that works in an absolute sense: the theory is not fully realised in the British constitution. It is only partly visible and because much of it depends on conventions, it becomes a difficult question to answer in detail. The Labour government has, since 1997, been introducing measures to try to formalise relationships between the government, Parliament and the courts with a view to creating a structure that more clearly differentiates the functions of each and regulates their relations with the other two. There is clearly no separation of powers between Parliament and the government (at least the political members of the government) as members of the government have to be members of Parliament. There is a much clearer separation of the judiciary, and judicial independence is an important feature of any democratic state. Recent steps to secure this by altering the role of the Lord Chancellor and the Lord Chief Justice and the creation of a Supreme Court have done much to protect the independence of the judiciary. Your conclusion on the question generally will depend on your view of the effectiveness of both law and conventions in securing a separation of powers.

3. What does the phrase the rule of law mean?

In one sense, this is a trick question, as it does not have any single meaning. It also means different things to different people. There is almost universal agreement that the rule of law is a good thing, as it prevents tyranny and anarchy. The difficulty comes in getting agreement as to the substance of the phrase. A number of meanings can be canvassed, from the very general idea that it signifies a preference for government by law rather than by force or anarchy to more detailed accounts. Many of the meanings ascribed to it use the term to relate to matters of form rather than substance – the rule of law is concerned with the way in which things are done rather than what they are. However, some versions go beyond form to argue that rules should have certain minimum content. Accounts of the rule of law often seek to argue what the rule of law should signify rather than describe what others think it does signify, and this can often confuse matters. Try to keep a clear distinction between these various matters as you think about this question.

4. What are the characteristics of constitutional conventions?

It is worth remembering that the term convention occurs in two contexts and has a different meaning depending on the context in which it is being used. The first is to signify a treaty, as, for example, in the European Convention on Human Rights. The second is to describe political practices that are routinely followed by those affected by them. It is the second of these that we are concerned with and it is important not to mix up the two meanings. The term constitutional convention is often used to describe conventions of this second type. The characteristics are difficult to pin down, but include the identification of a practice or behaviour which is followed because it is felt that it ought to be followed. As we are dealing with practices it is also difficult to establish precisely when a convention arises or whether any deviation from it is simply a failure to follow the existing convention or is in fact a step toward the establishment of a new convention. Conventions lack the precision of legal rules and do not have clearly identifiable and limited sources. The sanctions for a breach of convention are also political rather than legal.

5. What part do conventions play in the British constitution?

Remember all those metaphors about the way conventions operate within the constitution – flesh clothing bones, oiling machinery etc? They really give the clue as to the role played by conventions in the British constitution. Conventions are a key feature of the way in which the constitution operates in a number of ways. Whole parts of the constitution such as cabinet government,

choice of prime minister etc, are simply conventions rather than being based on a legal footing as they would be in other countries. Conventions work within a framework of law and enable it to operate more effectively. The interaction between law and convention is a characteristic of the way that laws are used, with the convention informing the use of the legal rule.

Chapter 3

1. What is the principle of parliamentary sovereignty?

This is the most important feature of the British constitution. It is the idea that Parliament can make whatever laws it wishes, and, in its pure form, is not subject to any legal limitations on its ability to make law. Further the law made by Parliament is the highest form of law recognised by the courts and takes precedence over the common law and over Parliament's previous legislation in the event of a conflict between two Acts of Parliament, as Parliament cannot bind its successors. The theory is tempered by political realities, however, in that Parliament has to recognise that, for example, economic forces or the pressures of international relations mean that Parliament cannot always do what it might wish. Legal limitations arising from membership of the European Union also have to be taken into account by the courts, and the courts also have duties arising from the Human Rights Act as to the interpretation of legislation. More generally, how the courts approach the task of interpretation can have an impact on whether legislation is applied in ways that Parliament might have envisaged.

2. Why is this principle so important in the British constitution?

It will be remembered that the principle of Parliamentary sovereignty is what lies at the heart of the British constitution in place of a document setting out the fundamental principles by which the state is governed. It provides the foundation of the constitution by enabling legislation passed by Parliament to take precedence over other forms of law. The recognition of the principle by the courts gives it legal significance as well as it being a political idea, and it is the legal aspects of sovereignty that we are concerned with. Even with the limitations on the principle mentioned above, it is still the basis of the British constitution.

3. What is the significance of the difference between Acts of Parliament and other forms of law?

Laws exist in a hierarchy, which is important in order to be able to resolve conflicts between them. A consequence of the principle of parliamentary sovereignty is that Acts of Parliament are the highest form of law in the UK. It therefore follows that Acts of Parliament take precedence over the common law and the principles of equity. Moving outside the domestic sphere however, a consequence of membership of the EU is that the principle of Community sovereignty operates to ensure that EU laws take precedence over Acts of Parliament in the event of conflict.

4. How have the EU and the Human Rights Act impacted on parliamentary sovereignty?

You should note that their impact has been different. Joining the European Community (as it then was) entailed subscribing to the idea of Community sovereignty. This means that European legislation prevails over any inconsistent law of a member state and is a necessary principle in order to promote unity in the application of European law across all member states. This has been achieved legally by virtue of s.2 European Communities Act 1972 and as such it can be argued that parliament has approved this particular limitation on its sovereignty. The position is very different with regard to the Human Rights Act which specifically incorporated the European Convention on Human Rights within the framework of parliamentary sovereignty, in particular by not giving the courts the power to overturn inconsistent legislation, but rather to refer it back to Parliament by means of a declaration of incompatibility. The power balance between the government, Parliament and the courts is clearly affected by these changes and you might like to reflect on the effect of this.

Chapter 4

1. How does the present electoral system operate?

In terms of its operation you should identify the basic components of the system; namely the division of the country into constituencies each returning one member of parliament elected by voters in the constituency casting a single vote for their preferred candidate, and the candidate with the most votes being elected to represent the constituency for a parliamentary term of up to 5 years. Candidates have to be nominated in order to stand for election and this is normally a matter for political parties, who put forward candidates in some or all constituencies. As a significant number of seats are "safe" in the sense that they will, in the ordinary course of things, return a member from a particular party, this effectively means that the election is under the control of the local party in relation to a large number of seats.

2. Is the present electoral system in need of reform?

This depends on your point of view. The fact that the present system has remained largely unaltered for a significant period of time might suggest that it is basically sound and if it seems to work then there is a strong case for leaving it alone. You will need to evaluate the arguments for preserving the present system to decide whether this view is sound. Particularly strong arguments relate to the link between the MP and the constituency, the simplicity of the system and the fact that it tends to produce a working majority for the government. These need to be weighed against the competing arguments, especially those relating to the limitations of the present system in terms of the lack of correlation between votes cast and seats obtained, the argument that having a government with a large majority is not necessarily desirable and the argument that smaller parties should be represented more proportionately. Even if you conclude that the present system is in need of reform you then have to decide what system might replace it: the various systems, of proportional representation or some mixed system, need to be evaluated. Ultimately, the question is resolved on the basis of the values you think are most important for the electoral system to display.

3. What are the functions of Parliament?

This can be divided in a number of ways. Parliament generally carries out a number of functions, including the making of legislation, debates and generally holding the government to account through these and other mechanisms, such as select committees and questions. As a national institution Parliament is a focus for the discussion of national issues. Individual members of parliament may use their position to deal with matters raised by their constituents, for example by raising the matter with a minister, tabling a question, putting forward a private member's bill or communicating with an individual or body on behalf of the constituent. Resolving problems, whether individual or collective, has traditionally been a major function of Parliament, which also, until the Supreme Court comes into operation, houses the final appeal court.

4. How successfully do you think it carries out these functions?

It is worth remembering that the government has a majority in the House of Commons and that this inevitably means that the ability of the opposition parties to hold the government to account will be limited. Further, the superiority of the House of Commons over the House of Lords means that the government's dominance extends to the whole of Parliament. This limitation extends to the activities of Parliament, including the making of legislation, but when looked at solely in theory fails to take into account the reality that the government for political reasons must take account of objections of the opposition parties and the House of Lords to its policies.

5. What functions does the present House of Lords perform and how successfully do you think it carries them out?

The functions of the House of Lords largely mirror and complement those of the House of Commons: the Lords engage in the making of legislation, debates and scrutiny of the government. On this last point, it is worth remembering that some government ministers will be members of the House of Lords. The House of Lords also, although this is a constitutional oddity that will soon disappear, houses the final appeal court in the domestic legal system. However, this will cease to be the case when the Supreme Court becomes operational.

6. Would a reformed House of Lords improve the working of Parliament or are the present arrangements satisfactory?

When the former Prime Minister, John Major, was asked about this, his response was to quote the old maxim "if it ain't broke don't fix it". As with many aspects of the British constitution the idea of having a chamber of the legislature composed of people largely there because of the circumstances of their birth or because they had been appointed by the government of the day might seem to be a recipe for ineffectiveness, but it could be argued that it brings into the political process those who might not otherwise become involved and thus brings a wider range of expertise to the deliberations of the House. However, whilst it may appear to work, it is offensive to democratic principles to have a chamber composed in this way and hence the moves to reform the House of Lords along democratic lines. Whilst the final form of the future criteria for membership has not been decided it seems clear that elected members will be a feature, though what proportion of the House will be elected is as yet undecided. The real issue is the power exercised by the House of Lords relative to the power of the House of Commons. At present the House of Commons enjoys superiority, confirmed in the Parliament Acts 1911–1949. However, the question for the future would be whether a reformed House of Lords would be entitled to exercise greater power than it does at present on the back of its greater democratic mandate.

Chapter 5

1. Who are the members of the executive?

   The political members of the executive are those Members of Parliament holding ministerial office. They are assisted by the civil service. This arrangement is replicated in devolved and local government.

2. What mechanisms exist to prevent abuses of power by the executive?

   Think about ways of challenging the government both through the courts as well as in Parliament. In the courts there are the processes of judicial review relating to the exercise of statutory powers, or an action for damages where the executive commits, for example, a breach of contract or a tort. Parliament has a number of mechanisms designed to subject the executive to scrutiny, including questions, committees, votes, debates etc.

3. What is the nature of the relationship between ministers and their civil servants?

   Ministers are politically accountable for the actions of their civil servants who are generally immune from the political process, although in recent years ministers have been more ready to refuse to resign where the failing is one caused by the civil service.

4. In what ways are ministers accountable for what they do?

   Accountability occurs largely through the conventions of ministerial responsibility. They are accountable to Parliament as members of the government

under the idea of collective responsibility. They are also individually responsible to Parliament for both their personal conduct and the conduct of their department.

5. What powers are available to the executive?

   Under the idea of the rule of law the executive can only exercise powers given to it by law, either in the form of statutory powers or of powers exercisable under the royal prerogative at common law. There will be issues relating to the extent and nature of those powers which the courts may determine. There may also be issues as to whether the government is acting constitutionally which, unless it involves a breach of law, is largely the province of Parliament.

Chapter 6

1. How are judges appointed? Do you think the present system is an improvement on the previous system?

   Judges are now appointed by the Judicial Appointments Commission rather than by individual ministers, with a view to establishing a more transparent system for appointments and ensuring that the judges represent the best of the talent available. Whether you think it represents an improvement on the previous system is a matter of opinion. In terms of whether the system produces better judges only time will tell.

2. How is the judiciary organised? Does the removal of the Lord Chancellor from his role as head of the judiciary make a difference to the judges?

   The judiciary, like the courts, is organised in a hierarchical system with the Lord Chief Justice at its head. Currently the most senior judges are the Lords of Appeal in Ordinary, (the Law Lords), then the Lords Justices of Appeal who sit in the Court of Appeal, then the High Court judges. These comprise the senior judiciary. Other forms of judge include the circuit judges, tribunal judges, district judges and other lower forms of judiciary such as recorders. The changes to the functions of the Lord Chancellor brought about by the Constitutional Reform Act 2005 now mean that the role of the Lord Chancellor is more focussed and removes the objections that the role offends the separation of powers. Whether this makes any long term difference to the way in which the judiciary operates is, at the moment, a matter of speculation.

3. Why is judicial independence from political interference regarded as so important?

Judges have historically, and to the present day, fulfilled an important role in adjudicating on disputes between the state and individual citizens, and have to be independent of political processes in order to do their job effectively. Being seen to be independent is in many ways as important as actually being independent of government. This principle is recognised in the European Convention on Human Rights, especially in Article 6, the right to a fair trial, of which independence of the adjudicator is a key component.

4. What is the test for bias? Why is it so important that judges should be seen to be impartial when trying cases? Can judges ever be totally impartial?

The test for bias as laid down in *Re Medicaments* and subsequently approved by the House of Lords is as follows: "The court must first ascertain all the circumstances which have a bearing on the suggestion that the judge was biased. It must then ask whether those circumstances would lead a fair-minded and informed observer to conclude that there was a real possibility, or a real danger, the two being the same, that the tribunal was biased." Judges need to be seen to be impartial as well as actually being impartial as there is an overriding need to uphold the integrity of the administration of justice and the principles of natural justice which require adjudication by an unbiased judge. Judges as human beings can never be totally impartial. The law on bias is concerned to identify those biases, actual or potential, that are unacceptable.

5. What powers do the judges have? Where do these powers come from?

Judges exercise power by virtue of their office as judges and from the court in which they sit. They derive these powers from statute or common law.

6. What limitations are there on the powers exercised by the judges?

Parliament can limit the powers of the judges by the ways in which it frames legislation even to the extent of excluding the jurisdiction of the courts. Courts are generally hostile to such measures and will try to find ways of interpreting them to enable them to hear claims brought by individual citizens. The courts recognise that there are limits to their jurisdiction in matters such as national security or where confidentiality is vital. Some of the lower courts have limits placed on their jurisdiction and this necessarily limits the power exercisable by the judges.

Chapter 7

1. Why was the Human Rights Act 1998 passed?

It was passed for a number of reasons, but largely to incorporate the European Convention on Human Rights into English law and to enable citizens to bring matters relating to their rights under the Convention before the domestic courts. Remember that formerly a citizen could not argue before an English court (as the Convention was not part of English law) that his rights under the Convention had been violated, but could only take a case to the European Court of Human Rights against the United Kingdom, something that required considerable resourcefulness and took a considerable amount of time.

2. How has the Human Rights Act incorporated the European Convention on Human Rights into English law?

It has done so with a view to preserving parliamentary sovereignty whilst recognising that the object of the Convention is to prevent abuses of state power. It has not given the courts a power to declare legislation to be invalid, but rather limits the power of the courts to making a declaration of incompatibility which then refers the matter to Parliament. However, the courts are given considerable latitude with regard to interpretation of legislation so as to be compatible with the Convention, so the power balance between the courts and Parliament is not as clear cut as it may appear. The concept of the state is given effect in the form of a public authority, signifying something exercising governmental power.

3. Which rights have been incorporated into English Law and in what circumstances can they be limited?

The Human Rights Act does not bring the whole of the European Convention on Human rights into English law. The term "Convention rights" which the Human Rights Act uses to signify those rights brought into English law, is explained in s.1 as the rights set out in Schedule 1 HRA, which means Arts 2–12 and 14 of the Convention, Arts 1 – 3 of the First Protocol and Arts 1–2 of the Sixth Protocol as read with Arts 16–18 of the Convention. The degree to which rights can be limited depends on the particular right in question. Some, such as Art 3 (prohibition on torture) cannot be limited, whilst many others are subject to limitations on specified grounds as long as these are effected by law and are necessary and proportionate.

4. What impact might the Human Rights Act have on public authorities and the courts?

As far as public authorities are concerned they are under a duty by virtue of s.6 to uphold the Convention rights in the way in which they act in the exercise of their powers. Failure to do so is unlawful and may expose the public authority to a claim through the courts by the victim. The courts are also under a duty by virtue of s.6 to uphold the

Convention rights, which exists independently of any such duty attaching to a party before the court. They also have duties under s.3 with regard to the interpretation of legislation so as to make it compatible with the Convention rights and in doing so, under s.2, to take account of, amongst other things, decisions of the European Court of Human rights. The courts have not been given a power to declare legislation that is not compatible invalid. They can however make a declaration of incompatibility under s.4, the effect of which is to leave it to Parliament to deal with the matter. The enactment of the Human Rights Act has involved a change in the power relationship between the government, Parliament and the courts, though the exact nature of that change is difficult to particularise. Have a look at some cases on human rights issues and decide whether you think, as some have suggested, that we are now governed by the judges rather than by Parliament and its members.

Chapter 8

1. Which human rights, protected by the European Convention on Human Rights, are relevant in this area?

A number are relevant, but Art 5, the right to liberty, is clearly engaged here. As with most of the rights under the Convention, it is capable of being limited on a number of grounds and clearly has been in English law as the police are able to interfere with individual liberty in a number of situations. It is worth remembering that the convention rights apply to both the law and the ways in which it is used by the police.

2. What limitations on those rights are permissible?

Under Art 5, limitations may be imposed on the right to liberty on the following grounds, of which the most relevant are:

"(b) the lawful arrest or detention of a person for non-compliance with the lawful order of a court or in order to secure the fulfilment of any obligation prescribed by law;

....

(c) the lawful arrest or detention of a person effected for the purpose of bringing him before the competent legal authority on reasonable suspicion of having committed an offence or when it is reasonably considered necessary to prevent his committing an offence or fleeing after having done so;"

This clearly leaves considerable scope to Parliament, the courts and the police to interfere with individual liberty, though whether statutes such as the Police and Criminal Evidence Act do so excessively is a matter for debate.

3. What powers do the police have to interfere with individual freedom?

You might consider the range of powers available to the police, drawing a distinction between those involving an arrest and those where action short of arrest has been taken such as powers of stop and search. This distinction is important in relation to the consequences that follow: arrest triggers a range of other powers in PACE that may be exercised such as powers of search of both the individual and of premises. Note the requirements that have to be followed in order that the powers are exercised lawfully and note also the effect of the Codes of Practice on the exercise of police powers.

4. Has an appropriate balance been achieved between giving the police enough power to do their job and giving individuals sufficient safeguards to uphold their human rights and prevent abuses of power?

The answer will depend on your perspective. There was and continues to be much talk of the law holding the balance between the powers of the police and the rights of suspects. Whether the law has been successful in achieving this will be affected by your view of where a proper balance lies.

Chapter 9

1. Which human rights are protected?

A number might be identified, but predominantly Arts. 5 (personal liberty), 10 (freedom of expression) and 11 (freedom of association).

2. What limitations on those rights are permissible?

According to the article in question, limitations must be necessary in a democratic society, must be made by law and must not be disproportionate. For example, public order is a basis on which restrictions may be placed on individual freedom.

3. What form do such limitations take in public order law?

Generally these are in the form of criminal offences, though the Public Order Act contains a number of administrative requirements which are backed by criminal sanctions. There are also the powers given to the police either by statute or at common law in relation to breaches of the peace.

4. What powers are given to the police to prevent disorder?

They have a wide range of powers to deal with public gatherings before they happen (e.g. under ss.11, 12 Public Order Act 1986) or at the time of such gatherings (e.g. under s.14 or at common law in respect of breaches of the peace) which cover a wide range of activity including requiring people to move to another location, arrest, preventing people from going to a specific place etc.

5. Has an adequate balance been achieved between giving the police sufficient powers to prevent disorder whilst upholding the right to free expression?

The answer to this will depend on your perspective. If you believe that the predominant purpose of the law is to prevent disorder, then you may want to argue that the police need greater powers than they currently enjoy and that the balance is too much in favour of those engaged in protests or other gatherings. If you believe that the object of the law is to promote the rights of individuals to gather together for lawful purposes, then you might argue that the law is too restrictive of this right.

Chapter 10

1. What is administrative law?

Administrative law is concerned with regulating the exercise of power by government in its widest sense so as to include not only central and local government but also other bodies exercising statutory powers. The powers exercised by government are largely statutory, though in the case of central government they also come from the common law in the form of the royal prerogative.

2. What matters does administrative law cover?

It covers the public law functions of government, and it covers the whole range of those activities that involve the exercise of discretion by the government. It also covers the question of whether the government has carried out any duties it is under.

3. What are the purposes of administrative law?

There is much debate about this. Some commentators see it as a mechanism for accountability, holding government and other public bodies to account for the exercise of power placed in their hands by statute or in the case of central government by the royal prerogative. Others see it as a mechanism for promoting good administration.

4. What is judicial review? How does it differ from an appeal?

The object of judicial review is to examine the legality of the exercise of statutory powers by government, and involves the court looking at the statutory provision in question and the way in which it has been used by the decision maker

in order to determine whether the decision maker has acted within the powers that have been granted by Parliament to that individual or body. It is not as such concerned with the question of whether the decision is right or wrong but rather with the broader question of whether the decision has been reached in a correct manner and is one within the range of possible decisions that a reasonable person could have come to. An appeal involves a rehearing of the case in order to determine whether the original decision was soundly based.

5. What other mechanisms exist to resolve or avoid disputes relating to administrative matters?

There are a number of non court based ways of dealing with disputes between individuals and public bodies, including complaints procedures, tribunals, inquiries, the various forms of ombudsman, and other forms of alternative dispute resolution such as negotiation.

Chapter 11

1. What is judicial review?

Remember that judicial review is a process whereby the legality of a decision can be examined. It differs from an appeal in that it is not in the form of a rehearing of the evidence and is usually solely concerned with matters of law. When exercising the function of judicial review the court is not concerned with the question of whether the decision is right or wrong but rather with the question of whether the decision was one the decision maker could lawfully have come to. As such, the question is largely, though not exclusively, concerned with the process leading to the making of the decision rather than with the decision itself, although if a decision has been reached which is contrary to reason then it can be overturned.

2. Who may bring a claim for judicial review and against whom may a claim be brought?

There are limitations on judicial review relating to both the person bringing a claim and the person against whom the claim may be brought. Only a person with sufficient interest can bring a claim – the object is to prevent busybodies from bringing frivolous claims and wasting the court's time. The claim may only be brought against a public body exercising public law functions. A public body has been fairly widely interpreted to include not only central and local government but also other administrative bodies that exercise statutory powers. Public law functions are essentially those undertaken by a public body when exercising statutory powers.

3. What type of dispute can be challenged by a claim for judicial review?

Remember that judicial review is a process concerned with public bodies exercising statutory powers, though also, in the case of central government, including the royal prerogative. The case is brought by the Crown on behalf of the individual against the public body. It can only be pursued where the public body is exercising public law functions which, in most cases, means they are exercising statutory powers. Where a public body is exercising functions in private law, for example in relation to individual contracts of employment or for goods or services, remedies lie in the ordinary claims for breach of contract etc that any individual or organisation might bring through a claim for damages.

4. What are the main procedural requirements involved in a claim for judicial review?

Claims for judicial review proceed in two stages, following the correct submission of appropriate forms. First there is a requirement that the clamant must obtain permission form the court to proceed. This is essentially a weeding out process to ensure that the court's time is not taken up with claims that have no merit. Very few cases fail at this stage, and being given permission does not necessarily mean that the claim will ultimately

succeed. The case then proceeds to a full hearing when the case is heard in full.

Chapter 12

1. On what grounds might a court declare a decision of a public body unlawful?

The principles of administrative law derive from the common law but have to be read in the light of the particular statutory provision in question. Where, for example, a statutory provision deals with issues such as whether the person should have a hearing, or what factors should or should not be taken into account, this will be followed insofar as it overrides the requirements of the common law. In the absence of such provisions, however, the court reads into the particular statutory provision the requirements of the common law in the form of the principles of administrative law. These may be classified in a number of ways (see e.g. *Associated Provincial Picture Houses v Wednesbury Corporation* [1948] 1 KB 223; *Council of Civil Service Unions v Minister for the Civil Service* [1985] AC 374) but they include the requirement to ensure that the law is interpreted correctly, that it is used for the correct purpose, that relevant considerations have been taken into account and that irrelevant maters have not been taken into account, that any procedural requirements have been observed and that generally the decision maker has acted reasonably. The Human Rights Act has added the requirement that courts must uphold the Convention rights and also take account of decisions of the European Court of Human Rights.

2. How do the courts apply those requirements in individual cases?

This is difficult to answer in the abstract, for ultimately it depends on the judge(s) hearing the case, who have considerable scope as to how they decide the case. This is because the principles of administrative law are very flexible both in their content and in the way in which they might be applied in any given case. The judges also, given the nature of the principles of statutory interpretation, have scope as to how to interpret the statutory provision in question. It therefore becomes very difficult to predict in advance which way a court is going to decide and on what basis, not least because there is not always agreement amongst the judges as to how to approach this task other than in a very general sense.

3. Are the courts consistent in the determination of cases of judicial review?

A glance at the cases will reveal that there will inevitably be inconsistency in the way in which individual judges approach the application of the principles of law to particular statutory provisions or to uses of the royal prerogative. The number of majority decisions in the higher courts indicates that the results in case of judicial review are not inevitable and depend on the view individual judges take of the merits of any claim. The wide

variety of statutory provisions etc and the way in which they are used means that there are always differences between individual cases in the way that they are argued before the courts. In the end, judicial review is an art rather than a science, though we should expect consistency in cases which are the same in all material particulars.

4. What is the impact of the Human Rights Act on judicial review?

There are several ways in which the Human Rights Act impacts on judicial review. The courts have their own duty to uphold the Convention rights under s.6, which includes, for example, not only securing a fair trial under Art 6 but also upholding other individual rights that may be in issue, such as the right to individual liberty under Art 5. The courts are also able to use concepts such as proportionality to extend the scope of judicial review. This has enabled the courts to take a more subtle approach than the more blunt *Wednesbury* principles.

Human Rights Act 1998
Schedule 1

The Articles

PART I   THE CONVENTION RIGHTS AND FREEDOMS

Article 2

Right to life

1. Everyone's right to life shall be protected by law. No one shall be deprived of his life intentionally save in the execution of a sentence of a court following his conviction of a crime for which this penalty is provided by law.

2. Deprivation of life shall not be regarded as inflicted in contravention of this Article when it results from the use of force which is no more than absolutely necessary:

   (a) in defence of any person from unlawful violence;

   (b) in order to effect a lawful arrest or to prevent the escape of a person lawfully detained;

   (c) in action lawfully taken for the purpose of quelling a riot or insurrection.

Article 3

Prohibition of torture

No one shall be subjected to torture or to inhuman or degrading treatment or punishment.

Article 4

Prohibition of slavery and forced labour

1. No one shall be held in slavery or servitude.

2. No one shall be required to perform forced or compulsory labour.

3. For the purpose of this Article the term "forced or compulsory labour" shall not include:

   (a) any work required to be done in the ordinary course of detention imposed according to the provisions of Article 5 of this Convention or during conditional release from such detention;

   (b) any service of a military character or, in case of conscientious objectors in countries where they are recognised, service exacted instead of compulsory military service;

   (c) any service exacted in case of an emergency or calamity threatening the life or well-being of the community;

   (d) any work or service which forms part of normal civic obligations.

Article 5

Right to liberty and security

1. Everyone has the right to liberty and security of person. No one shall be deprived of his liberty save in the following cases and in accordance with a procedure prescribed by law:

(a) the lawful detention of a person after conviction by a competent court;

(b) the lawful arrest or detention of a person for non-compliance with the lawful order of a court or in order to secure the fulfilment of any obligation prescribed by law;

(c) the lawful arrest or detention of a person effected for the purpose of bringing him before the competent legal authority on reasonable suspicion of having committed an offence or when it is reasonably considered necessary to prevent his committing an offence or fleeing after having done so;

(d) the detention of a minor by lawful order for the purpose of educational supervision or his lawful detention for the purpose of bringing him before the competent legal authority;

(e) the lawful detention of persons for the prevention of the spreading of infectious diseases, of persons of unsound mind, alcoholics or drug addicts or vagrants;

(f) the lawful arrest or detention of a person to prevent his effecting an unauthorised entry into the country or of a person against whom action is being taken with a view to deportation or extradition.

2. Everyone who is arrested shall be informed promptly, in a language which he understands, of the reasons for his arrest and of any charge against him.

3. Everyone arrested or detained in accordance with the provisions of paragraph 1(c) of this Article shall be brought promptly before a judge or other officer authorised by law to exercise judicial power and shall be entitled to trial within a reasonable time or to release pending trial. Release may be conditioned by guarantees to appear for trial.

4. Everyone who is deprived of his liberty by arrest or detention shall be entitled to take proceedings by which the lawfulness of his detention shall be decided speedily by a court and his release ordered if the detention is not lawful.

5. Everyone who has been the victim of arrest or detention in contravention of the provisions of

this Article shall have an enforceable right to compensation.

Article 6

Right to a fair trial

1. In the determination of his civil rights and obligations or of any criminal charge against him, everyone is entitled to a fair and public hearing within a reasonable time by an independent and impartial tribunal established by law. Judgment shall be pronounced publicly but the press and public may be excluded from all or part of the trial in the interest of morals, public order or national security in a democratic society, where the interests of juveniles or the protection of the private life of the parties so require, or to the extent strictly necessary in the opinion of the court in special circumstances where publicity would prejudice the interests of justice.

2. Everyone charged with a criminal offence shall be presumed innocent until proved guilty according to law.

3. Everyone charged with a criminal offence has the following minimum rights:

(a) to be informed promptly, in a language which he understands and in detail, of the nature and cause of the accusation against him;

(b) to have adequate time and facilities for the preparation of his defence;

(c) to defend himself in person or through legal assistance of his own choosing or, if he has not sufficient means to pay for legal assistance, to be given it free when the interests of justice so require;

(d) to examine or have examined witnesses against him and to obtain the attendance and examination of witnesses on his behalf under the same conditions as witnesses against him;

(e) to have the free assistance of an interpreter if he cannot understand or speak the language used in court.

Article 7

No punishment without law

1. No one shall be held guilty of any criminal offence on account of any act or omission which did not constitute a criminal offence under national or international law at the time when it was committed. Nor shall a heavier penalty be imposed than the one that was applicable at the time the criminal offence was committed.

2. This Article shall not prejudice the trial and punishment of any person for any act or omission which, at the time when it was committed, was criminal according to the general principles of law recognised by civilised nations.

Article 8

Right to respect for private and family life

1. Everyone has the right to respect for his private and family life, his home and his correspondence.

2. There shall be no interference by a public authority with the exercise of this right except such as is in accordance with the law and is necessary in a democratic society in the interests of national security, public safety or the economic well-being of the country, for the prevention of disorder or crime, for the protection of health or morals, or for the protection of the rights and freedoms of others.

Article 9

Freedom of thought, conscience and religion

1. Everyone has the right to freedom of thought, conscience and religion; this right includes freedom to change his religion or belief and freedom,

either alone or in community with others and in public or private, to manifest his religion or belief, in worship, teaching, practice and observance.

2. Freedom to manifest one's religion or beliefs shall be subject only to such limitations as are prescribed by law and are necessary in a democratic society in the interests of public safety, for the protection of public order, health or morals, or for the protection of the rights and freedoms of others.

Article 10

Freedom of expression

1. Everyone has the right to freedom of expression. This right shall include freedom to hold opinions and to receive and impart information and ideas without interference by public authority and regardless of frontiers. This Article shall not prevent States from requiring the licensing of broadcasting, television or cinema enterprises.

2. The exercise of these freedoms, since it carries with it duties and responsibilities, may be subject to such formalities, conditions, restrictions or penalties as are prescribed by law and are necessary in a democratic society, in the interests of national security, territorial integrity or public safety, for the prevention of disorder or crime, for the protection of health or morals, for the protection of the reputation or rights of others, for preventing the disclosure of information received in confidence, or for maintaining the authority and impartiality of the judiciary.

Article 11

Freedom of assembly and association

1. Everyone has the right to freedom of peaceful assembly and to freedom of association with

others, including the right to form and to join trade unions for the protection of his interests.

2. No restrictions shall be placed on the exercise of these rights other than such as are prescribed by law and are necessary in a democratic society in the interests of national security or public safety, for the prevention of disorder or crime, for the protection of health or morals or for the protection of the rights and freedoms of others. This Article shall not prevent the imposition of lawful restrictions on the exercise of these rights by members of the armed forces, of the police or of the administration of the State.

Article 12

Right to marry

Men and women of marriageable age have the right to marry and to found a family, according to the national laws governing the exercise of this right.

Article 14

Prohibition of discrimination

The enjoyment of the rights and freedoms set forth in this Convention shall be secured without discrimination on any ground such as sex, race, colour, language, religion, political or other opinion, national or social origin, association with a national minority, property, birth or other status.

Article 16

Restrictions on political activity of aliens

Nothing in Articles 10, 11 and 14 shall be regarded as preventing the High Contracting Parties from imposing restrictions on the political activity of aliens.

Article 17

Prohibition of abuse of rights

Nothing in this Convention may be interpreted as implying for any State, group or person any right to engage in any activity or perform any act aimed at the destruction of any of the rights and freedoms set forth herein or at their limitation to a greater extent than is provided for in the Convention.

Article 18

Limitation on use of restrictions on rights

The restrictions permitted under this Convention to the said rights and freedoms shall not be applied for any purpose other than those for which they have been prescribed.

PART III   THE SIXTH PROTOCOL

Article 1

Abolition of the death penalty

The death penalty shall be abolished. No one shall be condemned to such penalty or executed.

Article 2

Death penalty in time of war

A State may make provision in its law for the death penalty in respect of acts committed in time of war or of imminent threat of war; such penalty shall be applied only in the instances laid down in the law and in accordance with its provisions. The State shall communicate to the Secretary General of the Council of Europe the relevant provisions of that law.

Glossary

Affray—a person is guilty of affray if he uses or threatens unlawful violence towards another and his conduct is such as would cause a person of reasonable firmness present at the scene to fear for his personal safety

Arrest—occurs when one person deprives another person of his liberty and continues for as long as that deprivation of liberty continues

Assault—a person is guilty of assault if he causes another person to fear immediate physical harm. In practice however, the term assault is often used to encompass both the threat and act of physical violence (see battery)

Assault occasioning actual bodily harm—non-serious physical injury inflicted on a person by the deliberate action of another

Bail—the release of a person from police custody pending further stages in the criminal process. Courts can also decide whether to release a person on bail or detain him in custody following court hearings

Battery—the intentional or reckless use of physical force against another person, whether or not that person is injured as a result

Bill—a bill is the form in which an instrument which ultimately becomes an Act of Parliament starts while it is under discussion in Parliament

Breach of the peace—there is a breach of the peace whenever harm is actually done or is likely to be done to a person or in his presence to his property

Bylaws—laws that relate to the local authority area only

Civil list—the name given to the money allocated, on an annual basis, to the royal family to enable them to perform their official duties

Confession—a statement made by a suspect in which he admits that he committed the offence in question

Constable—any police officer, not just a person holding the rank of constable

Conventions—non-legal rules which are followed as a matter of political practice

False imprisonment—the unlawful confinement of a person, so as to remove their freedom of movement

Grievous bodily harm—very serious physical injury

Habeas corpus—a form of proceedings directed to a person who is detaining another requiring him to produce that other person before a court and to show some legal justification for the detention

Hansard—the name given to the verbatim published record of what is said in Parliament

Judicial Committee of the Privy Council—originally created as a committee of the Privy Council to hear appeals from overseas countries with a connection with the United Kingdom, latterly as members of the Commonwealth. It is now the final court of appeal in matters relating to devolution issues. The judges sitting in it are usually the judges of the House of Lords

Judicial deference—recognizes that some matters are so policy laden that they are best determined by the legislature or government rather than by the courts.

Malicious prosecution—a prosecution initiated without reasonable or probable cause

Malicious wounding—the intentional and unlawful wounding of a person

Manslaughter—the unlawful killing of another person which does not constitute murder

Margin of appreciation—a doctrine developed by the European Court of Human Rights which recognizes that certain matters may be decided by individual countries in the light of local conditions

Money Bill—a bill which in the opinion of the Speaker of the House of Commons is concerned solely with taxation and other matters related to public money

Murder—the unlawful killing of another person with 'malice aforethought'

Order in Council—a form of delegated legislation made under the authority of the royal prerogative

Ouster clause—a provision in an Act of Parliament that seeks to exclude the courts from exercising jurisdiction over any or all of the subject matter of the Act

Parliamentary sovereignty (or supremacy)—the principle that Parliament is the law making body with the highest authority in the UK and can make laws subject to no prior restraints; and that the courts cannot overturn laws made by Parliament

Proportionality—the idea that any interference with a Convention right must be no more than is necessary to achieve the legitimate objects of the state

Recuse—where a judge disqualifies himself from sitting in a particular case

Riot—where 12 or more persons who are present together use or threaten unlawful violence for a common cause and the conduct of them (taken together) is such as would cause a person of reasonable firmness present at the scene to fear for his personal safety, each of the persons using unlawful violence for the common purpose is guilty of riot

Spoiled ballot papers—ballot papers which are incorrectly completed

Trespass to goods—the unlawful interference with another person's possession of goods, either by taking them away, moving them, damaging them, or touching them, without permission

Trespass to land—the unlawful interference with another person's possession of land, by entering or remaining on it without permission

Trespassory assembly—though not explicitly defined, this is essentially one that is held on land to which those assembling have no legal rights and that gathers in contravention of an order under s. 14A Public Order Act 1986

Vicarious liability—the liability of a person for the acts committed by another, typically an employee

violent disorder—where 3 or more persons who are present together use or threaten unlawful violence and the conduct of them (taken together) is such as would cause a person of reasonable firmness present at the scene to fear for his personal safety, each of the persons using or threatening unlawful violence is guilty of violent disorder

Warrant—a document issued by a court authorizing the person to whom it is issued to do something

Index

DIRECTIONS: *straightforward law*

Studying the law can be a difficult task and as a student you want to know that you are on the right track and getting to grips with the key issues.

Books in the *DIRECTIONS* series effectively set you on your way. Without assuming prior legal knowledge, each book shows students where to start and offers a sufficiently detailed guide through the subject.

Each *DIRECTIONS* book is written by an experienced teacher or teachers who are passionate about making their subject understood. Topics are carefully and logically structured and clearly explained, making use of real life examples. Engaging learning features accompany the lively writing style, helping students effectively grasp each subject.

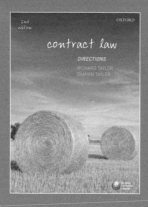

Titles in the series include:

- contract law
- English legal system
- equity and trusts law
- EU law
- human rights law
- land law
- public law
- tort law

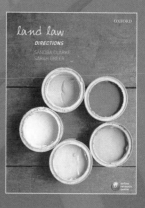

For further details about titles in the series visit

www.oxfordtextbooks.co.uk/law/directions/